What Happens Next?

WHAT HAPPENS NEXT?

Contemporary Urban Legends and Popular Culture

Gail de Vos

LIBRARIES UNLIMITED

AN IMPRINT OF ABC-CLIO, LLC
Santa Barbara, California • Denver, Colorado • Oxford, England

Library of Congress Cataloging-in-Publication Data

De Vos, Gail, 1949–
   What happens next? : contemporary urban legends and popular culture / Gail Arlene de Vos.
     pages cm
   Includes bibliographical references and index.
   ISBN 978–1–59884–633–1 (pbk.) — ISBN 978–1–59884–634–8 (ebook) (print)
1. Urban folklore. 2. Legends. 3. Mass media and folklore. 4. Literature and folklore.
I. Title.
GR78.D42   2012
398.209173′2—dc23   2012014930

ISBN: 978–1–59884–633–1
EISBN: 978–1–59884–634–8

16 15 14 13 12   1 2 3 4 5

This book is also available on the World Wide Web as an eBook.
Visit www.abc-clio.com for details.

Libraries Unlimited
An Imprint of ABC-CLIO, LLC

ABC-CLIO, LLC
130 Cremona Drive, P.O. Box 1911
Santa Barbara, California 93116-1911

This book is printed on acid-free paper ∞

Manufactured in the United States of America

This one is for my daughter Esther de Vos who accompanied this creative journey with one of her own.

Contents

Acknowledgments

Each book is truly a family affair. I could not have done this one without the research skills of and conversations with my daughter Taryn de Vos or without the support of my very patient husband, Peter, my daughter Esther, and my mother, Lillian Shukster. Others in my extended community, local and electronic, who thoughtfully participated in the journey in one way or another include: Ian Brodie, Carole and John Byrne, Verne Busby, Jan Harold Brunvand, Suzette Chan, Peter Dykes, Bill Ellis, Leanne and Ed Gugenheimer, Merle Harris, Arlene Lipkewich, Margaret Mackey, Linda M. McClure, Barbara Mikkelson, members of the International Society for Contemporary Legend Research (ISCLR), the Summer Village of Seba Beach Public Library and the outstanding Alberta Public Library system. Again, to my intrepid editor Barbara Ittner, a loud round of applause.

I also need to thank the wonderful Deborah Grabien, author extraordinaire, who I first met (electronically and through her Haunted Ballad mystery series) when researching and writing *Stories from Songs*. Conversations on Facebook and the very generous sharing of her short story added considerably to my overall enjoyment of this project (as did her sharing stories and novels of JP Kinkaid).

Large thanks go to authors Jenn Bennett, Elizabeth Bunce and Kate Chell Milford for giving me a glimpse into their individual creative processes in reworking the devil at the crossroads motif. A huge thanks also to musician and storyteller Joe Vickers, who took the story of the meeting with the devil at the crossroads to my classroom and beyond with his fine recording of his song. I wish also to thank my storytelling students who, in various assignments, led me to additional reworkings and allusions that I used in this book: Erin Mayko, Norm Dublanko, Laura Bowlby and Matthew Kerby.

Introduction

The stuff of legends—the supernatural, the horrific, the disastrous, the uncanny, the improbable, and the comical—is the stuff of our everyday attention and conversation.

—Oring (2008, 127)

In his *Encyclopedia of Urban Legends*, contemporary legend expert Jan Harold Brunvand writes of the popularization of the genre outside the realm of folklorists and other scholars, citing the 1998 film *Urban Legend* as a harbinger of the death of the oral-narrative genre, migrating "from *folk*lore into *popular* culture where they became stereotyped, standardized, exploited, commodified, and repackaged in a number of ways" (Brunvand 2001, xxvii). The film erupted on the scene two years after the publication of my first book on contemporary legends, *Tales, Rumors, and Gossip: Exploring Contemporary Folk Literature in Grades 7–12*. In the intervening years since its publication, I also monitored the trajectory of the genre as the term "urban legends" became commonplace and overused, even if the folkloric characterization of it has not always been understood by the media or layperson utilizing it. The results of my observations form the context of this book which focuses on the contemporary legend genre as it evolves from the traditional word-of-mouth performances of stories told about friends of friends who have extraordinary and frightening experiences in today's astounding and terrifying society to the predominantly electronically transmitted legends shaped by the medium.

The Popularization of the Genre

Gillian Bennett affirms that contemporary legends are narratives, "stories of some sort, with a beginning, middle and end, and traditional in that they were widely disseminated numerous times and places" (Bennett 2005, xii). This narrative aspect of contemporary legends has not changed in the intervening years or by the evolving transmission channels. Contemporary legends remain stories, although the mode of telling the legends has expanded exponentially, veering away from the ever adapting oral tale to the more fixed versions appearing on computer screens in e-mails, on blogs, on listservs, in social networking entries or on YouTube videos. One of the most observable benefits of the electronic transmission of contemporary legends resides in their availability for future researchers as core, stable texts. Contemporary legends, transmitted orally, are shaped to appeal to specific audiences and often changed through the narrator's attempt in remembering the details of the narrative. Contemporary legends that reveal considerable variation are those that spread orally, even if the narratives are also spread in Internet chat rooms or websites (Fine and Ellis 2010, 35).

Barbara Mikkelson, the voice at Snopes.com, confirms this development from the oral tradition to electronic transmission.

> The biggest change we've seen wrought to the genre has been due to the Internet. Prior to the online world, with the exception of Xeroxlore, urban legends circulated primarily in oral fashion— one person would repeat an interesting story as best he or she could remember it to another, who in turn would pass it along to others by the same method. In that fashion, small details were constantly changing, as the folks who passed along these legends unconsciously added details that made sense to them and subtracted ones that didn't. The online world, however, changed that because that which was circulated by email and through blogs, social media (e.g., Facebook) entries, and message board and newsgroup posts was in written form. Consequently, far less natural variation occurred, leaving many online-circulated legends almost set in stone. (Barbara Mikkelson, personal communication, July 7, 2011)

Ironically, numerous folklorists have credited the popularity of Brunvand's urban legend books with this perceived demise of the oral nature of the contemporary legend and its escalating recognition in popular culture. Linda Dégh states that Brunvand's five volumes, published between 1981 and 1993, inspired both the retelling of the traditional contemporary legends orally and in the media and the creation of fresh material with his network of correspondents. "As a consequence of book promotions, newspaper columns, television talk shows, and even a 1994 comic book version, Brunvand's books have inspired the adaptation (and abuse) of his popular horror and ghost legends. The movie industry in particular has taken interest" (Dégh 2001, 88). Dégh maintains that through his work, "urban legend" became a household term and gained prestige as a folklore genre.

Gary Alan Fine and Patricia Turner agree with Dégh, stating that Brunvand's series of popular books is instrumental in informing the general public about the existence of the legends (Fine and Turner 2001, 6). "In particular, journalists suddenly discovered that many of the stories they had tried in vain to authenticate were traditional" (Fine and Turner 2001, 7). Carl Lindahl mentions that Brunvand's "characterization of a legend as essentially a practically joke on gullible listeners reflects an arbitrary attitude toward the tellers" (Lindahl 1996, xiv). This, in fact, leads to the implication of urban legends as false stories or tales of little value other than as entertainment and an educational tool for the lay public. An unfortunate consequence is that the term "urban legend" becomes contaminated with notions of falseness and frivolity (Bennett 2005, 211). Brunvand's major message, claims Dégh, is that there is nothing to fear in these tales "because they never happened" (Dégh 2001, 45). A dramatic change in the public's attitude to contemporary legends accompanies this increasing public awareness of contemporary legends through Brunvand's corpus of work and films such as *Urban Legend*. "Around 20 years ago, before the word and the concept became commonly known, people tended to be too credulous. Nowadays they tend to be too suspicious" (Simonsen 2007, 189). Another impetus credited with this growing change in attitude and awareness of contemporary legends in North America is the terrorist attacks of September 11, 2001, which caused the lay population to be more aware of the role of rumors and urban legends in daily life (Donovan 2004, viii).

When conducting literature searches for contemporary legends it soon became apparent that they, or urban legends as they are most often referred to by non-folklorists, are researched and applied to fields as diverse as consumer behavior and marketing and for the purposes of providing catharsis for crime victims or others experiencing anxieties of a non-criminal nature. As Bill Ellis attests, contemporary legends are told in order to impose form on marginal experiences, aiding narrators and their audience in comprehending, controlling and sharing anxiety and creating community (Ellis 2001, 64).

> If one function of legend is to "name" previously undefined threats and so gain psychological control over them, then when people change their behavior based on such legends, they are engaging in magical practices. This is so even if the participants perceive them as "good common sense," since their actions do not act directly on the threat but simply reassure individuals that they are somehow controlling their fates. (Ellis 2001, 201)

Gary Alan Fine and Patricia Turner refer to folklorist Alan Dundes's persuasive argument that by transforming unacceptable impulses into a story that was claimed to have actually happened, narrators are able to express the inexpressible (Fine and Turner 2001, 17). Alternatively, Bernard Guerin and Yoshihiko Miyazaki conclude that "instead of telling such stories because they reduce anxiety or help us find meaning in uncertain events, the tellers utilize these very properties of anxiety and uncertainty to make a good story and improve their social relationships" (Guerin and Miyazaki 2006, 31).

> We suggest first that instead of anxious, ambiguity, or consequential situations causing or leading to rumours, the ambiguity and consequentiality of a situation are *utilized* for social conversation: Instead of putting effort into seeking meaningful interpretations of ambiguous or consequential events, people are putting effort into making good conversation and therefore good social relationships, and are using whatever conversational properties are available in the current material and the local context to do this. (Guerin and Miyazaki 2006, 30)

Other studies state that since contemporary legends frequently involve brand-name products or warn against consumer misbehaviour and the hazards of technology, they socialize consumers about the consequences of misusing resources or greediness in the accumulation of too many resources (Donovan, Mowen and Chakaborty 2001, 524). While the popularity of contemporary legends may be the result of the information they allegedly provide to aid people to avoid problems and escape danger, they are also utilized in marketing strategies as story lines for commercials (Donovan, Mowen and Chakaborty 2001, 522). The incorporation of contemporary legends in almost all facets of popular culture is explored in subsequent discussions throughout this book.

Contemporary Legends Redefined

> *Long ago we would say to our children that meeting your paramour for a midnight embrace was dangerous because that is when monsters roamed about most freely. Now we tell kids that if you go parking, the man with the hook for hand will gut you both.*
>
> —Mayberry and Kramer (2009, 54)

In *Tales, Rumors, and Gossip*, I quote David Buchan's definition of contemporary legends as:

> Stories told as true which circulate by word of mouth in contemporary society and exhibit traditional variation. They circulate in a wide variety of social groups, on every level of the socioeconomic scale and are prevalent among the educated. They contain both ancient and modern elements: they involve the phenomena of contemporary society but often demand belief in something unlikely or fantastically horrific or on occasion even supernatural. (de Vos 1996, xvii)

This definition was as relevant in 1996 as when Buchan first penned it in 1978; but some modifications are necessary to make it equally relevant today. The stories are still related as true but they, more often than not, circulate electronically, in print and in filmic and television versions. While often told as true, however, they are frequently recognized by their audiences as folkloric recordings of events, at least until they begin circulating anew as the result of an immediate horrific or terrifying current experience. As Bill Ellis maintains, "Unlike the folk song or the folktale, which might be learned in its finished form and maintained through a lifetime with only trivial changes, the very survival of the legend depends on its capacity to change" (Ellis 2001, 61). Orally transmitted contemporary legends are considered events which cannot be stabilized in form or frozen in time. Their written counterparts on the Internet, however, are considered objects, acquiring an independence of the sender or receiver and are reproducible in the same form. Fialkova and Yelenevskaya point out, however, that particularly with e-mail messages, "while narratives posted on the Internet can be saved in the original form, they are subject to modifications by addressees who often re-post the original but cut it, add their comments, or turn the message into a quasi-dialogue" (Fialkova and Yelenevskaya 2001, 76).

In his exploration on the use of the term "urban legend" among scholars, Sandy Hobbs searched the term on the Google Scholar website (scholar .google.com) to conclude that "the phrase is becoming quite widely used in academic publications to mean 'not true'" (Hobbs 2010, 5). The search for the term "contemporary legend" produces a significantly different outcome: all the articles and books listed were by contemporary legend scholars. "Most scholars in fields other than ours are probably unaware of the use of the term 'contemporary legend.' In contrast they are aware of the term 'urban legend' but in general do not treat it as a technical term" (Hobbs 2010, 5). While the term "urban legend" has a higher profile in popular culture, I continue to be more comfortable with the term "contemporary legend" and therefore it is the term of choice here.

Gillian Bennett states that the clash or confusion with the paranormal tends to result in "traditional" legends tales of ghosts, devils, saints and monsters whereas a second type of clash involving safety and danger, love and death, children and cruelty results in contemporary legends (Bennett 2005, xii). She believes that "though there are, of course, numerous exceptions, the characters and events in contemporary legends more often tend to be bizarre, scary, and macabre than overtly supernatural and are presented as topical and newsworthy reports from the everyday world, not the otherworld" (Bennett 2005, xii). However, both types of legends that reflect contemporary concerns and anxieties are considered between these covers. Ghosts, monsters and hatchet-wielding men rub shoulders with an extensive assortment of like, and not so similar, characters and creatures demonstrating the increasing interest in the paranormal and supernatural in North American society. Contemporary legends, narratives expressed as true experiences either face-to-face, with localization and variation, or electronically, citing specific and eminent locations without much deviation continue to circulate ardently in the twenty-first century. I find that the largest distinction between the contemporary legends discussed in *Tales, Rumors, and Gossip* and the ones in this book is the relative lack of "new" contemporary legends. We seem to be truly in a world of recycled material on all fronts.

Clearly, the content of contemporary legends has not changed as dramatically as their mode of transmission did. As discussed in *Tales, Rumors, and Gossip*, the legends are primarily anonymous, told as narratives in a conversational tone circulating among members of certain economic, family or cultural groups and include contemporary elements and details of everyday life with the bizarre details of the legends authenticated through the of actual names, places, dates and events to ground the tale in reality and reputable sources including the ubiquitous friend-of-a-friend. "The more unambiguous the source of the narrative, the more believable the narrative is likely to be. Likewise, the closer the connection of a narrator to his or her source, the more credible the account is likely to be" (Oring 2008, 133). They then exuded, and still now exude, a film noir tone in the telling with steamy, dark urban landscapes and ordinary characters facing unexpected twists and turns throughout the plots containing racial and gender stereotypes that often mirror modern racial attitudes and fears. The assertion on the website for the International Society for Contemporary Legend Research (ISCLR) states that members of the organization "are especially concerned with ways in which legends merge with life: real-life analogs to legend plots, social crusades that use legends or legend-like horror stories" (http://www.contemporarylegend.org).

Features of Contemporary Legends

> *Folklore is one of the oldest forms of conservation of cultural tradition and poeticized experience, it is a true reservoir of collective memory. The Internet is gradually assuming the latter role, too.*
>
> —Fialkova and Yelenevskaya (2001, 64)

As mentioned previously, the main differences in the last two decades are that the contemporary legends are no longer primarily communicated face-to-face and, because of the mode of electronic transmission, do not exist in such a myriad of multiple versions as before as they are often forwarded as is, instead of adapted and re-created with each retelling (de Vos 1996, 5–7). In addition to the elements of contemporary legends already reviewed, Bennett and Smith include the following: the outrageous content in the everyday setting and the immediate present; making the legends important; and discussable and entertaining stories that are often shaped along the lines of detective stories or jokes. Unlike the discussion earlier regarding the falseness embraced in the term, Bennett and Smith claim "it is almost impossible to be absolutely certain whether the events described in an urban legend ever took place, and most attempts to track the origin of a legend have failed" (Bennett and Smith 2007, xvii). The truth of the legends and their believability factor are highly dependent on the trustworthiness of the source of legend and the way the content reflected the world view of the audience. These tales are rarely told in first person.

> An urban legend is never experienced by the teller. It is always carried from someone else, a friend of a friend or a not-clearly documented news story another friend has heard. Some are outright, intentional hoaxes, but the collector of such tales can easily reap examples from those who really believe in the stories. When believed, they strongly reflect not only the desires and fears of the carrier of the tale, but also the carrier's ability or inability to analyze situations in a rational way. Thus, in a storyteller's voice, urban legends appeal to many listeners. (Davis 2004, 168)

The contemporary legends told, either face-to-face or electronically, contain the six principles Chip Heath believes are necessary for messages and ideas to stick or be memorable and therefore be transmitted to others as true and important tales. First of all, they need to be in story format. "Research shows that mentally rehearsing a situation helps one perform better when we encounter that situation in the physical environment. Similarly, hearing stories acts as a kind of mental flight simulator, preparing us to respond more quickly and effectively" (Heath and Heath 2007, 16). The stories need to engage emotional responses and to include elements of unexpectedness, generating interest and curiosity and violating people's expectations. "Compelling legends should have an emotional resonance for their audiences. They should present language, images, and messages that stir pre-existing emotional dispositions . . . They are more apt to persuade if they can capitalize on resident fears and connect with deep-seated wishes" (Oring 2008, 157). They need to be credible, with authenticity assured through the use of concrete details. Heath asserts that "naturally sticky ideas are full of concrete images—ice-filled bathtubs, apples with razors—because our brains are wired to remember concrete language" (Heath and Heath 2007, 16). Above all, the stories must be both simple and profound. People enthusiastically transmit contemporary legends largely because of these principles. Those that do not engage the audience emotionally, or with some aspect of belief or truth, lose momentum and vanish, sometimes to become relevant at another time or with another audience in the future.

When contemporary legends re-emerge in a cyclical manner, they are labelled "diving rumors." Ellis and Fine, using the broad term "rumor" when also referring to contemporary legends, assert that "like a skilled diver, these rumors appear, then plunge beneath the surface, only to reappear. People tire of stories once they know them, and move to other narratives. These rumors are then in remission until enough people have forgotten them and are readily available when a new trigger emerges that captures a similar theme" (Fine and Ellis 2010, 149).

Bill Ellis also considers contemporary legends as "emergent" since they grow out of social contexts. The legends emerge as news with their described events or beliefs directly relevant to the audience even though the motifs and structure of the tales are quite old. The legends are emergent in that their primary messages emerge out of specific social conditions and roles. "The best tellers—and the most popular legends—have the potential to transform social structures for better or worse. Hence legend telling is often a fundamentally *political act*" (Ellis 2001, xiv). The contemporary legends often embody an emergency as well, dealing with an urgent social problem (Ellis 2001, xiv).

When contemporary legends are related orally, narrators employ one of several methods to establish their own credibility and lack of gullibility. Contemporary legends often are accompanied by overt observations on their truth because of their extraordinary content. As a result of greater awareness of contemporary legends because of the growing presence of books and websites that aim at debunking stories, "many performances begin with statements such as 'This is *not* one of those urban legends but . . . ' which of course concedes exactly the same thing" (Fine and Ellis 2010, 109). Other narrators often introduce their story by highlighting its incredibility, followed by the evidence of their own experience that confirmed the incredible to be credible indeed. As a defensive strategy on the part of narrators, they offer alternative explanations of the action in the legend. "Narrators wish to protect themselves from charges of superstition and credulity" (Oring 2008, 136). Another method to assure the audience of the narrator's discernment and trustworthiness is the presentation of the narrator as a reluctant witness or interpreter of what was witnessed. This persistent self-questioning denotes truthfulness on the part of the narrator as does the practice of the narrator confessing to ignorance of the all of the facts themselves (Oring 2008, 137).

"A major function of legends . . . is to serve, individually and collectively, as convenient language for the experiences that lie, actually or potentially, at the very boundaries of existence. This stage of the legend is, practically speaking, uncollectable, unobservable, and untranscribable" (Ellis 2001, 62). Ellis believes that the fragmentary, incoherent plots are the norm rather than the exception among contemporary legends. Since the tellers assume that the essentials of the legendary context are familiar to their audiences, they often omit them, presenting instead only the outline of the plot which is then absorbed individually by members of the audience according to their own perceptions and beliefs (Ellis 2001, 9). Thus the legend exists in several different states: transient in which it provides the individual with a name for the marginality of an uncanny event or a social stress, where it translates this marginality into language by sharing it with others; and the resulting performance, repeated to convince or entertain, becoming a finished narrative. Once the legend becomes well known amongst the narrator's community, it transforms into a kernel narrative or a *metonym* rather than an extended narrative. "Legend metonyms show up everywhere but are often opaque to outsiders. To that extent, they define the boundaries both of the group's world and of its membership" (Ellis 2001, 64). Dormancy is the final state of existence when the legend no longer circulates as a legend because it is no longer relevant for the group. Instead it becomes a legend report (Ellis 2001, 61). Until, of course, it becomes relevant once again!

Gender Issues in Contemporary Legends

> *It is not surprising that, as is so often the case in contemporary legends generally, women are victims in these narratives much more frequently than they are agents. Neither is it surprising that in their construction of cars, hotels, malls and the Internet as male space, the legends punish women for their attempts to enter it.*
>
> —Tye (2005, 229)

In the last decade, several scholars explored contemporary legends in regards to gender issues. Diane Tye examines 21 contemporary legends, collected on Snopes.com, in which a woman acted by herself and that circulated in 2003. The women were either alone physically or isolated by their emotional distance from others. "The geographical locations of these legends suggest that female solitariness is a transient state for women for the legends' characters are on the move: leaving home, in or on the way to cars; in shopping malls, in hotels; or engaged in virtual travel on the Internet" (Tye 2005, 220). Tye ascertains that contemporary legends reinforce the notion that a woman's place is still in the home; away from the safety of home, she states women face all types of danger (Tye 2005, 222). Another source of danger for women, as attested to in the contemporary legends, is their use of the automobile. "Narratives of women victimized in their cars may be particularly powerful precisely because they speak to an area where some women fear taking control: driving" (Tye 2005, 224). If the lone woman safely leaves her home and survives driving the car, she frequently still faces grave danger by shopping. The lone women in the legends Tye examined are either self-indulgent single women or indifferent mothers who left their children somewhere else so they can enjoy the role of consumers or to stay in a hotel. "Like the legends linking women to cars and shopping malls, these narratives of women in hotels challenge their economic power" (Tye 2005, 227). In these legends the women are not just robbed of financial markers, but are almost always sexually assaulted or murdered in "forceful perpetuation of cultural images of women as consumers/consumed, rather than producers/creators" (Tye 2005, 229).

Although this study was undertaken over a decade ago, a quick search on the Snopes site demonstrates that there has not been a great deal of change in this undeniable message to date. One warning distributed by e-mail, for example, warns women traveling on business not to fill out the menu for room service as it can be used as an indicator for criminals that she is traveling alone. In her discussion about this legend, Barbara Mikkelson delineates the historical trends regarding female business travelers. Only 1 percent of business travelers in 1970 were female. This number rose substantially since then but this legend still has some resonance as at least twice as many females as males traveling on business orders room service (http://www.snopes.com/horrors/robbery/roommenu.asp). Another legend, circulating since 2003, warns women traveling alone about a possible serial killer or rapist that uses the trick of "dropped" five-dollar bills to try and lure them from the safety of their cars. The height of circulation of this legend was when a killer was on the loose in the Lafayette and Baton Rouge area. The fact that the killer had not been caught spawned numerous variants regarding the killer's presumed methods, including the false story that he utilizes a recording of a crying baby to lure women from their homes (http://www.snopes.com/crime/warnings/rapisttrick.asp).

Elissa Henken considers the effect of gender and gender shifts on the telling and reception of contemporary legends.

> While certain contemporary legends appear to be gender neutral (both men and women have eaten Kentucky-fried rat) and many are well established with one gender as the constant protagonist/ victim (women are the vulnerable main characters in their dorm rooms and cars—especially at shopping malls; men figure as scuba divers being dropped into forest fires and office workers surging the air currents to safety from the World Trade Center), still other legends, particularly those involving sexual activity, demonstrate various forms of gender shift. (Henken 2004, 237)

Henken's discussion of the gender roles in the "Welcome to the Wonderful World of AIDS" corpus of legends demonstrates that, while the narratives with both male and female protagonists provide the same warnings about HIV and those infected with the virus, they reflect very different expectations of appropriate situations concerning sexual activity and the supposedly ideal sexual encounter regarding the gender of its victim: women desire romance and courtship; men prefer the one-night stand (Henken 2004, 238). Henken also looks at contemporary legends that demonstrated gender shifts and declares that "when the protagonist of a legend is originally a female and shifts to being a man protagonist, that man is gay. However, when the legend originally features a male protagonist, no matter whether he is straight or gay, and then switches to a female protagonist, the punishment to crime ratio increases. The woman either incurs the same punishment for a lesser transgression or incurs a greater punishment for the same transgression" (Henken 2004, 246). Thus a double standard exists in the legends for homosexual and heterosexual males. Homosexual males are punished, in the legends, in much the same way and with the same severity as females, regardless of their sexual orientation. Heterosexual males are not subjected to the same stringent expectations (Henken 2004, 253).

William Nicolaisen, in his research on males in contemporary legends in North America, determines that not all males were accorded praiseworthy roles. He examines all of the relevant tales in Jan Harold Brunvand's first five volumes of contemporary legends to discover three distinct groups of characters that are featured more often than others. Like the legends involving lone women, many of the protagonists in this corpus of tales are "road users," which include all types of vehicles and users of vehicles, including car thieves and buyers of cars. The second group are a legion of philandering husbands and bridegrooms while the third group are made up from the criminal sector: bank robbers, burglars, subway attackers, killers, and escaped convicts (Nicolaisen 2005, 251).

> Even bearing in mind the essential purpose of contemporary legends—to entertain, startle, and engage through a selective emphasis on events bordering on believability and therefore also on eyebrow-raising accounts of the unusual and bizarre—the picture which emerges from the corpus of folk narratives . . . is essentially one of astonishing failure to succeed, even of a lack of resources to make potential success a possibility. (Nicolaisen 2005, 256)

Jeannie Thomas discovers gender bias in contemporary legends as well in her research on cemeteries. The legends mirror the dominance of visible and dramatic grave markers featuring young and beautiful females regardless of the age or position of the females buried at the gravesites. The statues of males, on the other hand, are more representative of the people buried under them. "Garbed in business suits, they are not beautiful, naked, sensual or eye-catching. Many are crafted and placed to indicate the prestige of the person whose grave they mark" (Thomas 2003, 21). The statues of males are less dramatic and garner less interest from spinners of legends and those engaged in legend tripping. The legends associated with legend tripping individualize the sculptures, and without any comprehension of the statue as a symbol, detail particulars of the statue's "life" before her untimely demise (Thomas 2003, 45). "The problem with the legends is that they do not present the life stories of the actual women buried at the site. Those stories are generally not told, and the women continue to remain anonymous and unknown despite the legend-tellers' belief that they are repeating a specific story" (Thomas 2003, 46).

Thomas, as did Tye and Henken, affirms that although many of the tellers of these contemporary legends were born after the women's movement in the 1960s, dated stereotypical views of women and their place in Western society are still passed on through the legends and materially, via the grave markers (Thomas 2003, 47). Nicolaisen postulates that many types of males also suffer from stereotypical views, although this finding is dependent more on their behaviour than their gender.

Influences of Electronic Transmission on Contemporary Legends

Contemporary legends are no longer the characteristics of the narrative culture of a nation, but they belong to a new strata of oral tradition with a world wide distribution. This is due to the increased mobility of our modern society, to tourism, and of course, to unlimited international communication and networks. Through these channels the stories about strange and curious events and mishaps are easily transmitted from continent to continent and become again a part of oral circulation and dissemination.

—Brednich (2001, 7)

One of the major reasons behind my writing this book is an exploration of the effect of technology and electronic transmission on contemporary legends. From a more simplistic past, when contemporary legends were often told as true and received as such, our Western world accepted them as an essential instrument to support discussions and supply allusions on as a widely diverse number of topics as platforms for these discussions and allusions. Jan Harold Brunvand comments that contemporary legends will continue to circulate as "funny, ironic, scary, and bizarre stories that are alleged to be true and told by our friends, family members, and neighbors are simply too beguiling to fade away, even if the mass media alone already supply us with an ample number of juicy narratives" (Brunvand 2000, 199). Frequently, as we observe, what the mass media offers is these same tales, wrapped in different narrative structures and formats, to augment and re-circulate the same canon of stories. What I found in my recent research is a revisiting, in content, of much of the same contemporary legends revitalized, reconceptualised and retold electronically, in celluloid, in print and visually by professionals and amateurs alike. While legends circulate and are debunked much more rapidly and widely today through the avenues of e-mail, blogs, discussion groups and social networking sites, their attractiveness has not declined.

> Sometimes media attention devoted to contemporary legends leads individuals to anticipate the demise of the genre. As more sophisticated means of sharing and disseminating information emerge, pundits have expected the disappearance of "mere" folklore. They reason that once people become familiar with the formulaic structure of rumors and legends, they will cease to be duped by them. But that has not been the case. Some people become adept at recognizing the rumors of *other* folk groups, but they often overlook the traditional beliefs that speak to their own concerns. (Fine and Turner 2001, 8)

Advancements in technology aid not only the spread and debunking of contemporary legends but also the study of the legends in their cyclic journeys. Research, now easily conducted through electronic means, means also that the transmission of contemporary legends is aided and abetted by anyone with the slightest interest in the topic. What happens next indeed?

What's Inside "What Happens Next?"

Although monitoring the virtual explosion of contemporary legends since the publication of *Tales, Rumors, and Gossip*, I had not actively considered writing another book on the topic. This book, therefore, came about as a result of several conversations with members of the ISCLR at our annual conferences and, in particular, the one held in Baddeck, Nova Scotia, Canada, in June of 2009, and with my editor, Barbara Ittner. I decided to focus on the visible evolution of the transmission of contemporary legends and the noticeable lack of fresh and new legend content.

The intent of this book is to provide, perhaps at times eclectic, background material to engage people interested in contemporary legends in further dialogue. I have not included all that is available about contemporary legends as they appear in our contemporary world, but tightened my focus to contemporary legends as they interest, influence and reflect young-adult audiences (as they are known in the library world). That being said, *What Happens Next?* should provide junior high and high school students and educators, librarians, contemporary legend scholars and others interested in the intersection of contemporary folklore and popular culture with ample material to aid in their own research, explorations and reworkings of the material in all media forms. I also hope that these legends will be continuously told, retold and reimagined in the oral tradition along the way.

This book is organized, for the most part, in broad thematic chapters. Chapter 1, containing a summary of media appearances of contemporary legends, focuses on contemporary legends in the horror genre in literature, film and television but also discusses the visibility of contemporary legends in other types of literature and the action of debunking the legends by various groups and methodology. The following chapter continues the discussion of contemporary legends in popular culture, exploring ostension, legend tripping and the commodification of folklore. Topics under consideration include further discussions on specific cinematic reworkings of contemporary legends, several examples of legend tripping as well as subjects as diverse as shoefiti, shagging bracelets, the Jersey Devil and Mothman. Netlore is the focus of chapter 3 in which e-mail messages, chain letters and photographic urban legends are reviewed. Numerous computer legends and hoaxes such as the "Nigerian Scam" and "The Grandparent/Emergency Scam" are explored in detail. Chapter 4 considers a wide variety of conspiracy theories and their relationship with contemporary legends. This chapter briefly looks at conspiracy theories as diverse as those surrounding the September 11, 2001, World Trade Center disaster, those indicating governmental interference outside of North America by Americans such as the legendary Chupacabra, the Grease Devils of Sri Lanka and the Stolen Kidney, and the ever present doomsday prophesies. The focus in chapter 5 is on ghostlore and scary stories, including dialogues on ghost hunting, ghost tourism and campus lore. The final chapter shines a spotlight on a specific folklore motif, "a meeting with the devil at the crossroads," in an endeavour to answer the question of it being considered a contemporary legend in its own right. Background on the blues musician Robert Johnson, who is most frequently identified with this item of folklore, is offered here as well as an annotated listing of the unanticipated number of current reworkings of the motif in popular culture. The Epilogue offers a brief and concise summary of this book with discussions of additional insights and, perhaps, oversights.

References

Bennett, Gillian. 2005. *Bodies: Sex, Violence, Disease, and Death in Contemporary Legend.* Jackson: University Press of Mississippi.

Bennett, Gillian, and Paul Smith, eds. 2007. *Urban Legends: A Collection of International Tall Tales and Terrors.* Westport, CT: Greenwood Press.

Brednich, Rolf W. 2001. "Where They Originated . . . Some Contemporary Legends and Their Literary Origins." Paper presented at ISFNR Congress, Melbourne, Australia. http://www.folklore.ee/folklore/vol20/legends.pdf (accessed October 19, 2010).

Brunvand, Jan H. 2000. *The Truth Never Stands in the Way of a Good Story.* Urbana: University of Illinois Press.

Brunvand, Jan Harold. 2001. *Encyclopedia of Urban Legends.* New York: Norton.

Davis, John L. 2004. "Introduction to Part Three: Urban Myths and Contemporary Tales." In *Texas Ghost Stories: Fifty Favorites for the Telling*, edited by Tim Tingle and Doc Moore, 167–70. Lubbock: Texas Tech University Press.

Dégh, Linda. 2001. *Legend and Belief: Dialectics of a Folklore Genre.* Bloomington: Indiana University Press.

de Vos, Gail. 1996. *Tales, Rumors, and Gossip: Exploring Contemporary Folk Literature in Grades 7–12.* Westport, CT: Libraries Unlimited.

Donovan, D. Todd, John C. Mowen and Goutam Chakaborty. 2001. "Urban Legends: Diffusion Processes and the Exchange of Resources." *The Journal of Consumer Marketing* 18 (6): 521–33.

Donovan, Pamela. 2004. *No Way of Knowing: Crime, Urban Legends, and the Internet.* American Popular History and Culture. New York: Routledge.

Ellis, Bill. 2001. *Aliens, Ghosts, and Cults: Legends We Live.* Jackson: University Press of Mississippi.

Fialkova, Larissa, and Maria N. Yelenevskaya. 2001. "Ghosts in the Cyber World." *Fabula* 42 (1/2): 64–89.

Fine, Gary Alan, and Bill Ellis. 2010. *The Global Grapevine: Why Rumors of Terrorism, Immigration, and Trade Matter.* New York: Oxford University Press.

Fine, Gary Alan, and Patricia A. Turner. 2001. *Whispers on the Color Line: Rumor and Race in America*. Berkeley: University of California Press.

Guerin, Bernard, and Yoshihiko Miyazaki. 2006. "Analyzing Rumors, Gossip, and Urban Legends through Their Conversational Properties." *The Psychological Record* 56: 23–34.

Heath, Chip, and Dan Heath. 2007. *Made to Stick: Why Some Ideas Survive and Others Die.* New York: Random House.

Henken, Elissa R. 2004. "Gender Shifts in Contemporary Legend." *Western Folklore* 63 (3): 237–56.

Hobbs, Sandy. 2010. "Scholarly Use of the Term 'Urban Legend.' " *FOAFTale News: Newsletter of The International Society for Contemporary Legend Research* 74:4–5.

Lindahl, Carl. 1996. "Series Editor's Preface." In *Contemporary Legend: A Reader*, edited by Gillian Bennett and Paul Smith, xi–xv. New York: Garland.

Mayberry, Jonathan, and David F. Kramer. 2009. *They Bite: Endless Cravings of Supernatural Predators*. New York: Citadel Press.

Nicolaisen, W. F. H. 2005. "Many Characters in Contemporary Legends: A Preliminary Survey." In *Manly Traditions: The Folk Roots of American Masculinities*, edited by Simon J. Bronner, 247–60. Bloomington: Indiana University Press.

Oring, Elliott. 2008. "Legendry and the Rhetoric of Truth." *Journal of American Folklore* 121 (480): 127–66.

Simonsen, Michele. 2007. "Review of Bengt af Klintbrg, *Glitterspray ouch 99 andra klinbergare*." In "Dossier: Rumors and Urban Legends," edited by Veronique Campion-Vincent. *Diogenes* 213:169–99.

Thomas, Jeannie Banks. 2003. *Naked Barbies, Warrior Joes, & Other Forms of Visible Gender*. Urbana: University of Illinois Press.

Tye, Diane. 2005. "On Their Own: Contemporary Legends of Women Alone in the Urban Landscape." *Ethnologies* 27 (2): 219–36.

CHAPTER 1

OVERVIEW OF MEDIA APPEARANCES OF CONTEMPORARY LEGENDS

Even with the increasing importance of the Internet in teen culture, television and films remain the two most prevalent media forms in teen life. For young people, the rise of home theatre systems built around video rentals, cable movie channels, and pay-per-view has made movies as pervasive to home life as television has been for decades.

—Clark (2003, 14)

In the decade since Clark's assertion, quoted above, streaming media, YouTube, DVDs, social networking sites, apps for telephones and continually developing other media accruements have equalized the playing field, making cinematic images totally portable. Within this active and lithe world of popular culture, contemporary legends surfaced, resurfaced, are told, retold and reworked as partial or complete narratives, and remain vibrant and significant for the general population. This chapter explores contemporary legends in the literary arts and the cinematic arts, with an emphasis on the horror genre in both literature and film because of the distinct connection between the horrific and a vast majority of contemporary legends.

> Horror tales, whether in the written word (books, e-mails, newspaper articles), filmed depiction (slasher film, newsreel) or oral telling (face-to-face interaction, newscaster) are not losing their appeal and can be found everywhere. Contemporary legends can be found on-screen—from movie screen to television screen to computer screen. The stories that were once told around glowing campfires or in darkened dorm rooms are now not only being depicted in films but also appearing online, in people's in-boxes. (McKechnie 2010, 171)

Contemporary Legends in the Literary Arts

Contemporary legends are easily located in all print formats and literary genres including graphic novels, short stories, poetry, picture books and novels intended for/appreciated by young-adult reading and listening audiences. Authors in the literary arts have embraced contemporary legends in at least four major ways. Firstly, contemporary legends provide a window into the concerns of the cultural time of the creation of texts written before the reader's contemporary time. These legends frequently seemed dated to current readers, but the legends illuminate the setting and time frame of the novel. Ian McEwan's adult novel *Solar* (2010) is a black comedy about a Nobel Prize–winning physicist, Michael Beard. In the story on climate change and environmental disaster, Michael Beard boards a train. Beard is inordinately fond of salt and vinegar potato chips (crisps) and is extremely surprised and discomforted when, while shovelling them into his mouth, the young man sitting opposite him helps himself to the chips. It was not until Beard leaves the train and puts his hand in his pocket to find his own package of chips that he realizes that he had been eating the ones belonging to the young man. Definitely a familiar contemporary legend that is not necessarily as current as it once was, "Kit Kat" struck a chord with readers and reviewers of this novel as many of them point to this brief episode in great detail. In an interview with McEwan, the author stated that:

> When I read my account at a literary festival, in the signing queue afterwards more than six or seven people said that had happened to them, or to someone they know. I decided to describe an encounter between Michael Beard and an urban legend professor, who insists that Beard's experience is inauthentic—which of course makes him very indignant. ("Ian McEwan in Conversation" 2010)

Tibor Fischer, in his review of the novel in *The Telegraph*, writes about flimsy charges of plagiarism against McEwan when the author read an excerpt of *Solar* at the Hay festival. The segment reworking the legendary "Kit Kat" was immediately compared to Douglas Adams's *Hitchhiker's Guide to the Galaxy* (1979), which also included a similar scenario but with cookies (biscuits) instead of crisps (Fischer 2010). "It doesn't matter finally whether McEwan had a recollection of Adams's biscuits buried away in his memory, because if you compare the writing, the treatment of the story couldn't be more different" (Fischer 2010). Of course, for those readers and listeners aware of the almost timeless contemporary legend, plagiarism would not be a consideration at all.

Another way that authors utilize contemporary legends in their writings is to have them act as a communicative device within the work, reflecting or foreshadowing one of the thematic story arcs in the story line. Contemporary legends here demonstrate the relationship between characters in the text or reveal character traits for one of the characters. In Patricia Smiley's short story "The Offer" (2009), for example, the characterization of the narrator is easily clarified with the following passage:

> Her bad luck had started with a letter out of the blue from the Nigerian minister of education. It seemed that he was having a problem transferring his son's college expense fund into the country in time to meet the enrolment deadline. If he failed, the young man's lifelong dream of attending the University of Washington would be destroyed. Would Mari be kind enough to help?

> The plan seemed simple enough. He would send her a check for
> thirty thousand dollars, which she would deposit in her savings
> account and then wire twenty-five thousand dollars to the son.
> The additional five thousand was hers to keep as compensation
> for her trouble She coveted the extra cash, because her car needed
> new tires and the dunning messages on her dentist's bill had turned
> impolite. (10)

"The Nigerian Money Scam," the contemporary legend painted in this descriptive
excerpt, is discussed in chapter 3. Another example of a familiar contemporary
legend is found in Laura Bickle's novel *Embers* (2010). "My mom was very cau-
tious. She was the kind of mom who took all of my Halloween candy to be
x-rayed for razor blades, made me wear an extra sweater, and insisted that I take
extra vitamin C" (111). Grouped with renowned wise-mother-adages, the "razor
blades in apples" and "tainted Halloween treats" have entered the lexicon of prover-
bial sayings and aptly aided in the characterization of the narrator's parent. Here,
and in countless other examples I have found in my readings, the contemporary
legend is merely referred to, not spelled out and not utilized as part of the plotline.
In other cases, contemporary legends have been employed in furthering the plot
but not for the plot itself. I have frequently found contemporary legends employed
in this manner in mystery novels written in the United Kingdom. Mark
Billingham, in *Bloodline* (2009), wrote:

> Just after lunch, a CPS lawyer named Hobbs called with depressing
> news. Eight months earlier, a young woman had been killed during
> an attempted car-jacking in Chiswick. She had got into her car after
> shopping, then stopped when she'd noticed a large piece of paper
> stuck to her rear windscreen. When she'd pulled over and got out
> to remove it, a man had jumped from the vehicle behind and
> attempted to steal her car. In trying to stop him, she had been dragged
> beneath the wheels and, a week after the incident, her husband had
> taken the decision to turn off the life-support machine. (190)

This contemporary legend, completely spelled out in this excerpt, has been circulating by e-mail at least since 2004. The entry in Snopes clearly marks it as a contemporary legend. They state that their law enforcement contacts were not familiar with
this type of carjacking. "Carjackings are generally crimes of opportunity, committed
by persons in need of quick cash or youngsters either out for a thrill or participating
in some rite of passage (such as a gang initiation)" ("Carjacking"). The planning and
execution of placing flyers on the back windshields is not indicative of the carjackers' mode of operation. While car alarms have made carjackers more innovative,
most drivers approach their vehicles in parking lots from the rear and would remove
any obstructions on the rear window before entering the vehicle.

     In other instances, the authors have used only allusions to popular contempo-
rary legends, secure that their reading audience would understand the references and
the rationale to that particular use. In the graphic novel *Y the Last Man: Motherland*,
one of a series of trade collections of the single-issue science fiction comic book created by Brian K. Vaughn and Pia Guerra, two characters are discussing the fact that
the world was now rat-free, particularly in the sewer. "Like the Pied Piper blew into
town. Only thing you have to worry about now is bugs, those stories about alligators
down here are just old wives' tales. Hopefully" (106).

Contemporary legends also serve as a frame of reference for the whole text. This is seen in the various reworkings of the "meeting of the devil at the crossroads" legend examined in chapter 6 and in the titles discussed later in this chapter.

Horror Literature

> Concern about the effects of reading "horror" stems from the fact that as a genre, it tends to be associated with kinds of knowledge and forms of experience regarded by many as unsuitable for children, notably those involving the occult or provoking high levels of fear or anxiety.
>
> —Reynolds (2001, 2)

While there are prolific mentions and reworkings of contemporary legends in publications aimed at adult audiences, the idea of contemporary legends, retold and reinvented, has gained a stronghold in horror literature for all ages. Horror literature, a work of fiction that contains a monster of some type, a monster that often has the effect of frightening the reader, does not have to have as its raison d'être the production of fear (Fonseca and Pulliam 2009, 3). Fonseca and Pulliam suggest that the various subgenres may be the best way to describe horror as a genre as they allow the reader, by supplying the pieces and giving a general framework for their interrelationships, to put the horror puzzle together (Fonseca and Pulliam 2009, 5). Rather than categorize the genre by style-based categories such as gothic horror, comic horror, splatterpunk, gentle reads and so on, Fonseca and Pulliam consider the type of monster (supernatural, human, metaphorical or a combination of all three) appearing in the story. Ghosts and haunted houses, a large and well-developed subgenre, are horror stories that deal with presences and absences. More than any of the other subgenres, this one lends itself to the short-story format (Fonseca and Pulliam 2009, 20).

> It is not unusual to find folklore in which the murdered dead return as revenging revenants, seeking to avenge themselves from beyond the grave. Most Americans grew up with similar stories of revenging revenants, usually told around the campfire or with flashlights being used for dramatic effect; these universal stories of "things that go bump in the night" come back to haunt us as adults, particularly when we are falling asleep in our beds—and suddenly we hear creaking noises when there is no physical evidence of a cause. (Fonseca and Pulliam 2009, 20)

The authors state that tales of ghosts feed a basic psychological need for affirmation that life existed after death. Because of this, they assert, ghost stories tend to be more psychological than other tales of the supernatural and rely more on atmosphere and suggestion and less on gore (Fonseca and Pulliam 2009, 21). Stories of ghosts and ghostlore are discussed in more detail in chapter 5 of this book.

Other subgenres identified by Fonseca and Pulliam include monster tales of golems, mummies, zombies, vampires and werewolves as well as mythical monsters and the "Old Ones" derived from classical mythology. Human monsters such as maniacs and sociopaths form another subgenre, as do "small town terror" and "villages of the damned" stories that frighten their readers with the realization that once a person is away from the sanctity and security of a civilization that plays by a known set of rules, anything can happen (Fonseca and Pulliam 2009, 7). Horror caused by the environment or by technology are accorded their own subgenres: ecological horror and technohorror. The latter subgenre, one of the most popular, includes tales of evil hospitals, military mistakes, mad scientists and alien invasions. Technohorror exploits the fear of the unknown that results from misused knowledge or scientific experimentation gone horribly wrong (Fonseca and Pulliam 2009, 7). Several contemporary legends factor largely in this subgenre of horror and are discussed in chapter 4. Demonic possession, Satanism, black magic and witches and warlocks formulate the subgenre the authors dub "The Devil Made Me Do It." These tales of black magic and demonic possession involve innocent people possessed by demons or the devil itself; tales of not so innocent people making deals with the devil at the crossroads for fame and fortune are discussed in chapter 6. Fonseca and Pulliam maintain that tales of Satanism and black magic could also be about witches, warlocks and others who willingly become involved with dark forces. Not all witches and warlocks practice black magic, and as a result, tales of those characters would not be classified as horror tales (Fonseca and Pulliam 2009, 6). Splatterpunk constitutes the subgenre of gross, where graphic sex and violence result from the decadent indulgences of bored mortals and immortals, rather than as shocking excesses of monsters that must be stopped (Fonseca and Pulliam 2009, 8). The final subgenres—comic horror, psychological horror, telekinesis and hypnosis—are fairly self-explanatory, as is everyday horror, situations that occur when the mundane becomes monstrous (Fonseca and Pulliam 2009, 8).

Young-adult readers, required by their stage of life to take chances, make decisions and evaluate risks, frequently appreciate frightening horror fiction that reflect their anxieties about and emotions around risk taking and decision making with their stories of extreme situations with exaggerated consequences (Reynolds 2001, 7).

> In an age when both the media and the public find it difficult to distinguish between reality and fantasy, a sober appraisal of beliefs in different types of supernatural enemies is most relevant. Such enemies may be defined as hostile, destructive forces coming from outside the familiar world, with power to influence or change individuals or events. Their supernatural nature renders them beyond the control of those who have no skill in magic or ritual. Supernatural enemies may be ambivalent in nature and not invariably hostile, but they are always potentially dangerous. They may not confine themselves to one form: they are often shape-shifters, able to appear as unfamiliar monsters or phantoms or in apparently familiar human or animal form, but they are always endowed with monstrous or terrifying characteristics. (Davidson and Chaudhri 2001, vii)

Selected Examples of Literature Incorporating Contemporary Legends

Most of the authors in this section have utilized the overall concept and significance of contemporary legends in modern society, but at the same time manufacture their own legends for their individual story lines.

Carman, Patrick. *Skeleton Creek*. New York: Scholastic, 2009.

Skeleton Creek, followed by *Ghost in the Machine*, *The Crossbones* and *The Raven*, is a multiplatform project written and produced by Carman. The series, consisting of novels, websites, blogs and other Internet platforms, tracks the adventures of Ryan and Sarah as they try to decipher the mysterious strange occurrences in their town of Skeleton Creek. Their investigation, due to an eerie accident effecting Ryan's mobility and ability to visit with Sarah, is told in two distinct and integrated methods: Ryan has written his thoughts and experiences in his journal while Sarah used a video camera, e-mailing clips from the videos to Ryan. Several Skeleton Creek websites (http://skeletoncreekfans.com/ and http://www.skeletoncreekisreal.com/) provide the readers of the print journals with Sarah's video investigation, and background information on the mysteries, the characters and the community of Skeleton Creek. In an interview with Erin McIntosh, the author stated that:

> The location, the Skeleton Creek dredge, is not only real a real place but you can go and tour it. And there is an actual—there was one person down through history who was killed on one of these dredges and his name was Joe Bush. So there is a lot of urban legend stuff floating around about the story, and I did that on purpose. I thought, well, might as well make it seem like there are some factual things about it. The fact that there's all this stuff floating around adds to the intrigue, makes it more interesting. . . . I had actually been to the dredge before, and I remembered wandering around and heard all the stories about it and the legends of it and what it was used for and I remember taking a lot of pictures and thinking, someday this is going to make a cool setting for a story. (McIntosh 2009)

Gaiman, Neil. "Bitter Grounds." *Fragile Things: Short Fictions and Wonders*. New York: William Morrow, 2006, 85–107.

Gaiman's challenging short story originally written for Nalo Hopkinson's 2003 anthology *Mojo: Conjure Stories* also appears in Joe Hill's horror anthology, *The Living Dead* (2008). The tale relates the adventures of the narrator, who, after hearing the legend from a professor about little coffee girls of Haiti who knock on people's doors to sell coffee, reluctantly assumes the identity of the missing professor. The narrator proceeds to the conference in New Orleans to deliver the professor's paper on "The Zombie Coffee Girls." During the discussion of the zombie coffee girl paper a member of the audience comments that the zombie coffee girls "were, she said, one with the Indian Rope Trick, just another of the urban legends of the past" (103).

The morning after his presentation at the conference, the narrator wakes up to find a zombie coffee girl at his door. The story concludes with the female zombie and the narrator walking off together "into the misty dawn" (Wagner, Golden and Bissette 2008, 380). Several mentions are made about folklorist, anthropologist and novelist Zora Neale Hurston as well as the legend of "The Vanishing Hitchhiker." " 'You know, this has that pristine urban legend quality, driving down country roads with a mysterious Samaritan. A Phantom Hitchhiker. After I get to my destination, I'll describe you to a friend, and they'll tell me you died ten years ago, and still go around giving people rides' " (87).

Hernandez, Gilbert. *Sloth*. New York: Vertigo, 2006.

Hernandez's graphic novel explores adolescent emotional concerns of fear, anxiety and joy with three teenage characters in a haunted lemon orchard in suburbia. Miguel, a disaffected young adult, resumes his relationship with his girlfriend, Lita, and band mate, Romeo, after coming out of a year-long coma. The threat of a supernatural and deadly "goatman" causes uncertainties among the characters, but before they could be resolved, the story begins again, this time with Lita coming out of the coma. In the third scenario, Romeo descends into a coma, leaving the legend about the goatman and the relationship of the three characters unresolved. Clean black-and-white art complemented the story line.

Booklist awards it a starred review, stating that this was "an ideal, somewhat challenging YA novel in graphic form; one sex scene" (Flagg 2006, 32). The review refers to the contemporary legend involvement as the three conducting a *Blair Witch*-like investigation of the goatman of the haunted lemon orchard. In their investigation, "they stumble onto the truth behind the urban legend . . . [with illustrated] sequences, particularly the nocturnal scenes in the mysterious orchard, as pictorially gorgeous as anything [Hernandez has] ever done" (32).

> Hernandez creatively suggests how young adults opt to escape the social and emotional pressures of growing into adulthood in the twenty-first century. Within the graphic novel, Hernandez touches on the volatile themes of abandonment, female discrimination in the workforce, love versus lust, teenage idolization, and adolescent self-esteem. Furthermore, Hernandez successfully depicts how the three main characters opt to "fade out" of society through self-induced comas, rather than the much glorified subject of teen suicide. This aspect of the graphic novel makes it a possible candidate for use in the classroom, preferably for twelfth-grade and college-level students. (Montoya 2009)

Hirshberg, Glen. "Mr. Dark's Carnival." *The Two Sams: Ghost Stories.* New York: Carroll & Graf, 2003, 93–139.

This short story, concerning a contemporary legend coming to life at Halloween, was nominated for the International Horror Guild Award and the World Fantasy Award. First published in *Shadows and Silence,* edited by Barbara and Christopher Roden (2000), it appears in *The Year's Best Fantasy and Horror #14,* edited by Ellen Datlow and Terri Windling (2001). Editor Ellen Datlow says of this story that it was inspired by one cathartic night of haunted-house hunting in Montana in 1989 and is one of several that the author tells his students every Halloween (Datlow 2001, 157).

The story, set in a college town in Montana famous for its Halloween celebrations, centers on a local contemporary legend about a strange carnival of undisclosed horrors. The narrator, a college professor, teaches his students about this local tradition and the legendary invitation to participate in the festivities. His horrific experience and discoveries about the haunted house are effectively told in this well-written and well-received tale.

Wooding, Chris. *Malice.* Illustrated by Dan Chernett. New York: Scholastic Press, 2009.

This first volume of the fantasy trilogy about a legendary comic book that was reportedly transporting its readers into a deadly alternative universe is written as a hybrid, partly in novel format and partly in comic book format. Reviewers of the novel often refer to a correspondence of the series to that of the *Ring* franchise and the "Bloody Mary" ritual. In order to enter the otherworld, the selected reader of the comic book *Malice* must gather ritual ingredients which are burned while the individual chants "Tall Jake, take me away" six times.

> "The chant was only a request. An invitation. Tall Jake would come when he was ready. It might be tonight; it might be tomorrow. Might be a week; might be never. But if he wanted you, if he chose you to play his horrible little game, he'd come when you were alone." (103)

Unbeknown to these prospective inhabitants of the otherworld, once they had completed the ritual, their experiences are recorded in future issues of the comic book. The comic book series, available from one hard-to-find comic book shop, is known only to young adults who have heard rumors of its existence.

> "What?" he protested. "It's just a stupid legend. You burn a few things, say the chant six times; Tall Jake comes to take you away. There's a million stories like that. I've heard ringtones that were scarier."
>
> Luke shook his head. "Listen, I'm not kidding. I said it, and some really weird stuff happened. (24)

Two middle-school-age protagonists, Seth and Katy, attempt to solve the mystery of the comic book and the world of *Malice.* Katy discovers secrets in the real world while Seth, sucked into the world of the contemporary legend, and a new friend undergo harrowing journeys and adventures seeking answers from within that world. There is a great deal of danger in this world, and not everyone who enters it returns to their former lives or even lives at all. A cliff-hanger ending leads into the second novel, *Havoc* (2010). The readership is still awaiting the conclusion of the fast-paced series at the writing of this entry.

In the beginning of the second novel when Seth returns to the real world for a very short visit, he scurries out from his village home into the storm.

> The lane where he lived was on a hill, and he followed it to the top, where it came to a crossroads. He had no idea where he was going, only that he had to get away. Lightning split the clouds in dazzling forks, and the storm roared in fury. The trees of the churchyard bowed and rustled as he passed. The shadows in the village were deep and thick, and he didn't know what might be hiding in them. (9)

Readers familiar with the contemporary legend of the meeting at the crossroads with the devil, discussed in chapter 6, will not be surprised to discover who Seth meets at that crossroads. The novels incorporate various other means of current communication in order to deliver the story; besides the comic book segments, transcriptions of chat conversations, notes in a wide variety of formats and storytelling sessions move the plotline quickly and purposefully forward.

> "They're probably just urban legends," said Alicia. "Like the one about the scary guy who keeps calling this girl when she's alone in the house. They trace the call, and it turns out to be coming—"
>
> "**—from inside the house!!!**" Philip cried in a fake wail of terror. "Yeah, like that." (52)

Perhaps related to the idea behind Wooding's trilogy is the legendary arcade game, *Polybius*, an Internet contemporary legend. According to the legend, the game was released in several suburbs of Portland, Oregon, in 1981. Playing the game caused the players to suffer from intense stress, horrific nightmares and suicidal tendencies. Shortly after its release, the game vanished without a trace, leaving no evidence of its existence. Before it disappeared, however, unknown data was collected from the arcade machines by men in black. The Wikipedia entry on the game declares that the original of the contemporary legend is unknown, but that some gamers thought it originated as a Usenet hoax, while others felt that it was a true contemporary legend growing out of the exaggerated and distorted stories of an early-release version of the game *Tempest*, retracted when it caused problems with photosensitive epilepsy, motion sickness and vertigo in the players. Mass-market attention to *Polybius* resulted in an article, "Secrets and Lies," published in *GamePro* (September 2003). Snopes.com debunks the legend as a current version of the "men in black" legends, circulating in the 1980s, collecting data in arcades. A *Polybius* game was featured in the episode "Please Homer, Don't Hammer 'Em" of *The Simpsons* (September 24, 2006). The front of the machine in the episode had "property of the US government" stamped on it. The *Polybius Theory* website, http://www.freewebs.com/polybiustheory/, offers detailed information regarding this legend.

Contemporary Legends in Film and Television

> *The general public evinces this interest in its consumption of books, television shows and films on legends; and there is an interest on the part of public institutions—government, industry, the press—to gauge the extent and understand the willingness of people to believe a host of unlikely events.*
>
> —Oring (2008, 127)

Both Paul Smith and Mikel Koven have written extensively on the ways contemporary legends have been utilized in current films. Smith identifies four major methods for this practice: embedded narratives, subplots, multiple plots and complete plots. Embedded narratives, similar to the way contemporary legends have been used in literature, occur when a character relates a contemporary legend in ordinary conversation or in a legend-telling scenario (Smith 1999, 140). Mikel Koven considers this type of usage to be *dialogic* motifs, occurring in fictional contexts with great verisimilitude to actual legend transmission (Koven 2008, 101). For Koven, any film not directly based on a contemporary legend text but using legendary materials within its narrative would be considered an embedded narrative (Koven 2008, 102). Since contemporary legends are concise by their very nature, they have been frequently embedded as narrative asides (spoken within the dialogue) or embedded action (ostension). The natural brevity of contemporary legends means that an individual legend is usually insufficient for a feature-length film, but would certainly act as a single-strand narrative in short films and YouTube videos. An example of this is the short award-winning horror film *Side Effect* (2008), written and directed by Liz Adams, based on the contemporary legend of "The Hippy Babysitter." Contemporary legends are utilized in other films as an integral part of the film's subplot or, combined with other individual contemporary legends, to create a single film or series of television programs. Smith likens this third method of multiple plots to a print anthology, "much in the way a writer would put together a collection of related short stories" (Smith 1999, 144). Individual contemporary legends are used as the basis for complete films in Smith's fourth category.

Koven further subdivides this latter category into four main narrative strategies: extended narratives, resultant narratives, structuring narratives and fusion narratives. Films that utilize extended narratives take the contemporary legend as a starting point and extend it further, depicting "what happened next" or the repercussions of the incident. The film *The Curve/Dead Man's Curve* (1998) focuses on the legend of the college suicide rule and extends the narrative much beyond the traditional story (Koven 2008, 102). Resultant narratives give the background story for the contemporary legend with the actual legend acting almost as a punch line to the film. "Ideally under this narrative strategy, we have identified with our protagonist(s) and so are more receptive to the horror of what happens to them once the legend aspects are revealed" (Koven 2008, 103). The films *Paradise Lost/Turistas* (2006) and *The Harvest* (1993), both focussed on the "kidney theft" contemporary legends, exemplify this narrative strategy. Structuring narratives utilize contemporary legends as a structuring framework for the film's narrative. The "suicide rule," mentioned earlier and discussed in chapter 5, is the structural framework for *Dead Man on Campus* (1998) (Koven 2008, 104). Fusion narratives do exactly that: two different contemporary legends are fused together to extend the narrative. More than two contemporary legends change the categorization to multi-strand narratives. The film *Alligators* (1980) fuses the two contemporary legends, "alligators in the sewer" and "pet abductions for medical experiments," for the story line (Koven 2008, 102).

As mentioned earlier, because of their succinct length most individual contemporary legends cannot be the basis for full-length films. Therefore other narrative techniques have been employed to transform the legends into film: multi-strand narratives and anthology films. The film *Urban Legend* embodies the most obvious example of multi-strand narrative films, fusing together numerous legend texts, both dialogically (through discussion of the legends by the characters in the film) and ostensively (told through action). The *Urban Legend* film has been referred to several times in other discussions in this book, particularly as an example of cinematic ostension since the film is entirely about ostension; the characters making various legends "real" by enacting the events within the legends that the characters had heard and told (Koven 2008, 105). Anthology films, on the other hand, do not fuse contemporary legends together in one narrative but treat each story as unique and, usually with some type of framing device or uniting symbol or character, presenting them as a collection of tales. Several films, such as *Campfire Tales* (1997), *Tales from a Golden Age* (2009) and *Trick 'r Treat* (2009), follow this basic narrative structure. Anthology films celebrate the short-story quality of contemporary legends and treat each story as distinct, using any of the techniques of the single-strand or embedded narratives (Koven 2008, 111). *Haunted Universities* (2010) is based on four contemporary legends and horror stories set in universities in Thailand. The four tales related to their studies, each based on a different contemporary legend popular in Thailand, are experienced by different students. The anthology film is framed with the story of Muay who, when taking an internship with an emergency service organization, becomes involved with some terrifying incidents surrounding universities. The Thai contemporary legends in this film may not be immediately recognizable for North American audiences, but the overall theme and idea of the film would certainly be accessible.

> We are not always presented with a narrative as such, for while contemporary legends are essentially a composite of plot, text, beliefs, and attitudes, in the hands of the filmmaker the presentation of an extended narrative is not always what is required. Instead, we are sometimes simply offered a recognizable *allusion* to a narrative that, in itself, is never fully expressed. (Smith 1999, 147)

Televised and Filmic Contemporary Legends

Popular culture has been one of the chief disseminators of contemporary legends in our society, through not just film but television programming as well. Both types of cinematic presentation draw on contemporary legend materials for their story lines but also, by retelling and reshaping the legends, redistribute them to a new generation (Koven 2008, 69). Less concerned with academic perspectives on folklore, the producers of these programs tend to fuse all elements of folk tradition together with little attention paid to cultural meanings or specific phenomena behind such lore, falling victim to "folklore fallacy" arguments (Koven 2008, 78). Postings on fan websites, discussion blogs and chat rooms tend to rectify some of the erroneous beliefs and misrepresentations within some of these programs but, for those viewers who are not actively participating in other aspects of their television and film viewing, their understanding of contemporary legends would be compromised. Koven expounded on discussions by *X-File* fans about the use of folklore in the series as demonstrating an *active* television readership. These discussions, and the ones for subsequent programs such as *Supernatural*, reflect the types of debates that folklorists named as essential defining characteristics of the contemporary legend as genre (Koven 2008, 80). However, I quickly discovered when discussing contemporary legends with students that most of the time their perception of the legends reflects those that they passively consume. This opportunely results in plenty of "teachable moments."

This extremely selective and subjective collection of titles consists of contemporary legends that have had a regular appearance in programs or were a major component of films not considered part of the horror genre or ghostlore. Titles in these other two categories are discussed elsewhere.

Freaky Stories *(Television Series)*

This Canadian animated series, hosted by two puppets, Larry, a cockroach, and Maurice, a maggot, focuses on contemporary legends and other scary stories. Every episode, now available for viewing on YouTube, begins with "This is a true story, and it happened to a friend of a friend of mine." Germane contemporary legends told in the series included "Mexican Pet," "Beehive Hairdo," "The Hook," "Humans Can Lick Too," "The Vanishing Hitchhiker," "The Choking Doberman," "Alligators in the Sewer" and "Have You Checked the Children," a babysitting horror tale. One episode includes the legend of a young man at a super-market who is duped by an elderly woman into paying for her groceries. This latter contemporary legend is retold, in a great spirit of fun, by Tom Waits on his album *Orphans: Brawlers, Bawlers & Bastards* (2006). Waits tells the tale of "Missing My Son" rather than singing it on his album. At least four different videos of him doing so are readily available on YouTube.

MythBusters *(Television Series)*

> We originally started out with the scarecrow idea of urban legends and we branched from that into common misconceptions and things like movie physics and stuff like that. At this point we're also finding fertile territory in things like idioms, idiomatic phrases like "needle in a haystack" ... It comes from everywhere, it comes from the fans, it comes from people yelling at me in the street and from news stories that we read.
>
> —Dilworth (2009)

The long-running series, shown on Discovery Channel and collected on DVD and posted on YouTube, focuses on uncovering the truth behind contemporary legends, rumors and unbelievable moments in film and YouTube videos. Hosted by Jamie Hyneman and Adam Savage, the series features a team of special effects and subject experts and, in most cases, a great deal of explosives. For example, on the episode of the "the exploding toilet," once the contemporary legend was related folklorist Heather Joseph-Withan appeared, offering background information about the legend. Also available are numerous books and science kits related to the television series. The earlier episodes focus more on contemporary legends as is demonstrated in the first DVD collection, *MythBusters Collection 1*. Among the legion of legends Savage and Hyneman explored, the following are particularly relevant: "The Exploding Toilet," "Cell Phone Dangers at Gas Stations," "Dangers at Suntan Salons," "Pets in Microwave Ovens" (this one was not actually tested but was discussed on the show that explored other legends relating to microwave ovens), numerous Cokelore legends, "Pop Rocks and Drinking Soda" and "Death Cars." One of the investigated contemporary legends is particular pertinent to me: "Barrel of Bricks." Snopes.com classifies it as a humorous contemporary legend, a "loony letter" which clarifies an accident report when calamity resulted when a dim-witted person tried to hoist a barrel of bricks to the top of a building. The letter, which has resurfaced many times over the years, floated as an e-mail message in 1997 but is traced back as far as an 1895 newspaper (Mikkelson 2008). It appeared in David Foster Wallace's novel *Infinite Jest* (1996), Laurel and Hardy's film *Way Out West* (1937), the film *Babe: Pig in the City* (1998) and the video for "Squares" by Beta Band (2001). It also made an appearance in my daughter's first-year class as a bricklayer, related in the form of a Workman's Compensation Board report and, since that time, on multiple job sites in a variety of formats (de Vos, personal communication, 2009).

Besides access through various websites, sanctioned and other, as well as several *MythBusters* Facebook pages (over 4.5 million people "liked" the main Facebook fan page at this point in time), there have also been a large number of people following Adam Savage's Twitter feed. "For some of the nearly 100,000 followers of 'MythBusters' star Adam Savage's Twitter feed, communicating with him has proven to be more than just your average back-and-forth. For some, it's been a way to submit ideas that he and his Discovery Channel show costars have used for actual episodes" (Terdiman 2009). Savage is also quoted as stating that Twitter allowed him to have significant dialogues with his fans that are more civilized than the show's official forums, which often attract negative commentary. Hyneman, on the other hand, finds all of the social networks distracting and does not participate with fans on any of them (Terdiman 2009).

The Simpsons *(Television Series)*

> *Stories about Bart are so bad that the school board thought he was nothing but an urban legend.*
>
> —"Simpsons Urban Legends"

Haynes Lee, in the "Simpsons Urban Legends" online guide, crosschecks most of the contemporary legends that appear in *The Simpsons* with a variety of resources including Snopes.com. Unfortunately, the actual episodes in which the contemporary legend appeared are not indicated in these entries. Contemporary legends in the series that correspond to those discussed in this book include: "Babysitter and the Telephone Call," "Alligator in the Sewers," "Shoefiti," "Kidney Heist," "Poisoned Halloween Candy," "Razor Blades in Apples" and "Bloody Mary," or in this case, "Bloody Margie." In *Treehouse of Horror IV*, the Halloween special reworked the classic story of "The Devil and Daniel Webster," which is considered in chapter 6 of this book.

Tales from the Golden Age *(2009)*

Inspired by contemporary legends circulating during the Communist era in his home country of Romania, Cristian Mungiu writes five short screenplays, directed by five different directors, for this collective film. In Romania, the film is released as two separate entities divided by the basic theme of the story: tales of love and tales of authority. While North American audiences are not familiar with legends such as "The Legend of the Greedy Policeman" in which the killing of a pig without arousing suspicions of the neighbors was the main focus, or "The Legend of the Official Visit," where an entire village is thrown into disarray when the upcoming presidential motorcade would be passing through it, they would likely be fascinated at this glimpse of folklore, and politics, in a different culture. For young-adult audiences, the episode "The Legend of the Air Sellers," regarding a student scam, would be accessible, relevant and recognizable. In an interview with BBC News reporter Emma Jones, award-winning director Cristian Mungiu states that since he wanted to make a film for his audience, he opened the project up to other Romanian directors and to the public. "We got a lot of buzz on Twitter and Facebook, with people posting up stories and memories from their youth and adolescence. I thought it was important to get these stories made, before we forget about them" (Jones 2009).

Horror Films

> *Human nature seems to crave knowledge that is seemingly unknowable; perhaps people look to the supernatural when there do not seem to be satisfactory answers to their questions in the everyday "real" world. Regardless of the reason, this interest has led people to the séance table, to fortune-tellers, and to haunted houses. It also leads people to read books such as this collection of ghost stories and has spawned an entire segment of the entertainment industry as well, which brings horror fiction and horror movies to a wide and eager audience.*
>
> —McCormick and Wyatt (2009, 6)

Koven cites Larry Danielson, stating that many horror movies draw heavily on "stories which are not ghost or witch stories—they usually do not deal with the supernatural—which are told because of the effect of horror they produce in the listener. Usually the emphasis is on the grisly or strange rather than on the supernatural" (Koven 2008, 13). Brigid Cherry, in her overview on horror, categorizes cinematic horror into seven distinct subgenres: the gothic; supernatural, occult and ghost films; psychological horror; monster movies; slashers; body horror, splatter and gore films; and exploitation cinema. She defines gothic horror films as based on classic tales of horror, often adapting pre-existing monsters or creatures from novels and mythology, and psychological horror as films that explore psychological states and psychoses, including criminality and serial killers (Cherry 2009, 5). Monster films feature invasions of the everyday world by natural and secular creatures leading to death and destruction (Cherry 2009, 5). Films that explore abjection and disgust of the human body, involving mutation, disease or aberrant and fetishistic behaviour such as cannibalism or sado-masochism, are categorized as body horror, splatter and gore films. This category includes films featuring postmodern zombies (Cherry 2009, 6). Cherry defines exploitation cinema as films focused on extreme or taboo subjects, including violence and torture, Nazi death camps, rape and other sexual assaults upon women (Cherry 2009, 6).

Tsai claims that American horror films were long obsessed with bodies, with the roots of the genre traced to the Gothic tradition and literary classics that helped shape the paradigms over the last two centuries (Tsai 2008, 6). She briefly traces the evolution of the modern horror movie scene in the 1970s where films dealt with new psychological fears such as mother-children relationships and fear of the female body exemplified by *The Exorcist* (1972) and *Carrie* (1976). This latter film, along with *The Texas Chain Massacre* (1974) and *Halloween* (1978), highlights the genesis of the slasher film (Tsai 2008, 8). "The events of 9/11 are thought to have changed Americans' perceptions of what is frightening. Like the shock and panic of the 21st century's terrorist attack, cinematic horror now offers a new direction in Asian horror inspiration: Japanese horror remakes" (Tsai 2008, 8). At the same time, she continues, ghost films could not escape American horror's obsession with the death of the body: "American's [sic] treatments of ghosts are either images of corporeal embodiment or internally as psychological otherness. Not to mention that American ghosts, unlike those of Japan, are rarely gendered as female" (Tsai 2008, 9).

> The function of horror—to scare, shock, revolt or otherwise hor-
> rify the viewer—also means that filmmakers are constantly push-
> ing at the boundaries in order to invent new ways of arousing
> these emotions in audiences (who over time will naturally learn
> what to expect from a specific type of horror, a process that may
> well lead to viewers becoming used to or even bored with the for-
> mula) and thus keep the scares coming. (Cherry 2009, 4)

Most horror films, with their predictable outcomes in a set, time-bounded narrative, have followed the same functional patterns as Ouija boards for adolescents
and "Bloody Mary" ritual games for pre-adolescents (Koven 1999, 164). For young
adults, horror films function as contemporary initiation rites; going to a "scary
movie" has been considered ritualistic, often following seasonal markers such as
Halloween, and a rite of passage (Koven 2008, 19).

> As anthropologist Victor Turner argued, in modern society the
> experience of watching films together can, in some ways, serve
> the same functions as the older rituals that marked rites of passage.
> Specifically, he wrote of the ability of film to call forth in its audi-
> ence a sense of luminal moments, that time of transition in rituals
> where the past is forgotten and the participants are able to envision
> a new future. An important appeal of confronting the stories of the
> supernatural in teen culture, then, may have references to a need to
> feel competent and powerful in the face of powers beyond one's
> control. In today's situation, this occurs in the context of peers
> who share similar fears and are bonded together as those fears are
> invoked and symbolically overcome. Thus, perhaps the séance of
> the late-night communal television-viewing of horror films gives
> adolescent boys an opportunity to demonstrate their fearlessness
> while girls, due to changing gender conventions, can either dem-
> onstrate their own fearlessness or their need for reassurance from
> the boys. (Clark 2003, 6)

The marketing of horror reflects the diverse emotional effects of different
types of horror, particularly the revulsion and disgust of gore films; the shock and
dread of slasher films; and the shiver sensation of supernatural horror films
(Cherry 2009, 47). It will be interesting to observe how the ongoing presence of
these films available on the Internet, YouTube or a streaming service such as
Netflix changes the emphasis and effect of future marketing promotions of the horror genre. John Carpenter, renowned director of horror films such as the *Halloween*
series, states, "Folklore is translated into a twentieth-century medium, the movies,
as opposed to being told around a campfire. Now, there it is right in front of you
on the screen. The horror film is always reinvented by the new generation. Then
you keep seeing it again and again until it wears out. Then somebody else comes
along and reinvents it" (Mayberry and Kramer 2009, 16).

Lynn Schofield Clark stresses that horror films and television programs, like
séances and other supernatural activities, offer young adults chances to vicariously
participate in rebellion at the same time as they control their fears through the symbolic defeat of evil monsters and supernatural spirits. With the defeat of these
uncanny beings, the viewers' social order is ultimately restored. The horror genre
sanctions the audiences considering acceptable or troublesome consequences for

society as a whole (Clark 2003, 63). I focus on two of the film categories that were most relevant to young-adult audiences and to the discussion on contemporary legends: slasher films and, principally in chapter 5, supernatural, occult and ghost films.

Supernatural, Occult and Ghost Films

> Horror is the genre of film where scepticism about the paranormal is consistently vanquished.
>
> —Edwards (2001, 88)

Cherry defines these films as those that involve the interventions of spirits, ghosts, witchcraft, the devil and other entities into the real world, often featuring uncanny elements (Cherry 2009, 5). Films and television programs with strong supernatural elements present young adults a chance to experience and relieve fears about death, the afterlife and other forces in life that they believe are beyond their control (Clark 2003, 63). Several films fitting into this category have been included in the section on selected films below while many others are covered in the discussions on mass-mediated ostension in chapter 2 and the discussions on ghostlore in chapter 5.

Slasher Films

Films that portray "groups of teenagers menaced by a stalker, set in domestic and suburban spaces frequented by young people, [with] the only a survivor a female who (in the early cycles) has not participated in underage sex" are classified as slasher films (Cherry 2009, 6). Mikel Koven subdivides the slasher film into three distinct types: the "Scooby-Doo" films; "psycho character studies"; and "psycho killers" or "terror tales" (Koven 2003). "Scooby-Doo" films are named after the animated television series dealing with a gang of teenagers who solve non-supernatural mysteries disguised as paranormal legends to distract people from the illegal operations of some adults. Koven asserts that the horror films of this category are in reality gory murder mysteries with the human killer using some type of legend to distract others from discovering their identity (Koven 2003). The second type of slasher film, the "psycho character study" that attempts the exploration of the psyche of a psychotic killer, has been fairly uncommon. The third type is indicative of the popular perception of slasher films—the killer is known to both the audience and the characters in the film. "Terror tale" films are neither mysterious nor psychological explorations as little is revealed regarding the killers' motivations or their back stories. This subgenre, featuring well-known films such as *Halloween* (1978), *Friday the 13th* (1980) and *The Burning* (1981), also reveals its connection to oral urban legends (Koven 2003). Koven illuminates the connections between contemporary legends and this third type of slasher film with a discussion of *The Burning* (1981) and the Cropsey legend which at the time of the publication of his article was virtually unknown outside of the local area. This unfamiliarity with the legend, of course, changes drastically with the release and dynamic web presence of the film *Cropsey* (2009), discussed in chapter 2.

Koven agrees that there are fundamental differences between an orally transmitted contemporary legend and a horror movie based on a contemporary legend; but both formats demonstrate "the ideological functions of maintaining categories of normalcy and transmission of belief traditions" (Koven 2003). He maintains that in all of the terror tale films and legends, when someone wanders off—from the campsite, the university campus, home or school—that person is at risk from psychotic killers. "This potentiality of violence, for the on-screen characters in slasher movies and for the 'friends-of-a-friend' of urban legends, and for us listeners/viewers, underlines that these narratives are predicated upon what is *possible*, and assuming we do not wish to end up as grist for these killers' mills, need to heed their narrative interdictions" (Koven 2003). McKechnie agrees that slasher films and contemporary horror legends share a similar structure and story line. She maintains that a fundamental difference between the two formats reflected the differences in transmission and the length available for the telling in a feature film (McKechnie 2010, 85).

> The female survivor is a central figure in slasher films and contemporary legends. In both, she manages to avoid being murdered. But it is *how* she manages this that highlights the difference between the two genres. In contemporary legends she passively relies on the help of rescuers who are usually male, but it is her apparent evolution beyond this in slasher films that makes her seem a stronger figure than her contemporary legend counterpart. In slasher films she rises up to fight back against her assailant. (McKechnie 2010, 89)

Another major difference is that the killers in the contemporary legends are undeveloped and unnamed characters. Often the gender is indeterminate as well. In the slasher film equivalent, the killers are usually given names and have a definite physical presence. Killers in most of the oral legends are never seen by the protagonists in the legends. They remain hidden throughout the legend, and the danger they present is concealed along with the descriptions of the murders as they occur. These details are left to the imagination of the individual members of the audience. Slasher films, because of their length and their intent, feature multiple murders while the contemporary legend usually hinges on the one killing. "Whether or not this murder is the work of a serial killer, and thus this victim is but one of many, the focus of the legend is on one particular murder. It is this particular victim's death that forms the crux of the legend. Any further murders would only serve to lengthen, and perhaps even complicate, the plot" (McKechnie 2010, 121).

Gary Alan Fine and Patricia Turner suggest that the success of the slasher film *Candyman* (1992), which embraces numerous contemporary legends but focuses on "Bloody Mary," inspired others to produce similar types of cinematic reworkings of folklore. Fine and Turner mention *The X-Files*, *Urban Legend*, *Dead Man on Campus* and *I Saw What You Did Last Summer* as examples a decade ago (Fine and Turner 2001, 1). The number of titles of films and television programs incorporating folklore, and specifically contemporary legends, has swelled substantially since then. They state that the reworked contemporary legends in *Candyman* and others testify to the powerful presence of contemporary legends. At the same time, the authors caution their readers that the folklorists in the film committed a crucial error. While focusing their efforts on the collecting and debunking of the contemporary legend, the cinematic folklorists overlooked the underpinning truths of the story. "Consequently, the very real history of race and class hostility that permeates this section of inner-city Chicago ensnares them in the form of the violent Candyman figure" (Fine and Turner 2001, 3). The DVD *Candyman: Special Edition* (2004) includes several features regarding the making of the film and the background of the story itself. The feature, "Sweet to the Sweet: *The Candyman*

Mythos," discusses the short story by Clive Barker, "The Forbidden," that was the genesis of this film, commenting that the story was born and developed out of the concept of extreme racism. In another feature, "Books of Blood," author Clive Baker expounds on the fact that most horror films were developed through contemporary legends via short stories.

Film critic Mark Kermode charts the history of the slasher movie in the documentary *Scream and Scream Again: A History of the Slasher Film* (2000), available in five parts on YouTube. Mikel Koven reports that for Kermode, the contemporary legend "The Hook" worked as a morality archetype for the entire body of slasher films. "Within this documentary film, and following Kermode's introduction, is a montage retelling of this legend by a variety of horror movie filmmakers including Wes Craven, William Lustig, Sean Cunningham, John McNaughton, and Tobe Hooper; each filmmaker relates a sentence or two of the story" (Koven 2003).

Making Their Own Horror Videos

> By watching horror movies and by making movies of their own, students enrich their perceptions of legend quests. Some horror movies, such as Shirley Jackson's The Haunting *(1999)* and Stephen King's Rose Red *(2002), involve exploration of a spooky place. The Blair Witch Project *(1999)* not only shows college students venturing into a haunted domain in Burkittsville, Maryland, but also suggests that their adventure really happened. Such filmed enactments of legend quests increase students' expectations.
>
> —Tucker (2007, 204)

Elizabeth Tucker asserts that while students enjoy visiting the sites immortalized by horror movies, they enjoy making their own horror films even more. A quick search of YouTube bears out this finding. The videos posted on that site and others are of various lengths, involve diverse narrative techniques and are of varied quality. The overreaching commonality is intrigue with the horrific possibilities of contemporary legends. As mentioned in the discussion on legend tripping, local landmarks offer good potential for these video creators, especially if the landmarks are in secluded locations (Tucker 2007, 207). Frequently, films, television programs and print reworkings of contemporary legends contain the amateur video-making motif as the reason d'être for the character's involvement in the horrific situation in the first place. Not only has the ubiquitous Internet aided in this process, but the increasing availability of digital technology has made producing their own videos much less complicated.

Examples of Horror and Slasher Titles Incorporating Contemporary Legends

The films and television programs included here are not examined in much detail in the above discussion nor in the following chapters, with the exception of the *Supernatural* franchise that figures prominently in several other conversations.

Campfire Tales *(1997)*

Similar in structure to the 1991 anthology film of the same name, this horror film contains three short vignettes that are framed as stories told around the campfire. Two contemporary legends are featured here: "The Black (or Red) Ribbon," about the young girl wearing a ribbon to keep her head on her shoulders, is reworked in "The Locket"; and "People Can Lick Too," in the segment of the same name. The story line in the second segment involves a conversation on a chat line between a pre-teenage girl and her "new friend" that ends with disastrous and, for those familiar with this contemporary legend, predictable results.

The Ring (Ringu) *(1998) and* The Ring *(2002)*

> *The basic hook of* The Ring *is a simple one, centered on a fictional urban legend succinctly expressed by one of the film's characters: "There's this videotape out there, and if you watch it, you get a phone call from a girl telling you that you will die in seven days ... And then seven days later you die."*
>
> —Lacefield (2010, 1)

In Japanese popular culture, contemporary legends have continued to be relevant, and the core story of *Ringu* was familiar to a large part of the population, even to those on the periphery of exposure to the film (G. Wright 2010, 45).

Ringu, based on Koji Suzuki's horror novels, became a multimedia franchise in Japan alone including three *Ringu* movies, a Japanese television series and a manga series written by Hiroshi Takahashi. The manga series incorporates elements from both *Ringu* and the television series. When the film *The Ring* was released in 2002 in North America, it became the fifth-highest-grossing horror film of all time, nearly single-handedly reviving the sector of the film industry dominated by film franchises such as *Friday the 13th*, *Halloween* and *Scream* (Lacefield 2010, 1).

> Where *The Ring* succeeded was in marrying the vengeful ghost scenario with the sanitized teen-pitched genre revival of [Wes] Craven's films. In doing so, it got back to the very basis of what made the horror genre work in the first place—the mystery element, the feeling that there is something inexplicable lurking just beneath the surface of normal everyday living. (Mees and Sharp 2004, 262)

Ringu not only focuses on the contemporary legend genre but also incorporates the idea behind the ubiquitous chain letters. The title of the film, more accurately translated as "The Chain," epitomizes chain letters when the protagonist realizes, at the end of the film, that the curse could be avoided by copying the video tape and sending it to someone else, with the warning that the recipient must also make a copy and pass it on within the week, accompanied with the warning and instructions to continue the chain (Ellis 2004, 233 n. 9). The plotline of *Ringu* finds parallels in the real world of chain letters, computer viruses and bootleg videos (Mees and Sharp 2004, 260). Technology is directly implicated in the horror with the curse activated by the watching of the videotape and the curse announced by telephone. Technology is not just an alienating barrier or a worthless substitute for sight and knowledge but an actual conduit for the paranormal (Cherry 2009, 194).

Nakata's *Ringu* became the most successful Japanese horror film ever made, as well as one of the most well-known Japanese films in the international market, aiding in rejuvenating the Japanese horror industry (Lacefield 2010, 4). The psychological horror in *Ringu* is much more intense than the terror generated by the

American remake, which depends more heavily on visual effects (Brown 2006, 368). *The Ring* could be considered an act of repackaging artistic ideas and images as commodities. "The ideas and meaning of the original are often treated as a fixed entity, and the remake stands as a mirror of the ideas. But a conversion is also necessary for the remake to make an impact on current audiences" (Tsai 2008, 5). The most obvious changes made to enhance cultural understanding are the images on the cursed video tape. The series of images on the original video tape are a series of montages referencing Japanese folklore and horror stories situated in the Edo period: "a bright moon filling the ocean-blue sky; a woman brushing her long black hair in front of a mirror; mirror shifts its place on the wall and reveals a reflection of a girl dressed in a white *katabira* (a plain, unlined kimono); a floating *kanji* (ideograms) describing a volcanic eruption appears; lament men crawling away; a man whose head is covered with a white square cloth; a close-up shot of the word *sada* (chaste) in the pupil; and the videotape ends with a shot of a well" (Tsai 2008, 35). The video tape in *The Ring* includes several overlapped images from the Japanese original, such as the same mirror at the opposite side and the pupil of an eye, although a horse's eye instead of a human one, and the final shot of the well. A different cinematic text is presented with the glare of the moonlight replaced by the light of a circle or ring, later discovered to be the internal view from the bottom of a well; disjointed images of the external view of a house, a cliff, a needle penetrating an index finger; maggots; a pig's tale; a burning tree; a chair swirling upside down in the air; a falling-down ladder; and ocean waves breaking on stones. "Elements that are associated with Japanese cultures, such as *Kanji*, volcanoes, and kimonos, are taken out and replaced by maggots, blood, and a ladder (suggesting bad luck if walked under). Unlike Sadako's manifestation of the montage, most of the abstract images in *The Ring* are not given any explanation by the narrative" (Tsai 2008, 36).

Ringu's narrative is derived, largely, from the established tradition of the Japanese female ghost story (Wee 2010, 82). *The Ring*, on the other hand, reflecting a more American moral perspective, follows the tradition of popular American supernatural horror films (Wee 2010, 91). *Ringu* reflects Japanese cinema's link to classical art forms such as Kabuki and Noh theatre, "forms that depict the continuing influence of Japanese folktales on contemporary cultural productions. The figure of Sadako borrows from the traditional tales of *yurei*, familiar narratives that are prominent in both classical Japanese theatre and cinema" (Wee 2010, 96). The key themes and characters, identifiable to *Ringu* audiences, based on the foundations of the ghost story laid down in *Tales of Ugetsu* and other classical tales, include the vengeful ghost with long black hair; the haunted houses; themes of abandonment and alienation; and doomed love (Balmain 2008, 32). A direct influence from kabuki theatre can be seen through the story of Oiwa, or *Tokaido Yotsuya Kaidan* (Ghost Story of Yotsuya), and Oiwa's manifestation in a lantern. "Ghosts today also materialize through media such as televisions, cell phones, and photographs. Situating postmodern ghosts as emerging from technological media can be considered analogous to Oiwa's use of the lantern" (Tsai 2008, 12). "The continuing significance of the central theme of the *Ring* films—the linkage between media technologies and the supernatural—has continued in popular horror films such as . . . *Paranormal Activity* (2009)" (Lacefield 2010, 2). The film franchise continues to utilize developing technology as well: the proposed release of the newest instalment of the *Ringu* series, *Sadako* 3D, announced at a press conference in Tokyo in February 2011, states that the 3D technology vividly portrays Sadako crawling out of the television set.

The unexplained deaths of a small group of teenagers that began both the novel and the cinematic adaptations of *Ringu* reflect media users in Japan and the United States known, in marketing terms, as "early adapters." Teenagers, the primary market for horror films, have always been the most susceptible to the genre's curses and creatures, from a radioactive blob to a psychotic slasher. "In the past these threats generally came from some anti-teen elsewhere—an external world of adult science or traumatized killer's pre-Oedipal sexuality" (Sconce 2010, 216). Occult software, the newest source of horror, was reflected in a decade of haunted medium programming on the television front that followed on the heels of these films.

Supernatural *(Television Series)*

> *The saturation of popular culture with supernatural narratives is not simply a result of producers' playfulness with technology; it is of course a result of the stories' marketability. Audiences are apparently fascinated by the idea of something outside the realm of natural ontology.*
>
> —Petersen (2010)

Supernatural, premiering on September 13, 2005, follows the adventures of two brothers, Dean and Sam, who fight demons and other monsters each week in the hour-long episodes. The two brothers travel throughout the United States to defeat beings of evil and to save innocent people. Many episodes during the first three seasons are essentially ghost stories, in which the brothers serve as "ghostbusters," either exterminating vengeful spirits or helping spirits of those wrongfully murdered to "find peace." Other story lines have the brothers encountering monsters and creatures with origins in folklore, either local or from other cultures and eras, and urban legends, such as Bloody Mary and Hookman (Engstrom and Valenzano 2010, 72). The themes and motifs within this series resound in the conventionality of interrelated gothic and horror modes in general. Partnered with Kripke's well-documented awareness of cinematic and television genres, the multitude of supernatural television programming that began airing around the same time demonstrates a long tradition of the gothic in popular culture addressing national fears as a type of haunting or possession by the "Other" (J. Wright 2008). Included in this convention are series such as *Medium* (2005–) and *Lost* (2004–); themes such as the Route 66 tradition in literature and film after Kerouac, referenced in the *Supernatural* episode, "Route 666"; and the law-and-order programs such as *NCIS* (2003–) and *Criminal Minds* (2005–) that emerged post–September 11 indicating that although danger was everywhere, various agencies are working to protect the general population (J. Wright 2008).

The popularity of The *X-Files* (1993–2002) facilitated a renewed interest in the paranormal, ghostlore and contemporary legends. This interest in the paranormal is also reflected in other television programming such as *Ghost Whisperer* (2005–), *Fringe* (2008–) and *True Blood* (2008–), which deals with supernatural beings and the afterlife in different ways (Petersen 2010). Both *Charmed* and *Supernatural* incorporate a range of ancient symbols and languages into their narratives. Often elements, symbols and names in *Supernatural* borrowed from actual religious history and folklore are revealed to the audiences by the Winchester brothers in their searches through old books and scriptures to find information about the demons they were going to hunt (Petersen 2010). Engstrom and Valenzano analyze the types of antagonists the Winchester family fought in the first 60 episodes of the series. The most frequent category of antagonist is that of creatures or monsters such as witches, shapeshifters and vampires. Ghosts or vengeful spirits constitute the second category while demons from hell, humans and curses or cursed objects populate the last three categories (Engstrom and Valenzano 2010, 75). Many of these monsters and ghostlore figures are reconfigured characters from contemporary legends. Contemporary legends serve as a driving force in *The X-Files and Supernatural*, both produced by Kim Manners. "The reworking of urban legends in *Supernatural* underlines how familiar aspects of American culture are drawn in and seen from new perspectives as part of a general strategy. Although some elements of the show encourage humor, other elements evoke other emotions, such as empathy or sorrow" (Petersen 2010).

Evidence of the show's popularity, aside from its average 2 million-plus viewing audience, includes the fan publication *Supernatural Magazine*, published by Titan magazines, a series of companion novels and books, various fan sites and SuperWikis available on the Internet, not to mention show-related merchandise such as calendars, coffee mugs, T-shirts, statuettes, throw blankets, trading cars and series-specific jewellery (e.g., pentagram earrings and necklace) and costume accessories, such as "Sam's Jelly Bracelet," and Dean's Protective Amulet" (Engstrom and Valenzano 2010, 72). The contemporary legends in the series have been discussed, explained and retold on these countless websites, blogs, message boards and social networking sites as well as in *Supernatural Magazine* which also provides fans with "educational material regarding the origins of the urban legends and monsters featured in episodes" (Engstrom and Valenzano 2010, 73). The authors apparently feel that curious fans might seek more information after reading the "Myths and Legends" column in the publication (Engstrom and Valenzano 2010, 81).

A thematic teaching unit was recently developed for high school students revolving around the *Supernatural* television program. The impetus behind the unit was critical thinking.

> The hypothesis is that as you teach students to think *critically* by watching *critically*, then they will be able to translate that skill into reading *critically*, and eventually writing *critically*. TV episodes serve as a hook to get students engaged (using a medium the students are quite familiar with though maybe not critically) and then as a portal to other literary pieces based on theme, topic and general literary devices. Using graphic organizers and web communities, journal activities, research and Fan Fiction, all fitting themes of the program, every moment of class students are engaged in an active learning community (there is no passive sitting with your head on the desk in the dark!) and educational standards are met using 21st Century Literature. ("Teaching Literature Supernaturally" http://tls4students.org/)

Supernatural as discussed in other chapters and sections of this book demonstrates, along with the popularity of the program, the successful incorporation of contemporary legends throughout the history of the show.

Trick 'r Treat *(2009)*

This film, written and directed by Michael Dougherty, is an anthology of four Halloween-related tales tied together by the character of Sam, a minute trick-ortreater wearing a burlap pumpkin mask. The film, awarded the Audience Choice Award at the Los Angeles Screamfest (2008) and the Silver Audience Award (2009) at Toronto's After Dark Film Festival, is based on Dougherty's short film *Season's Greetings* and spawned its own reworking of a graphic novel by the same name. The graphic novel, adapted by Marc Anderyko and illustrated by various artists, was published by DC Comics the same year. Since the film had not yet been made, Anderyko worked from the screenplay, interpreting the visual possibilities in his own way. Anderyko has been quoted as saying both the graphic novel and the film were made with love of all things Halloween by all involved (Snellings 2009). Dougherty provides the introduction for *Trick 'r' Treat: Tales of Mayhem, Mystery, and Mischief* (2007) as well as commentary on his filmmaking process and the ideas behind the film originally to be released in 2007. The film, once made, was released direct to video. Only the Blu-Ray version, however, includes the "The Lore and Legends of Halloween," offering background information on the holiday itself and the original film short that was the genesis of the film.

The film begins with a storytelling session of contemporary legends told by three friends in a coffee shop. The third episode, "The Halloween School Bus Massacre Revisited," involves legend tripping to an abandoned rock quarry, the site of a local legend regarding the bus crash and murder of eight mentally challenged children by their parents. "Meet Sam," the final episode in the film, reworks the contemporary legend of "razor blades in apples," making sure that the Halloween candy is checked for foreign substances.

Urban Legend *(1998)*

The killer in this film bases the methodology of killing the victims on certain contemporary legends. It is followed by *Urban Legends: Final Cut* (2000) and the direct-to-video *Urban Legends: Bloody Mary* (2005). "While this film could not exist with the contemporary legends themselves, its depiction of them has served as the variants transmitted by people who have viewed it, including some of my informants ... Thus one film has managed to influence which variants of several contemporary legends are transmitted" (McKechnie 2010, 51). McKechnie's research demonstrates findings similar to mine when speaking with young adults about contemporary legends. Most of my audiences are also familiar with the variants presented in the film, and as with the Disneyfication of folklore, often do not realize that there are other versions. Contemporary legends appearing in the film, among a plethora of others, include "Killer in the Backseat," "Lights Out! Gang Initiation," "Bloody Mary," "The Boyfriend's Death," "Aren't You Glad You Didn't Turn on the Lights?" and the "Kidney Heist."

Urban Legends *(Television Series)*

Originally aired in Canada in 2007, the 30-minute show, hosted by Michael Allcock, features three dramatized contemporary legends each week. The audience is invited to speculate on which one of the three dramatizations is true. Syfy television programming advertised their new series, *Urban Legends*, in the spring of 2011. The series, hosted by David Hewlett, is basically the same series as the Canadian one, with a different narration track. Along with known contemporary legends such as harvesting body fat for cosmetic companies and organs for transplants, the program dramatizes popular superstitions and twisted crime narratives as part of the offerings.

Although the series is not yet available for live streaming or downloading at http://www.syfy.com/rewind, other relevant programs were found the at that site. Back episodes of *Paranormal Witness, Haven, Ghost Hunters International, Fact or Fiction: Paranormal Files* and *Haunted Collector* are available for Internet users in the United States. Unfortunately for Canadians, there is a licensing barrier for these programs.

When a Stranger Calls *(2006)*

Based on the contemporary legend of "The Babysitter and the Man Upstairs," the film is a remake of *When a Stranger Calls*, released in 1979. The horror story follows Jill, a teenager, and her babysitting misadventures after the film depicts a scene on the other side of town where another babysitter and the three children under her care are murdered. The two story lines are united when Jill is attacked by the same killer. The police, tracing the telephone calls made to Jill, discover that they originated from inside the house, and manage to rescue Jill—or do they?

Darwin Awards

The Darwin Awards, frequently considered a subgenre of contemporary legends, are named for evolutionary theorist Charles Darwin. These stories of people who had either seriously injured or killed themselves by doing something extremely stupid or absurdly dangerous are, for the most part, tales of self-inflicted death. The actors in these stories have effectively removed "their faulty genes from society's collective gene pool" (Masterson 2003, 35). The awards began as an e-mail newsletter in the early 1990s; the first archive was started at Stanford University in 1994; and the official website, http://www.darwinawards.com/, continues to collect and store nearly 400 Darwin Awards, from that time until the present, for easy access. Since their first appearance, the legendary stories have "migrated from the realm of written folklore to modern oral legendary, and ... are now often performed alongside 'stupid criminal' stories and stories of heists gone awry" (Masterson 2003, 35). Not only do the Darwin Awards have a website presence, they also have a Facebook fan page, numerous volumes of books and at least one film, *The Darwin Awards* (2006), dedicated, as stated on their website, to the "improvement of the human genome" and "honoring those who accidently remove themselves from it." The contemporary legend mentioned earlier in this chapter, "The Bricklayer," is one of the most popular entries on the website. Another popular tale is "Dynamite Ice Fishing." Perhaps because I live on the edge of a lake renowned for ice fishing for much of the year, this one highly appeals to me and my fellow villagers: Two guys are out ice fishing with their dog and decided that drilling a hole would take too long so they throw a stick of dynamite out onto the ice. The dog retrieves the explosives and drops it under the truck, blowing a hole in the ice that sinks the truck.

Debunking and Confirming Contemporary Legends

While the Internet has served to increase the velocity and volume which urban legends circulate, it has also enhanced debunking practices and the relative cultural power of debunkers to believers and promulgators. Since believers and promulgators pass on these stories with, for the most part, sincere

belief that they are true, they are usually not prepared for
debate in the way debunkers are.

—Donovan (2004, 112)

Over the years, contemporary legend scholars have bemoaned the fact that
many of the articles and books regarding contemporary legends focus on what the
stories meant or whether the legends were true or not. In their collection of contemporary legends, Bennett and Smith state that their book, unlike many urban legend
books and websites, was not designed as a "rumor-buster." "This is because, we
do not see untruth as a defining criterion of urban legends; rather, we think that
one of the things that help to define a legend is *uncertainty* about whether it is true
(the 'If it's true, it's important, but *is* it true' principle)" (Bennett and Smith
2007, xx). The overall purpose of my book is not to debunk or "prove the truthfulness" of the contemporary legends discussed within these covers, but since
debunking has played an important role in shaping their social meaning, some attention must be paid to the practice. Besides, the visibility, influence and prestige of
debunkers have increased significantly in the last two decades, particularly
with the rise of the Internet. "Word-of-mouth narratives, or those sent via e-mail,
are now commonly considered for the category of urban legend when they are out-
landish, audacious, or unusually clever tales that purport to be read" (Donovan
2004, 111).

The development of the Internet ensured that dialogue about contemporary
legends is no longer limited to the interpersonal. Contemporary legends are now
transferred between websites and online contacts rather than between acquaintances. An increased interest due to the media's active promotion of the cult of celebrity has also brought attention to contemporary legends that includes recognized
individuals such as musicians, actors, and politicians (Inglis 2007, 591).

Jan Harold Brunvand has been consulted by media sources and the lay public
as an expert on urban legends since the early 1980s. The plethora of newspaper columns, books, articles and presentations Brunvand has provided on the topic of contemporary legends has made his name synonymous with urban legends. "Brunvand
found that he had his hands full, though, as he probably spent just as much time
writing about urban legends as he did debunking the claims of those "friends of a
friend" stories" (Stine 1999). Brunvand's anthologies and the various others published in the last two decades are educational and entertaining but lacking in
scholarly documentation, classification and interpretation. "The texts are not verbatim transcripts of field-recorded legends or copies of media sources but rather are
retold, summarized, or abstracted versions of the originals, without professional
commentaries that contextualize the performance and the performers" (Dégh
2001, 96). A revised, updated and expanded version of Brunvand's *Encyclopedia
of Urban Legends*, sent to his publisher at the same time as I was finishing this book,
has attempted to rectify this. He adds about 100 new entries, including several for
countries not previously covered, and includes many sample texts of legends in
the entries so readers will have more full-text examples for reference instead of
the summaries and paraphrases of stories in the previous volume (Brunvand,
personal communication, April 12, 2011).

In the last two decades, the contemporary legend debunking community has
undergone a rapid transformation as a result of an increased awareness of contemporary legends and the explosive growth of the Internet (Donovan 2004, 114).
Donovan has reassured her readers that "seasoned participants in debunking news

groups and websites tend to be interested in the study of urban legends—their history, evolution, and innovation—and are often more amused rather than aggravated when a legend fails to fall in the face of repeated debunking" (Donovan 2004, 115). The newsgroup alt.folklore.urban (AFU) emerged on Usenet in the early 1990s. It provides a place for correspondences from other newsgroups to discuss suspected misinformation. As the Internet has grown, so has the volume of messages on the newsgroup. The group still has a slight online presence at http://groups.google.com/group/alt.folklore.urban/topics?pli=1.

The most frequently referenced online expert on contemporary legends is Urban Legends Reference Pages, perhaps more recognizable as Snopes.com, administered by Barbara and David Mikkelson. The website, heavily referenced throughout this book, determines the validity of contemporary legends. They rate the contemporary legends as true, false, ambiguous, unclassifiable or of indeterminate origin, and categorize them in broad categories. An internal search engine makes this site easy to use, and the well-researched entries on each of the legends are frequently updated.

Another reliable debunking "service" that, like the Snopes.com newsletter, arrives regularly in my e-mail in-box as a subscription, is the urban legend reference pages at About.com. David Emery, a freelance writer and "avid chronicler of urban legends," states on his website About.com: Urban Legends: "On this site we'll debunk, deconstruct, and, wherever possible, simply revel in the strangest, scariest, funniest, most popular tall tales, rumors, and hoaxes people see fit to share, both on-line and off . . . in what promises to be a constantly entertaining, ever-enlightening exploration of the urban legends and folklore of the digital age" (Emery). Entries offer information on recently circulating contemporary legends along with variants of the legends, relevant photographs and sources for further information. A fairly comprehensive listing of hoaxes, scams and a few contemporary legends can be found at Hoaxbusters (http://www.hoaxbusters.org/) while an equally comprehensive listing of e-rumors, with links to more information, has been found at Truth Or Fiction (http://www.truthorfiction.com/). This latter site, founded by Rich Buhler, has devoted itself to tracking rumors and contemporary legends transmitted through forwarded e-mails and establishing their validity.

Regardless of the information contained on debunking sites and in other materials, Donovan maintains that, as a group, debunkers spend little time examining the significance of contemporary legends to those who believe in their truthfulness or on the symbolism of the legends, but are mainly concerned with the culture of gullibility (Donovan 2004, 119). The debunkers have been an essential element in the current dissemination and understanding of contemporary legends as they added to the meaning of these contemporary legends by stabilizing them through archiving and by forcing believers to strengthen their arguments, affecting the language of new cycles of contemporary legends (Donovan 2004, 119).

> The publications of seemingly endless collections of texts for the use of the common reader has shifted from the hands of folklorists to those of journalists and collectors/editors with no interest in scholarly research, only in providing material for dinner-party anecdotes. They want to entertain, frighten or amuse their readers with the most ugly, nasty and sensational narratives. Films like "Urban Legends" or the "Blair Witch Project" have contributed to public acknowledgement of modern legends as a separate genre and as an integral part of contemporary society. (Brednich 2001, 9)

International Society for Contemporary Legend Research (ISCLR)

While discussions regarding contemporary legends can be found in a myriad of folklore journals, as well as within diverse academic disciplines, and on countless websites, blogs, social networking sites and elsewhere written by scholars and lay people interested in the topic, one professional society dedicates itself to the study of contemporary legends. The mission statement of the society, as stated on the website, maintains that ISCLR "encourages study of so-called 'modern' and 'urban' legends, and also of any legend that circulates actively. Members are especially concerned with ways in which legends merge with life: real-life analogs to legend plots, social crusades that use legends or legend-like horror stories, and search for evidence behind claims of alien abductions and mystery cats" (http://www.contemporarylegend.org/). Membership in the society, open to all those interested in contemporary legendary, includes the newsletter *FOAFtale News*, archived online at http://www.folklore.ee/FOAFtale/, the annual peer-reviewed journal, *Contemporary Legend*, and the opportunity to attend and present papers at their annual conference which alternates between North American and European locations. The *Contemporary Legend* journal promotes and encourages research on contemporary legends, as well as providing a forum for those who are working in the area. Here "legend" is interpreted in its broadest sense to include Sagen, dites, popular rumors, sayings and beliefs as well as narratives; while "contemporary" refers also to legends in active circulation in a given community (http://www.contemporarylegend.org/). Book reviews, an annual bibliography of books, essays and theses regarding contemporary legends, along with sections on contemporary legend in popular culture have also been featured in the journal. In addition, an active Facebook presence is available for dissemination and discussion of emerging and reoccurring contemporary legends.

References

Balmain, Colette. 2008. *Introduction to Japanese Horror Film*. Edinburgh: Edinburgh University Press.

Bennett, Gillian, and Paul Smith. 2007. *Urban Legends: A Collection of International Tall Tales and Terrors*. Westport, CT: Greenwood Press.

Brednich, Rolf W. 2001. "Where They Originated . . . Some Contemporary Legends and Their Literary Origins." Paper presented at ISFNR Congress, Melbourne, Australia, http://www.folklore.ee/folklore/vol20/legends.pdf (accessed October 19, 2010).

Brown, Alan. 2006. *Ghost Hunters of the South*. Jackson: University Press of Mississippi.

"Carjacking." Snopes.com. http://www.snopes.com/crime/warnings/carjack.asp (accessed September 12, 2011).

Cherry, Brigid. 2009. *Horror*. London: Routledge.

Clark, Lynn Schofield. 2003. *From Angels to Aliens: Teenagers, the Media, and the Supernatural*. Oxford: Oxford University Press.

Davidson, Hilda Ellis, and Anna Chaudhri. 2001. *Supernatural Enemies*. Durham, NC: Carolina Academic Press.

Datlow, Ellen. 2001. "Editorial Comment on 'Mr. Dark's Carnival.' " *The Year's Best Fantasy and Horror #14*, edited by Ellen Datlow and Terri Windling, 156–82. New York: St. Martin's Press.

Dégh, Linda. 2001. *Legend and Belief: Dialectics of a Folklore Genre*. Bloomington: Indiana University Press.

Dilworth, Joseph, Jr. 2009. "The PCZ Interview with MythBusters Jamie Hyneman and Adam Savage." *Pop Culture Zoo*. http://popculturezoo.com/2009/10/the-pcz-interview-with -mythbusters-jamie-hyneman-and-adam-savage/ (accessed September 14, 2011).

Donovan, Pamela. 2004. *No Way of Knowing: Crime, Urban Legends, and the Internet.* American Popular History and Culture. New York: Routledge, 2004.

Edwards, Emily D. 2001. "A House That Tries to Be Haunted: Ghostly Narratives in Popular Film and Television." In *Hauntings and Poltergeists: Multidisciplinary Perspectives,* edited by James Houran and Rense Lange, 82–119. Jefferson, NC: McFarland.

Ellis, Bill. 2004. *Lucifer Ascending: The Occult in Folklore and Popular Culture.* Lexington: University Press of Kentucky.

Engstrom, Erika, and Joseph M. Valenzano III. 2010. "Demon Hunters and Hegemony: Portrayal of Religion in the CW's *Supernatural.*" *Journal of Myth and Religion* 9 (2): 67–83.

Fine, Gary Alan, and Patricia A. Turner. 2001. *Whispers on the Color Line: Rumor and Race in America.* Berkeley: University of California Press.

Fischer, Tibor. 2010. "Solar by Ian McEwan: A Review." *The Telegraph,* March. http://www.telegraph.co.uk/culture/books/7359254/Solar-by-Ian-McEwan-review.html (accessed September 15, 2011).

Flagg, Gordon. 2006. "Review of *Sloth.*" *Booklist* 102 (18): 32.

Fonseca, Anthony J., and June Michele Pulliam. 2009. *Hooked on Horror III: A Guide to Reading Interests.* Westport, CT: Libraries Unlimited.

"Ian McEwan in Conversation." 2010. *Random Reads,* March 9. http://randomhouseindia.wordpress.com/2010/03/09/interview-with-ian-mcewan/ (accessed September 15, 2011).

Inglis, Ian. 2007. " 'Sex and Drugs and Rock'n'Roll': Urban Legends and Popular Music." *Popular Music and Society* 30 (5): 591–603.

Jones, Emma. 2009. "Tales from the Golden Age." BBC News. http://news.bbc.co.uk/2/hi/entertainment/8350110.stm (accessed September 15, 2011).

Kermode, Mark. 2000. *Scream and Scream Again: A History of the Slasher Film.* Directed by Andrew Abbott and Russell Leven. Also available on YouTube at http://www.youtube.com/watch?v=8EcBO37LnD4, Part 1.

Koven, Mikel J. 1999. *Candyman* Can: Film and Ostension. *Contemporary Legend* n.s. 2: 155–73.

Koven, Mikel J. 2003. "The Terror Tale: Urban Legends and the Slasher Film." *Scope: An Online Journal of Film and TV Studies.* http://www.scope.nottingham.ac.uk/article.php?issue=may2003&id=259&section=article (accessed September 12, 2011).

Koven, Mikel J. 2008. *Film, Folklore, and Urban Legends.* Lanham, MD: Scarecrow Press.

Lacefield, Kristen. 2010. "Media Anxiety and the *Ring* Phenomenon." In *The Scary Screen: Media Anxiety in* The Ring, edited by Kristen Lacefield, 1–25. Surrey, England: Ashgate.

Mayberry, Jonathan, and David F. Kramer. *They Bite: Endless Cravings of Supernatural Predators.* New York: Citadel Press, 2009.

Masterson, Justin. 2003. "At Least That's How I Heard It: Rhetorical Devices as Clues to a Narrative Agenda in Conversational Legend Performance." *Midwestern Performance* 28 (2): 28–41.

McCormick, James, and Macy Wyatt. 2009. *Ghosts of the Bluegrass.* Lexington: University Press of Kentucky.

McIntosh, Erin. 2009. "Winter Blog Blast: Patrick Carman." Miss Erin. http://misserinmarie.blogspot.com/2009/11/winter-blog-blast-tour-patrick-carman.html (accessed September 16, 2011).

McKechnie, Rhiannon. 2010. *With Terror in Their Hearts: A Structural and Textual Analysis of Gender, Transmission, and the Enjoyment of Horror in Slasher Films and Contemporary Legends.* Thesis, Master of Arts, Folklore Department, Memorial University of Newfoundland.

Mees, Tom, and Jasper Sharp. 2004. *The Midnight Eye Guide to New Japanese Film.* Berkeley, CA: Stone Bride Press.

Mikkelson, Barbara. 2008. "The Barrel of Bricks." Snopes.com. http://www.snopes.com/humor/letters/bricks.asp (accessed September 15, 2011).

Montoya, Cira. 2009. "Student Review and Lesson Ideas." *EN/SANE World.* http://
ensaneworld.blogspot.com/2009/04/student-review-and-lesson-ideas-sloth.html
(accessed September 15, 2009).

Oring, Elliott. 2008. "Legendry and the Rhetoric of Truth." *Journal of American Folklore*
121 (480): 127–66.

Petersen, Line Nybro. 2010. "Renegotiating Religious Imaginations through Transformations
of 'Banal Religion' in 'Supernatural.' " *Transformative Works and Cultures* 4.
http://journal.transformativeworks.org/index.php/twc/article/view/142 (accessed
September 14, 2011).

"Polybius" (video game). Wikipedia. http://en.wikipedia.org/wiki/Polybius_%28video_game
%29 (accessed September 16, 2011).

Reynolds, Kimberley. 2001. "Introduction." In *Frightening Fiction*, edited by Kimberley
Reynolds, Geraldine Brennan and Kevin McCarron, 1–18. Contemporary Classics of
Children's Literature. London: Continuum.

Sconce, Jeffrey. 2010. "Haunted Networks." In *The Scary Screen: Media Anxiety in* The
Ring, edited by Kristen Lacefield, 215–20. Surrey, England: Ashgate.

"Simpsons Urban Legends." The Simpsons Archive. http://www.snpp.com/guides/
folklore.html (accessed September 15, 2011).

Smith, Paul. 1999. Contemporary Legend on Film and Television: Some Observations.
Contemporary Legend n.s. 2:137–54.

Snellings, April. 2009. "Graphic Novel "Trick 'r Treat" Celebrates All Things Halloween."
Metro Pulse. http://www.metropulse.com/news/2009/oct/21/graphic-novel-trick-r
-treat-celebrates-halloween/?print=1 (accessed September 14, 2011).

Stine, Scott Aaron. 1999. "The Snuff Film: The Making of an Urban Legend." *CSI* 23 (3).
http://www.csicop.org/si/show/snuff_film_the_making_of_an_urban_legend/
(accessed September 16, 2011).

Terdiman, Daniel. 2009. " 'MythBusters' Ready to Storm Fall TV Season." CNET News,
October 1. http://news.cnet.com/8301-13772_3-10364928-52.html#ixzz1Y2fxGSCm
(accessed September 15, 2011).

Tsai, Peijen Beth. 2008. *Horror Translation: From Nakata Hideo's Ringu to Gore
Verbinski's* The Ring. Thesis for Master of Fine Arts, Department of Media Study,
State University of New York at Buffalo.

Tucker, Elizabeth. 2007. *Haunted Halls: Ghostlore of American College Campuses.* Jackson:
University Press of Mississippi.

Wagner, Hank, Christopher Golden and Stephen R. Bissette. 2008. *Prince of Stories: The
Many Worlds of Neil Gaiman.* New York: St. Martin's Press.

Wee, Valerie. 2010. "Cultural Constructions of the Supernatural: The Case of *Ringu* and *The
Ring.*" In *The Scary Screen: Media Anxiety in* The Ring, edited by Kristen Lacefield,
81–96. Surrey, England: Ashgate.

Wright, Greg. 2010. "Tracing the Transference of a Cross-Cultural Media Virus: The
Evolution of *Ring.*" In *The Scary Screen: Media Anxiety in* The Ring, edited by
Kristen Lacefield, 45–61. Surrey, England: Ashgate.

Wright, Julia M. 2008. "Latchkey Hero: Masculinity, Class and the Gothic in Eric Kripke's
Supernatural." *Genders* 47. http://www.genders.org/g47/g47_wright.html (accessed
September 14, 2011).

CHAPTER 2

OSTENSION, LEGEND TRIPPING AND COMMODIFICATION OF FOLKLORE

This chapter extends the discussion initiated in chapter 4 of *Tales, Rumors, and Gossip* which explores the topics of ostension and legend tripping and the legends of Bloody Mary, Poisoned Halloween Treats and Mercantile Legends.

Definition of Terms

While the term "ostension" remains a term basically used by folklorists and other legend scholars, the phrase "legend tripping" has gained wide currency outside of the academic sphere, particularly in online discussions and on websites. Before exploring the world of contemporary legends coming alive, however, these terms need to be briefly clarified.

Ostension "refers to the process by which people act out themes or events found within folk narratives" (Fine 1991, 179). The story, instead of purely being told (represented through storytelling), is shown as a direct action (presented) (Koven 2007, 184). People act on the legends, using them as blueprints or maps for behaviour with the new narratives of their experiences being told and retold to validate the original legend (de Vos 1996, 56).

Pseudo-Ostension refers to the process of "imitating the outlines of a known narrative to perpetuate a hoax" (Ellis 1989, 208). Rather than acting out a belief, people terrify their friends at a legend-tripping site by pretending to be the ghost or monster that they are seeking.

Quasi-Ostension involves the misinterpretation of events occurring naturally in terms of an existing contemporary legend (Ellis 2001, 163).

Proto-Ostension occurs when a person appropriates a contemporary legend alleged to have happened to someone else and claims it as a memorate (a personal experience tale) (Ellis 2001, 163).

Mass-Mediated Ostension "implicitly recognizes an audience by encouraging some form of post-presentation debate regarding the veracity of the legends presented. There is also an implicit recognition of the fictive form of this narration (a fiction film), but equally a recognition that the stories upon which certain films are based come from 'genuine urban legends' " (Koven 2007, 185).

Legend Tripping refers to an organized (although sometimes spontaneous) activity in which individuals make a journey to a place where "uncanny" events are believed to have occurred in the interest of testing a local legend (Holly and Cordy 2007, 345).

Commodification, the marketing of folklore, has two major qualifiers: the object must have "folk antecedents" and be mass produced to sell or promote (Floyd 2011, 46). "Commodification denotes the process which something goes through, in this case a belief tradition, in order to serve as a commodity, something of use, advantage or value" (Leary 2003, 100). The specific purpose of commodification is not to disseminate information or experiences but rather to promote items or entertain (Leary 2003, 100).

Commodification of Contemporary Legends

> When [folklore] becomes popular culture it moves beyond the network of origin through the deliberate agency of individuals who may not themselves be part of the originating group. As part of popular culture, broader referents of knowledge or behavior are interpretable in at least a limited way, whether or not they are actively used by individuals in the larger society. (This is where much adaptation of folklore and traditional materials for advertizing [sic] purposes comes in—it is evocative and perhaps attractive because of the recognition that there is more than meets the eye here).
>
> —Brewer (1994, 8)

Commodification of folklore is not a new phenomenon by any means; folklorists and social scientists have long documented how and why elements of contemporary legends and other items of tradition have been adapted, adopted, satirized and so on by advertisers on television, radio, newspapers and the Internet to market products. Linda Dégh acknowledges that newspaper advertisements "use content units, motifs, episodes, whole stories, cycles and conglomerates in developing their own stylistic conventions and formulas" (Dégh 2001, 182). What is, perhaps, a more recent practice is the marketing of the contemporary legend itself in print and visual media (television, film and YouTube videos), through tourism and via assorted merchandise. In the last two decades there have been infinite collections of contemporary legend texts, intended for lay readers, with the authorship transferring from "folklorists to those of journalists and collectors/editors with no interest in scholarly research, only in providing material for dinner-party anecdotes" (Brednich 2001, 9). These publications, along with the earlier corpus of contemporary legend compilations by Jan Harold Brunvand, have made the term "urban legend" a household phrase, although the popular understanding of this term may be diverse and in disagreement to that of scholars. At the same time this plethora of print resources has gained ground, advancements in technology have had a large impact on the commodification of contemporary legends and the paranormal. The new wave of films, television programming and paranormal-focused websites not only aids in the revival of interest in the supernatural but also assists in re-creating new interpretations and variants of these items of traditional folklore.

A fairly recent, and universal, occurrence is the establishment of a cottage industry regarding haunted pubs, inns and hotels and highways. "The idea of whole communities being ghost-infested is an obvious product of modern tourism. It is a reversal of the historic position where communities desired to be rid of their spirits ... [They] now boast of the number of ghosts they have" (Davies 2009, 64). Many of these publicized haunted places accentuate their ghostly connections with ghost tours, historical and paranormal theme parties, murder mystery nights and séances (Goldstein 2007, 183). Diane Goldstein's belief is that this current wave of commodification of the paranormal and the selling of location's associations with the supernatural developed as a result of three concurrent cultural measures: the rise of baby boomer spirituality and New Age interest in diverse belief traditions, the shifting focus to increasingly violent and reality-based television, and the shift in tourist consumer patterns (Goldstein 2007, 193). It is no longer uncommon for travelers to seek out paranormal adventures.

> A well-known story among Kyoto taxi drivers is the one about the ghost who appears as a young lady and hails a taxi for a ride. According to one sightseer's experience in the ancient capital, "I took a trip to Kyoto looking for ghosts. A taxi driver said he picked up a young woman along the banks of the Kamo River and started taking her to a place called Midoro Pond. When they entered the dark Tadasu Forest, the driver looked back at the woman, but he saw nothing there except for a damp spot on the seat where she had been sitting." If the Kyoto cabbies are to be believed, this perpetually on-the-go phantom still haunts them to this day. (Farrell 2009)

Popular sites for hauntings are promoted as possible legend-tripping excursions. For example, the above anecdote is followed by the enquiry: "Why not make your trip to the ancient capital even more special by checking out some of these sites? See the directions at the end of this article for help finding your way" (Farrell 2009). Extended discourse on the commodification of ghostlore in popular culture, ghost hunting and ghost tourism is continued in chapter 5 of this volume.

Several major concerns regarding the commodification of folklore have risen for folklorists and legend scholars. Foremost is popular culture's tendency to gather its imagery from diverse and multiple folkloric elements, motifs and supernatural beings and combining them in a way that would not be found together in tradition. "Ghosts, vampires, werewolves, witches, zombies and monsters hang out together in popular culture in ways that tend to turn a blind eye towards history, cultural variation, and patterns of tradition and transmission" (Goldstein, Grider and Thomas 2007, 211).

A second concern is that these folkloric traditions will become trivialized through stereotyping and sensationalism or that they will become invented traditions as a result of commodification practices (Goldstein 2007, 195). "In the re-creation of traditional culture for a market audience, tradition is by definition fragmented, re-engineered, and reinvented as experiences for visitors to enjoy. Most tour operators will admit that they alter the narratives, deleting confused or boring parts, and occasionally merging two or more narratives to heighten dramatic effect" (Goldstein 2007, 200). Further examples of commodification emerge in other discussions later in this chapter as well as throughout the rest of this book.

Motivated by desires to inform, entertain, obtain profits and seek truths, producers perpetuate the tradition by writing books and articles, advertising, creating television and movie specials and interacting on the World Wide Web. Thus they obtain their desired secondary gain through mass dissemination geared towards academic or commercial purposes (Leary 2003, 116).

Examples of Ostension and Pseudo-Ostension

> *Ostension is present whenever someone creates [a] "found narrative" out of real life or whenever someone creates a stir by manufacturing evidence for legendary events. Such cases test the boundaries of "life" and "legend" by staging actions that the players represent as real and that the audience overtly accept as such. Yet such performances may not always be fiction: they may inspire real-life actions with lasting results.*

—Ellis (2001, 161)

One of the major developments in the ongoing discussions on contemporary legend in the last two decades is the articulation and actualization of ostension in and outside of folkloric circles. Both contemporary legends and ostensive action could have a tremendous impact. As Theo Meder states, "We tell, hear, see and read legends, but we believe, experience, re-enact and live legends too. The notion of *ostension* is used to comprehend the mechanism of legends we live. For other kinds of legends the notion of *proto-ostension* is used, namely when people tell legends as if they were personally involved—because they *believe* so, because they *want* to believe so, or because they want *others* to believe so" (Meder "Ethnic Conflict").

Jonathan Floyd discovered that several different ostensive enactments of the Almo massacre legend, in Idaho, do in fact aid in altering the perception of the actual historical event. The legend claims that in 1861 a large wagon train was moving west through the area when they were set upon by Shoshoni and Bannocks near Almo Creek. Circling for protection, the pioneers were soon short of water and were shot as they tried to obtain the precious liquid. Six of the travelers did manage to escape, surviving on rosebuds and roots until rescued by Mormon settlers. Upon returning to the site they discovered that they were the only survivors; all others had been killed.

Floyd first looks at the play of children, close to the time of the actual historical event, who engaged in a simple form of adolescent legend tripping re-enacting the massacre in the area. Secondly, he examines the legend as told by an amateur historian who took various groups of tourists in a string of cars imitating a wagon train to the legendary site. While the children do not use the legend for economic gain, the legend here is told to tourists to bolster the tourism experience; the enactment involved planning and a number of people (Floyd 2011, 62). The third example of ostension is the historical re-enactment of the Indian attack similar to the one depicted in the legend. This event "orchestrates a massive publicity event for the area as a potential destination and his re-enactment is high drama with a division of spectators and players, which requires a great deal of planning" (Floyd 2011, 62).

It would seem that a natural progression of ostensive action as related to the Almo massacre is observable in the three accounts chosen here in two major ways, the first being that the ostensive action becomes more complex as time goes on, and the second being that the people engaging in the ostensive action are more and more distant from Almo, both geographically and by family ties. While the other forms of enactment like Rice's legend tripping and Dayley's pseudo-legend-trip seem to have been more informal and communally enacted, Dawson's saga has a distinct separation between spectators and players, as well as roles that are complex and scripted. The importance of commodifying the image of the "Old West" through an Indian massacre in the saga is evident in the time and effort used to create Dawson's enactment, as the complexity and theatrical nature of it could be considered what Bill Ellis would term high drama. (Floyd 2011, 52)

In 1938, citizens of the area erected a marker to commemorate the massacre. However, in 2010 the citizens of the area came to realize that the legendary massacre had never taken place. "I would contend that just as folklore in general adapts to the ever-changing world and culture around it, so especially do legends and the way in which people draw meaning from and interact with them" (Floyd 2011, 12). This is definitely a case where the osculating ostension of a legend developed a life of its own.

A more recent concrete ostensive marker is the sculpture created by Maarten de Reus for the Vellertheuvel in Apeldoorn (Gelderland) called "Cage-with-no-puma-in-it." The contemporary legend of Winnie the Puma circulated in the Netherlands during the summer of 2005. Many people allegedly spotted the puma but it was, naturally, never caught. The sculpture, a construction of steel wire, shows a puma in a cage when seen from a distance, but the puma fades away the closer one gets to the cage. During the presentation of this work of art in 2008, the local pop group Springvloed sung their "Puma Song" (Meder 2011, 11). In an ironic form of folkloric ostension, artist and filmmaker John Lundberg created a website called "ostension" to explain and clarify the term, stating that much of his artwork revolved around the idea of ostension. "This site attempts to describe what ostension is and explain what it has to do with contemporary/urban legends. Ostension encompasses a wide range of subjects including, crop circles, AIDS, mind control, ghosts, satanism, alien abductions, cults, etc." (http://www.ostension.org/).

Bloody Mary

In the discussion of "Ostension and Bloody Mary" in *Tales, Rumors, and Gossip*, I briefly explore the history of the game, the legend and the occurrences of mirrors in folklore and literature. Three functions of the ritual game are identified: to actively challenge and conquer fears; to allow opportunities to increase peer group status; and to develop a mechanism for coping with the supernatural (de Vos 1996, 67). Since the publication of that book, I have had countless additional discussions with young people of various ages regarding "Bloody Mary." When conducting contemporary legends sessions in the secondary school system, numerous students related their experiences, both positive and negative, with great glee while others hid their heads in terror at the very thought of calling her. There is little agreement with any age group as to the back story of Bloody Mary and, in fact, many of the students had very little concern regarding the reason behind the murderous ghost. Instead they are just interested in seeing "what would happen." Several popular folkloric elements in the Bloody Mary legend mentioned in the television program *Supernatural* include a ghost of a woman murdered right after her wedding, who might have been pregnant, who can be summoned by repeating that you had killed her baby. "If you do it, the story goes, and Mary appears, one of two things can happen. Either she's going to tell you something about your future, or she's going to tear your face off and kill you" (Irvine 2007, 21). The show also refers to divination by mirror, and the superstitions regarding mirrors are one of the reasons why a mirror is involved in the Bloody Mary story (Irvine 2007, 22).

Alan Dundes believed that the ritual, as performed by young girls, is connected to the onset of the first menses. His rationale for this theory includes the age of the female participants and the location of the ritual. According to his interpretation, the ritual is anticipatory, warning young girls what to expect when they attained puberty, and it explained why the bathroom was the room of choice for the ritual: the flushing of toilets and the "explicit and repeated emphasis on the sudden appearance of blood" (Dundes 2002, 85). "The taboo status of menstruation and the 'shame' wrongly associated with its presence meant that . . . little girls are often kept in the dark about it, a metaphor which is apt in the light of the darkness imposed as part of setting the stage for Bloody Mary rituals—which are either performed at night, e.g., midnight, or in bathrooms during the day with the lights turned off" (Dundes 2002, 90).

However, despite Dundes's emphasis on the young females performing the ritual, I have discovered that players of the ritual included both genders. Most of my female university students recall playing it when they were younger and terrifying themselves in the process, while many of the male students recall "aiding" the "spooky" aspect of the legend by creating noises and so on while others called on the spirit in the mirror. None of these students referred to recent experiences with Bloody Mary. In her research with college students, Libby Tucker found that her students did in fact perform the mirror ritual. She claims that, because of the popularity of the movie *Candyman*, Bloody Mary became a form of ostensive play for this age of student as well as they act out the summoning scene with vigour and humor (Tucker 2005, 197).

While there are parallels between preadolescents' Bloody Mary rituals and college students' sightings of ghosts in mirrors, the age states are different; the images seen in mirrors are different as well. Pre-adolescent girls see an aggressive mother figure who threatened to inflict pain, an early initiation into the perils of female maturity. College students, farther from the protection of the home, see aspects of their adult selves that are evolving: male/female identities, sexual relationships and social roles (Tucker 2005, 199).

Along with the persistence of the ritual of Bloody Mary, the popularity of the legend continues to be a force in popular culture as can be attested by the examples later in the chapter. It also joins hands with another persistent and shifting traditional item of folklore discussed in chapter 3: chain letters or chain e-mails. This obnoxious and overtly threatening chain e-mail, aimed at children and adolescents, was circulating in 2008:

THIS EMAIL HAS BEEN CURSED ONCE OPENED YOU MUST SEND IT

You are now cursed. You must send this on or you will be killed. Tonight at 12:00 am, by Bloody Mary. This is no joke. So don't think you can quickly get out of it and delete it now because Bloody Mary will come to you if you do not send this on. She will slit your throat and your wrists and pull your eyeballs out with a fork. And then hang your dead corpse in your bedroom cupboard or put you under your bed. What's [sic] your parents going to do when they find you dead? Won't be funny then, will it? Don't think this is a fake and it's all put on to scare you because your [sic] wrong, so very wrong. Want to hear of some of the sad, sad people who lost their lives or have been seriously hurt by this email?

CASE ONE–

Annalise [Surname Removed]: She got this email. Rubbish she thought. She deleted it. And now, Annalise dead.

CASE TWO–

Louise [Surname Removed]: She sent this to only 4 people and when she woke up in the morning her wrists had deep lacerations on each. Luckily there was no pain felt, though she is scarred for life.

CASE THREE–

Thomas [Surname Removed]: He sent this to 5 people. Big mistake. The night Thomas was lying in his bed watching T.V. The clock shows "12:01am," The T.V misteriously [sic] flickered off and Thomas's bedroom lamp flashed on and off several times. It went pitch black, Thomas looked to the left of him and there she was, Bloody Mary standing in white rags. Blood everywhere with a knife in her hand then disappeared. The biggest fright of Thomas's life.

Warning ... NEVER look in a mirror and repeat—"Bloody Mary. Bloody Mary. Bloody Mary ... I KILLED YOUR SON." Is it the end for you tonight! YOU ARE NOW CURSED

We strongly advise you to send this email on. It is seriously NO JOKE. We don't want to see another life wasted. ITS [sic] YOUR CHOICE ... WANNA DIE TONIGHT? If you send this email to ...

NO PEOPLE—You're going to die.

1–5 PEOPLE—You're going to either get hurt or get the biggest fright of your life.

5–15 PEOPLE—You will bring your family bad luck and someone close to you will die.

15–25 OR MORE PEOPLE—You are safe from Bloody Mary.

** DO NOT FORWARD COPY AND PASTE. RENAME THE SUBJECT (Bloody Mary Curse)

The Halloween Sadist

Jan Harold Brunvand defines the "Halloween Sadist" contemporary legend, while thoroughly debunked by folklorists, sociologists and law enforcement officials, as resulting from sadistic people preying on children at Halloween through the agencies of poisoned candy and razor blades or needles in apples. Brunvand claimed 10 years ago that "despite broad dissemination of such findings in the academic and popular press, warnings against these so-called Halloween sadists still appear each October, and organized efforts to eliminate trick-or-treat or to submit Halloween treats to X-ray checks continue in many communities" (Brunvand 2001, 187).

Ironically, the same warnings are still appearing currently although some articles are hedging their claims with comments suggesting that it is better to be safe than sorry. "A primary reason 'The Halloween Sadist' continues to circulate by word of mouth is because the media gives validity to the legend. Police departments issue warnings as well, which gives this particular legend some truth" (Cruz 2008, 16). Joel Best states that Halloween sadism was best seen as a contemporary legend but concerns about Halloween were heightened when any recent and relevant crimes sharpened public anxieties. Illustrations of this include the 1982 Tylenol poisonings and the legends following the September 11, 2001, attacks warning against visiting malls on Halloween (Best 2008). A compilation of news items in the media of contemporary legends during the last two days of October 2010 include over a dozen reports of Halloween sadism. The diverse reports warn against marijuana-laced Halloween candy in Los Angeles, numerous incidents of tampered candy that later proved to be hoaxes and numerous cases of razor blades, safety pins and needles in Halloween swag. Unfortunately, while the articles covering the discovery of these items made front-page news coverage, the subsequent articles debunking the claims are, as frequently happens, buried where very few people will find them.

In his research on reported incidents of Halloween sadism in the newspapers from 1958 to 2008, Best found that there are intensified reports from 1969 to 1971 (31 in the three years) and again in 1982 (12), but for most of the other years there are very few reports, from none to three or four in a year. This certainly is not the epidemic of cases that is suggested by the media and the legends. Best pointed to five deaths attributed to Halloween sadism in North America. I discuss the most famous case, that of eight-year-old Timothy O'Bryan in 1974, in *Tales, Rumors, and Gossip*. Timothy died after ingesting cyanide-laced Halloween candy. Investigations reveal that he had received the candy from his father who had recently taken out a life insurance policy on his son. The father was convicted and executed for the murder (Best 2008). The most recent death occurred in Vancouver, British Columbia, in 2001. After eating Halloween candy, a four-year-old girl died suddenly. The police advised the parents to throw out all of the Halloween treats. However, no evidence of poisoning was found in the pathology tests, and the autopsy showed that the child died of a streptococcus infection (Best 2008).

The theme of the *Food Network Challenge*, aired on October 31, 2010, was "Extreme Urban Legend Cakes." Four professional cake designers attempt to win a $10,000 prize awarded by a panel of judges which included contemporary legend expert Lynne S. McNeill. McNeill served as the reviews editor for the peer-reviewed journal *Contemporary Legend*. In an interview with David Emery, McNeill states:

> Judging urban legend-themed cakes is by far one of the most unique applications of a folklorist's skills that I've ever been asked to make, and it was easily one of the most fun. I was thrilled that the Food Network recognized that a folklorist would make a good guest judge for this topic (or even that they knew there was such a thing as a folklorist at all—many people don't!), and I'm hopeful that this recognition is a trend that catches on in popular media. (Emery 2010)

Ostensive Abuse

> *Events provoke stories; but it is far more likely that stories provoke events. Some forms of ostension are relatively benign; others can be deadly. As far back as 1978, evangelist Kurt E. Koch averred that devil-worshipping baby-sitters in the United States had actually roasted a baby in an oven.*
>
> —Ellis (2001, 164)

Examples of ostensive abuse, often involving criminal activity by over-exuberant legend trippers, has long been discussed by folklorists and sociologists. One fairly benign example, from the Netherlands, involves a haunted, deserted farm in Brummen (Gelderland), mentioned in a list of 10 haunted houses in the Netherlands on http://nl.wikipedia.org/wiki/Spookhuis. According to the legend, when the farmer disapproved of his son's choice of wife, the son hanged himself on a tree and his ghost returned to haunt the farmer. Although the farmer moved away from the area, the revenant continues to haunt the place. "Tenants who use the barn as a stable, and the neighbours, have never experienced any haunting episodes, but they did have problems with (drunk) youngsters who came hunting for ghosts in the dead of night" (Meder 2011, 128). When the alleged haunted farm was added to a legend safari bus route, neighbours experienced a mild form of ostensive abuse, so much so that one neighbour attached a sign to her door stating: "No ringing for ghost stories" (Meder 2011, 128).

A much more malevolent illustration is the case of Mary Partington in Lincoln, Nebraska, in the 1960s. "She became the victim of a kind of adolescent 'ostensive frenzy' growing out of legend tripping that caused not only destruction to her property, but more significantly extreme personal and emotional suffering on her part" (Summers 2000, 20). Wynne Summers describes her youthful legend-tripping experiences on Mary's property. The proscribed ritual includes arriving late at night, creeping up to the windows, peeking in and banging on them and the doors, screaming and then running back to the car and racing as fast as possible away from the home (Summers 2000, 20). "She had been the victim of Lincoln teenagers [sic] rituals for years starting in the sixties. They regarded her property as a place they could invade at will, breaking and entering, riddling the sides of her house with bullet holes, stealing inside at night and taking 'trophies'—any of Mary's personal possessions that made good objects to later show to friends" (Summers 2000, 21). Mary Partington's major transgression was that she was eccentric, was different from her neighbours in that she did not demonstrate any interest in modern conveniences and lived in a fairly isolated old farmhouse. "By her very eccentricity and forceful insistence on living as if she were still locked in the early 1900s, she almost invited teen ritual and performance, in the guise of the ostensive legend trip" (Summers 2000, 25). The ostensive abuse finally resulted in Mary leaving the home she so loved. Her experience becomes legendary in its own right as the site of her former home became a stop for organized ghost tours decades later. "One October evening decades ago, she shot an intruder trying to get through her window. She was forced to move, and the house was razed. But they say that sometimes on Oct. 24, when the conditions are right, you can see the outline of the house" (Story, 2009). The factual story of Mary Partington's life and experiences is the focus of Frances G. Reinehr's 1989 book *Bloody Mary, Gentle Woman*. Mary received the nickname of "Bloody Mary" after she shot and killed the intruder. She was not charged with a crime on the grounds of self-defence (Nebraska State Historical Society 2007).

Mass-Mediated Ostension

In presentations and articles regarding contemporary legends and films, Mikel Koven argues for consideration by folklorists of the varied natures of manifestations of contemporary legends in film, labelling these appearances as cinematic ostension. Koven believes that a legend dramatized through film is a type of ostension since the legend is *shown* through actions rather than having the story *retold* in narration.

This cinematic ostension "implicitly recognizes an audience by encouraging some form of postpresentation debate regarding the veracity of the legends presented. There is also an implicit recognition of the fictive form of this narration (a fictive film) but equally a recognition that the stories upon which certain films are based come from 'genuine urban legends' " (Koven 2008, 139). Later he modifies the terminology as he feels that the former term semantically excluded television or other forms of popular culture. He thinks that "mass-mediated ostension" is a more appropriate and less restrictive term. Although Koven does not mention specific formats other film and television, original YouTube video productions featuring contemporary legends also correspond to the revised terminology. "Mass-mediated ostension recognizes that *presented* legend materials, whether dramatised or 'documentary,' is the medium through which extra-textual debates surrounding the legend's veracity occur" (Koven 2007, 185). The visualized text functions like a traditional oral storyteller, creating a complex relationship among the legendary traditions, the television, film or YouTube video, and the members of the audience watching the show (Koven 2007, 183). The responses of audiences are subsequently captured not only in face-to-face interactions with other members of the audience but in blog entries, by Twitter and Facebook commentary and in fan fiction constructs after the fact.

As has been discussed elsewhere in this book, forms of mass-mediated ostension are less concerned with academic perspectives on folklore. Thus the creators of these programs, films and videos tend to "to fuse all elements of folk tradition into a single homogenous mass with little attention to cultural meanings or the phenomenon behind such lore" (Koven 2008, 78). Koven is surprised that contemporary legends appeared rather infrequently within the relatively large corpus of horror movies. Contemporary legends are, of course, copyright free and are "good, gross, frightening, and suspenseful stories" (Koven 2008, 111).

The following movies and television programs are often mentioned as exemplifying mass-mediated ostension in the literature. As many of them are referenced throughout the various discussions of specific legends in other parts of this book, only a brief discussion of the ostensive activity is offered here. All of these titles are available on DVD, and their trailers and numerous excerpts from the films and programs are also available through YouTube.

Candyman *(1992)*

Based on a short story "The Forbidden" by Clive Barker, *Candyman* is the first film in a trilogy which includes *Candyman 2: Farewell to the Flesh* and *Candyman 3: Day of the Dead*. The protagonist, Helen Lyle, while conducting research on contemporary legends for her thesis, attempts to summon the one-armed Candyman (an infusion of "The Hook" and "Bloody Mary" legends) from a mirror with not unexpected horrific results.

Urban Legends *(1998)*

This film, more than any other title discussed here, embodies the design of mass-media ostension of contemporary legends: a killer is utilizing, as a model, the various ways of dying as described in diverse contemporary legends, to murder the victims. Also part of a trilogy, this film is followed by *Urban Legends: Final Cut* and *Urban Legends: Bloody Mary*. The last film in the trilogy went directly to video without being shown in theatres. Contemporary legends alluded to or shown in the first film include "the Killer in the Backseat," "Bloody Mary," "The

Babysitter and the Man Upstairs," "Pop Rocks," "Death of Little Mikey," "The Boyfriend's Death," "Spider Eggs in Bubble Gum," "Gang Initiation Headlights," "Aren't You Glad You Didn't Turn on the Lights?," "The Pet in the Microwave" and "The Kidney Heist." The movie, although not well received by critics, inspired the Indian film *Whistle* (2003) and is continually referred to in fan discussions of contemporary legends.

The X-Files *(1993–2002)*

This American science-fiction series, created by Chris Carter and featuring FBI agents Fox Mulder (David Duchovny) and Dana Scully (Gillian Anderson), focuses on the investigation of paranormal phenomenon which includes "monster of the week" episodes that often featured traditional creatures drawn from the well of world folklore. The ostensive use of folklore in this series, however, resembles the invented and fragmented commodified folklore discussed earlier in this chapter. Thus the folklore in this series are "narratives that are more 'Frankenstein-like' monsters, cobbled together from any handy source, than a representation of the narrative tradition these stories emerged from" (Koven 2008, 38).

Most Haunted *(2002–10)*

Most Haunted is a British paranormal reality television series which inspired a number of satellite programs. The series is both " *about* the folklore of the supernatural and the ostensive presentation of such phenomena . . . a kind of televised 'legend-trip' " (Koven 2007, 186).

> The highly artificial legend and memorate section of each *Most Haunted* episode is more than just contrived television. It creates this "generally scary condition" in the location prior to the investigation proper. In terms of quasi-ostension, by beginning the investigation in the tradition associated with the location being investigated, any phenomena, natural or supernatural, encountered during the night will be interpreted from the perspective of that legend tradition. This section of the episode, then, primes the pump, as it were. (Koven 2007, 191)

Supernatural *(2005–Present)*

"*Supernatural* does not simply retell folk narratives, but actually *performs* the stories . . . what Koven calls 'mass-media ostension' " (Tosenberger 2010). There is no doubt that this television series embraces traditional folklore and the ostensive use of folklore and relies heavily on contemporary legends.

> The series not only uses ostension because it is a mass-media text that dramatizes folk narratives, it also actively and consistently depicts ostension as a process. Almost every episode features the majority of the characters performing ostensive acts—and Sam and Dean, at least, are fully conscious of this ostension. *Supernatural* relies heavily upon existing legend texts, and the majority of every episode involves Sam and Dean investigating the folklore record to determine which ostensive action will be

most efficacious in defeating the creature of the week. (Tosenberger 2010)

Tosenberger asserts that the series often sets traditionalist views of folklore against more nuanced and postmodern understandings of folk research, folk groups and folk material. "And," she claims, "because *Supernatural* adheres much more closely to the existing folklore record than do other notable shows influenced by supernatural folklore . . . it encourages fans of the series to do their own investigations—and transformations—of both the series and the folklore that inspires it" (Tosenberger 2010). An extended example of ostension is the fact that the fans also investigate the folklore itself, and comment on and correct, if they feel it is necessary, the presentation of the traditional material in the individual programs. The Library section of the SuperWiki, http://www.supernaturalwiki.com/index.php ?title=Category:Library, was a prime repository of such commentary (Tosenberger 2010).

Blood Oath *(2007)*

This low-budget horror film, recently released on DVD, follows four friends as they pursue a local legend of the cursed Krupp family. The legend, regarding the family's deal with the supernatural in order to have a child, has had horrific repercussions on the area in the past. The friends, blissfully legend tripping, soon unleash the horror on themselves.

Cropsey *(2009)*

This example appropriates the long-standing and locally well-known contemporary legend of the "Cropsey Maniac" for both the title and the genesis of the documentary horror film. The traditional legend of the Cropsey maniac involves a respected member of the community who, in order to avenge the accidental death of a family member, stalked various summer camps in New York state, first as an axe-wielding man and, later, as a revenant (Haring and Breslerman 1977, 15). In their examination of the legend as told in summer camps, Haring and Breslerman identify the major motifs of the legend: the central character is always a respected adult male "typifying the values of the older generation from a middle-class adolescent's point of view" (Haring and Breslerman 1977, 17); the first death that acted as the initial action of the story is always accidental and involves a family member; Cropsey reacts pathologically to the news of the death and commences his bloody revenge; although authorities attempt to capture Cropsey, he continually eludes them, even after his death, to haunt the neighbourhood. The authors conclude that the story fulfilled several functions for both the campers and the counsellors:

- It permitted moments of imagined melodrama as an escape from the scheduled camp life.
- It promoted feelings of solidarity among listeners: "The setting and main actor of the story appear *outside* the camp or school grounds, and the action of mayhem and insanity is of a type of solidly condemned by the society to which the hearers belong" (Haring and Breslerman 1977, 21).
- It integrated new campers into the camp society by introducing them to local traditions, solving the problem of continuity in a situation of annual change.
- It explicitly ensured conformity to the accepted cultural norms, particularly the prohibition against leaving the camp grounds (Haring and Breslerman 1977, 21).

In a more recent look at the legend, Libby Tucker maintains that the Cropsey Maniac still terrorizes New York campers. "Anyone who has access to the Internet will quickly learn that the answer to that question [of contemporary relevancy] is 'yes' " (Tucker 2006b). Tucker also extends the commentary by Haring and Breslerman regarding the function of the Cropsey legend.

> Another key ingredient [was the] insistence that the listener may be targeted for death within a certain period of time, just because he or she has lived in Cropsey's domain. The growing number of stories that identify Cropsey as a ghost seem to suggest that he is ever-present and inescapable. Adolescents test their bravery by talking about him; even adult camp alumni shiver slightly when mentioning his name. (Tucker 2006b)

The film *Cropsey*, resulting from a discussion between two people about their recollections about their local legend, make it universally recognized. For filmmakers Joshua Zeman and Barbara Brancaccio, however, the legendary maniac had morphed into an escaped mental patient, with either an axe or a hook for a hand, who lives in the old abandoned Willowbrook Mental Institution and appears at night to snatch children off the streets (http://cropseylegend.com). The film's directors were aware, also, of the film *The Burning* (1981) which incorporates the legend in its lead character, Cropsey, a disfigured camp caretaker who has been burned in a prank and continually takes his revenge on camp counsellors with garden shears. The misguided prank, shown in the opening sequence, and the story of his revengeful acts told around the campfire by a counsellor during an overnight excursion, propel the action of this earlier film.

Variants of the legend are frequently mentioned in the film reviews of *Cropsey*. Michele Orange writes that he was "an axe-wielding (or alternately hook-handed) bogeyman known . . . to troll the woods looking for disobedient children; over time his name became a shorthand for all manner of evil" (Orange 2010). John Anderson comments that the film is "named for the mythic bogeyman of Hudson Valley campfire stories [and] is the cinematic version of peeking under the bed and not breathing a sigh of relief" (Anderson 2010). "Cropsey was the name of a generic killer figure—wielding an axe, or a hook hand, take your pick—woven by slumber-party storytellers and recounted to children. A basic urban legend, but rendered all the stranger for the events that actually *did* occur near the site of the Willowbrook State School, an institution for children with mental retardation in central Staten Island that was closed in 1987 due to wicked abuses to patients" (Bowery Boys 2010). Steve Dollar of the *Wall Street Journal* also remarks on the legendary identity of the character, blending several different legends and versions together: "Staten Island's own bogeyman—the escaped mental patient of lore with a hook for an arm who, after the tragic death of his son, snatched up wayward children in a vengeful range. He was an urban legend" (Dollar 2010). In a recent interview with Josh Zeman, Don Lewis states:

> The film is ostensibly about the "Cropsey" urban legend that's been floating around Staten Island kids for years. The story, which was likely spawned by kids but likely perpetuated by adults to keep kids safe, revolves around an old, dilapidated mental institution said to be haunted by an escaped mental patient named Cropsey. He would come out late at night and snatch kids off the

streets and murder them without any remorse. While the area did have its share of missing children, none were ever found. Then the legend seemed to come to life as a murdered child was found and a creepy local "Boo Radley" type figure named Andre Rand was arrested. What followed was a sensationalized trial that took the area by storm and, luckily for us, filmmakers Josh Zeman and Barbara Brancaccio were there to capture it all. (Lewis 2011)

These reviews, and others, also make reference to the film as a "chilling horror documentary [which] proves some urban legends are real" (O'Leary 2010). However, there are also numerous comments regarding the use of the legend in the title as more of an attention grabber than an in-depth study on the legend. "So the documentary, *Cropsey*, is very much a case of bait-and-switch. The movie is called *Cropsey* and the text of the film suggests that the 'urban legend' of Cropsey is real ... but it makes no attempt to find if there is, actually, a historical Cropsey" (Muir 2010). Muir, in fact, is quite dismayed regarding the fact that the title of the movie, for him, is misnamed as "they opened with the supposition that maybe, just maybe, Cropsey's urban legend is real. And then they don't follow through on any of it" (Muir 2010). Another reviewer says that the film, chronicling approximately two decades, was "prefaced by the story of Cropsey and the time-honored tradition of legend tripping, a common practice involving the nighttime dalliances of children trying to scare each other with visits to frightening locales. This was explored in the film *Candyman*, albeit in a much more mature manner, so it's no surprise that *Cropsey* manages to instil genuine frights in the audience" (McHargue 2010). McHargue concludes that "Cropsey is an incredibly rich and informative 'whodunnit' filled to the brim with social commentary, all while exploring the horrifying reality of popular—and seemingly fictional—motif of urban legends in horror cinema" (McHargue 2010). Folklorist Bill Ellis, in a note to the ISCLR listserv, affirms that he was interviewed on camera as part of the project and was assured that the contemporary legend perspective he provided proved influential to the film (Ellis, "Documentary on NTC Cropsey Maniac Legend-Trip," personal communication, April 23, 2009). The final words of the film definitely reiterate the ostensive intent of the film directors, ensuring that *Cropsey* is a prime example of mass-mediated ostension: "The power of the urban legend is that it doesn't claim to be the truth rather that the truth is a range of possibilities and it is up to the audience to decide."

Shoefiti

The term "shoefiti," a composite of shoe and graffiti referring to the act of flinging shoes over a telephone wire or power wire to hang by their laces, is considered to be a global example of ostensive behaviour. Photographs of the hanging shoes populate the Internet as do discussions of the myriad of rationales behind this mysterious, secret activity. Almost all of these discussions label shoefiti as a contemporary legend regardless of the fact that there is rarely any narrative structure attached to the reasons for the activity. One website dedicated to shoefiti photographs and sightings, http://www.shoefiti.com, established in September 2005, collects pictures of shoe sightings, and links to mentions of shoefiti in the media, allusions and reworkings of shoefiti in popular culture including the name of a band in Madrid, a photo book covering the shoefiti scene in Columbus, Ohio, and, among other things, commodified items for sale on eBay. The archive for the "shoefiti theories category" contains at least 20 postings as of September 2011.

Cathy Preston considers shoefiti as unsanctioned community art objects because "though community-based, the object is not institutionally sanctioned" (Preston 2007, 11). She maintains that these sites also became the objects of story-telling of both personal narratives and contemporary legends. While several commentaries indicate that this is an activity that began in this decade, Arthur Goldstruck asserts that "the idea of shoes on phone lines identifying drug-dealers or gang activities goes back decades. In 1996, Cecil Adams, author of *The Straight Dope* (book, web site and column) listed more than a dozen theories for the 'truth' behind the phenomenon" (Goldstruck 2010). The South African versions of shoefiti discussed by Goldstruck share the same elements and the same theories in this global contemporary legend.

Rationales for Shoefiti

The most cited reason for shoes hanging on a wire is as an indicator for a local crack house or gang-related locations. Often these comments are made by police personnel but, if these rationales are indeed true, would it not make police work much easier? Other reasons are much more innocent and encompass a wide variety of rites of passage: celebrating the end of the school year or graduation, retiring from the military or a job, celebrating a forthcoming marriage, marking the loss of virginity or marking a move from the present neighbourhood to a better one. Some beliefs and tales centre on the paranormal, signifying of death of a loved one or an attempt to keep the property safe from ghostly presences. Still others explain that it is a fun way of getting rid of unwanted footwear or to tease younger children by tossing their shoes out of reach. All of the narratives are in agreement, however, that the activity must be done secretly and under the cover of darkness.

Recently, there has been a rash of newspaper articles examining this phenomenon with queries regarding the rationale for the activity, questions regarding the safety of removing the shoes from the wires and the civic responsibilities of people affected by shoefiti encounters. Various communities attempt to have a system in place to have the shoes removed within a certain time frame since many people felt the hanging shoes lowered their property values due to the negative connotations associated with the activity. Others worry about the danger to public safety with rainstorms, electrical storms and power outages as well as the act of removing the shoes from power lines itself. While some reports declare the dangling shoes as harmless, the *German Herald* reported that two Germans in Koln (Cologne) were in critical condition with severe burns after using a fishing rod to pull a pair of running shoes from a train power cable. The name and ages of the two men are given in this concise article but there is a definite contemporary legend aura to it ("High Voltage Tops," 2011).

The appearances of shoefiti on the Internet exploded with the advent of the digital camera and YouTube but have gone far beyond the simple documenting of photographs or videos. This documentation, of course, is the result of observers of shoefiti, not the practitioners of it, as the first rule of shoefiti is to not to be caught. In a recent Internet search, there are equally diverse arrays of products depicting shoefiti offered online as there are photographs including art prints, paintings, fabrics, sculptures, birthday cards, T-shirts and other items of clothing.

An Ostensive Leave Taking

Upon retirement from Penn State University, Bill Ellis, folklorist and contemporary legend scholar, decided that he needed a ritual to mark the transition.

Noticing two pairs of old tennis shoes dangling from a network of heavy wires on his commute to and from his home, he "thought it might be an appropriately ostensive act for me to add a third pair of shoes as a token of my taking leave from Pennsylvania" (Ellis, personal communication). He discusses his rationale for selecting shoes, his recording the dates of employment on the shoes and his practice sessions, stating that it was not as easy as it might seem to have the shoes remain on the wires and the experience itself during the late evening.

> As my eyes adapted to the dark I could see the criss-cross of wires clearly. Through the web they made, stars glittered in the clear night sky. I was utterly alone ... Once, twice, I swung the shoes back and forth, then, my adrenaline surging, I launched them together up into the starry night. To my astonishment, one of the shoes hit the thick wire dead center. The other one, traveling below it, passed under the cable, came to the end of the tied shoelaces, jerked, and did a pretty little arc, up, back, and around, looping neatly over the wire. Securely tethered twenty feet up, the shoes rocked back and forth, and the other two pairs also jiggled, as if welcoming the newcomer. ... I did what decorum required: I pulled out my digital camera and took a couple of flash photographs, in case the authorities came by later and took down the sneakers. (Ellis, e-mail communication)

Ellis quotes a comment from one of his personal informants regarding shoefiti: "When you leave some place for good, tie a pair of old shoes together and throw them over a wire, as a sign that you're not coming back" (Ellis, "Sneakers on the Wire: An Ostensive Leavetaking," e-mail communication, May 24, 2009).

Shoefiti as an Adapted Art Form

Fairly recently, two knitting enthusiasts from Vancouver, British Columbia, published a book of instructions for knitting and crocheting graffiti. Entitled *Yarn Bombing*, the cover depicts a pair of knitted sneakers hanging from a wire, ostensibly a power line, as a tree and wide sky provides the background to the shoes. Yarn Bombing, a covert textile street art, celebrates "knit graffiti" which is explained as an international guerrilla movement whose international members create stunning works of art out of yarn and send them freely to public spaces. The book includes interviews with members of the group as well as over 20 patterns to create from yarn. The book, written by Mandy Moore and Leanne Prain, was in its third printing by Arsenal Pulp Press in 2009.

Shoe Trees

Related to shoes on a wire are shoes tossed into trees, often mimicking the mysteriousness of shoefiti but just as often including messages, poems, greetings and accomplishments inscribed on the shoes with a permanent marker. RoadsideAmerica.com includes the sites of shoe trees in their online guide to offbeat tourist attractions. Several of these sites such as the Shoe Tree in Salem, Michigan, include a legend with the shoe tree: a serial killer dispatched young children for their footwear. According to various Internet sites, shoe trees are found all over the United States, in Canada and in England. A recent car advertisement for

Volkswagen Canada GT shown in Canada and available on YouTube includes a visual reference to a shoe tree.

Shag or Sex Bracelets

Also referred to as gel bracelets and jelly bracelets, these vibrantly colored thin rubbery bands are inexpensive and easily obtainable by young people. The bracelets, popular since the 1980s when Madonna was seen wearing them, can be worn singly or interconnected on wrists, on ankles or around the neck and should not to be confused with the wider "charity awareness bands." It is only in the last decade, however, that the bracelets became the subject of contemporary legends linking them to sex codes, games and the premature sexualisation of young people. According to these legends, each color of the bracelet is linked to a specific sexual act, ranging from the fairly innocent hugging and kissing to more aggressive forms of sexual intercourse. When a bracelet is snapped or broken, the wearer of the bracelet is then expected to perform that specific act. While none of the myriad of news stories and Internet sites indicate that young people actually utilized the jewellery to proclaim their willingness to engage in the sexual acts, educators, police and politicians, as early as 2003 and as recently as 2010, issue warnings to parents about the meanings of the bracelets. Barbara Mikkelson states that the banning of the bracelets in schools is "an attempt . . . to return children to a time when they weren't so focused on sex . . . Such codes and rumors also serve to desensitize kids to the physical side of love, to lose awareness of its importance and specialness as sex becomes (at least in their minds, thanks to this undercutting) a mundane, meaningless activity one would properly engage in with anyone, even someone of short acquaintance" ("Sex Bracelets" 2009). A quick survey of Internet sites on this topic demonstrates that there are no standard meanings attached to the colors of the bracelets. Mikkelson reports that middle school and high school students deny any truth to the legends and are shocked that adults would think that they would be so cavalier with sexual favors. Parents, on the other hand, have often banned their children from wearing the bracelets as a result of the media frenzy created by both reputable and tabloid journalism in North American, Australia and Europe.

Examples of Legend Tripping

> At some distance from traditional religion are the séances, Ouija boards, and levitation that have long been a part of teen girl sleepovers, and "legend tripping" (visiting cemeteries, purportedly haunted houses, and other creepy places) that has been an established practice in teen boy life since the introduction of the automobile gave them increased mobility and autonomy. All of these practices serve as challenged to the ways in which authorities like teachers, parents, and the police oversee and discipline public spaces for young people. Also, they each play with (and to some extent rebel against) the definitions and practices of the afterlife that have long been the concerns of traditional monotheistic religions.
>
> —Clark (2003, 6)

Legend trips refer to short expeditions to sites that have supernatural or scary narratives associated with them. The trip experience usually includes the telling of scary and site-specific legends to get participants in the right mood. Usually the legend sites centre on visible objects, varying from visits to cemeteries, remote roads and bridges, tunnels, deserted and "haunted" houses and landscapes. "The object or place may be known and referred to by a descriptive name such as Dead Man's Hollow, Screaming bridge, or the Devil's Backbone, but more often the name does not reflect its legend connections" (Dégh 2001, 156). Legend trips serve as tests of legends about haunted locations. "If uncanny or frightening experiences occur, then they serve to confirm the truth of the original account. It is true that most legend-trip narratives are legends in their own right and often displace or suppress the narratives that charter the legend trip in the first place" (Oring 2008, 138).

Often the participants act out aspects of the legend and follow prescribed rituals that may be unique to that legend and place. The distinguishing feature of legend tripping that separates them from other types of tourism, for the most part, is the perilous element and the deliberate flirting with danger and the supernatural. Legend tripping is differentiated from the drama of ghost tours and other commodified ostension in that there is no clearly marked separation between the roles of players and spectators in legend tripping. Everyone involved in legend tripping are spectators. "There may be differences in the way adolescents' perceive the events witnessed, some seeing them as genuinely supernatural, others taking the trip as mere entertainment and pretending to be sacred. But no one (except perhaps the ghost) is enacting drama" (Ellis 2001, 166). A secondary distinguishing demarcation is the rationale for the legend trip as a ritualistic effort to test and delineate the boundaries of the known world (Ellis 2001, 166).

Tim Prizer argues that legend trips are more than ostension, where oral traditions became social events or actions, but are a form of performance in their own right relying on techniques of framing that attempts to convince or dissuade an audience of supernatural manifestation (Prizer 2004, 70). This framing corresponds to the tripartite structure of the legend trips themselves: the oral encounter with the story; the participation in the legend trip event itself; and the interpretative narratives after the experience (Prizer 2004, 81). The introductory storytelling about escaped maniacs, ghosts, witches or curses associated with the site sets the scene for the trip. Personal-experience stories about previous legend trip encounters are told along with the traditional tales to enhance the scare factor. In many cases historical accuracy is not a concern of either the teller or the members of the audience. The enactment of the legend trip constitutes the second component of the legend trip structure, and its effectiveness is dependent upon the threatening and remoteness of the site and the amount of tension and uncertainty generated by the trip and the stories previously told. Because of this heightened nervous anticipation, something usually happens at the site which affects the participants and their understanding of that "happening." The third stage, the telling and retelling of the events of the legend trip, has always been an essential element. However, with the advent of the popularity of uploading videos of legend trips on YouTube, this third stage becomes much more viral and the cyclical nature of the legend trips themselves becomes more pronounced. Libby Tucker notes that television programs such as *Fear Factor* encouraged videotaping of the legend quests and the uploading of these concrete examples to YouTube, resulting in a much wider dissemination of both the foundation legend and the various legend quest experiences. Because of technological advances and the popularity of the online environment, legend trippers no longer have to actually visit the site to experience vicariously the thrills and enhanced comprehension of the activity itself. (Tucker 2006a, 34) Tucker prefers the term "legend quest" rather than "legend tripping" because, in her research, the underlying rationale for participants include the wish to comprehend the mystery of death, to query the horror of domestic violence and to articulate the relationship between humans and technology. Tucker adds that there is definitely a strong emotional component attached: "an attempt to feel both thrilled and afraid under relatively safe circumstances" (Tucker 2006a, 34).

Internet sites and literature about legend trips and the activity of legend tripping are perhaps some of the fastest-growing by-products of contemporary legends at this time. "In this digital age, college students can easily preview locations they want to visit by surfing the Internet" (Tucker 2007, 185).

> Just as Ouija boards and tarot cards can be viewed as a playful entry to a magical world, so too can [the television series] *Supernatural*. Ellis discusses legend-tripping, which is another entry to the supernatural realm as it "generates excitement with an alternative, play-like redefinition of reality in terms of a super-natural 'dare.' Teens need not believe that they are visiting a real witch's grave or putting themselves in real danger. By means of the legend-trip, they temporarily escape what they perceive as a restrictive, adult-oriented, everyday world" (Ellis 2004, 137–8). *Supernatural* offers viewers a similar escape, but of course it does so without the trouble of actually having to visit a graveyard in the dead of night. (Petersen 2010)

Developing technology enhances the legend-tripping experience for people who do not want to brave the elements outside their realm of comfort: webcams are set up in "haunted" places for continuous or drop-in viewing; tweeting and blogging entries involve a wide assortment of people, not all initially part of the legend-tripping experience that has also, in many cases, been captured on video and uploaded to YouTube and other websites. These more passive legend trippers engage in the legend trip in a similar manner to those that actively seek out the experiences: they engage in the dialogue with the community and add new stories to the ongoing repertoire of tales building around specific legend-tripping sites. The computer-mediated discussions, accordingly, have three distinct stages: the telling of the legend, the story of the virtual legend-tripping experience and the discussion of the legend trip with others who had also experienced it (Goldstein 2011).

Several people have made legend tripping their career, incorporating all three stages as performance. Jeff Belanger, proclaimed by his publisher as "one of the most visible and prolific legend researchers today" (Belanger 2011, back matter), published an informal guide to finding UFOs, monsters, ghosts and urban legends, and maintains an active Facebook page, website and tour schedule on this activity. Belanger, in essence, represents an ostensive example of the legend-tripping trend. He pays lip service to the folkloric definition of legend tripping (as found on Wikipedia) but broadens the term, "turning it from a somewhat negative endeavour to a positive" (Belanger, 2011, 4). Most legend scholars, however, do not label legend tripping as either a negative or a positive force, but rather examine both the legend behind the journey and experiences of the journey itself to better understand the phenomenon. "The extreme variability of these legends itself suggests that the trip, not the legend, is the most important thing in the tradition. The stories alone thus cannot be understood without setting them into the context of this more complex folk tradition of deviant plan" (Ellis 2004, 114).

Jeannie Thomas contemplates that unusual grave markers tend to become the subject of legends, and those markers that are depictions of human beings become a focus for legend-tripping excursions because there is a suggestion that the statue "may have some sort of 'life story' to tell. The construction of that story emerges as a legend" (Thomas 2003, 47). Donald Holly and Casey Cordy's research focuses on visitor activities at vampire gravesites in southern Rhode Island. "It is believed," they write, "that one can summon the ghost of Mercy Brown by peering through an opening in a nearby gravestone while changing three times, 'Mercy Brown, are you a vampire?' " (Holly and Cordy 2007, 345). The Exeter, Rhode Island, case of Mercy Brown (1892) allegedly influenced Bram Stoker, author of *Dracula* (1897) (Nickell 2009).

> George Brown lost his wife and then his eldest daughter. One of his sons, Edwin, returned and once again became ill, so George exhumed the bodies of his wife and daughters. The wife and first daughter had decomposed, but Mercy's body—buried for three months—was fresh and turned sideways in the coffin, and blood dripped from her mouth. They cut out her heart, burned it, and dissolved the ashes in a medicine for Edwin to drink. However, he also died, and Mercy Brown became known as Exeter's vampire. (Nickell 2009)

Holly and Cordy identify other methods to summon spirits from their graves which include offending them by urinating on the gravesites, vandalizing their tombstones and performing sexual acts at the site. Bill Ellis addresses rituals and vandalism as frequent by-products of adolescent legend trips: "A legend-trip to a graveyard (particularly one that involves drunken partying or fornication) is a ritual act that presupposes a supernatural threat that is meant to be defied. It often involves the social creation of a fetish—a bone, stone, or other artifact—that is a physical manifestation of the site's supernatural power" (Ellis 2004, 123).

> This is not to say that *all* vandals are involved in legend-trips, or that all legend-trippers desecrate cemeteries. But the atmosphere of antisocial "fun" set up by this ritual activity clearly extends to gravestone smashing and removal, grave-disturbing, and something close to animal sacrifice. The rite of legend-tripping is much better documented and attested in the years before the present Satanism scare than any occult tradition involving grave-robbing. ... legend-tripping actually appropriates official definitions of "Satanism" so that, paradoxically, efforts to stem such activities may instead heighten the "black magic" elements that teens include. (Ellis 2004, 134)

Carl Lindahl's research on the haunted railroad crossing site near San Antonio, discussed below, demonstrates that legend trips are taken very seriously by a wide age range of participants who respect both the legend and the legend site. And, as Linda Dégh expounds,

> It may have been believed earlier that only adolescents and young adults go on legend-trips as part of their coming-of-age ceremony ... we have since learned that adults also desire the

experience. This is why they passionately visit sites of spiritual gratification. Adults join pilgrimages, visit and worship at places of miracles and saintly apparitions and engage in vacation tours to experience haunted historic monuments at home and abroad. This "wonderlust" not only turns international and national tourism into a lucrative business, but it also strengthens the personal dedication of individuals to particular legend sites. (Dégh 2001, 211)

San Antonio Ghost Tracks

> *When Danny drove out to the site to rendezvous with a film crew from Actuality Productions in connection with the Discovery Channel project, he also found a steady stream of people driving up in their automobiles to experience the phenomena themselves.*
>
> —Barnett (2003, 4)

One of the most popular legend-tripping sites in Texas is the isolated railroad crossing at the southern extreme of San Antonio. At this intersection in the 1930s or 1940s, the legend maintains, there had been a tragic accident involving a school bus and an oncoming train. The ghosts of the children linger at that spot to aid any car that may be stopped on the tracks by pushing the vehicles to safety over the tracks. Tiny handprints on the back of these vehicles are a common motif to this legend, and dusting for these handprints became part of the ritual of legend trippers at the site. To assist in finding the handprints, people sprinkle a fine powder over the trunk and rear bumper before stopping their vehicles at the crossing. Snopes.com states that "although the city of San Antonio has long claimed this folktale as its own, pointing to the railway crossing where Villamain Road becomes Shane Road where cars seem to behave strangely and close to a set of streets named after children (Bobbie Allen, Cindy Sue, Laura Lee, Nancy Carole, and Richey Otis), the bus accident that sparked the legend took place in a city more than a thousand miles away" ("Helping Hands" 2007). The actual site of the 1938 accident is said to be Salt Lake City, Utah, with wide media coverage of the tragedy that affected the citizens of San Antonio who adopted and adapted the legend for their own. The San Antonio location works as the core of the train tracks legend was a "gravity hill" phenomenon. "People who visit the scene by car drive slowly (and at least seemingly) upward along a gradual incline toward the tracks. Stopping short of the rails, the driver shifts the car into neutral, and the car seems to roll uphill and over the tracks in defiance of gravity" (Lindahl 2005, 166). Lindahl asserts that this legend and legend trip site attracts diverse groups of participants.

> Among the hundreds of thousands who have visited the train tracks south of San Antonio, there are many who come simply to experience the thrill of a gravity hill; such legend-trippers have no particular knowledge of or interest in the tales of ghostly children. For many Hispanics, however, the train tracks mark a semisacred site that verifies a constellation of culture-specific beliefs . . . Hispanic pilgrims bring an entire constellation of beliefs and practices with them to the tracks, and they discover a pattern

of intertwined social messages alongside the handprints left by the ghostly children on their cars. (Lindahl 2005, 180)

Those who treated this as a pilgrimage return to the site again and again. Lindahl found that these pilgrims share their quest with their own children who then continue the tradition as they mature and have their own children (Lindahl 2005, 179). Lindahl reports his own experiences at the site in his article. Folklorist Jeannie Thomas also went legend tripping at this site while attending a conference of the ISCLR in 2001 after Carl Lindahl gave a paper at the conference and organized a legend trip to the site.

> Once the car has been "pushed" over to the other side, the driver pulls off the road and all the occupants get out to inspect the trunk lid to see if the ghostly children left their finger prints in the powder ... Our car, driven by Carl Lindahl, was adorned with a heavy dusting of powder and did appear to move uphill ... It occurred to me that the powder could highlight any pre-existing prints, but we pulled over, and at first glance there were no finger-prints on the trunk. Later, a little boy came over to look at our car, and we noticed a sole fingerprint not long after he disappeared. The actions of this little boy and several others brought me into different kinds of human interactions that I had previously ex-perienced in the San Antonio area. (Thomas 2007, 55)

She records that everyone who was at the site is looking for evidence or testing the truth of the legend in the same way that the folklorists are doing. "This was also accomplished by interacting with all the other strangers at the tracks. We all got out, looked at each other's cars, and talked to each other" (Thomas 2007, 56). In an on-line article on Legends of America, the anonymous author states that there are numerous negative consequences associated with this particular legend-tripping site.

> As the curious from all over the country come to witness the para-normal phenomena, law enforcement are constantly forced to deal with traffic problems at the site, especially around Halloween. Area residents have grown extremely weary of the congestion and the drugs and alcohol that seemingly accompany many of the visitors. Unfortunately, a criminal element has also entered upon the scene as reports of car-jackings, purse snatchings and worse, are perpetrated on the many curious and unsuspecting ghost hunters. (Weiser 2010)

At a recent conference of the ISCLR, a legend-tripping experience was organ-ized at a much different legend trip site, one that includes a gruesome murder and hexes in the hills of Pennsylvania, discussed next.

Rehmeyer's Hollow

Also known as Hex Hollow, the site of Nelson Rehmeyer's murder in 1928 remains an active legend-tripping location in York County in central Pennsylvania. Nelson Rehmeyer, known in the community as a pow-wow doctor, a practitioner of folk healing and magic, was thought to have placed a hex on John

Blymire. Blymire and two accomplices, John Curry and Wilbert Hess, paid a late-night visit to Rehmeyer at his home to gain a few locks of his hair and his copy of the book *Long Lost Friend* to break the hex. This quest quickly went wrong, and the three men, after murdering and mutilating Rehmeyer, set his body on fire. In an attempt to completely destroy the evidence, the men covered the burning body with a mattress and closed all the windows in the house. Unfortunately for them, this served to quench the fire, and several days later, after the body was found, they were arrested, quickly tried and imprisoned. The house, now owned by Nelson Rehmeyer's great-grandson, Ricky Ebaugh, stands there still and is thought by locals to be haunted. Adolescent thrill seekers still flock to the location late at night. Not particularly welcomed, the legend trippers soon discover that the house is surrounded by no-trespassing signs and warnings that trespassers would definitely be prosecuted.

At the 2011 conference of ISCLR in Harrisburg, Pennsylvania, Charlotte M. Albert presented a paper on "Hex Hollow: The Rehmeyer Witch Legend of Southern York County," with background on the history of the murder, the legend tripping in the hollow and séances at the gravesite. Sitting in the audience were three members of the Rehmeyer family who joined in the discussion after Albert's paper was given. The discussion encompassed personal-history narratives, family history, legend trip experiences and the "Hex Hollow Halloween Ride." The family refer to the trial as the "O. J. Simpson" trial of the times, a theme echoed on several online blogs. Later that afternoon, Albert, McGinnis and the family members, now joined by Nelson's niece who was 12 years old on the night of the murder, and her great-great-granddaughter, and a five-car caravan of conference attendees followed the legend-tripping script. We made our way to Nelson's home and stood respectfully on the road taking pictures of the site. The family warned us that Ricky Ebaugh, who knew we were coming, would not be pleased with any signs of trespassing. We stood respectfully at the roadside, just off the property line, and revisited the story that we had heard earlier that day. We then followed the winding road past homes that belonged to other members of the family to the cemetery where Nelson Rehmeyer is buried. More background stories were exchanged and pictures were taken at each stop, documenting our daylight journey through the past. The cemetery is now closed after nightfall to deter legend seekers, so our time spent on the journey and in the cemetery was finite. Although there are several references on the Internet in 2007 to the house becoming a historical site and open to tours, this has not been actualized yet.

There are numerous websites dedicated to this murder, considered one of the famous haunted sites in Pennsylvania, and obviously fascinated with the hex connection since the murder and the resulting trial were fairly straightforward, with one omission. The reason for the murder, the hex and all mention of witchcraft, were not allowed by the judge to be brought forward at the trial. The stated motive for the murder was robbery. Blymire and Curry were convicted of murder in the first degree while 14-year-old Hess got murder in the second degree. One of the family members spoke of his meeting with Hess after his release from prison. He did not identify himself to Hess and was, at the time, close to the same age as Hess was when Rehmeyer died.

J. Ross McGinnis, in his compendium of primary source documents and analysis titled *Trials of Hex*, describes the community's fascination with the case in his foreword:

> Unprecedented and unparalleled, the events leading up to the
> climactic days of January 1929 tested the character of the

community, as well as the fabric of its institutions. The story is fact. It has all of the essential ingredients of a fascinating tale of mysticism and the occult; a brutal, bloody, vicious murder done in the name of the ancient, primitive and satanic power of witchcraft and superstition. ... Never before had an alleged witch been murdered in cold blood in order to break a curse. Not since medieval Europe and the witch trials of Salem, Massachusetts, had serious thought been given to witchcraft and the occult. Not since an earlier period in human history, when primitive people engaged in blood feuds and believed that there was a dark and malignant destiny that could be invoked by practitioners of black magic by means of formulas and incantations, had people killed to break a spell or a curse. Never before had the people who killed a witch been brought to trial for murder ... A curse as old as time led to a murder that created confusion and panic. The legal system provided a forum that not only contained the crisis but also provided the community with an opportunity to demonstrate insight and understanding in a situation that no prophet could have foretold and no writer of fiction could have imagined. (McGinnis 2000)

Stull Cemetery

The infamous Stull Cemetery with its long history of ghost, devil and witch legends is the impetus for the location of the home for Sam and Dean Winchester in the television series *Supernatural*. The Winchester family hailed from Lawrence, Kansas, just down the road from the old cemetery. There is not much left of the tiny village, but the number of haunted uncanny residents linked to the old abandoned church and the cemetery have been circulating for at least a century. An article, published in the University of Kansas student newspaper in November 1974, angered residents of the area with the reported tales of devil worship, memory loss after visiting the cemetery and mischievous uncanny spirits ("The Legend"). The article also asserts that it is one of the two places on earth where the devil makes a personal appearance twice a year: the spring equinox and Halloween ("Top Ten"). "On March 20, 1978, more than 150 people waited in the cemetery for the arrival of the devil. The word also spread that the spirits of those who died violent deaths, and were buried there, would return from the grave" ("Top Ten"). An article in the *Kansas City Times* reported, in 1980, that the devil appears in Stull Cemetery because of the murder of the mayor in the old stone barn in the cemetery in the 1850s. The barn was later converted into a church which was later gutted by fire. An old decaying crucifix, still hanging from one wall, is thought to sometimes turn upside down when visitors step into the building at midnight ("Top Ten"). What is missing from the article is the historical fact that neither the Deer Creek Community nor Stull had a mayor. Others maintain that the devil appears to visit a witch buried in the cemetery. An old headstone, inscribed with the name "Wittich," is located close to the old church.

Countless other tales circulate about this location. Some tales claim that the devil's only half-human haunted child, possibly a shapeshifter, is buried in the old Stull cemetery. This child was conceived, perhaps, by the union of the devil and the witch. Legends also assert that the original name of the town was "Skull," transformed to the present name in an attempt to hide the mystical and diabolical nature of the area. In fact, the original name of the town was "Deer Creek Community" until 1899, when it was renamed in honor of the first postmaster, Sylvester Stull ("Ten Top").

> One of the strangest stories about Stull supposedly appeared in Time magazine in either 1993 or 1995 (depending on the version you hear). This story claims that Pope John Paul II allegedly ordered his private plane to fly around eastern Kansas while on his way to a public appearance in Colorado. The reason for this, the story claims, was that the Pope did not want to fly over "unholy ground." ("Top Ten")

According to reports, by 1989, the legend trippers on Halloween night became so overwhelming that the Douglas County sheriff's department, called in for crowd control, ticketed people for trespassing. The police response resulted from the presence of nearly 500 people the year before which had culminated in physical damage to the church and gravestones. Ten years later, reporters from a local newspaper and television news crew joined the legend trippers at the cemetery; the police department requested them all to leave before midnight ("Top Ten"). The old stone church was torn down on March 29, 2002. While the church no longer stands, the reputation of the cemetery remains, gaining fresh life with the connection to the Winchester family, particularly after the battle waged in Stull Cemetery when Sam was used as a vessel by Lucifer (season 5, episode 22), and the online presence of their fans.

Screaming Tunnel at Niagara Falls

Niagara, Ontario, is considered the most haunted region in Canada (Collins-Koehn 2011). The Screaming Tunnel in Niagara Falls, built by the Grand Trunk Railroad in the early 1900s in an ill-fated attempt to connect Niagara Falls to Toronto and New York City, is one of the most infamous locations in this haunted region. With the financial problems after World War I, the tracks were never laid, leaving the rough-cut stone tunnel, 16 feet high by 125 feet long, in the middle of nowhere ("Screaming Tunnel"). Legend trippers and ghost tourists who went into the middle of the tunnel at night and light a match find that it will be extinguished instantly by the wind, while a piercing scream echoes off the stone walls. Numerous contemporary legends explain the scream. The most popular legend tells of a family who resided in a farmhouse near the tunnel. When their home caught on fire, the family fled into the tunnel. The young daughter, screaming with her hair and clothes in flames, collapsed and died near the middle of the tunnel. In another variant, the young girl is chased and burned by her angry father when he lost the custody battle during his divorce. In another gruesome legend, the young girl is raped and then burned by her assailant in an attempt to hide the evidence of his deed. A kidnapped young girl is featured in yet another peculiar variant. Her kidnapper, a butcher, held her captive in his house near the tunnel until she manages to escape into the tunnel. Wearing a pig's mask, the butcher catches the girl and sets her on fire in the middle of the tunnel.

Some local residents refer to the tunnel as "Stinky Tunnel," possibly due to the garbage left behind by teens who party in the tunnel but most likely to sulphur pools located near the tunnel (Fleury 2008). Many people know the tunnel as the temporary place of refuge for Christopher Walken in the film *Dead Zone* (1983). The legendary setting continues to have an ongoing presence on paranormal and tourism websites and on YouTube.

The screams of the young girl heard inside the tunnel are reminiscent of the cries of babies heard on many bridges across the United States. Marilyn Hudson states that most folklorists located the earliest "cry baby" tales in Maryland, Ohio, Illinois and New Jersey in the early part of the twentieth century. The advent of the Internet produced numerous Cry Baby Bridges everywhere (Hudson 2011). The common elements of the legend include a woman (sometimes a couple) crossing a bridge during a rain- or snowstorm, or the couple are fighting, or the woman is consumed with depression, and the baby accidently is thrown off the bridge. Reminiscent of the La Llorona tale, cries of the woman and/or the baby haunt the bridge. Hudson refers to the belief of many folklorists that the legends emerged during the "roaring twenties" when many old customs, manners and norms were eradicated and the arrival of the automobile made it possible for young people to venture further afield. "The Crybaby Bridge motif is most probably an early 20th century invention to convey moral values, warn of sexual indiscretion, and safeguard human life" (Hudson 2011). Cry Baby Bridges are also frequently the destination of legend trippers and, even more frequently, videos uploaded on YouTube.

Legend Tripping in College Tunnels

> Legends about tunnels saturate [North] American campuses because they transform the generic experience of college into a distinctly local experience. In the process of developing an institutional identity, college employees, alumni, college publications, and students generate these legends.
>
> —DeFruscio and McCormick (2005)

Although the tunnel legends are localized at the various campuses, the majority of them encompass three major plotlines: the playing of pranks in tunnels, the participation in role-playing games such as Dungeons and Dragons and an alleged connection to the Underground Railroad (DeFruscio and McCormick 2005). They also almost always include a challenge (particularly a physical challenge) as a central theme, resulting in traditional legend-tripping behaviour (DeFruscio and McCormick 2005). The following three comments epitomize this widespread legendary tradition:

> The steam tunnels at A&M have long been rumored to host secret society meetings and store weapons. However, adventurous students that have been lured out of bed in the wee hours of the morning know that these stories are full of hot air. ... I think because very few students and staff actually know what's underneath the school it has prompted many legends. (Skelto 2009)

> As we wondered about the tunnels, we stumbled across a WSU alumnus from the 1990s who not only (risking possible expulsion) snuck down a manhole to explore our subterranean campus, but with his friends (they called themselves MoleNet) made a map and video of their excursions. They had some interesting discoveries—a bomb shelter, three dead cats, and a mysterious laboratory. (Sudermann 2010)

In the late 60s and early 70s tunnel running was a cheap date. You could get into practically any building on campus. And an enterprising engineering student . . . actually mapped a variety of routes. The whole activity came to a screeching halt with the paranoia around VietNam war protests. Rumor was that if you flicked on one of the light switches your position would be revealed to the campus police. Consequently, many of the more gullible suffered bumps and bruises, mainly from running into one of the many valves and connectors. (Sudermann 2010)

Cryptozoology and Legend Tripping

Because humans have the ability to find monsters virtually everywhere and in every shape, the world is replete with intricate monster stories from all eras . . . And just as our ancestors did, we continue to find monsters everywhere. Some are preserved in modern monster myths, often known as urban legends or campfire tales, which relate the exploits of the Bogeyman, the notorious Hook, and an assortment of vengeful ghosts.

—Blackman (1998 as quoted in Leary 2003, 17–18)

Many organized legend trips are focused on sightings of cryptozoological creatures by members of cryptozoological organizations. Due to the magnitude of material on Bigfoot, discussion on this most infamous figure is not integrated here but two other well-known creatures, in both folklore and popular culture, are included: the Jersey Devil and Mothman.

The Jersey Devil

In 1735, Mrs. Leeds of Estellville, New Jersey was not overly enthusiastic when she found out that she was pregnant with her thirteenth child and declared that if she was going to have another child, it might as well be a devil. And, indeed, it was! It was born with an animal's head, a bird's body and cloven hoofs instead of feet. "Cursing its mother (it could speak at birth), it promptly flew up the chimney and took up residence in the swamps and pine barrens of southern New Jersey, where it has lived ever since."

—Coleman (2001, 235)

Another legend involving the birth of the Jersey Devil incorporates the curse on Mrs. Leeds (or Shrouds) during her pregnancy as a result of her practicing witchcraft or insulting a minister, with the deformed, winged child flying out of the home immediately after its birth (Newton 2005, 217). "The deadly combination of belief in witchcraft and misogyny created one of the most enduring of American folkloric traditions in the eighteenth century. The so-called Jersey Devil, rumored even today to haunt the pine barrens of southern New Jersey, grew out of set of folk stories circulating in New England in the decades following the Salem executions" (Poole 2009, 19).

There have been more than 2,000 sightings of the Jersey Devil by reputable and credible sources, including Joseph Bonaparte, oldest brother of Emperor Napoleon, but none of the sightings have ever been confirmed by photographic or scientific evidence. This creature, with its leathery wings, cloven hoofs and horns, reportedly has inhabited the New Jersey Pine Barrens since that first flight. "The Jersey Devil assaults anyone who enters its habitat. There are numerous reports of teenagers, hunters, and explorers venturing into New Jersey's forests only to be threatened by the monster. Some disappear altogether" (Blackman 1998, 83). Over the centuries, the name Jersey Devil has been applied to any supposed monster, beast or paranormal creature in the state of New Jersey. "Eventually the Devil was held responsible for every major calamity that befell the state, and some people even maintained that its appearance presaged the coming of war. On a less cosmic scale it was said that its breath could sour milk, kill fish, and dry up corn-fields" (Coleman 2001, 235).

Folklorist Charles Skinner predicted in 1903 that the Jersey Devil sightings would cease in the twentieth century, but he was soon proved wrong by subsequent reported encounters in 1909, 1926, 1951, 1991 and 2008. In fact, in 1909 there was such a frenzy of sightings and published eyewitness accounts in the media that the Philadelphia Zoo offered a $10,000 reward for the capture of the creature. This reward has never been collected and apparently currently remains available (The Jersey Devil—Fact or Fiction). Cryptozoologist Loren Coleman affirms that he is "convinced of this much: The Jersey Devil is more than just a legend, more than a centuries old folktale, more than a convenient gimmick for hucksters to use in fooling the unsuspecting. It is all these things, true, but it is also one thing more: a mystery" (Coleman 2001, 244). There are a plethora of articles and books including descriptions and discussions on the Jersey Devil. Scott Poole includes a brief discussion on the Jersey Devil that connected the stories to misogynistic assumptions about women and their bodies in his book *Satan in America: The Devil We Know*. He also states that folklorists and anthropologists had done the primary work on the Jersey Devil (Poole 2009, 224).

This regional, yet international, monster has a wide YouTube presence along with numerous other programs searching for the truth of the Devil such as *Destination Truth: The New Jersey Devil* (Season 3, Episode 12). This episode welcomes Kris Williams from *Ghost Hunters* and had the team checking the DNA from biological remains collected at the museum as well as flying over the Pine Barrens in order to locate the creature. While no conclusive proof or sightings were forthcoming, there are enough eerie noises and movement to suggest a real possibility of something lurking in the area. *Monster Quest: Leeds Devil* explores the legendary creature and sightings, including that of footprints in the snow in 2004, and made it available for viewing at http://www.history.com/shows/monsterquest/inter-actives/monsterpedia-jersey-devil. Explorations of the legend also appear in *Lost Tapes*, in *Freak Encounters* and on various YouTube excerpts and legend-tripping videos. *Coast to Coast AM* has an interview with Loren Coleman talking about his book, *Monsters of New Jersey*, coauthored with Bruce Hallenbeck (Stackpole Books, 2010), where Coleman states that the Jersey Devil could be described as a feral human/Bigfoot creature. The interview was available at http://www.coasttocoastam .com/show/2010/09/06.

Amongst the multitude of active websites dedicated to or incorporating the legend of the Jersey Devil, there are also several exhibits on the topic with folklorists offering lectures on the subject. Folklorist Stephen Winnick from the Delaware Valley Regional Folklife Center presented a lecture for the opening reception of the traveling exhibit "Tales of the Jersey Devil" at the Wheaton Arts Center on November 22, 2002, and again at the American Folklife Center in Washington, DC, in 2005. In his years at the Delaware Valley Regional Folklife Center, Winnick investigated its presence and persistence in folklore and popular culture. Excerpts of his talk from a 2004 episode of *History Hunters* can be viewed on YouTube. The traveling collection includes visual representations in drawings, paintings and sculptures. Also included in the opening reception was a presentation by Harry Leeds on the perception of the Jersey Devil legend in the Leeds family.

Both organized and spontaneous legend-tripping excursions to the Barrens searched in vain for this elusive creature. If one is determined to go independently, "always travel with a bright lantern, which a handful of researchers insist can dissuade the monster from attacking. Others claim that holy items, such as the Bible and a crucifix might also ward off the creature" (Blackman1998, 87). Probably a more gratifying experience would result by registering for the program "Jersey Devil Hunt," Pinelands Adventures, Pinelands Preservation Alliance: Protecting and Exploring New Jersey's Pine Barrens, which begins "with an old-fashioned campfire (bring your hot dogs & marshmallows). We calm our nerves with some good, old-time music. Then, with a little ghostly light from the moon, we search the woods, cautiously, for that most infamous denizen of the Pine Barrens. All hunts begin at 7 p.m. at a remote location in Wharton State Forest." More information can be obtained at http://www.pinelandsalliance.org/exploration/adventures/ (June 3, 2011). There are ample opportunities for those who are more serious about the search for the Jersey Devil as well. The Devil Hunters, a group of official researchers dedicated to discovering the truth on the Jersey Devil, follow up on suspected sightings, offer excursions (hunts) and monitor online dialogue with people all over the world at their website "The Devil Hunters," http://www.njdevilhunters.com. The stated goal of this group, established in 1999, is to answer questions surrounding the Jersey Devil and its legend. The site, however, has not been updated since 2009. Dan Barry, reporting in his column "This Land," explains: "They explore that dark piney chasm between fact and legend, acting upon what most of us, at one time or another, have thought: Something's out there" (Barry 2008). When not investigating sightings they visit traditional devil haunts in the area, including the location of Mother Leed's home.

Countless allusions to and adaptations of the Jersey Devil can be found in popular culture including computer games, music videos and song lyrics, not to mention the National Hockey League team. Commodification of the legend has resulted in local store names, T-shirts, Boy Scout patches, posters, postcards and the like.

Mothman

> *Mothman: winged, humanoid being; an entity of prophesy; an omen; a warning; an angel; an alien; or a military experiment.*
> —Lee (2008, 215)

Mothman first appeared on the McClintic Wildlife Sanctuary near Point Pleasant, West Virginia, in 1966. The two couples who first sighted the creature, Steve and Mary Mallette and David and Linda Scarberry, were chased by it as they drove their vehicle frantically away. The name Mothman was given to the creature by an unnamed copy editor at a local newspaper in homage or, perhaps as a parody, to a popular television program at the time, *Batman*. While the eyewitness story was not totally accepted as true, many people traveled to the sanctuary to see for themselves. None of the curiosity seekers, however, ever saw it. "The Mothman, it seemed, was only spotted when it wanted to be—always the pursuer, never the quarry" (Asfar 2003, 178). It did materialize to people who were actively seeking it until December 1967, when it stopped abruptly. Many theorists thought that the Mothman's appearance was prophetic in nature, and with the collapse of the Silber Bridge on December 15, 1967, it was no longer needed. When the bridge collapsed, 67 people fell into the river and 46 of them died, some of whom were minor witnesses in the Mothman saga.

Other theories are put forth such as that of Loren Coleman who declared, in a 2002 article in *USA Today*, that the sightings continue but were no longer reported (http://www.lorencoleman.com/mothman_file.html). Coleman's identity as an expert cryptozoologist was formed with the publicity of Mothman in the light of the upcoming *Mothman Prophecies* film in 2001. Loren Coleman posted a blog entry on the death of Linda Scarberry on March 6, 2011. Along with notice of her death, he discusses her renowned witnessing of the Mothman on November 15, 1966, and his ongoing relationship with her during his own investigations on the creature. Reagan Lee, who maintains Mothman Flutterings (http://orangeorb.net/blog/), a regularly updated blog focused on current Mothman sightings and imagery, asserts that the Mothman phenomenon was possibly the result of a kind of covert military presence. "The Mothman phenomena shares many similarities with other paranormal and Fortean events. There seems to be a military, or at least, some kind of covert human manipulation involved, yet this doesn't account for everything about the experiences" (Lee 2008, 221). Skeptics, dismissing any ideas of folklore or a hoax, explain the creature as a misidentified Sandhill crane. The surrounding area apparently had a large problem with the cranes during the 1960s.

Commodification of Mothman

Although the Mothman Museum website has not been updated since 2009, it contains a great deal of information on the legend, and the museum remains open to the public (http://mothmanmuseum.com/). The Mothman Festival, established in 2001, is held on the third weekend every September. The festival includes guest speakers, vendor exhibits and tours focusing on the relevant areas of Point Pleasant. Their website includes links to the Mothman Museum, their Facebook page and various other activities focusing on Mothman (http://www.mothman festival.com/).

Mothman appears in various RPG games over the years and as a plush toy and collectable figures. Accompanying Mothman in the set of figurines, among others, are Eye Witness, Silver Bridge and Point Pleasant. On a slightly larger scale, a 12-foot-tall stainless-steel sculpture of the Mothman by Robert Roach is located in Point Pleasant and is accompanied by a full-text version of the legend. Mothman Christmas ornaments and beanbag toys are sold by Point Pleasant businesses.

Selected Resources on the Mothman

The legend of the Mothman has a strong Internet presence: blog accounts of the bridge disaster; archived newspaper articles from a variety of countries; discussions on various theories, particularly those of skeptics commenting on possible birds that may have been mistaken for the Mothman and those of conspiracy theorists; and numerous postings of sightings. Loren Coleman has collected and maintained "The Mothman File" with republished full-text articles from newspapers during 2001–2 regarding the *Mothman Prophecies* film (http://www.lorencoleman.com/mothman_file.html). There are numerous video and audio clips available online as well but most of them are duplicates of each other. The same witnesses are interviewed and the basic story is the same. Some of the interviews bring up the curse of Cornstalk and make references to UFOs and Men in Black, but most leave the question of the Mothman open to interpretation. The Curse of Cornstalk, the Shawnee warrior, was allegedly placed on the Point Pleasant area just before he was assassinated by militiamen in 1774.

> And as he lay their [*sic*] dying in the smoke-filled room, he was said to have pronounced his now legendary curse. The stories say that he looked upon his assassins and spoke to them: "I was the border man's friend. Many times I have saved him and his people from harm. I never warred with you, but only to protect our wigwams and lands. I refused to join your paleface enemies with the red coats. I came to the fort as your friend and you murdered me. You have murdered by my side, my young son. . . . For this, may the curse of the Great Spirit rest upon this land. May it be blighted by nature. May it even be blighted in its hopes. May the strength of its peoples be paralyzed by the stain of our blood." ("Haunted West Virginia" 2002)

The curse, supposedly lasting 200 years, became the validation behind many of the unfortunate disasters since that time: floods, severe fires and a murderous hostage situation at the Mason County Courthouse in 1977. The Mothman Museum asserts that there is some evidence that the curse was a plot element of a local play during the early 1990s ("Curse").

The Mothman legend has also been the focus of several television investigatory programs. *MonsterQuest: Mothman* (Season 4, Episode 5) uses nighttime surveillance, perception tests and forensic sketching in its determination of the mythical or realistic nature of the creature and is readily available on DVD and YouTube. Other Mothman sightings on the television screen include *Paranormal State* (season 1, episode 17), *Lost Tapes: Mothman* (season 2, episode 12), *SciFi Investigates Mothman* (season 1, episode 103) and *Unsolved Mysteries: Mothman (Unexplained)* which first aired in 2002. Recently, there have been several illustrated books on monsters that incorporate only brief information on Mothman but provide an opportunity for creative interpretations of the folkloric figure. Many of these slight volumes include discussions of conspiracies, prophesies and debunking. Monographs exploring the legend in much greater detail included:

Coleman, Loren. *Mothman and Other Curious Encounters.* New York: Paraview Press, 2002. Coleman focuses on placing Mothman in context by discussing other sightings of giant winged creatures such as Thunderbirds.

Colvin, Andrew. *The Mothman's Photographer: The Work of an Artist Touched by the Prophesies of the Infamous Mothman.* Charleston, SC: Booksurge LLC, 2005. When photographer Andrew Colvin realized, in 2001, that the 9/11 attacks had been accurately predicted by a childhood friend who was one of the eyewitnesses to a Mothman sighting, he spent the next five years documenting his experiences growing up in paranormal West

Virginia. This volume contains almost 300 images. According to the product description for the book, "Colvin has been known mostly for his theory that Mothman was once revered worldwide as a crime-fighting deity (who sends visions, dreams, and messages to ordinary humans)."

Colvin, Andrew. *The Mothman's Photographer II: Meetings with Remarkable Witnesses Touched by Paranormal Phenomena, UFOs and the Prophesies of West Virginia's Infamous Mothman*. Charleston, SC: Booksurge LLC, 2005. Based on the first half of the 32-hour video series documenting his experiences growing up in West Virginia, the book includes Mothman plus many other paranormal phenomena of the area.

Keel, John. *The Mothman Prophesies*. 1975. Keel provides the chronology of the Mothman and apparent related paranormal events in the area, including UFO activity, Men in Black encounters, poltergeist activity and sightings of other legendary figures such as Bigfoot and black panthers, and the December 15, 1967, collapse of the Silver Bridge spanning the Ohio River. This book has had numerous editions since the original publication.

Sergent, Donnie, Jr., and Jeff Warmsley. *Mothman: The Facts Behind the Legend*. Toronto: Hushion House, 2002. Written by two natives of Pont Pleasant, West Virginia, the book attempts to answer many of the questions revolving around the Mothman sightings and includes eyewitness reports, previously unpublished information and photographs.

Steiger, Brad. *Real Monsters, Gruesome Critters, and Beasts from the Darkside*. Canton, MI: Visible Ink, 2011. Steiger includes a chapter entitled "Mothman—Harbinger of Death" containing several illustrations of the Mothman.

Literary and Visual Adaptations

Due to the vast number of literary and visual adaptations of the contemporary legends discussed in this chapter, it is necessary to limit the annotations to demonstrate the variety of reworkings rather than to be as inclusive as possible.

Legend Tripping

Bray, Libby. "Bad Things." In *The Restless Dead: Ten Original Stories of the Supernatural*. Edited by Deborah Noyes. Cambridge: MA: Candlewick Press, 2007, 131–55.
"It was Brian's idea to go devil worshipping. The newspaper had reported the story all week: out on Route 211, past the cemetery, they'd found the mutilated cattle, all of them cut wide open in a ritual fashion. Rumors raced through the town like a flash flood" (131). After such a beginning as this, Bray's control of the characterizations, the plot and her language takes her readers on their own legend trip along with Brian and his friends as they attempt to catch the Satanists. When one of Brian's friends, Danny, meets with his own dead brother along Route 211, things begin to disintegrate for Danny in a very large way.
Bray states that the story was inspired by a real incident:

> When I was in high school in North Texas, there were some cow mutations that took place on the outskirts of town, and the rumors of satanic rituals ran fast and furiously—absolutely catnip for a bunch of bored, imaginative sixteen-year-olds. So my friend Les picked us all up in his pickup, and we drove out there to play chicken with the devil worshippers, who never materialized. Mostly, we drank beer, listened to bad metal bands, and talked honestly. And what could be scarier than that? (269)

Ewert, Ivan. "Waterheads." In *Close Encounters of the Urban Kind*. Edited by Jennifer Brozek. Lexington, KY: Apex, 2010, 48–57.
The story of legend tripping on an old bridge takes a definitely odd turn when the light-hearted adventure intermingled with an alien presence. "You ever break down on that bridge

at night—you ever turn off your lights, even for a moment—their little ones will swarm right over you and fetch you where nobody's ever like to find you" (48). The author claims that the core concept of the story, based on an actual legend surrounding the Concord Bridge in Cobb County, Georgia, is not changed much in his reworking of the legend. He found only one reference to the legend online but heard from his relatives and friends in the area about their own adolescent adventures with the Waterheads (57).

Teitelbaum, Michael. "Bridge of Sorrow." *The Scary States of America*. New York: Delacorte Press, 2007, 224–32.

"Before Halloween last year, I thought our town ghost story was just that—a story. But after what happened to me and my girlfriend, I know it's true" (225). In a La Llorona-type of tale, the narrator is told about the infanticide of a woman's children in her attempt to marry a man who wanted nothing to do with children. As a result of his disgust with her actions, the mother runs to a nearby bridge, stabs herself in the stomach and leaps to her death in the deepest depths of the river. Her cries and wailing can be heard when crossing the bridge at night. The narrator and his girlfriend, dressed in their Halloween costumes, decide to frighten their friends as they cross the bridge on the way to the Halloween party, but they are the ones who became frightened by the howls, the churning red water of the river and the ghostly apparition. As they try to escape, the ghostly presence attacks their car but they make it to safety, only to notice a bloody knife deeply plunged into the backseat of the car.

Bloody Mary

The figure of Bloody Mary figures largely in paranormal television programming. The ritual is also parodied in the animated program *South Park* where the show's creative team substitutes chanting "Bloody Mary" with saying "Biggie Smalls" in the mirror three times in an attempt to summon him. *Supernatural* (season 1, episode 5) focuses on "Bloody Mary" as discussed earlier. She also makes an appearance in the film *Urban Legend*.

"Chick Flick." *Charmed*. Season 2, episode 18.

The sisters fight a demon who is bringing horror movie characters to life, including Bloody Mary. Bloody Mary does not last long as the sisters soon push her out the window and kill her. All of the monsters must be killed in the same manner as they are in the original horror films. This episode includes the character but does not incorporate her legend in the least.

Christensen, Jo-Anne. "Bloody Mary." *Campfire Ghost Stories*. Edmonton, Alberta: Lone Pine, 2002, 38–44.

During Kelly's 14th birthday slumber party, Kelly and her friends do everything they can to ignore Kelly's younger sister's presence until they decide to play "Bloody Mary" with her. The older girls think it will be a treat to have Carmen, Kelly's sister, become so frightened that she would leave them alone on her own accord, but what happened in the bathroom that evening makes Kelly and her friends scream as well. One of the more chilling reworkings of this contemporary legend.

Domingo, Dominick R., and John Stecenko. *The Legend of Bloody Mary*. Directed by John Stencenko, 2008.

Ryan's sister, Amy, went missing eight years previously after playing the game "Bloody Mary" by stumbling onto a website about a witch going by that name. Now, in an effort to help Ryan finally deal with his sister's disappearance, his girlfriend engages the help of Father O'Neal, a priest and an archaeologist, to uncover the truth of the legend. An interesting take on the legend, concentrating more on the story of Mary Worth as the source of the spirit and how to quiet her, than the horror aspect of a girl pulling someone into the mirror realm.

"Don't Try This at Home." *Ghost Whisperer*. Season 3, episode 2.
    When individual members of a group of girls are frightened into a coma, the remaining girl, claiming that the ghost of Bloody Mary is responsible, engages the interest of the ghost whisperer. His investigation into a local girl, named Mary, buried at the turn of the last century, and the supposed Bloody Mary of legend, allows him to discourage the angry spirit from her revengeful behaviour. The episode ends with the "real" Bloody Mary showing herself.

"Road Kill." *Supernatural Animated*. Season 1, episode 2.
    Dean and his father investigate a case in which a girl was found with her eyes scratched out, all the reflective surfaces taped over in her house and messages from her friends to stop calling them about the one time they called on Bloody Mary when they were younger.

Halloween Sadism

Koontz, Dean, and Fred Van Lente. *Odd Is On Our Side*. Illustrated by Queenie Chan. New York: Ballantine, 2010.
    This graphic novel instalment from the Odd Thomas franchise is a prequel to the novels also featuring Odd, a character who can see dead people. Set at Halloween, the story line provides the opportunity for a flashback to a previous tragedy featuring death by poisoned Halloween treats. Although the perpetrator of the incident had been convicted, the town since provides a "safe Halloween" celebration for the children rather than have them go house to house to gather their bounty. This piece of history is told around the dinner table when one of the characters asks why trick-or-treating was no longer a practice. Apparently Norman Turley, an extremely proud gardener, decides to permanently stop the children from trampling his garden each year as they go trick or treating. The manga style art is realistic and effectively utilizes black backgrounds when needed. In an excerpt of a discussion between the two authors, Dean Koontz responds to Fred Van Lente's proposal that there is a religion-based motive for the poisoning by maintaining that "the Odd Thomas stories try to avoid both politically correct villains and needlessly negative characterizations of whole groups" (185). He then suggests the gardening connection and a plant poison to poison the candy.

"Scary Sherry: Bianca's Toast." *Psych*. Season 1, episode 15.
    A subplot of this episode involves a father taking his children to the police station to x-ray their Halloween candy for razor blades.

Rehmeyer's Hollow

Apprentice to Murder. 1988.
    This thriller film, starring Donald Sutherland, is based on the book *Hex* by Arthur Lewis. In this "true story" a series of murders occur in a tiny isolated community, and suspicion immediately falls on the local self-styled faith healer and mystic. "You would have to already know the legend in order to see the similarities" (de Vos, personal communication, September 5, 2011).

Lewis, Arthur. *Hex*. New York: Trident Press, 1969.
    The author takes the side of the murderer John Blymire and presents him as the victim rather than the assailant.

Mercy Brown: Vampire

Kiernan, Caitlin R. *The Red Tree*. New York: ROC, 2009.
    The horror novel, intended for mature readers, employs the idea of legend tripping, photoshopping images and contemporary legends to narrate Sarah's experiences in Rhode Island. The author frequently makes asides regarding folkloristic observations. For example, in the "preface" written by the editor regarding this "found manuscript," the narrator declares:

And, oddly (or so it seems to me), there is little evidence that local teens and other curiosity seekers have targeted the Wright Farm for nightly visitations, vandalism, or, to employ the vernacular of folklorists, "legend tripping."[1] Indeed, given local traditions of ghosts, witches, and even vampires,[2] I find the general absence of "urban myth" surrounding the farm nothing short of remarkable. (7)

The footnotes in the above excerpt and included as footnotes at the end of this entry, are incorporated in the entire novel, adding a pseudo-academic feel to the reading experience. The legendary vampire Mercy Brown plays a role in the novel. The narrator highlights many of the paranormal activities of the area. "Mercy Brown and the plague of consumptive vampires, all the phantoms, witches, ghost towns, shunned pastures, the haunted cemeteries, and whatnot. The usual New England spookfest. Hell, there's even supposed to be some sort of swamp monster luring about in a bog around Gloucester or Chepachet" (105). In her author's note, Kiernan mentions her fascination with an enormous oak tree near Exeter, Rhode Island.

There were a number of peculiar objects set all about its base—dismembered doll parts, empty wine bottles, a copy of the New Testament missing its fake leather cover, faded plastic flowers, and other things I can't now recall. For no reason I could put my finger on, I found the site unnerving, and I didn't linger there. Perhaps it was only the tree's relative proximity to the Exeter Grange Hall and Chestnut Hill Baptist Church. The state's most famous "vampire," Mercy Brown (1873–1892), is buried in the church's cemetery. Or perhaps my disquiet arose from the simple, unsolvable mystery of those random objects scattered about the base of the tree. (383)

Kiernan, Caitlin R. "As Red as Red." In *Haunted Legends*. Edited by Ellen Datlow and Nick Mamatas. New York: Tor, 2010, 75–93.

This short story furthered the material explored by the folklorist in Kiernan's novel *The Red Tree*, discussed in the previous entry. In fact, the author's afterword in this collection is a quote from one of the characters in that novel. The short story's narrator, a folklorist, is researching Mercy Brown and other consumptive vampires in her study of the psychology behind the hysteria and superstitions of the time (77). Her research, however, becomes derailed when she observes a ghostly presence outside of the library window.

Teitelbaum, Michael. "Death of a Vampire." *The Scary States of America*. New York: Delacorte Press, 2007, 306–14.

The narrator is told the story of Mercy Brown from one of his informants who had an adventure when on a family road trip to Rhode Island. "Local superstition was that when one family was hit hard by tuberculosis, the cause might be a dead family member rising from the grave to devour the living" (309). Other superstitious beliefs of that time include the curing of tuberculosis by digging up the body of a relative who died from the disease and burning the corpse's heart, mixing the ashes with water and drinking the result. In order to save his son, Edwin, Mercy's father digs up the bodies of her mother, her sister and herself. Only Mercy's body is still fresh, warm and still filled with blood. Following the directives of the superstition, Mercy's heart is drained of blood, burned and the ashes consumed by her brother in the unsuccessful attempt to save his life. "However, no one else in Exeter contracted tuberculosis after that day" (310).

Encouraged by the legend, the storyteller searches for Mercy Brown's grave. "For all the fuss about the legend, it was kinda hard to find the grave. No big markers, no line of tourists, no plastic gravestone replicas for sale. Just a normal stone slab with her name and birth and death dates carved into it" (311). However, attempting a rubbing of the headstone proves to be rather more difficult for the storyteller and she is haunted by her experience and, perhaps Mercy herself, once she returns home.

San Antonio Ghost Tracks

Christensen, Jo-Anne. "Children of the Tracks." *Campfire Ghost Stories.* Edmonton, Alberta: Lone Pine, 2002, 26–31.

Four young people arrive at the railroad crossing, park the car on the tracks and sprinkle flour over the trunk of the car. The driver, Paul, then tells his passengers the tale of a tragic accident that took place at that exact location. The setting here is at an unnamed location, not San Antonio, and instead of a school bus accident, it involves a father, his pickup truck and his five children. The children are all killed but had subsequently helped push other vehicles out of danger when they were also in that same predicament. "And everybody around here things the same thing: those people were saved by the spirits of those little kids who died when the train hit them." (29) Immediately after telling the story, Paul switches off the car engine and stays there in the path of the oncoming train. His friends flee the car and watch in horror and then in relief as the car gently rolls off the tracks. "On the chrome bumper, in the heavy dusting of white flour about which they had all forgotten, there they were: five distinct sets of child-size handprints" (31).

Cleveland, Brian and Jason. *Fingerprints.* Directed by Harry Basil, 2006.

The film centers on a teenage girl, Melanie, who has just returned home from rehabilitation. She moves to her family's new home in the town of Emerald, where her father was a part of the crew constructing a highway over the old train tracks. After her sister told her of the legend, Melanie begins seeing the ghost of Julie, one of the dead children, and becomes more and more involved in mysterious occurrences in the town.

Mantooth, John. 2010. "Shoebox Train Wreck." In *Haunted Legends.* Edited by Ellen Datlow and Nick Mamatas. New York: Tor, 2010, 109–20. Republished in a collection of short stories by the author in *Shoebox Train Wreck* (Toronto: Chizine Publications, 2012).

Told in the first person, this story evokes the guilt still felt by the train engineer after the tragic meeting with the school bus. In the intervening years he has created panoramas of the six victims in shoe boxes, not only keeping his feelings of guilt alive and well stoked but also keeping the spirits of the dead children from accessing their final rest.

From the author's afterword:

> As a school bus driver, I was drawn to the legend of San Antonio's "Ghost Children." Train tracks are anathema to bus drivers, and stalling on the tracks while an oncoming train bears down on you is something we fear in the silences of our routes, long after the last child has been safely delivered home. Telling the story from the train engineer's point of view was one of those writing surprises that happen without explanation, but in retrospect, now seems inevitable. In researching the legend and legends like it, I found myself wondering how the principals involved in such an accident would feel about their true tragedies playing second fiddle to these maudlin legends. Soon, I was mulling over issues like guilt and forgiveness and how even sentimental ghost stories might have something to teach us about ourselves and the way we deal with tragedy, communal guilt, and personal recovery. (119)

Teitelbaum, Michael. "Tiny Helping Hands." *The Scary States of America.* New York: Delacorte Press, 2007, 337–43.

An e-mail conversation between the narrator and his cousin transmits the legend of Shane Road in San Antonio, Texas, and, when next visiting his cousin, sparks a legend trip to the site. Because the narrator had checked the wrong train schedule, he and his cousin are stalled on the tracks in front of an oncoming train. Just in time, however, the car is pushed off the tracks and they can see tiny handprints on the edges of the front windshield and the side windows.

Tingle, Tim, and Doc Moore. "Children of the Tracks." *Texas Ghost Stories: Fifty Favorites for the Telling*. Lubbock: Texas Tech University Press, 2004, 224–27.

Told from the point of view of the sole survivor of the bus accident 25 years earlier, the bus driver realizes that he must return to the site of the accident to face his nightmares. By doing so, he also helps the victims, alive and ghosts, to finally gain some rest after the tragedy.

The authors noted the legend-tripping activities associated with the legend.

Shoefiti

August, John. *Big Fish*. Directed by Tim Burton, 2003. Based on a novel by Daniel Wallace.

In this film, a young girl in the town of Spectre throws the shoes of protagonist Edward Bloom over telephone wires to discourage him from leaving the town.

Bate, Matthew. *Flying Kicks*. 2010.

This awarding-winning Australian short film examines the shoefiti trend. "The film is like a global Chinese whisper in a way. Somewhere along the line there may have been a grain of truth and these theories get passed along, especially on the internet ... I heard from people in Argentina who said it was a mafia symbol, or in Spain that the local mafia were using it as a symbol that they have a deal with the local cops where if they saw a pair of sneakers in a particular neighbourhood then the cops had to stay out of there" (http://www.abc.net.au/news/stories/2010/07/22/2960865.htm).

Gruley, Bryan. *The Hanging Tree: A Starvation Lake Mystery*. New York: Touchstone, 2010.

The novel opens with the discovery of a woman hanging from the shoe tree near the town. The victim, ironically, had started the shoe tree over 20 years before, when she climbed into the tree to hang one of her boyfriend's football cleats tied together with one of her high-top sneakers in the old oak to celebrate their relationship.

> Soon more shoes began to appear in the tree. At the high school, hanging shoes became a spring ritual for graduating seniors, which naturally prompted a brief, futile attempt by the police to stop it, seeing as the kids' hangings usually involved beer and sometimes ladders. But adults hung shoes in the tree, too, especially after a night at Enright's Pub. Out-of-state tourists saw the tree and pulled over and hung their own shoes and flip-flops, their equivalent of writing in the guest book at a rental cottage. Sometimes when a romance soured, one of the two lovers would bother to shinny into the tree and slice a pair of shoes away. (8)

Henkin, Hilary, and David Mamet. *Wag the Dog*. Directed by Barry Levinson, 1997.

Shoefiti features, in this film, as a spontaneous tribute to Sgt. William Schumann, played by Woody Harrelson, who had purportedly been "shot down behind enemy lines" in Albania. Shoefiti is used here as a propaganda weapon to manipulate the news media.

Tunnel Legends

Caldwell, Ian, and Dustin Thomason. *The Rule of Four*. New York: Dial Press, 2004.

The novel "opens with a group of college friends deciding to break the stress of studying and thesis writing with a game of laser tag in the steam tunnels that crisscross the underground of Princeton University's campus" (DeFruscio and McCormick 2005).

"The Jersey Devil"

Avalos, Stefan, and Lance Weiler, writers and directors. *The Last Broadcast*, 1998.

This pseudo-documentary takes place in the Pine Barrens, and while the film mentions the Jersey Devil, it offers no background details of the legend.

Carter Chris. "The Jersey Devil." *X-Files*. Season 1, episode 5.

Scully and Mulder investigate murders thought to be the work of the Jersey Devil. Carter wants to present the Jersey Devil as an evolutionary throwback (Lowry 1995, 110). The "episode avoids asking about the veracity of the story but instead posits what such a story would look like *should* it be true. What would the Jersey Devil look like, literally in(corp) orated, in the *flesh*?" (Koven 2008, 71).

Davis, Douglas G. *Carny*. Directed by Sheldon Wilson, 2009.

In this horror film the director of the Carnival captures the Jersey Devil and puts it on display, at least until it gets loose. In Australia, the film was known as *Jersey Devil*.

DiGerolamo, Tony. *The Jersey Devil Comic Book*. South Jersey Rebellion Productions, 1996. 12 issues.

"Based on the legend, it follows the exploits of a mysterious hermit named J.D. who thinks he is the Jersey Devil. J.D. lives in the Pine Barrens and through him we are retelling the ghost stories connected to the myth in modern times" (http://www.thefixsite.com/jersey-devil/jdcomic.html, June 5, 2011).

Ford, Jeffrey. Down Atison Road. In *Haunted Legends*. Edited by Ellen Datlow and Nick Mamatas. New York: Tor, 2010, 167–82.

"You will, of course, have heard of the Jersey Devil. He's for the tourists. The place is thick with legends far more bizarre and profound. If you learn to look and you're lucky, you might even witness one being born" (169). While this story does not focus on the Jersey Devil, it is very evocative of the Pine Barrens and the large paranormal possibilities that may be found within. The author proclaims that the Jersey Devil is definitely not the weirdest anomaly in New Jersey, stating that it is a shame that the Devil got all the publicity because there are literally hundreds of other legends that existed in and around the Barrens that are lesser known but equally fascinating. "The strange wilderness has been shaping legends since humanity first set foot here. They crisscross and interconnect like a web" (181).

Lamb, Cynthia. *Brigid's Charge*. Corte Madera, CA: Bay Island Books, 1997.

Lamb, a direct descendant of Deborah Leeds, the woman frequently accused by history of being the mother of the Jersey Devil, crafts a reworking of the origin legend incorporating the Jersey Devil and the Celtic goddess Brigid in her historical fiction novel intended for mature readers about women's spirituality.

Maryk, Michael, and Cliff Robertson. *13th Child: Legend of the Jersey Devil*. Directed by Thomas Ashley and Steven Stockage, 2002.

In a manner reminiscent of the uncanny, I wrote this entry for this direct-to-video horror film on September 10, 2010, the date Cliff Robertson, the cowriter and star of this film, and many others, died. The Jersey Devil in the film is tied to his brother's life and cannot be dispatched unless his brother, over 200 years old, is also killed. The film is based on the book *The Jersey Devil* by James F. McCoy and Ray Miller Jr. James F. McCoy was interviewed on Coast to Coast AM (January 19, 2009) speaking of the history of the Jersey Devil on the centennial of the sightings in the Delaware Valley. The interview is archived at http://www.coasttocoastam.com/show/2009/01/19.

Teitelbaum, Michael. "Devil in the Dark." *The Scary States of America*. New York: Delacorte Press, 2007, 233–40.

According to the young narrator, the Jersey Devil is one of the oldest and most dangerous paranormal creatures every reported. When posting a call on his blog for reports on sightings and stories about the creature, he receives an assignment written by a student in Leeds Point, New Jersey. In the assignment, the student, Lauren, relates much of the available research on the New Jersey Devil as well as her own experience seeking out more information from an elderly woman who is reputed to have seen the creature herself. The woman's father had frightened the creature away with a shotgun and it was never seen by the woman again. At the end of the interview, Lauren realizes that the elderly woman, Margaret Leeds, was a direct descendant of Miranda Leeds, the person who allegedly gave birth to the Jersey

Devil. "Maybe the creature wasn't violently attacking the Leeds farm at all—maybe it just wanted to come home" (240).

Mothman

Alexander, Alma. "I Am Sorry for Talking So Rarely to Strangers." In *Close Encounters of the Urban Kind*. Edited by Jennifer Brozek. Lexington, KY: Apex, 2010, 202–14.

When Bess was six years old, she overheard her father speak of killing a monster and, when later that evening she met the pregnant mate of the moth-like creature, Bess agrees to take care of their progeny. Year after year the cocoons hatch and leave, vanishing from sight, "disappearing somewhere into myth and legend" (208). Bess becomes careless when the last cocoon hatches, and her father immediately destroys it although she tries to save it. Years later, after the death of her parents, Bess comes to an understanding about her mother and the power of parental love. The author states, in the afterword, that "the urban legend being followed here is the Mothman. The visions of the Mothman as reported in various sightings do have variations, but on the whole are remarkably internally consistent, enough for there to be a basis for assuming in this in this story that the creature is a physical reality" (214).

Fear, Brad. *A Macabre Myth of Moth-Man*. Birmingham, IN: AuthorHouse, 2008.

The first instalment of a five-book saga chronicles the mishaps of a half-man, half-insect detective.

Hatem, Richard. *The Mothman Prophesies*. Directed by Mark Pellington, 2002.

Based on the novel by the same name by John Keel, the film follows the adventures of an investigator reporter who, after he and his wife are involved in a car accident, arrive in Point Pleasant, West Virginia, obsessed with the Mothman.

Lambert, Chad, et al. *Return to Point Pleasant*. Ape Entertainment, 2008.

This graphic novel follows the adventures of time traveling scientists as they investigate 200 years of paranormal folklore in the Point Pleasant area.

Lee, Sonny, and Patrick Walsh. *Mothman*. Directed by Sheldon Wilson, 2010.

A group of teenagers from Point Pleasant attempt to frighten a younger sibling around the campfire with the story of the Mothman pulling a person underwater and drowning him or her. When the young boy drowns in a prank by the teens, they disguise it as an accident. Ten years later one of the teens returns to report on the Mothman Festival, triggering off a series of revengeful attacks by the Mothman. Other nods to the area's corpses of legend such as Chief Cornstalk and the Silver Bridge are incorporated in the made-for-television film. Here Mothman is definitely not a figure of prophesy but one of great destruction.

Meyers, Bill. *Angel of Wrath: A Novel*. The Voice of God series. 2009.

The author incorporates elements of the Mothman legend in this novel marketed as Christian suspense.

Spotnitz, Frank. "Detour." *X-Files*. Season 5, episode 4.

While traveling to a conference, Sully and Mulder stop at a roadblock to help with an investigation of attacks by assailants with glowing eyes. "The creature reminds Mulder of the Mothman of Point Pleasant, West Virginia, and in a couple lines of dialogue he cites the Mothman and its hometown by name ("I've got an X-file dated back to 1952 on it"). Apart from having red eyes, the creatures don't really resemble the Mothman in either appearance or behavior." (http://everydayislikewednesday.blogspot.ca/2012/03/another-moth man.html (accessed March 17, 2012).

Teitelbaum, Michael. "Mothman: Strange Creature, Alien . . . or Both?" In *The Scary States of America*. New York: Delacorte Press, 2007, 374–82.

Background information on Mothman is provided for the reader through an instant messaging transcript between the narrator and his friend, CreatureFan. "For years after the first Mothman sightings, lots of reports of electronic disturbances came in from houses near the plant. Passing cars continue to lose radio signals and headlights, or just stall out altogether" (377). Accompanying the back story is a tale told by a young boy who had been lost in the woods in the area and found, in the old TNT plant rumored to be the Mothman's lair, a huge nest. Next to the nest he discovers a huge putrid pile of small-animal remains, and before he can go any further, he discovers the beast that made the nest—the Mothman. The experience is terrifying, but the creature suddenly stops as a red glow appears in the sky and the creature vanishes. When the boy makes it safely to a nearby house, the resident tells him that the creature is definitely the Mothman and that they think there is a definite connection between it and aliens. The boy's mother does not believe his story until the red glow appears in the sky, their car stalls and the headlights blink out.

Endnotes

1. See the relevant entry, "legend trip," in Jan Harold Brunvand's *American Folklore: An Encyclopedia*, Garland Reference Library of the Humanities, vol. 1551 (New York: Garland, 1995), 439–40.

2. Michael E. Bell, *Food for the Dead: On the Trail of New England's Vampires* (New York: Carroll & Graf, 2001).

References

Anderson, John. 2010. "Long Shadows of a Borough's Boogeyman." *New York Times*, May 30. http://www.nytimes.com/2010/05/30/movies/30cropsey.html (accessed July 6, 2011).

Asfar, Dan. 2003. *Haunted Highways*. Edmonton, Alberta: Ghost House Books, 2003.

Barnett, Virginia and Daniel. 2003. "The San Antonio Ghost Children: Exploring the Facts behind an Urban Legend." *The North Texas Skeptics* 17 (11): 3–5.

Barry, Dan . 2008. "In the Wilds of New Jersey, a Legend Inspires a Hunt." *New York Times*, September 8. http://www.nytimes.com/2008/09/08/us/08land.html (accessed June 3, 2011).

Belanger, Jeff. 2011. *Picture Yourself Legend Tripping: Your Complete Guide to Finding UFOs, Monsters, Ghosts, and Urban Legends in Your Own Backyard*. Boston: Course Technology, Cengage Learning.

Best, Joel. 2008."Halloween Sadism: The Evidence," http://dspace.udel.edu:8080/dspace/bit stream/handle/19716/726/DSpace.revised%20thru%2008.pdf;jsessionid=4E05012395 7986F049130687B2B03921?sequence=3 (accessed September 25, 2011).

Blackman, W. Haden. 1998. *The Field Guide to North American Monsters: Everything You Need to Know about Encountering over 100 Terrifying Creatures in the Wild*. New York: Three Rivers Press.

Bloody Mary Curse Chain Email. http://www.hoax-slayer.com/bloody-mary-curse-chain-email.shtml (accessed July 4, 2011).

Bowery Boys. 2010. "Review of Cropsey." http://theboweryboys.blogspot.com/2010/07/cropsey-urban-legend-intersects-with.html (accessed July 5, 2011).

Brednich, Rolf W. 2001. "Where They Originated . . . Some Contemporary Legends and Their Literary Origins." Paper presented at ISFNR Congress, Melbourne, Australia. http://www.folklore.ee/folklore/vol20/legends.pdf (accessed October 19, 2010).

Brewer, Teri. 1994. "Preface: The Marketing of Tradition." *Folklore in Use: Applications in the Real World* 2 (1): 1–11.

Brunvand, Jan Harold. 2001. *Encyclopedia of Urban Legends*. New York: Norton.

Clark, Lynn Schofield. 2003. *From Angels to Aliens: Teenagers, the Media, and the Supernatural.* Oxford: Oxford University Press.

Coleman, Loren. 2001. *Mysterious America: The Ultimate Guide to the Nation's Weirdest Wonders, Strangest Spots, and Creepiest Creatures.* New York: Paraview Pocket Books.

Collins-Koehn, Laurie. 2011. "Haunted Niagara: Urban Legends or a Glimpse into the Paranormal?" http://www.niagarafallsreview.ca/ArticleDisplay.aspx?e=3209243 (accessed September 10, 2011).

Cruz, Meredith E. 2008. *Fear of Crime and Belief in Urban Folklore: An Exploration of Urban Folklore and Fear.* Thesis, Master of Science in Criminology, the University of Texas at Dallas.

"Curse of Cornstalk." http://www.mothmanmuseum.com/MothmanLives/mothmanhistory/history/unusual.html.

Davies, Owen. 2009. *The Haunted: A Social History of Ghosts.* Basingstoke, Hampshire, UK: Palgrave Macmillan.

DeFruscio, Vince, and Charlie McCormick. 2005. The Underground Seen: Tunneling Legends on College and University Campuses. *Journal of New York Folklore* 31 (Fall–Winter). http://www.nyfolklore.org/pubs/voic31-3-4/undergrd.html.

Dégh, Linda. 2001. *Legend and Belief: Dialectics of a Folklore Genre.* Bloomington: Indiana University Press.

de Vos, Gail. 1996. *Tales, Rumors, and Gossip: Exploring Contemporary Folk Literature in Grades 7–12.* Westport, CT: Libraries Unlimited.

Dollar, Steve. 2010. "Staten Island Boogeyman Haunts Anew." *Wall Street Journal,* May 28. http://online.wsj.com/article/SB10001424052748704269204575270783660589168.html (accessed July 6, 2011).

Dundes, Alan. 2002. "Bloody Mary in the Mirror: A Reflection of Pre-Pubescent Anxiety." In *Bloody Mary in the Mirror: Essays in Psychoanalytic Folkloristics.* Jackson: University Press of Mississippi, 76–94. Originally published in *Western Folklore* 57 (1998): 119–35.

Ellis, Bill. 1989. "Death by Folklore: Ostension, Contemporary Legend and Murder." *Western Folklore* 48 (July): 201–20.

Ellis, Bill. 2001. *Aliens, Ghosts, and Cults: Legends We Live.* Jackson: University Press of Mississippi.

Ellis, Bill. 2004. *Lucifer Ascending: The Occult in Folklore and Popular Culture.* Lexington: University Press of Kentucky,.

Emery, David. 2010. "A Halloween Treat from Food Network Challenge: 'Extreme Urban Legend Cakes.'" About.com: Urban Legends. http://urbanlegends.about.com/b/2010/10/28/food-network-challenge-extreme-urban-legend-cakes.htm (accessed September 24, 2011).

Farrell, Alex. 2009. "The Occult World of Ancient Kyoto." *Japan Today,* June 4. http://www.japantoday.com/category/travel/view/the-occult-world-of-ancient-kyoto (accessed June 14, 2011).

Fine, Gary Alan. 1991. "Redemption Rumors and the Power of Ostension." *Journal of American Folklore* 106:179–81.

Fleury, Maureen K. 2008. "The Screaming Tunnel at Niagara Falls." http://www.suite101.com/content/the-screaming-tunnel-a51813 (accessed September 10, 2011).

Floyd, Jonathan A. 2011. "The Legend of the Almo Massacre: Ostensive Action and the Commodification of Folklore." *All Graduate Reports and Creative Projects.* http://digitalcommons.usa.edu/gradreprts/29 (accessed June 21, 2011).

Goldstein, Diane E. 2007. "The Commodification of Belief." In *Haunting Experiences: Ghosts in Contemporary Folklore,* edited by Diane E. Goldstein, Sylvia Grider and Jeannie Banks Thomas, 171–205. Logan: Utah State University Press.

Goldstein, Diane E. 2011. "Crying Babies, Tiny Handprints and Terror on the Web: Virtual Legend Tripping." Conference Paper, Perspective on Contemporary Legend 29th International Conference, Harrisburg, Pennsylvania, May 26.

Goldstein, Diane E., Sylvia Grider and Jeannie Banks Thomas. 2007. *Haunting Experiences: Ghosts in Contemporary Folklore.* Logan: Utah State University Press.

Goldstruck, Arthur. 2010. "Legends from a Small Country." http://thoselegends.blogspot
.com/2010/08/shoes-on-line.html (accessed May 31, 2011).

Haring, Lee, and Mark Breslerman. 1977. "The Cropsey Maniac." *New York Folklore* 3
(1–4): 15–27.

"Haunted West Virginia: The Cornstalk Curse." 2002. http://www.prairieghosts.com/
cornstalk.html (accessed September 10, 2011).

"Helping Hands." 2007. http://www.snopes.com/horrors/ghosts/handprint.asp (accessed
May 30, 2011).

"High Voltage Tops." 2011. http://germanherald.com/news/Germany_in_Focus/2011-02-28/
598/High_voltage_Tops (accessed May 31, 2011).

Holly, Donald H., Jr., and Casey E. Cordy. 2007. " What's in a Coin? Reading the Material
Culture of Legend Tripping and Other Activities." *Journal of American Folklore* 120
(477): 335–54.

Hudson, Marilyn A. 2011. "Cry, Baby, Cry." http://mystorical.blogspot.com/2011/06/cry
-baby-cry.html (accessed September 10, 2011).

Irvine, Alex. 2007. *The Supernatural Book of Monsters, Spirits, Demons, and Ghouls*. New
York: Harper Entertainment.

The Jersey Devil—Fact or Fiction. Atlantic County, New Jersey County Government.
http://www.aclink.org/HISTORY/mainpages/jerseydevil3.asp (accessed June 3,
2011).

Koven, Mikel J. 1999. *Candyman* Can: Film and Ostension. *Contemporary Legend* n.s.
2:155–73.

Koven, Mikel J. 2007. "*Most Haunted* and the Convergence of Traditional Belief and Popular
Television." *Folklore* 118 (August): 183–202.

Koven, Mikel J. 2008. *Film, Folklore, and Urban Legends*. Lanham, MD: Scarecrow Press.

Leary, Frances. 2003. *The Honey Island Swamp Monster: The Development and
Maintenance of a Folk and Commodified Belief Tradition*. Master of Arts Thesis,
Department of Folklore, Memorial University of Newfoundland.

Lee, Regan. 2008. "Mothman and Other Synchronicities: Dreams, Coincidences and High
Strangeness." *Dark Lore* 2:215–21.

"The Legend of Stull, Kansas." http://ghosthauntings.org/legend_of_stull_kansas.aspx
(accessed September 10, 2011).

Lewis, Don R. 2011. "Truth Is Stranger Than Fiction: An Interview with 'Cropsey'
Filmmaker Josh Zeman." http://www.filmthreat.com/interviews/37161/ (accessed
July 6, 2011).

Lindahl, Carl. 2005. "Ostensive Healing: Pilgrimage to the San Antonio Ghost Tracks."
Journal of American Folklore 118 (468): 164–85.

Lowry, Brain. 1975. *The Truth Is Out There: The Official Guide to the X-Files*. New York:
Harper.

McGinnis, J. Ross. 2000. *Trials of Hex*. Waterford, MI: Davis/Trinity.

McHargue, Brad. "Denver Film Presents: 'Cropsey.' " http://blog.moviefone.com/2010/07/
05/denver-film-presents-cropsey/ (accessed July 5, 2011).

Meder, Theo. 2011. "In Search of the Dutch Lore of the Land: Old and New Legends
throughout the Netherlands." *Folklore* 122 (2): 117–34.

Meder, Theo. "Ethnic Conflict Hoaxes in Dutch News Media: *Memes* and *Ostension*: Legend
and Life Interacting." http://members.chello.nl/m.jong9/ostension.htm (accessed
July 1, 2011).

Muir, John Kenneth. 2010. "Cult Movie Review: Cropsey." http://reflectionson
filmandtelevision.blogspot.com/2010/08/cult-movie-review-cropsey-2009.html
(accessed July 6, 2011).

Nebraska State Historical Society. 2007. "Nebraska's Perfectly Peculiar People." http://
www.nebraskahistory.org/sites/mnh/weird_nebraska/nebraskas_perfectly.htm
(accessed June 30, 2011).

Newton, Michael. 2005. *Encyclopedia of Cryptozoology: A Global Guide to Hidden Animals
and Their Pursuers*. Jefferson, NC: McFarland.

Nickell, Joe. 2009. "Searching for Vampire Graves." *CSI: Committee for Skeptical Inquiry* 33 (2). http://www.csicop.org/si/show/searching_for_vampire_graves/ (accessed September 9, 2011).

O'Leary, Devin D. 2010. "Film Review: Cropsey." http://alibi.com/film/33205/Cropsey.html (accessed July 6, 2011).

Orange, Michelle. 2010. Review: A Bogeyman Gets His Close-Up in *Cropsey*. http://www.movieline.com/2010/06/review-a-bogeyman-gets-his-close-up-in-cropsey.php (accessed July 5, 2011).

Oring, Elliott. 2008. "Legendry and the Rhetoric of Truth." *Journal of American Folklore* 121 (480): 127–66.

Petersen, Line Nybro. 2010. "Renegotiating religious imaginations through transformations of "banal religion" in "Supernatural." *Tansformative Works and Cultures* 4. http://journal.transformativeworks.org/index.php/twc/article/view/142 (accessed September 14, 2011).

Poole, Scott W. 2009. *Satan in America: The Devil We Know*. Lanham, MD: Rowman & Littlefield.

Preston, Cathy. 2007. "Panty Trees, Shoe Trees, and Legend." *FOAFTALE News: News Letter of the International Society for Contemporary Legend Research* 67 (May): 11–12.

Prizer, Tim. 2004. "Shame Old Roads Can't Talk": Narrative, Experience, and Belief in the Framing of Legend-Trips as Performance. *Contemporary Legend* n.s. 7:67–97.

"Screaming Tunnel." http://www.nflibrary.ca/ForAdults/LocalHistoryMaterials/LegendsFolkloreofNiagaraFalls/ScreamingTunnel/tabid/237/Default.aspx (accessed September 10, 2011).

"Sex Bracelets." 2009. http://www.snopes.com/risque/school/bracelet.asp (accessed June 2, 2011).

Skelto, Rebekah. 2009. "Legends Add Interest to Campus History." http://www.thebatt.com/2.8485/legends-add-interest-to-campus-history-1.1181526 (accessed June 29, 2011).

Story, Sheila. 2009. "Lincoln Ghost Tours helps relieve fear of ghosts." *Lincoln Journal Star* http://journalstar.com/news/local/article_2567ae14-c1be-11de-ale2-001cc4c03286.html (accessed March 17, 2012).

Sudermann, Hannelore. 2010. "WSU Myths and Legends." http://wsm.wsu.edu/s/index.php?id=793 (accessed June 30, 2011).

Summers, Wynne L. 2000. "Bloody Mary: When Ostension Becomes a Deadly and Destructive Teen Ritual." *Midwestern Folklore* 26 (1): 19–26.

"The Top Ten Haunted Cemetery or Graveyards in the United States." http://www.hauntedamericatours.com/toptenhaunted/toptenhauntedcemeteries/ (accessed September 10, 2011).

Thomas, Jeannie Banks. 2003. *Naked Barbies, Warrior Joes, and Other Forms of Visible Gender*. Urbana: University of Illinois Press.

Thomas, Jeannie Banks. 2007. "The Usefulness of Ghost Stories." In *Haunting Experiences: Ghosts in Contemporary Folklore*, Diane E. Goldstein, Sylvia Grider and Jeannie Banks Thomas. Logan: Utah State University Press, 25–59.

Tosenberger, Catherine. 2010. " 'Kinda Like the Folklore of Its Day': *Supernatural*, Fairy Tales, and Ostension." *Transformative Works and Cultures* no. 4. http://dx.doi.org/10.3983/twc.2010.0174 (no longer available online, accessed June 23, 2011)

Tucker, Elizabeth. 2005. "Ghosts in Mirrors: Reflections of the Self." *Journal of American Folklore* 118 (468): 86–203.

Tucker, Libby. 2006a. "Legend Quests." *VOICES: The Journal of New York Folklore* 32 (1–2): 34–38.

Tucker, Libby. 2006b. "Cropsey at Camp." *VOICES: The Journal of New York Folklore* 32 (3–4). http://www.nyfolklore.org/pubs/voic32-3-4/gspirits.html (accessed July 6, 2011).

Tucker, Elizabeth. 2007. *Haunted Halls: Ghostlore of American College Campuses*. Jackson: University Press of Mississippi.

Weiser, Kathy. 2010. "Ghost Children upon San Antonio's Railroad Tracks. Legends of America: A Travel Site for the Nostalgic & Historic Minded." http://www.legendsofamerica.com/tx-ghostlychildren.html (accessed June 17, 2011).

CHAPTER 3

FOLKLORE AND THE INTERNET: NETLORE

---

*U*rban legends have found their way into the media for years, and this form of retelling the stories is a means for oral popular culture to survive and prosper in an increasingly media-saturated society. It is a way of holding onto a culturally-relevant oral tradition. The existence of urban legends in cyber-space is indicative of our attempts to ensure the continuity of tradition while embracing change.

—Fernback (2003, 43)

Urban legend expert Jan Harold Brunvand argues that the contemporary legend is losing its vitality as an oral-narrative legend and that it has mostly migrated from "*folk*lore into *popular* culture where they became stereotyped, standardized, exploited, commodified, and repackaged in a number of ways" (Brunvand 2001a, xxvii). He maintains that performances of contemporary legends are now being shaped by the Internet rather than face-to-face communication. This has certainly been the case in the intervening years. However, the majority of scholarship on contemporary legends written in the last decade has woven within it the realization that the Internet and other relevant technological innovations offer an exciting potential for the transmission of all types of folklore, including contemporary legends. Elizabeth Tucker affirms that those studying supernatural narratives, for example, are beginning to comprehend how the legends are shared and the legend characters developed through the Internet (Tucker 2009, 69). And, since the contemporary legends have virtually relocated themselves in popular culture and online culture, they need to be studied and discussed where they reside. "We should also do our best to educate the media and the public about the distinctions between rumors, myths and legends, although this may prove as unsuccessful as efforts to restrict the use of the term 'folklore' itself" (Brunvand 2004b, 19). A quick online search for the terms "folklore," "rumors," "myths" and "legends" brought forth items that do not fit the authorized definitions. There is a great deal of culling of hits involved when conducting research online because of the proliferation of Internet resources such as wikis, social networking, photo sharing and folksonomy (collaborative tagging, creating and managing tags to annotate and categorize content) where users no longer need to know any computer programming to add material and use terms indiscriminately or misuse them entirely.

Others have stated that these mediated legends are an example of what Ong (1982) referred to as secondary orality. "It is a re-emergence of an oral character in communication that represents a blend of literate, oral, and electronic cultures in contemporary discourse" (Fernback 2003, 37). These mediated legends share elements associated with oral contemporary legends: they are traditional, socially relevant and applicable to current social norms and situations (Fernback 2003, 33). They also, as has been established throughout the discussions in this book, exist in multiple variants online and in popular culture. People, when e-mailing, blogging or posting on a discussion board or social networking site, frequently make use of folklore as a cultural frame of reference, particularly when they are responding to ambiguity and anxiety (Bronner 2009, 25). "The Internet has become America's rumor bazaar. Increasingly consumers do not need to claim they heard a rumor from television talk shows; they can announce that 'it was on the Internet' " (Fine and Turner 2001, 112). Fine and Turner speculate on the effect the Internet and the attribution of sources to the Internet will have on the credibility of sources and conclude that while this remains to be seen, a compelling story always outweighs its source (Fine and Turner 2001, 112). The Internet plays a huge role, not only in the dissemination of contemporary legends but also in the debunking of them; although, as Brunvand points out, "even when a story is identified and revealed as a mere legend, that doesn't stop it from being forwarded and retold" (Brunvand 2004a, 237). Despite the many directives from a myriad of sources to check possible contemporary legends with responsible websites such as Snopes, the mediated transmission of contemporary legends has not abated. In fact, the unforeseen central function of the antihoax websites is the online preservation of the legends and e-mail hoaxes as they reproduce the texts as part of the debunking dialogue.

E-mail itself shares many characteristics of the oral tradition and as such becomes a productive medium for disseminating contemporary folklore to the huge networks of friends and acquaintances connected through their computers (Kibby 2005, 789). Widespread communities on Facebook, Twitter, blogs and personal home pages are also actively involved in relating, shaping and disseminating contemporary legends along with their closely related cousins, e-mail hoaxes and chain letters. The major difference between the orally transmitted contemporary legends and those transmitted electronically is that the societal fears and prejudices contained within them are expressed much more abrasively due to the virtual anonymity of the person posting the narrative (Blank 2007, 19). "Clearly, both chain letters and e-mail hoaxes follow the conventions of the urban legend genre, which underscores the rationale for studying urban legends and other folk narratives on the Internet" (Blank 2007, 19).

Russell Frank reflects that the current visual and aural narration of contemporary legends, other forms of folklore and newslore through technological transmission has not changed the content but resulted in a new branch of folklore that is without antecedent (Frank 2011, 194). This new branch he considers netlore.

> Every new communication medium becomes a new way to transmit folklore. Jokes and stories told face-to-face can easily be told and quickly spread over the telephone, and though jokes and stories may arise that involve the phone itself—the urban legend about the babysitter who takes a call from a murderer on the premises comes to mind—it is hard to see how the medium has given rise to new *forms* of folklore. Fax machines and computers, on the other hand, have not only served as media for the communication of folklore

but provided the tools for the creation and transmission of new forms of folklore. Forms of expression like the composite photograph, the phony document, or the video production may not be new, but computer applications have so reduced the cost and labor-intensiveness of producing them that they are available to amateurs and may be disseminated by amateurs on a scale that was simply not possible before. (Frank 2011, 215)

For folklorists and others fascinated with contemporary legends, the Internet offers the three-D's of netlore: dissemination, debunking and discussion. This chapter focuses on diverse examples of current netlore including e-mail hoaxes, chain letters, telephone and cell phone legends, and scarelore such as gang initiation legends and fears regarding traveling radiation resulting from the 2011 earthquakes in Japan.

Definition of Terms

Netlore is folklore that is not oral, not communicated face-to-face and not passed from generation to generation. Nor does it exhibit much variation. It is folklore because "as expressive behavior it is a form of subversive play, circulating in an underground communicative universe that runs parallel to and often parodies, mocks, or comments mordantly on "official" channels of communication such as the mass media" (Frank 2011, 9).

Newslore consists of "folklore that comments on, and is therefore indecipherable without knowledge of current events" (Frank 2011, 7). Newslore occurs in multiple formats: jokes, digitally altered photographs, mock news stories, press releases or interoffice memoranda, parodies of songs, poems, political and commercial advertisements, movie previews and posters, still or animated cartoons and short live-action films, and contemporary legends (Frank 2011, 7). Frank comments that video and audio newslore came later than the text-based and still images and are not what he argued was the golden age of newslore from the 1990s through to the early 2000s (Frank 2011, 230, n. 3). Newslore is both ephemeral and traditional, directly responding to current events and fading with the news coverage of those events, and often recycled images and texts applied to earlier events (Frank 2004, 634).

Hoaxes are documents, actions or artifacts intended to deceive the public. Those that appear on the Internet can be viewed as a subset of folklore legends, but the key factor that separates the hoax from a contemporary legend is that the hoax is a deliberate deception. Most hoaxes on the Internet are classified as chain letters, computer virus and software hoaxes, medical hoaxes, rumors, legends and jokes (Dunn and Allen 2005, 88).

E-mail hoaxes, messages containing false or at least problematic information, are passed on via the forward function of e-mail programs (Heyd 2008, 1). They spread deceptive, outdated or imprecise warnings, promises, threats or supposedly relevant information with ease, yet are communicated exclusively from private user to private user (Heyd 2008, 2).

Chain letters appear in various forms. Some call for the recipient to forward information to others in a group (usually by way of warnings or threats if information is not directly passed on to a certain number of people) while others tie in to a recipient's gluttony or play to a recipient's compassion (Dunn and Allen 2005, 88). Similar to contemporary legends, chain letters and chain letter parodies are rife with attestations of authenticity and firmness on the importance of forwarding the message immediately (Frank 2011, 227). They exploit irrational anxieties and wishes of recipients, promising credible rewards or threatening missed opportunities, injury or other malevolence.

Debunking consists of discrediting "true" assertions as being false, embellished or ostentatious and is usually associated with skeptical investigations of UFOs, paranormal phenomena, cryptozoological claims, conspiracy theories and contemporary legends. Mythbusters, Snopes and the Skeptics Society are three reputable resources testing and discussing the validity of contemporary legends.

Photographic urban legends, digitally altered photographs, circulate among friends via e-mail and turn up on netlore sites, just as jokes and contemporary legends do, as well as on websites run by pranksters and propagandists (Frank 2011, 217). The photographs must meet three criteria to be considered photographic urban legends. They must tell a story, be extraordinary yet believable and express, at least indirectly, anxiety about threats to our safety and health (Frank 2011, 217).

Types of Netlore and Newslore

While it may seem obvious that much contemporary folklore responds to current events, it is easy to forget that, strictly speaking, the lore responds not to the events themselves but to accounts of the events ... it is important to recognize that newslore may be a response to how that story is told—to what is left out as well as what is included—as much as it is a response to the occurrence itself.

—Frank (2011, 92)

Since a large majority of people are continually linked to electronic media of one sort or another, it is imperative to be cognisant of the different types of newslore and netlore that persistently make their appearances.

Computer Legends, Viruses and Warnings

E-mail hoaxes cannot exist without the Internet. These narratives are exclusive to the Internet. The Internet is the premier forum for studying urban legends, chain letters, hoaxes and jokes

—Blank (2007, 17).

In the intervening years since the term urban legend became a buzz word or catch-all phrase for all things suspect, strange or misunderstood, the legends regarding computer use and misuse have run rampant. Now, however, since more people are becoming computer savvy, the warnings and hoaxes play on people's fears and anxieties of viral conspiracies and the dangers of online communication and contamination. There is a very good reason behind spam filters, firewalls, security software packages, and due diligence. Almost weekly, e-mail in-boxes overflow with messages of dire emergencies from banking institutions the recipient has never utilized, PayPal alerts regarding misuse or unauthorized use of non-existent accounts, requests for aid regarding missing children, women or items, or covert supplications for financial windfalls. Often warning missives arrive from people one knows and trust but who are misguided in their enthusiasm to protect their friends from danger and disaster. Internet connectivity should be accompanied by mandatory educational material regarding the disadvantages of some netlore and newslore. But, would anyone read it?

E-mail Hoaxes and Social Network Warnings

It happened fast, really fast. Within hours of the destruction of the World Trade Center in New York on September 11, 2001, there were reports of online solicitations from "representatives"

*of charities and relief agencies. Fortunately, many savvy recipi-
ents of such solicitations by e-mail and telephone were reluctant
to give their credit card information to these solicitors and com-
plained to law enforcement authorities. With good reason, it
seems. The very next day ScamBusters posted: [a warning of
these spammers and advice to those who received e-mail and
telephone solicitations].*

—Ebbinghouse (2002, 97)

Not all e-mail hoaxes originate with the digital medium. "There are well established cases where a classic urban legend (kidney theft, syringes in cinema seats,
etc.) have made it into the digital medium; reciprocally, tales that began as e-mail
hoaxes may make the transition if users begin to retell them orally" (Heyd 2008,
78). Virus hoaxes and giveaway and charity e-mail hoaxes that depend on the fictional
"e-mail tracker" element are less likely to be transmitted orally. However, most of
these hoaxes are closely related to contemporary legends in their folkloric content,
number of variants and cyclic relevance. "These hoaxes have made great headway
across cyberspace, flooding inboxes with fake tales about free money, community
safety concerns, and false reports of celebrity deaths" (Blank 2007, 17). According
to researchers, the explosion of e-mail hoaxes occurred between 1997 and 1999.
Variants of many of the current e-mail hoaxes, the charity e-mail hoaxes and giveaway
e-mail hoaxes, were also established at this time (Heyd 2008, 4). Two significant
topics that developed later were the approaching millennium, with the Y2K bug, and
the World Trade Center attacks of September 11. Many of the hoaxes circulating after
9/11, however, were recycled from hoaxes regarding previous catastrophes.

Three basic types of e-mail users are identified in the literature: forwarders,
spikers and readers. Forwarders read whatever arrives in their e-mail in-box and
then pass it along to members of their own network of e-mail friends. Spikers, on
the other hand, delete all forwarded material unread while readers read the forwarded materials but are reluctant to forward items imprudently and therefore do
so only if they ascertain somehow that the messages have validity (Frank 2011,
10). This support is one of the prime functions of a website such as Snopes.com.
Effective e-mail hoaxes are almost totally dependent on the first type of e-mail user.
Since a major identification element in an e-mail hoax is the instruction explicitly
stated in the text to "forward this to everyone you know" or a similar phraseology,
the wording would be lost on the spiker while the reader would consider forwarding
the message as a waste of time for any possible recipients (Heyd 2008, 20). Phishing
e-mails and spam do not encourage forwarding: the success of Nigeria scam
e-mails, discussed in more detail later in this chapter, depends on the confidential
treatment of the message routinely requested in such mails (Heyd 2008, 21). Scam
e-mails, much like the hoax e-mails, offer products and services that are inaccurate
and fraudulent but, unlike hoaxes, have very real consequences for those who
respond, such as loss of money and, in some cases, loss of life.

Types of E-mail Hoaxes

E-mail hoaxes are deceptive messages, pure and simple. Their nucleus is a
false proposition or one that is outdated, imprecise or unverifiable. If the message
warns of a virus, the peril would be non-existent; if it offers rewards of any kind,
it would be impossible to claim them; and if it targets compassion for a missing or
ill child, the person would be illusory (Heyd 2008, 23). There are three distinct

types of e-mail hoaxes circulating on the Internet since its conception: virus hoaxes, giveaway hoaxes and charity hoaxes.

Virus Hoaxes

Often considered the typical type of e-mail hoaxes, virus hoaxes developed alongside hacker culture and concerns about online security and safety. They usually warn against (non-existent) security threats that appear in an e-mail message and often contain references to well-known software or Internet security companies to boost their credibility factor (Heyd 2008, 31–32). As people become more acclimatized to the online environment, these types of e-mail hoaxes declined in number.

Giveaway Hoaxes

This type of e-mail hoax names a major company, ranging from software companies to food manufacturers, that reimburses participants with money or other offerings if they forward the e-mail to a certain number of people within a set time limit, in a similar manner to chain letter communications. The rationale behind the e-mail is stated as market research or an analogous narrative, and the success of the stated initiative would be monitored by a professed "e-mail tracking" (or sometimes "tracing") system which does not exist (Heyd 2008, 33).

Charity Hoaxes or Sympathy Hoaxes

Two major types of these hoaxes, the "sick child" and the "missing child," have been circulating online since at least 1997. In the "sick child" hoax, a child, or sometimes the parents, afflicted by something through no fault of the child and needing financial aid, would receive financial help by an organization, corporation or unspecified "billionaire" if the e-mail is forwarded a certain number of times. Heyd states that this type of armchair activism could have been inspired by legitimate click-to-donate websites (Heyd 2008, 34). The "missing child" hoax informs the recipient about a lost or abducted child and requests dissemination of the information. Differentiation between e-mail hoaxes and genuine alerts that are actually grounded in reality is, and remains, crucial, particularly as the Amber Alert program for missing children, installed in the United States in 1996, circulates real search alerts via e-mail (Heyd 2008, 34). Unfortunately, false Amber Alert e-mails also continue to circulate. At the time of this writing, checking Snopes.com for the term "Amber Alert" produced over 20 hits, including the fake Amber Alert for licence plates 72B 381 (gray car) and 98B 351 (2006 Mitsubishi Eclipse). Several of the hits concern Amber Alerts that had been cancelled but continue to circulate by e-mail, while others are still valid and legitimate.

Current Examples of E-mail Hoaxes

Out of the plethora of hoaxes circulating during the writing of this chapter, I selected a few from those that were current and came to my e-mail directly from friends.

Fake Amber Alerts

In the discussion on the "Ashley Flores" "missing child" sympathy hoax, Barbara Mikkelson of Snopes.com states that the earliest texts of this alert, circulating in 2006, did not incorporate the basic information that would be included in an authentic alert: where and when the child went missing, a physical description of the child and contact information for the parents and the police department issuing the alert. Only an ambiguous statement is provided: a deli manager from Philadelphia had a 13-year-old daughter who had been missing for two weeks. Mikkelson reports that on the one day alone, May 19, 2006, their website had over 25,000 searches from readers looking for information about the missing child (Mikkelson 2011a). An adapted version continued to circulate in subsequent years. "As of March 2011, nearly five years after the original 'missing Ashley Flores' message was first set loose on the Internet, the hoax was still going strong, with this article remaining one of the most searched-for articles on our site" (Mikkelson 2011a). Other debunking sites and contemporary legend discussion sites include information regarding this particular hoax. A similar hoax containing phraseology from the Ashley Flores text began to circulate in 2007 about a missing boy, Evan Trembley. Again, obvious clues point to this being a hoax: basic information is missing about the alleged disappearance; contact information is a non-functioning Yahoo e-mail account; none of the organizations that tracked missing children have any record of a missing child by this name; and the information regarding the police force supposedly searching for him is incorrect (Mikkelson 2009b).

An abducted-children alert originating in the United Kingdom circulating on Facebook in March 2011 was deemed false by the Warwickshire police. The text message and message on Facebook claims that the young boy and girl had been snatched by people in a white van with a red dragon motif on it. The police used the opportunity to issue a reminder about "stranger danger" although the abduction story was false (" 'Abducted Children' Alert" 2011).

"Strawberry Quick" Panic

> The tale told in the "Strawberry Quick" alert has the earmarks of an urban legend: lack of detail (children supposedly were rushed to the hospital after ingesting meth they mistook for candy, but we're not told when, where, or to whom this happened); implausibility (why flavor a drug that is typically snorted or smoked, let alone offer it in "chocolate, peanut butter, cola, cherry, grape and orange" as well as strawberry?); similarity to other urban legends (such as the old one about poisoned Halloween candy); and the closing admonition to "pass this email on to as many people as you can."
>
> —Sullum (2010)

Sometimes hoaxes gain reputable affiliation because of fears of the members of an organization. In his blog, Jacob Sullum reports on the strange adventures of the Texas PTA and the methamphetamine-laced drug marketed to school-age children called "strawberry quick." Apparently, the PTA was called to task regarding their passing information about this contemporary legend that had been debunked previously by Snopes.com, the drug policy organization Join Together, the Drug Enforcement Administration and Texas Crime Stoppers (Sullum 2010). In their repeal of their original warning, they state that "strawberry quick" did not exist in Texas. They do not reveal the fact that it is a contemporary legend, not existing anywhere. Dr. Jane Maxwell, with the Gulf Coast Addiction Technology Transfer Center, University of Texas at Austin, when consulted on the existence of "strawberry quick," affirmed that strawberry quick is a "myth," and an urban legend (Sullum 2010). The PTA statement assured that "rumors about new drugs or drugs targeted to children can occur in this field, but the fact that 'strawberry quick' is not present in Texas in no way invalidates the urge to caution and to be fully aware regarding drug and alcohol promotion or usage amongst our Texas children. Forewarned is forearmed" (Sullum 2010). However, as Sullum remarks rather acerbically, "after trying to stir up a panic about an urban legend, the Texas PTA blames Texas Crime Stoppers, which in turn blames a juvenile probation office in Central Texas. That's a nice example to set for the kids: When you're caught pre-varicating, shift the responsibility to someone else" (Sullum 2010). This contemporary legend went viral on Facebook during February 2012 with copious warning postings and commentaries about the danger and the fact that it was an urban legend.

"Le-a"

An e-mail, explaining the correct pronunciation of the name "Ledasha," which had been circulating during 2008 and 2009, popped up in e-mail in-boxes again in late 2011. As the fairly consistent message states: "My aunt/cousin/college room-mate is a teacher/nurse/social worker in Georgia/Louisiana/Detroit. She had a student/patient whose name was written Le-a. She asked, 'Is that pronounced LAY-uh?' And the girl's mother got all offended: 'It's Ledash! The dash don't be silent!' "

According to Barbara Mikkelson, the comment from the mother positions the speaker as African American, and that a racist and disapproving aspect of the message is clearly expressed in the comment appended to many of the forwards: "And we let these people vote!!" (Mikkelson 2009c). At this point in time, there has been no affirmation of anyone carrying this name.

"Nigerian Scam"/"Advance Fee Fraud"/"419 Fraud"

> Found when the protagonist was checking his email: "come-ons from that seemingly massive group of African princes who needed but a small loan to claim their long-lost fortunes (doesn't it always take $50,000 to become a multimillionaire?)."
>
> —Parks (2011, 129)

Discussion of this prolific e-mail scam or hoax is included to illuminate the major differences between a hoax and a scam. The scam is also referred to as the Advance Fee Fraud, the 419 Fraud (after a formerly relevant section of the Nigerian Criminal Code) and, in Europe, the Nigerian Connection. This scam attempts to persuade the unsolicited recipient to send money in exchange for a com-mission on a significantly larger amount of money that needed to be quickly removed from a bank or other financial institution. The original letter, first appear-ing in the early 1980s, involved a request for help from an official of a government agency, usually the central bank, in Nigeria. The country in question now could be any one of many, the agency resembling any official-sounding name, and the target company or individual receiving the letter technologically, via e-mail rather than through the post (Chuck 2002, 114). "419 scammers impersonate real people, espe-cially Nigerian political figures, whom they plainly consider corrupt, and therefore fun to impersonate, or actually serious about weeding out corruption, and therefore fun to impersonate" (Edelson 2006, 8). Edelson affirms that if the prospect responded, a team is immediately available to keep up the discourse and to produce bogus certificates. "Victims are induced to meet the scammers in Lagos, Amsterdam or Johannesburg. Some have been held for ransom and even killed" (Edelson 2006, 18).

A typical variant of this scam arrived in my spam folder in my e-mail in-box while I was writing this section.

> From: <misslucia00@pop.com.br>
> Date: 2011/6/16
> Subject: From Miss Lucia Albert Odienne.
> To:
>> From Miss Lucia Albert Odienne.
>> Compliment of the Season.
>> How are you and your family members I hope you are all fine? My name is Miss Lucia Albert (18yrs). I am the only surviving child of late Mr. & Mrs. Albert Odienne, may their soul rest in perfect peace. I am an under graduate studying at Ashesi university college Ghana in our neighboring country. My mother died when I was (3yrs) but my late father was a politician a former Mayor; he was assassinated due to the political crisis in this country on September 6th 2010 by the unknown persons, by the members of the Government of the former president on his way back from Korhogo in the Northern Area part of this country. They claim that my father has not been supporting the Government of Laurent Gbagbo to resist France and United Nations from taken over the country.
>> I have the sum of Ten Million Dollars ($10,000,000.00) which was acquired by my late Father, he deposited the money into suspense account in a bank outside in my country which I shall detail you in your confirmation to assist me further. I seek your permission to remit this amount into your account so that I could come to your country for investment and to further my studies. I am willing to offer you 20% of the total sum for your desire to assist me. Presently I am on exile in a refugee in Cotonu Benin Republic. Please do respond immediately you receive this email for more information regarding the transfer.
>> Respectfully yours,
>> Miss Lucia Albert Odienne.

Edelson provides a checklist to aid the reader in recognizing the legitimacy of these appeals, stating that it is a scam if only one of these elements is present:

- Does the proposal come from a stranger who found you "through the internet," or in a "business directory," or among the files of his father (a murdered cocoa merchant), or scribbled in the diary of the Sultan of Brunei?
- Is the email From: and To: the same person?
- Is the letter addressed to "CEO" even though you're a retired dentist or truck driver?
- Does the writer claim to be the wife, son, lawyer, or banker of a General, Chief or Prince?
- Do the words "secret" or "confidential" appear?
- Do other addresses appear in the "copied to": section of this "confidential" email?

• Does the writer use a free email service (Yahoo, Hotmail)? (Edelson 2006, 65)

Other warning signs include odd spellings, flowery phrases and awkward modes of language use in the body of the e-mail.

> With all the resources of the Web available to most people and organizations with e-mail, why don't more folks uncover the story of this scam for themselves? You may well ask. There are sites all over the Web describing the Nigerian letter in detail. Still, according to the 419 Coalition, a Nigerian based group that actively fights the scam, the letter is reportedly the third largest industry in Nigeria, and has cost the world more than five billion dollars over the past 15 years. Not to mention costing at least 15 people their lives. (Chuck 2002, 116)

As mentioned, there are abundant websites focusing on the Nigerian (419) scam. Scam Detectives, from the United Kingdom, http://www.scam-detectives. co.uk/, include sectors on e-mail scams, employment scams and charity scams. The major e-mail scams discussed on the site include phishing e-mails, designed to gather usernames and passwords for financial institutions and credit cards on a fake website to enable scammers to access those accounts; dating scams; viruses and malware; lottery scams; and advance fee frauds, discussed here.

Interview with a "Scammer"

In an interview conducted on January 22, 2010, with a Nigerian 419 scammer, the scammer identifies himself as a gang member with strong English and computer skills. There was a disclaimer regarding this conversation, but regardless of its authenticity, it offers intriguing possible background aspects of this scam. Excerpts from a series of three interviews follow:

> First you need to understand how the gangs work. At the bottom are the "foot soldiers," kids who spend all of their time online to find email addresses and send out the first emails to get people interested. When they receive a reply, the victim is passed up the chain, to someone who has better English to get copies of ID from them like copies of their passport and driving licenses and build up trust. Then when they are ready to ask for money, they are passed further up again to someone who will pretend to be a barrister or shipping agent who will tell the victim that they need to pay charges or even a bribe to get the big cash amount out of the country. When they pay up, the gang master will collect the money from the Western Union office, using fake ID that they have taken from other scam victims. ("Interview with a Scammer, Part 1")

> Once I had spent some time as a "foot soldier" (*sending out initial approaches and passing serious victims to other scammers) I was promoted to act as either a barrister, shipping agent or bank official. In the early days I had a supervisor who would read my emails and suggest responses, then I was left to do it myself.

I had lots of different documents that I would use to convince the victim that I was genuine, including photographs of an official looking man in an office, fake ID and storage manifests, bank statements showing the money, whatever would best convince the victim that I, and the money, was real. I think the English term is to "worm my way" into their trust, taking it slowly and carefully so I didn't scare them away by asking for too much money too soon. ("Interview with a Scammer, Part 2")

We had something called the recovery approach. A few months after the original scam, we would approach the victim again, this time pretending to be from the FBI, or the Nigerian Authorities. The email would tell the victim that we had caught a scammer and had found all of the details of the original scam, and that the money could be recovered. Of course there would be fees involved as well. Victims would often pay up again to try and get their money back. ("Interview with a Scammer, Part 2")

The biggest thing I can say is to delete the emails and never to reply. Once you reply your email address *will* be put on a list and sold to other gangs, even if you never reply again. It just tells them that the address is real and that somebody reads email going to that address. If they can't get you with 419 [advance fee fraud] they will try phishing or viruses to get your banking details and take your money that way. I used lots of different stories to get people to send money. I used the dying widow story a lot, saying that I was an old lady dying of cancer and had fallen out with my children. I wanted to give my money to charity and didn't trust them to carry out my wishes, so was looking for someone outside of the country to make sure it went to the right place. So whatever the story is, make sure you delete the email, because you can be sure it is a scam. ("Interview with a Scammer, Part 3")

A recent variant on this scam is the romance scam, or Internet seduction, in which a con artist joins an online dating service or a social networking site and gains the trust and affection of the target. He or she claims interest in meeting or building a serious relationship, but in order to do so, he or she needs funds from the mark. Other variations include Craigslist services, lotteries and fake banks. Even more insidious is this variation using the Internet Relay system for the deaf.

Special services allow the deaf to use Web pages to connect with specially trained operators, who place telephone calls on their behalf and act as translators. Several relay operators say the system is often abused by criminals—many from Nigeria—who use it to place free international phone calls. Also, the fact that a relay operator is placing the call can put merchants off their guard. Some fall for the ploy, and find themselves shipping Bibles or wedding dresses to Nigeria, anything that can be sold for a small profit. (Sullivan 2005)

Selected Resources on the "Nigerian Scam"

Several books have been penned on this topic including Charles Tive's *419 Scam: Exploits of the Nigerian Con Man* (iUniverse, 2006); Chidi Igwe's *Taking Back Nigeria from 419: What to Do about the Worldwide E-Mail Scam/Advance Fee Fraud* (iUniverse, 2007); and *Mountains of Gold: An Exploratory Research on Nigerian 419-Fraud* by Yvette M. M. Shoenmakers, E. De Vries Robbe and A. P. Van Wijk (Amsterdam: SWP, 2009).

Barbara Mikkelson discusses the "Nigerian Scam" at Snopes.com (http://www.snopes.com/fraud/advancefee/nigeria.asp) and includes links to information about the scam from the U.S. Secret Service, the Federal Trade Commission and the Better Business Bureau. Other websites that offer detailed and essential information about this scam include Scambusters (http://www.scambusters.org/NigerianFee.html), Nigerian Scam (http://www.nigerianscam.com) and Nigeria-The 419 Coalition Website (http://home.rica.net/alphae/419coal/). This latter website includes links for country-specific information for reporting fraud attempts for Australia, Belgium, Canada, the Netherlands, South Africa, the United Kingdom and the United States. Both the Canadian government (http://www.antifraudcentre-centreantifraude.ca/english/recognizeit_advfeefraud.html) and the Royal Mounted Canadian Police websites (http://www.rcmp-grc.gc.ca/scams-fraudes/west-ouest-africa-eng.htm) contain detailed information about how to recognize the "Nigerian/West African Fraud" as well as directives for reporting the fraud attempts. The RCMP site requests that these letters and e-mails received by Canadians be forwarded to the Canadian Anti-Fraud Centre to aid them in the strategic targeting of would-be fraudsters.

Social Network Warnings

Social networking sites are often considered dangerous by people unfamiliar with the phenomenon regardless of how often reassurances are offered regarding personal security theft and computer viral activity as a result of indiscriminately clicking on embedded links on the social networking page. Several worms have surfaced on Facebook recently: "Koobface Virus," "Profileye Worm" and "Error Check Worm," to name a few.

"Koobface Virus," an anagram for Facebook, is a virus that results from clicking on a fake message from a friend directing the user to watch a video on YouTube or view a photo. The link takes the user to a site telling him or her to update his or her software in order to view the video or photograph. Clicking on the update begins a cyclical pattern that infects the user's friend list. This virus also affects people using Friendster, MySpace, Bebo, Tagged and LiveJournal, to mention only a few. "Profileye Worm" and "Error Check Worm" are very similar in that they are disguised as Facebook applications that, if one added them to the Facebook profile, worm their way into collecting profile data and spreading it across Facebook. Profileye suggests that the user check to see who has viewed the user's profile by installing the application, while "Error Check Worm" claims that a known Facebook user had faced errors when checking the recipient's profile and to view the error's message. Other variants include "stalker apps" that post messages such as "I've just seen who checks me out most here on Facebook! You can see who stalks you too!" Clicking on the accompanying link reposts the message on the walls of all the recipient's friends. These types of scams are referred to as clickjacking scams. One that circulated widely during March 2011 was an invitation to view a video of a whale "smashed into a building" during the tsunami in Japan following the earthquakes. Clicking on this video replicated the posting on the profile pages of others. The bottom line in these cases is not to believe everything that one reads or is posted on one's social networking page!

Chain Letters

Chain letters, now mostly transmitted via e-mail, text messaging and social networks such as Facebook, are relatively effortless compared to the chain letters of the past. Before, the recipient had to make physical copies of each of the messages that were to be forwarded to the chosen recipients, but now, a mere click on the keyboard does it all. Chain letters, then and now, include a list of names and instructions for the receiver to remove the name at the top of the list, add their name to the bottom of the list and forward the adapted message to a certain number of people. The chain letter promises good luck, often unspecified, to those who continue the chain and dire bad fortune to those who break the chain by refusing to forward it. The basic outline includes an invocation or hook: an admonition to pray, trust the Lord or other expression of faith and friendship followed by a statement of origin regarding the chain letter itself. The origin statement includes the name of a person who allegedly began the chain, how many times the letter had circulated bringing good fortune to those who cooperated and the specific number of people this particular letter must be forwarded to immediately. These instructions are followed by several anecdotes demonstrating the good fortune that came to others along with warnings regarding the misfortunes that befell those who broke the chain as well as the mechanics of the actual directives as mentioned earlier (Dégh 2001, 189). The hook "heightens the reader's emotional awareness to the message's content after which the message attempts to influence the recipients' behavior by evoking their greed, sympathy, or fear. Once this is achieved, a request to resend the transmission is implemented and the recipient is faced with the decision to continue the transmission or ignore it" (Blank 2007, 16). The included warning or threat functions as insurance that the chain letter will be forwarded as quickly as possible.

Besides the luck-generating (or ill luck avoidance) chain letters described previously, there are several other categories of contemporary chain letters. The money-generating chain letters, also known as pyramid or Ponzi schemes, promise untold riches to those who participate in their circulation. Others are altruistic, seeking benefit for others rather than financial enrichment or enhancement of good fortune, and include prayers for the suffering and collections made on behalf of charitable groups or those in need themselves. A prevalent example of the altruistic chain letter is the dying child hoax such as the "postcards for Buddy" messages circulating in the 1990s and the Jessica Mydek plea repudiated by the American Cancer Society. The following excerpt has been posted on the American Cancer Society's website in which the society offers a disclaimer regarding the chain letter appeal. The society assures people that they had never endorsed the effort and mentioned several variants, including one that had a picture of "Tickle Me Elmo" accompanying the appeal. The text of the original message reads as follows:

LITTLE JESSICA MYDEK IS SEVEN YEARS OLD AND IS SUFFERING FROM AN ACUTE AND VERY RARE CASE OF CEREBRAL CARCINOMA. THIS CONDITION CAUSES SEVERE MALIGNANT BRAIN TUMORS AND IS A

TERMINAL ILLNESS. THE DOCTORS HAVE GIVEN HER SIX MONTHS TO LIVE.

AS PART OF HER DYING WISH, SHE WANTED TO START A CHAIN LETTER TO INFORM PEOPLE OF THIS CONDITION AND TO SEND PEOPLE THE MESSAGE TO LIVE LIFE TO THE FULLEST AND ENJOY EVERY MOMENT, A CHANCE THAT SHE WILL NEVER HAVE. FURTHERMORE, THE AMERICAN CANCER SOCIETY AND SEVERAL CORPORATE SPONSORS HAVE AGREED TO DONATE THREE CENTS TOWARD CONTINUING CANCER RESEARCH FOR EVERY NEW PERSON THAT GETS FORWARDED THIS MESSAGE. PLEASE GIVE JESSICA AND ALL CANCER VICTIMS A CHANCE.

IF THERE ARE ANY QUESTIONS, SEND THEM TO THE AMERICAN CANCER SOCIETY AT ACS@AOL.COM.

This particular chain letter with its heartbreaking story appears to have struck an emotional chord with online users. Although we are very concerned that the American Cancer Society's name has been used to manipulate the online public, we applaud the good intentions of all who participated in this letter. We are pleased to note that there are so many caring individuals out there and hope that they will find another way to support cancer research. Jessica Mydek's story, whether true or false, is representative of that of many cancer patients who benefit daily from the efforts of legitimate cancer organizations nationwide. (http://www.ou.edu/oupd/acsmidek.htm)

Still other chain letters promise "something for nothing" with appeals to augment the bank account or bring fame to those who participate. Basically practical jokes, this type of chain letter includes e-mail tracking hoaxes and *Guinness Book of World Records* hoaxes. An increasingly frequent type of chain letter is not meant to prompt recipients to forward the chain letter but is a piece intended for humor and parody, meant solely for entertainment (Mikkelson 2009a).

Photographic Urban Legends

Two types of purposefully altered photographs aimed at perpetuating a hoax have historically been of interest to folklorists. The first are spirit photographs, alleged to capture the paranormal manifestations on film, and the second are tall tale photographs that typically depicted gigantic fruit or vegetables on a farm wagon or train, or beasts like the jackalope, half jackrabbit and half antelope (Frank 2011, 216). With the advent of the Internet and digital photography, however, a third type of hoax photograph emerged: the photoshopped image. The terms "photoshopped" and "photoshops" derive from the ubiquitous software program "Photoshop" which allows users to alter, enhance and otherwise manipulate digital images. Photoshops, in this instance, are defined as narrative photographs that, like many photographs in the news, appear to be strange but true. Unlike the news photographs, however, they are photoshopped, the images manipulated, and are fakes that generate consideration by illustrating current fears and anxieties. These are considered folklore "because as expressive behavior they are a form of subversive play, circulating in an underground communicative universe that runs parallel to and often parodies, mocks, or comments mordantly on such 'official' channels of communication as the mass media" (Frank 2003, 122). To be considered photographic urban legends, these photoshopped images must tell a story. "A photo of an occurrence, however—whether it shows something that has already happened, or something that is happening or about to happen—implies a plot as defined by Georges: 'a series of incidents set in a specific locale and presented in a logical time sequence that builds to a kind of climax' (1976:9)" (Frank 2003, 123). As Frank points out, digitally altered photographs are not the only images circulating on the Internet. Often real photographs, with false back stories, become illustrated contemporary legends. Snopes.com categorizes photographs and video clips under the heading "Fauxtography" and includes a wide array of subheadings such as accidents, advertisements, Hurricane Katrina, the 2004 tsunami and supernatural and paranormal phenomena. Some of the images in their files are not hoaxes at all but are authentic images submitted by their readers. While editing this section of the book, a Facebook friend circulated a link to a blog entry entitled "15 Animals You Won't Believe Aren't Photoshopped." The item, posted August 15, 2011, had been viewed by 261,246 people when the link to the blog entry arrived. However, without any explanation, the posting had been removed by September 9, 2011.

An even more immediate image circulated after Hurricane Irene in late August 2011. The image was of a great white shark prowling the flooded streets of Puerto Rico. The photograph appeared on Reddit.com on August 24, and was debunked as a hoax the same day. The shark is just the latest entry in contemporary legends and netlore of aquatic predator sightings in urban areas suffering from flooding: sharks and alligators were reportedly swimming in downtown New Orleans after Hurricane Katrina (2005), and flesh-eating piranhas swam in a flooded Nashville shopping mall after escaping from a storm-damaged aquarium (2010). Perhaps equally unbelievable but definitely true were the sea lions moving rather frantically through a shopping mall in Edmonton during a Christmas Seal campaign in 1973. While no photographs captured the occasion, my husband's well-meaning fund-raising event resulted in similar sightings.

Russell Frank ascertains that there are two distinct types of humorously digitally altered photographs that emerged following the terrorist attacks of September 11. The first, newslore of vengeance, consists of fantasies of annihilation or humiliation aimed at Osama bin Laden or Afghanistan, where it was rumored he was hiding. Newslore of victimization, the second type, expresses incomprehension at fate or chance for people who lived and died in the attack (Frank 2004, 633). These digitally altered photographs, along with other items of newslore, illuminate the relationship between folklore and news, challenge mainstream news media representations of public reaction to the events and highlight the role of the Internet as "a communication underground where such challenges to the hegemony of the mainstream news media may be mounted" (Frank 2004, 634). In his study on the September 11-based "photoshops," the preferred term among the people responsible for these images, Frank found that more than half of them deal with revenge in one form or another. This chapter, however, focuses on his example for the second category, the newslore of victimization.

"Tourist Guy"

The photograph, that of the "Tourist Guy "or "Accidental Tourist" as it is labelled by Snopes, depicted a doomed tourist posing on the observation deck of a World Trade Center tower moments before a hijacked airline smashed into the building. Apparently, the intact camera was later found in the wreckage of the towers.

The original Tourist Guy image was plausible, at least at first glance, more urban legend than joke. The apparent motive of the first wave of e-mailers was not to amuse but to appal. Once the picture had been debunked, however, the sense of victimization gave way to relief: Tourist Guy, like the rest of us, had survived. The endless permutations of Tourist Guy that followed, coinciding with the reduced sense of imminent threat as the days and weeks after September 11 passed without follow-up attacks, seemed to place September 11 in historical context: as horrific as it was, we had come through other horrific events. We would come through this one as well. The jokes do more than express anxiety; they grapple with it. (Frank 2011, 81)

Chicago Sun-Times columnist Richard Roeper refers to these images as "photographic urban legends" (Frank 2004, 650). Frank cites, from various sources including Netlore and Roeper, the following questions and observations about the photograph that exposed it as a hoax. The original photograph and the resulting image gallery of variants and permutations can be found at http://Touristof Death.com (August 15, 2011) and at http://www.snopes.com/rumors/photos/ tourist.asp (August 15, 2011).

- Why isn't the fast-moving aircraft blurry in the photo?
- Why doesn't the subject (or the photographer, for that matter) seem to be aware of the plane's high-decibel approach?
- The temperature was between 65 and 70 degrees that morning. Why is this man dressed for winter?
- How did the camera survive the 110-story fall when the tower collapsed?
- How was the camera found so quickly amidst all the rubble?
- Why has this one-of-a-kind, newsworthy photo not appeared in any media venue?
- There was no observation deck on the north tower, and the deck on the south tower wasn't scheduled to open until 9:30 that day.
- The American Airlines jet shown in the photo is a Boeing 757, but the American Airlines plane that struck the tower was a Boeing 767. (Frank 2004, 650–51)

When revealed as a hoax, the photograph did not vanish from the Internet and e-mail messages but quickly gave way to parodies of the hoax. Instead of an airplane, Tourist Guy stands before a subway car or a hot-air balloon, or the Stay-Puft Marshmallow Man from the *Ghostbusters* film of 1984 that rushes towards him on the observation tower. Or, instead of being on the tower, he visits other disasters: the crash of the Concorde in 2000; the Kennedy motorcade in Dallas in 1963; the crash of the Graf zeppelin in 1937; the sinking of the *Titanic* in 1912 and in the 1997 movie of that disaster; as well as in Abraham Lincoln's box in Ford's Theatre in 1865 among others (Frank 2004, 651).

Photographic Parodies: "Roaming Gnomes"

Other parodies involving photographs and photoshopped images circulate widely on the Internet. One popular example is that of "Roaming Gnomes." In *Tales, Rumors, and Gossip*, I briefly examine "Roaming Gnomes" as an example of ostension. Then, and now, lawn ornaments, particularly those of gnomes, disappear from various private properties, to return later after a whirlwind vacation accompanied by documented photographic proof of their journeys (de Vos 1996,

61–62). Bennett and Smith consider this story a practical joke or hoax, extremely popular in Australia and the United Kingdom but not in the United States (Bennett and Smith 2007, 28). It was, however, a well-known phenomenon here in Canada during the late 1980s and 1990s. But the roaming gnomes' photographic chronicled journeys did not entirely vanish. Murphy the garden gnome, for example, traveled to 12 countries before returning home to Gloucestershire, England, in 2008. Now, with the advent of digital cameras, photographs of the roaming gnomes colonize Internet sites. Also, because of the ease of digitally altering photographs, the roaming gnome does not actually need to travel to be included in many of the images depicting him in various tourist spots.

Besides the photographic images of these traveling gnomes, there are numerous clubs and organizations dedicated to "roaming gnomes," the most prominent being the Garden Gnome Liberation Front (also known as the Front for the Liberation of Garden Gnomes—*le Front pour la Libération des Nains de Jardin* [FLNJ]) first introduced to France in 1997. After several years of relatively quiet, the Front "liberated" 20 gnomes from a Parisian garden show in 2000, demanding that the gnomes be released into their natural habitat and not be deemed cheap yard decorations. In 2006, 80 gnomes were again stolen in France. There are active branches of the Liberation Front in other areas of Europe as well.

Various products and advertising campaigns have been developed utilizing the idea of the yard gnomes being kidnapped and going on vacations. In 2004, a widely distributed advertisement asking for information regarding a missing garden gnome circulated which included a toll-free hot line and website address (http://www.whereismygnome.com). More than 308,000 people visited the website featuring postcards of the gnome in exotic locations, while another 140,000 people called the hot line in the following weeks. The advertisements, website and toll-free telephone line were part of a new Travelocity advertising campaign. The lawn ornament is still being utilized as an icon for the company to this day. A search on the online photo-sharing site, Flickr, for the term "roaming gnomes" brought forth almost 2,500 results on August 17, 2011. Consumers can also adopt fridge magnet "gnomes on the go" at http://www.gnomeonthego.com website. Each of the magnets has a unique tracking number that can be entered on the website so its travels can be followed by all. The introduction on the site credited the movie *Amelie* as the inspiration for these "flat" traveling gnomes.

Additional Netlore Examples

A myriad of examples can be included in this section, but space restrictions demand a judicial decision in establishing criteria for selection which includes: contemporary relevance, widespread distribution and longevity of the specific contemporary legends.

Contemporary Legends Reflecting Domestic or International Crisis

Contemporary legends proliferate in times of domestic or international crisis. This phenomenon is exemplified by legends circulating immediately in the aftermath of the September 11 attacks on the World Trade Center and the 2011 earthquake disaster in Japan and the resultant fear of radiation leaks from nuclear fallout.

"The Grateful Stranger"

Diane Goldstein reports that among the numerous and varied legends circulating immediately after September 11, many of the narratives focused on the theme of foreknowledge (Goldstein 2009, 237). The most widespread of these relates the tale of the "Grateful Stranger" in which a woman who performs a simple kindness for a stranger is rewarded by his telling her to avoid a certain place on a certain day. The first wave of tales told about Middle Eastern male protagonists who warn people about staying out of shopping malls that Halloween. This version circulated orally and electronically in North America, deterring shoppers from the malls and Halloween activities in those malls (Goldstein 2009, 238). Another variant circulating at the same time had a Middle Eastern male disappearing from his apartment prior to September 11 but leaving a note for his girlfriend or wife warning her not to fly on that date nor to go to any shopping malls on October 31. Specific mentions of Halloween in the shopping mall warnings are part of a larger tradition of Halloween contemporary legends from warnings about razor blades in Halloween treats to the rumors regarding the psychopaths roaming around various college campuses planning to kill dorm residents (Frank 2011, 74).

Current variants of the "Grateful Stranger" legend include warnings about drinking Coca-Cola after a certain (shifting) date, text messages circulating in New York during the first week of January 2009 regarding visiting Manhattan and, in May 2011, two warnings regarding the Paris Metro and attending Tea Party events because of anticipated terrorist attacks. The variants circulating during the Israeli attack on Gaza in January 2009 specifically targeted the Jewish population around New York City. Warnings to avoid specific locations such as bridges and tourist locations and the entire Manhattan area on a certain date proliferated during that time. "Officials said they knew of no credible threats matching any version of the story, which New York Deputy Police Commissioner Paul Browne dismissed as an 'urban myth' " (Emery "The Grateful Tourist"). Barbara Mikkelson also assures her readers that these rumors are not grounded in reality but are expressions of fear about events that might unfold and that more harm was about to come, and, also, an aspect of wishful thinking (Mikkelson 2011d). Goldstein affirms that foreknowledge stories contain the wish that people can protect themselves from terrorism by advance knowledge of approaching danger (Goldstein 2009, 241). There seems to be a marked difference, however, in the foreknowledge legends of September 11 and the variants that preceded or followed them. "The September 11th foreknowledge stories seem to provide stark contrasts in public relations to terrorism versus our reactions to other disasters or historical war parallels. Information is still a commodity but those who have it or seem to have it are the enemy" (Goldstein 2009, 245).

"Acid Rain Fallout"

Immediately after reports of the possible meltdown of the Fukishima Daiichi nuclear power plant after the March 2011 massive earthquake in Japan, countless news reports and e-mail messages circulating internationally and in North America highlighted the terror the world collectively faced. From false maps showing the projected path of fallout across the western coastal areas of North America to shortages of ionized salt in Asian shops, newslore items struggled to both reassure and horrify their readers regarding the environmental repercussions of the disaster. Snopes.com assures their readers that "as of March 17, 2011, government officials debunked false information circulating widely and affirmed that any radiation that might reach the United States would have extremely minor health consequences" ("Nuclear Fallout Map" 2011).

David Emery, in his March 15, 2011, About.com urban legends column, also posted that these false warnings of health threats spread through Asia via text messages, e-mail, Facebook and Twitter despite government assurances that there was no imminent danger (Emery "Nuclear"). The messages, alleged to have originated from a news flash from the British Broadcasting Corporation (denounced as a hoax by the BBC), read:

> Japan Government confirms radiation leak at Fukushima nuclear plants. Asian countries should take necessary precautions. Remain indoors first 24 hours. Close doors and windows. Swab neck skin with Betadine where thyroid area is, radiation hits thyroid first. Take extra precaution radiation may hit Philippines starting at 4 pm today. Please send to your loved ones.

These messages were quickly disseminated all over Asia creating panics in various countries. Almost as quickly, warnings against the "acid rain" e-mail hoaxes were published by reliable sources such as the *Los Angeles Times* (March 19, 2011), the *Philippine Star* (March 15, 2011) and the *Times of India* (March 15, 2011), but people tended to forward the hoaxes regardless, just to be on the safe side. A purchasing frenzy on additional items such as iodized salt and diapers was also reportedly a result of these false hoaxes. In Korea, for example, it was believed that diapers manufactured in Japan after the nuclear explosions would be contaminated with radioactive materials. State education officials in the Philippines issued an advisory on March 16, 2011, to public schools not to panic because of unfounded text messages and e-mails and that all text messages must be verified before any action is undertaken. The Polytechnic University of the Philippines in Manila suspended classes the day before because of the text rumors, prompted, officials maintained, because of the multitude of calls from concerned parents. More recently, on July 5, 2011, it was reported that customers were avoiding used cars from Fukushima Prefecture because of the rumors that vehicles were radioactively contaminated. Interestingly, the original article was no longer available online a month later although there were numerous references to the news report from Mainichi, Japan, still available in a search in August 2011.

Scarelore

> *In modern legends, the forest has been replaced by an urban landscape peopled with drug dealers, kidnappers, paedophiles, Satanists and unspecified bad people. These characters lurk in shopping malls (usually in the parking lots), in suburban neighbourhoods (usually in abandoned houses) and along the roadside. Contemporary legends see children threatened by drugs (particularly heroin and LSD), by syringes and hypodermic needles, by knives, axes and razor blades, and by gangs using petrol bombs as part of bizarre gang initiations ceremonies.*
>
> —Croft (2006, 1056)

Scarelore, a major category of forwardable folklore, incorporates dire messages warning the recipients of dangers that reflect the fears, anxieties and obsessions of contemporary society (Kibby 2005, 781). Many of these warnings circulated orally in previous renditions such as the legend of the "attempted abduction." "One problem that could result from a belief in this legend is a heightened sense of fear in these various parks and stores. Another fear that could be created is a heightened fear of strangers as well as minorities. ... The legend also victimizes the young and innocent, which is a large concern in society" (Cruz 2008, 11). As Rolf Brednich stated at the beginning of this century, the Internet has become the prime breeding ground for a new generation of contemporary, sometimes even dangerous, legends (Brednich 2001, 9). This forecast has certainly had legs, with an increasing number of instances of scarelore appearing as emerging legends or as legends clothed in updated garments to make them even more relevant.

"Bumping the Bumper"

> New gang initiation . . . . they bump your car. You stop; they shoot you. This started last night (3/26/2008). Warn your family and friends. Letters are being passed out today in North Dallas schools. If this happens to you, you need to keep driving until you get to a public place where people are milling around. Do not stop! Call the police as you continue driving. Tell them where you are, what direction you are heading, and describe the car that bumped you if you can.

One variant of the e-mail warning encourages the receiver to forward the warning to all friends and family members saying "it is better to receive this email 25 times and it saves your life, than to ignore it and get killed" (Mikkelson 2011c).

Other gang-related contemporary legends that appear on Snopes.com and are considered false include targets randomly selected at Wal-Mart, by someone knocking on doors and asking for directions, throwing bricks at cars to get them to stop and spreading deadly poison on pay phone buttons. It seems that regardless of the vast amount of debunking about gang initiation legends circulating, people's fears and anxieties of gang-related concerns will override legitimate reassurances from politicians, police forces and folklorists.

"Burundanga"

This warning of criminals in various North American cities using Burundanga-soaked business cards to incapacitate their victims began circulating by e-mail in 2008. Burundanga, an extract of the datura plant from Colombia, contains alkaloids such as scopolamine and atropine, has no scent and needs to be inhaled or swallowed in order to affect females in the manner as described in the warnings: a strong odor that causes dizziness and disorientation after a few minutes of accepting the business cards. Burundanga, however, must be inhaled or ingested, or the person have prolonged topical contact with it, in order for it to have an effect. Barbara Mikkelson points out that the alkaloids are powerful toxins that can, at lower doses, produce dry mouth, dizziness and blurred vision and in higher doses can cause delirium and unconsciousness; but the drug is not available in North America. It is believed to be used in Colombia by robbers and rapists to render potential victims tractable, allowing the criminals to have them empty their bank accounts or act as drug mules for those who gave it to them. Typically, the drug is slipped into the food or drink of intended victims, or is packed into cigarettes or sticks of gum which are then offered to the targets, not embedded in a business card (Mikkelson 2011b).

> The [American] Embassy continues to receive reports of criminals using disabling drugs to temporarily incapacitate tourists and others. At bars, restaurants, and other public areas, perpetrators may offer tainted drinks, cigarettes, or gum ... Avoid leaving food or drinks unattended at a bar or restaurant, and be suspicious if a stranger offers you something to eat or drink. (Mikkelson 2011b)

Copycat reports of such crimes taking place followed the widespread dissemination of the e-mail warnings. Police reports maintain that the events did not happen as reported and that the victims were not in danger from any type of drug-embedded pieces of paper. Mikkelson equates the copycat reports from this legend to those that followed the case of the perfume robbers legend circulating previously (Mikkelson 2011b). When discussing this latter legend, Meredith Cruz states that because of the relative newness of the legend, folklorists had not had the opportunity to research it. After collecting several versions on the Internet, she found several themes that correspond with the Burundanga business card tale. "The victim is often female, she is lured by 'discount perfume sellers,' who are robbers, she is knocked unconscious by a chemical and she is robbed" (Cruz 2008, 12).

"Dangerous Canola Oil"

E-mail and Facebook warnings have circulated since 2001 regarding the dangers of using Canola oil by consumers because of the toxic nature of this "genetically engineered plant developed in Canada from the rapeseed plant, which is part of the mustard family of plants." While the family relationship of rapeseed and mustard is factual, this example of scarelore is utilizing the probable correlation of poisonous mustard gas in the minds of readers. The scarelore also points out that Canola is not the name of a natural plant but a "made-up word from the words Canada and oil." While this is also factual, what the message does not state is that rapeseed was renamed in 1986 to distance the original name from the negative connotations of the word "rape." Most Canadians quickly adopted the new name for the crops, seeds and cooking oil without a quibble. The skeptical detective discusses this warning, with information gathered from Snopes.com on January 9, 2010, possibly as a consequence of inquiries resulting from a number of cooking blogs that include warnings about the dangers of canola oil in recipes (Angela 2010).

"Egged Windshields"

Gang members throw raw eggs at windshields with the knowledge that if the motorist attempts to clean the egg off with the car's wipers, he or she will make the situation worse and will be forced to stop and pull over. When my husband's windshield was hit by an egg thrown from the ditch along the highway this past spring, he did not pull over, but because of the location of the impact, he did not have to clear his windshield with the help of the washer fluid. Upon reporting the incident to the local RCMP attachment, he was told that there was nothing they could do about it since he did not stop and locate the miscreants. They apparently were not aware of the connection to the gang initiation legend. The warnings circulating about the egging all caution recipients against using their windshield wipers and fluid as it mixes with the egg and definitely impedes visibility. "This is a new technique used by gangs, so please inform your friends and relatives. These are desperate times and these are unsavoury individuals who will take desperate measures to get what they want. *Please BE SAFE AND NEVER STOP YOUR VEHICLE*" (collected via e-mail and Facebook, January 13, 2011).

"Gang Initiation" (Lights Out!)

A ubiquitous contemporary legend warning, transmitted orally, by fax machines and flyers, and by electronic means such as e-mail, social networking sites and personal web pages and blogs has been circulating since the early 1990s. The warning claims that prospective gang members are being initiated by killing the drivers of cars who innocently and helpfully flash their headlights at them to notify them that their vehicles are being driven at night without any lights. The warning caused a major scare in the United States and Canada when it first circulated, and then it went dormant for about five years until it gained prominence again with the release of the 1998 film *Urban Legend* in which it was a key plot device. Jan Harold Brunvand does not credit the film with the resurgence of this legend, but instead attributes it to cluttered bulletin boards and desk drawers that have not been cleared of the older warnings. "Urban rumors and legends that have such printed or published texts often return without warning, or seemingly without any actual incident to spur their reappearance" (Brunvand 2001b, 242). Bill Ellis reports a variant that countered the gang involvement:

> When American legends were actively circulating that held that gangs would follow and murder the occupants of any car that blinked its lights at them, the author heard a counter-rumor that police were encouraging the spread of this story for their own purposes. Since motorists often warned each other of speed traps by blinking their lights at each other, this counter-rumor held, any "urban legend" that discouraged this practice would allow police to issue more speeding tickets. (Ellis 2005, 125)

Many police departments and newspapers actually attempt to alleviate anxiety of the gang initiation warning by issuing denials, but this seems only to fuel the fears further and not everyone takes heed of the genuine warnings about the false ones. Most of these hoax warnings include names and contact information of credible people such as police officers which resulted in cautionary information being circulated on the police websites denying their authenticity. On November 20, 1998, Canada's Minister of Defence, Art Eggleton, issued an urgent security warning for all Ontario Members of Parliament regarding this piece of folklore. Later that day, his office issued an update advising recipients that the original story was a hoax. By 2004 the initiation hoax was circulating in Britain, Mexico, and beyond. Fears of teenage and gang crimes, racism, urban problems and attacks on foreigners are topics underlying the hysteria produced by this hoax (Brunvand 2000, 104). Howell reaffirms the prominent role of gangs in contemporary urban youth culture. Youth gangs are feared by the general public, admired and emulated by many young people and provide constant fodder for the media (Howell 2007). Barbara Mikkelson asserts that while there have been instances of initiations into street gangs that lead to the murder of random victims, they have been rare and do not involve gang hopefuls being commanded to take the lives of the haphazardly selected (Mikkelson 2011c). Joel Best and Mary Hutchinson concur, stating that newspaper accounts use initiation rites to explain unsolved crimes (Best and Hutchinson 1996, 383).

All of the contemporary legends mentioning gang initiations contain several similar elements: demands that the initiates commit violence against random strangers; the victims are most often women or children; the violence seems pointless and its only purpose is to fulfil the demands of the initiation rite; and gang members are frequently identified as members of ethnic minorities while their victims, implicitly if not explicitly, belong to the white majority (Best and Hutchinson 1996, 389).

"Halloween Gang Initiations" or "Red October"

> I just received a text from a friend whose mother works as a court official in NYC. Her mom got a memo this morning stating that the Bloods are having their gang initiation in NYC this weekend and that they will be targeting 20–30 women, doing drive-by shootings from a silver SUV. Please send this along to any girl you know living in NYC area and be safe & alert this weekend. Hopefully this won't even happen but I just wanted to pass it on regardless. (Collected via e-mail, October 2008)

Modifications on this contemporary legend include similar updated techniques and circulated in October 2009 on Facebook with non-specific geographic information instead of the earlier messages targeting specified states and cities.

"Infant Car Seat"

> So I just got a phone call from my mom who lives out in Alberta saying they just got e-mails warning women about new gang initiations. A woman in Red Deer was driving down the highway and saw an infant car seat on the side of the road with a blanket draped over it. She didn't stop but drove to the nearest RCMP detachment and reported it. Turns out it is a new gang initiation to get women to stop on the side of the road for an infant car seat (which is usually placed near a grassy or wooded area) with a doll in it. Once the women stop, the gang grab them and rape, beat and leave them for dead. Disgusting!!! This woman had an instinct not to stop and good thing she didn't. So please don't stop for an infant car seat on the side of roads call your RCMP or police. (Collected via e-mail and Facebook, September 15, 2010)

The same message has circulated regarding warnings against "National Gang Week." A March 2010 version combined the "fake baby in a blood soaked car seat" warning with one about eggs being thrown at motorists' windshields. Versions in circulation in August 2010 repositioned the co-joined warning about baby car seats and eggs thrown at windshields into one issued in Europe.

"Killer Clowns"

Sandy Hobbs and David Cornwell examine the legend of the killer clowns that had circulated in Scotland in 1991. The legend concerns children being approached by ill-intentioned adults dressed as clowns (Hobbs and Cornwell 2001, 207). In examining the variants they had collected regarding this legend, they discovered that the most common methodology used was clowns giving or offering children candy. However, what happened next is not always consistent in the stories, or even mentioned (Hobbs and Cornwell 2001, 207). There are several references in the collected variants to the "Chelsea Smilers" legend, discussed as "Smiley Gang" in chapter 5 of this volume, but only a few of the variants mention extreme violence. The story seemed to drop out of sight in the catchment area in June 1992, only to resurface around Halloween in 1994. "At one of the schools, the head, unaware of the existence of the rumour, had caused consternation when he appeared at a Halloween party dressed as a clown" (Hobbs and Cornwell 2001, 211). The authors cite the discussion by Loren Coleman in his book *Mysterious America* (1983) in which he wrote about stories of threatening clowns in vans in the United States during the early 1980s and other sources demonstrating the earlier widespread dissemination of the story in other parts of the globe.

By 2004 the clown story circulating in North America became infused with even more audacious criminal activity as the killer clown is now disguised as a life-size clown doll or statue within the safe boundaries of the home. According to Barbara Mikkelson, the contemporary legend exists in two forms. In the first one, similar to the older legend of the babysitter and the man upstairs, it is the babysitter who appears to be the person at risk, while in the second variant, it is the children who are the target (Mikkelson 2004). Some versions in this second type carry an unmistakeable paedophilic element with a frightened child reporting being touched inappropriately by something in its room, while others only hinted at the sexual element by concluding the story with a comment that the "clown" was revealed to be a sexual predator wanted in several states (Mikkelson 2004). David Emery reports a chain-letter variant of this legend: "If you don't repost to 10 peeps within 5 minutes the clown will be standing next 2 your bed at 3:00 a.m. with a knife in his hand" (Emery "The Clown Statue"). Both Emery and Mikkelson mention a rather tentative connection to the real assassin, John Wayne Gacy, who had been labelled by the media as the "Killer Clown" for his habit of hosting neighbourhood parties at which he dressed as a clown. However, the clown costume was never utilized as part of his murdering spree.

"UPS Uniforms and Terrorism"

There has been a huge purchase, $32,000 worth, of United Parcel Service (UPS) uniforms on eBay over the last 30 days. This could represent a serious threat as bogus drivers (terrorists) can drop off anything to anyone with deadly consequences! If you have ANY questions when a UPS driver appears at your door they should be able to furnish VALID I.D.

Additionally, if someone in a UPS uniform comes to make a drop off or pick up, make absolutely sure they are driving a UPS truck. UPS doesn't make deliveries or pickups in anything, except a company vehicle. If you have a problem, call your local law enforcement agency right away!

TAKE THIS SERIOUSLY! Tell everyone in your office, your family, your friends, etc. Make people aware so that we can prepare and/or avoid terrorist attacks on our people! Thank you for your time in reviewing this and PLEASE send to EVERYONE

on your list, even if they are friend or foe. We should all be aware!
(Via e-mail April 29, 2011)

Barbara Mikkelson reports that this e-mail has been circulating since 2003 as
the result of a number of uniforms offered for sale on eBay at that time. "Because
our new terrorist-aware mode of thinking affects how we perceive events, many
people skipped over other potentially less terrifying explanations (e.g., uniform collectors adding to their stock . . .) and went straight to the assumption that UPS uniforms were being snapped up by terrorists" (Mikkelson 2011e). The April 2011
posting quoted above first appeared on the Los Angeles Police Department site,
lending credence and currency to the legend. The posting was speedily followed
by an update regarding the warning with the comment "This 'INFO' is apparently
an Internet Myth."

Telephones and the Contemporary Legend

With advances of any popular technological devices, similar to microwave
ovens first hitting the marketplace, a wide variety of rumors and legends circulate
about their inherent dangers. Contemporary legends regarding cell phones include
warnings about cell phones touching off explosions at gas stations. Despite the warnings posted at gas stations about this possibility there have been no documented
instances of a cell phone causing a fire or explosion anywhere. E-mail warnings tell
how cell phones can unlock any car equipped with remote keyless entry systems
(false); how eggs and popcorn can be cooked using activated cell phones (false); that
a child died during a routine operation because someone used a cell phone in the hospital (false); and that forwarding a text message to 10 other people obtains a substantial credit on your cell phone bill (false). The latter hoax is a direct successor to the
"giveaway hoaxes" which were popular in e-mail in-boxes earlier. A constructive
and true story involving the use of a cell phone circulated during January 2011.

> While walking home from the bus stop this week, a 13-year-old
> Norwegian school boy stumbled upon four wolves. In the end,
> it may have been his love of heavy-metal music by the band
> Creed that saved his life. . . . Remembering his parents' advice,
> Walter pulled the earphones out of his mobile phone, turned the
> volume all the way up and blasted heavy metal music over its
> miniature speakers. At the same time, he yelled as loud as he could
> while flailing his arms about wildly to scare off the pack of wild
> animals. (http://www.spiegel.de/international/zeitgeist/0,1518,
> 740680,00.html, August 17, 2011)

The story was reposted and repeated on various blogs following the online
publication of the article. However, in true contemporary legend tradition, as
David Pescovitz reports on the blog site "boingboing," certain details were changed
in the process including the last name of the boy and the band played over the
speakers (Pescovitz 2011).

"Grandparent"/"Emergency" Scam

For those who do not travel around with their phones on their person, danger
may come from someone dialling land lines at random.

Con-artist:	"Hi Grandma/Grandpa."
Victim:	"Hi."
Con-artist:	"Do you know who this is?"
Victim:	"John?"
Con-artist:	"Yeah."

The headline in my local community weekly paper, *The Village Voice*, submitted by the RCMP on January 25, 2011, was familiar to me: " 'Grandparent'/ 'Emergency' Scam PCD Update." The article summarizes the telephone scam that had been targeting senior citizens across North America for several years. A grandparent or elderly person receives a phone call from someone claiming to be one of his or her grandchildren. The caller states that he or she is in trouble, in jail, in a car accident, etc., and needs money. If the con artist is successful, money is wired, usually through Western Union, to a variety of locations. The author of this article claimed that over the past six months, 38 incidents were reported around the Edmonton, Alberta, region where I reside. Eleven people fell for the scam, transferring approximately $54,000 to unknown callers during that time. In December 2009, nine incidents were reported with five individuals transferring approximately $29,000 of their funds as a result of the telephone calls. On September 6, 2011, an article submitted by the Breton [Alberta] RCMP to the same local newspaper ascertained that the calls to seniors were still being made regarding the grandparent scam. The article strongly suggests that anyone receiving these types of calls should immediately call the local police department.

Although technically this is a scam rather than a contemporary legend, the stories told about the victims' and others' experiences with the phone calls circulated among the senior population. My mother delighted in telling me about two of her friends, in another part of the province, who received similar calls. Both of them were told by their "grandchildren" that they were too embarrassed to ask their parents for help and that they should not mention the call or request for funds to them. While some research had been done regarding the back stories supplied for these two grandmothers, one grandmother realized very quickly that it was a scam and hung up on the caller. The second grandmother was about to go to the bank when she thought critically about the call and realized that the grandson the caller had mentioned as a driver in a car accident could not have been driving as he is blind. Panic and concern had blinded her at first to the scam!

The government of Canada website includes the verbatim script for the "grandparent scam" included above and encourages people to contact the Canadian Anti-Fraud Centre (Phonebusters) if they receive such a call (http:// www.phonebusters.com/english/recognizeit_emergency.html). Among the other frauds discussed on the site is the "Nigerian Letter Scam" discussed earlier. The Scam Detectives from the United Kingdom discuss the scam in an online entry dated May 25, 2011 (http://www.scam-detectives.co.uk/blog/2011/05/25/elderly-targeted-in-cruel-grandparent-scam/). Snopes.com calls the scam "The Family Way," reminding their readers to verify all such calls and pleas before reacting. A quick search online will garner countless examples of the scam and as equal a number of debunking sites and places to contact on all continents to report suspicious occurrences.

Two other current telephone call scams reference lowering interest rates on credit cards and alleged calls from Microsoft Windows. The latter claims that they had received a report about a virus that had been downloaded to the listener's computer. They offer assistance in resolving the problem, instructing the listener to download software from the website. Anyone who followed the recommended instructions would now be the proud recipients of an active virus.

"Stolen Passport" Scam

Although this scam has been making the rounds for several years through e-mail messages, it is integrated here because of the inclusion of telephone numbers as part of the message. The latest round, utilizing the name of a successful author of children's books, Alma Flor Ada, circulated on the child_lit listerv followed by a warning to the membership that the message was not authentic. A quick search on debunking sites show that the message, almost word for word, has been sent using a variety of other names.

> Apologies for having to reach out to you like this, I made a quick trip to London, UK and had my bag stolen from me with my passport and credit cards in it. The embassy is willing to help by letting me fly without my passport, I just have to pay for a ticket and settle Hotel bills. Unfortunately for me, I can't have access to funds without my credit card, I've made contact with my bank but they need more time to come up with a new one. I was thinking of asking you to lend me some quick funds that I can give back as soon as I get in. I really need to be on the next available flight. I can forward you details on how you can get the funds to me. You can reach me via email or May field hotel's desk phone, the numbers are +447024029894 or +447024030611.

As Russell Frank comments, a contemporary legend, in this age of electronic reproduction, become more of a written phenomenon than an oral one, with some legends deriving their authority from assuming the guise of supposedly authoritative written genres, such as news stories, business memoranda and press releases, and visual genres such as the news photograph (Frank 2011, 220).

> Where the typical written legend aggressively asserts its factuality through the use of exclamation points, the sender's expression of disdain for junk e-mail, or even claims that the story has been certified by Snopes, the stories that parody official forms of communication rely on the rhetorical trappings of those forms . . . We can debate whether these parodies are subgenres of the contemporary legend, but they certainly possess some of the essential features of legends: they are narratives (implicitly so in the case of the phony news photo), they are fictions presented as matters of fact, and their subject matter tends, broadly, to engage with one modern bedevilment or other. (Frank 2011, 220)

Literary and Visual Adaptations

The contemporary legends in this chapter are not reworked with the same enthusiasm as the corpus of other contemporary legends discussed in this book. While there are numerous allusions to them in books of all genres, written for all reading audiences, this section focuses on story lines that more fully embody the legends.

E-mail Hoaxes

Wadlow, Jeff, and Beau Bauman. *Cry Wolf*. Directed by Jeff Wadlow, 2005.

In this slasher film which blends the idea of contemporary legends with modern technology, a group of students play a game called Cry Wolf. After a murder is committed on the campus, in order to deflect attention from their group, one of the students suggests creating a fake e-mail informing everyone about a serial killer who travels from campus to campus killing students. They describe the killer in great detail and the message goes viral. The film demonstrates how quickly and effectively a mediated e-mail can spread a contemporary legend, considered by many of the recipients as a true warning.

"Gang Initiation" (Lights Out!)

Pelland, Jennifer. "Headlights." In *Close Encounters of the Urban Kind*. Edited by Jennifer Brozek. Lexington, KY: Apex, 2010, 65–75.

Three teenage boys, getting ready to leave town after they finish high school, go for a ride in the country. The three, formerly friends, are not particularly at ease with each other when one becomes angry and pulls out a gun. "You know that Crips initiation ritual. The one where you drive with your headlights off, and then kill the first person who flashes their lights at you?" "Okay, first of all, that's a total myth. And second, you think pretending to be a Crip is a good idea? On what planet?"(69).

Unfortunately for the other two, it is the driver who has the gun. He switches off the headlights, and when an oncoming car flashes its lights at them, he chases it. The car vanishes, and when the boys go looking for it, a car chases them, stalking them and flashing its lights at them. When the narrator awakes, he finds himself captured by an alien and has to make a choice regarding sacrificing himself or one of his friends. His choice changes the direction of his life forever.

The author's afterword briefly discusses the contemporary legend of the gang initiation ritual, directs the reader to snopes.com and states that "to be honest, I think I chose it because it was the first urban legend that sprung to mind" (75).

"Killer Clowns"

Gutman, Dan. "I'm Not Afraid." In *Half-Minute Horrors*. Edited by Susan Rich. New York: Harper, 2009, 106–7.

In this very concise story, the first-person narrator assures his audience that he has not been frightened by the dark, the echoes, the noises, the cobwebs or the smells and dripping blood when he was legend tripping during Halloween at the old Granger Mansion. The only thing that frightened him is the clown!

Livings, Martin. "Lollo." In *Close Encounters of the Urban Kind*. Edited by Jennifer Brozek. Lexington, KY: Apex, 2010, 1–18.

When the children Jenny is babysitting are terrified of the clown statue, she throws a blanket on it but thinks that it is perhaps the strangest clown she had ever seen. When she mentions it to their mother later that evening when she phones, Jennifer is informed that they do not have a clown statue in their home. Examining the doll in an effort to control her own fears, Jenny soon realizes that she has every reason to be frightened. Interspersed with Jenny's story, provided as background noise, is the soundtrack from a nature documentary discussing specimen collections and their importance to those who studied the flora and fauna of a strange community.

In the afterword, the author states that he had encountered problems coming up with an idea for a story for this anthology until he stumbled across the story of a babysitter complaining to the parents about a clown statue, and being told that they did not own such a thing. "In the legend it's usually a psychopath, or sometimes a drunk circus midget. But my immediate, if odd, reaction was, how would an alien race infiltrate an ordinary house in order to examine the inhabitants or to collect samples" (18).

"Roaming Gnomes"

Bray, Libba. *Going Bovine*. New York: Delacorte Press, 2009.

> Some of my students have this project. They stole a yard gnome from somebody's lawn and have taken him on vacation all over the world. They pass him off to whoever's going on a trip next. (28)

The roaming gnome is a distinctive character in this award-winning young-adult novel. When the group of "heroes" kidnap Balder, the gnome, taking him with them on their road-trip adventure, they get much more than they bargain. Balder immediately informs the narrator, Cameron, "You and your friends are not to take any unauthorized pictures of me. I do not wish to show up on your Internet page posed in front of any national monuments or next to dubious signage with some obnoxious caption underneath. I've had quite enough of that" (259). Bray plays with Norse mythology with this character; not only is Balder a Norse god, tricked into the false form of a gnome by Loki, but the advertisement in the newspaper publicizes Valhalla Yard Gnomes, "Lawn Ornaments fit for a God" (173). After Balder is rescued, he grumpily informs Cameron that he was asleep during the rescue mission. "Next thing I knew I woke up in a strange hotel room with those three idiots. They took photographs of me on top of the minibar and e-mailed them to all their friends. Posing me with chocolate bars and soda cans. Can you imagine?" (393).

Jeunet, Jean-Pierre and Guilluame Laurant. *Amelie*. Directed by Jean-Pierre Jeunet , 2001.

After a gnome disappears its owner receives anonymously mailed photographs of the garden creature taken in different tourist locations around the world in a subplot of this French romantic comedy. There is some speculation by journalists that this film was used as inspiration for subsequent incidents of roaming gnome activity; an ostensive reaction to the film, rather than to the earlier stories and news reports.

Reitman, Jason and Sheldon Turner. *Up in the Air*. Directed by Jason Reitman, 2009. Adapted from the novel of the same name, written by Walter Kirn, published in 2001.

A subplot, involving a cardboard cutout of the main character's sister and her fiancée photographed in tourist locations, is referred to as "kind of like that gnome in the French movie."

References

" 'Abducted Children' Alert on Facebook Was False, Say Police." 2011. http://www .thisistamworth.co.uk/Abducted-children-alert-Facebook-false-say-police/story-12616564 -detail/story.html (accessed September 8, 2011).

Angela. 2010. "Is Canola Oil Dangerous?" The Skeptic Detective. http://skeptic detective.wordpress.com/2010/01/09/is-canola-oil-dangerous/ (accessed September 9, 2011).

Bennett, Gillian, and Paul Smith. 2007. *Urban Legends: A Collection of International Tall Tales and Terrors*. Westport, CT: Greenwood Press.

Best, Joel, and Mary M. Hutchinson. 1996. "The Gang Initiation Rite as a Motif in Contemporary Crime Discourse." *Justice Quarterly* 13 (3): 383–404.

Blank, Trevor J. 2007. "Examining the Transmission of Urban Legends: Making the Case for Folklore Fieldwork on the Internet." *Folklore Forum* 37 (1): 15–26.

Brednich, Rolf W. 2001. "Where They Originated . . . Some Contemporary Legends and Their Literary Origins." Paper presented at ISFNR Congress, Melbourne, Australia. http://www.folklore.ee/folklore/vol20/legends.pdf (accessed October 19, 2010).

Bronner, Simon J. 2009. "Digitalizing and Virtualizing Folklore." In *Folklore and the Internet: Vernacular Expression in a Digital World*. Edited by Trevor J. Blank. Logan: Utah State University Press, 21–66.

Brunvand, Jan Harold. 2000. " 'Lights Out!': A Faxlore Phenomenon." In *The Truth Never Stands in the Way of a Good Story*. Chicago: University of Illinois Press, 95–107.

Brunvand, Jan Harold. 2001a. *Encyclopedia of Urban Legends*. New York: Norton.

Brunvand, Jan Harold. 2001b. "Lights Out!" In *Encyclopedia of Urban Legends*. New York: Norton, 241–42.

Brunvand, Jan Harold. 2004a. *Be Afraid, Be Very Afraid: The Book of Scary Urban Legends*. New York: Norton.

Brunvand, Jan Harold. 2004b. "The Vanishing 'Urban Legend.' " *Midwestern Folklore* 30 (2): 5–20.

Chuck, Lysbeth B. 2002. "Welcome to the Dark Side: How E-Commerce, Online Consumer, and E-Mail Fraud Rely on Misdirection and Misinformation." In *Web of Deception: Misinformation on the Internet*. Edited by Anne P. Mintz. Medford, NJ: Information Today, 113–48.

Croft, Robin. 2006. "Folklore, Families and Fear: Exploring the Influence of the Oral Tradition on Consumer Decision-Making." *Journal of Marketing Management* 22:1053–76.

Cruz, Meredith E. 2008. *Fear of Crime and Belief in Urban Folklore: An Exploration of Urban Folklore and Fear*. Thesis, Master of Science in Criminology, the University of Texas at Dallas.

Dégh, Linda. 2001. *Legend and Belief: Dialectics of a Folklore Genre*. Bloomington: Indiana University Press.

de Vos, Gail. 1996. *Tales, Rumors, and Gossip: Exploring Contemporary Folk Literature in Grades 7–12*. Westport, CT: Libraries Unlimited.

Dunn, Henry B., and Charlotte A. Allen. 2005. "Rumors, Urban Legends and Internet Hoaxes." *Proceedings of the Annual Meeting of the Association of Collegiate Marketing Educators*. Dallas, TX: The University of Tennessee at Martin, 85–91. Available online at http://www.sbaer.uca.edu/research/acme/2005/10.pdf (accessed March 21, 2012).

Ebbinghouse, Carol. 2002. "Brother Have You Got a Dime? Charity Scams on the Web." In *Web of Deception: Misinformation on the Internet*. Edited by Anne P. Mintz. Medford, NJ: Information Today, 97–112.

Edelson, Eve. 2006. *Scamorama*. New York: Disinformation.

Ellis, Bill. 2001. *Aliens, Ghosts, and Cults: Legends We Live*. Jackson: University Press of Mississippi.

Ellis, Bill. 2005. "Legend/Antilegend: Humor as an Integral Part of the Contemporary Legend Process," In *Rumor Mills: The Social Impact of Rumor and Legend*. Edited by Gary Alan Fine, Veronique Campion-Vincent and Chip Heath. New Brunswick, NJ: Transaction, 123–40.

Emery, David. "The Clown Statue/the Clown Doll." About.com: Urban Legends. http://urbanlegends.about.com/od/horrors/a/clown_statue.htm (accessed September 9, 2011).

Emery, David. "The Grateful Terrorist." About.com: Urban Legends. http://urbanlegends.about.com/od/crime/a/grateful_terror.htm (accessed September 9, 2011).

Emery, David. 2011. " 'Nuclear Rain' Rumors Spread in Asia." http://urbanlegends.about.com/b/2011/03/15/nuclear-rain-rumors-asia.htm (accessed September 9, 2011).

Fernback, Jan. 2003. "Legends on the Net: An Examination of Computer-Mediated Communication as a Locus of Oral Culture." *New Media & Society* 5 (1): 29–45.

Fine, Gary Alan, and Patricia A. Turner. 2001. *Whispers on the Color Line: Rumor and Race in America*. Berkeley: University of California Press.

Frank, Russell. 2003. " 'Worth a Thousand Words': The Photographic Urban Legend and the Illustrated Urban Legend." *Contemporary Legend* n.s. 6:119–45.

Frank, Russell. 2004. "When the Going Gets Tough, the Tough Go Photoshopping: September 11 and the Newslore of Vengeance and Victimization." *New Media Society* 6: 633–58.

Frank, Russell. 2011. *Newslore: Contemporary Folklore on the Internet*. Jackson: University of Mississippi.

Goldstein, Diane E. 2009. "The Sounds of Silence: Foreknowledge, Miracles, Suppressed Narratives, and Terrorism—What Not Telling Might Tell Us." *Western Folklore* 68 (2/3): 235–55.

Heyd, Theresa. 2008. *Email Hoaxes: Form, Function, Genre Ecology*. Amsterdam: John Benjamins.

Hobbs, Sandy, and David Cornwell. 2001. "Killer Clowns and Vampires: Children's Panics in Contemporary Scotland." In *Supernatural Enemies*. Edited by Hilda Ellis Davidson and Anna Chaudhri. Durham, NC: Carolina Academic Press, 203–17.

Howell, James C. 2007. "Menacing or Mimicking? Realities of Youth Gangs." *Juvenile and Family Court Journal* 58 (2). http://www.famm.org/Repository/Files/Howell_2007_gang_Myths%5B1%5D.pdf (accessed June 12, 2010)

"Interview with a Scammer, Parts 1–3." 2010. Scam Detectives. http://www.scam-detectives.co.uk/blog/2010/01/22/interview-with-a-scammer-part-one/ (accessed September 9, 2011).

Kibby, Marjorie D. 2005. "Email Forwardables: Folklore in the Age of the Internet." *New Media Society* 7 (6): 770–90.

Mikkelson, Barbara. 2004. "Clown Statue." http://www.snopes.com/horrors/madmen/statue.asp (accessed September 21, 2011).

Mikkelson, Barbara. 2009a. "Chain Linked." http://www.snopes.com/luck/chain.asp (accessed August 12, 2011).

Mikkelson, Barbara. 2009b. "Evan Trembley." http://www.snopes.com/inboxer/missing/trembley.asp (accessed September 8, 2011).

Mikkelson, Barbara. 2009c. "Le-a." http://www.snopes.com/racial/language/le-a.asp (accessed September 8, 2011).

Mikkelson, Barbara. 2010. "Lights Out!" http://www.snopes.com/crime/gangs/lightsout.asp (accessed August 12, 2011).

Mikkelson, Barbara. 2011a. "Ashley Flores." http://www.snopes.com/inboxer/missing/ashleyflores.asp (accessed September 8, 2011).

Mikkelson, Barbara. 2011b. "Burundanga." http://www.snopes.com/crime/warnings/burundanga.asp (accessed September 21, 2011).

Mikkelson, Barbara. 2011c. "Deadly Pullover." http://www.snopes.com/crime/gangs/pullover.asp (accessed September 9, 2011).

Mikkelson, Barbara. 2011d. "Stalk Tip." http://www.snopes.com/rumors/warning.asp (accessed August 12, 2011).

Mikkelson, Barbara. 2011e. "Uniform Behavior." http://www.snopes.com/rumors/upsuniforms.asp (accessed August 12, 2011).

"Nuclear Fallout Map." 2011. Snopes.com. http://www.snopes.com/photos/technology/fallout.asp (accessed September 9, 2011).

Ong, Walter. 1982. *Orality and Literacy: The Technologizing of the Word*. London: Methuen.

Parks, Brad. 2011. *Eyes of the Innocent*. New York: Thomas Dunne.

Pescovitz, Davis. 2011. "Boy Uses Creed to Fend Off Wolves." http://boingboing.net/2011/01/26/boy-uses-creed-to-fe.html (accessed September 9, 2011).

Sullivan, Bob. 2005. " 'Nigerian Scams' Keep Evolving." Msnbc.com. http://www.msnbc.msn.com/id/8171053/ns/technology_and_science-security/t/nigerian-scams-keep-evolving/ (accessed June 16, 2011).

Sullum, Jacob. 2010. "Texas PTA Blames Texas Crime Stoppers for 'Strawberry Quick' Panic." January 6. http://reason.com/blog/2010/01/06/texas-pta-blames-texas-crime-s (accessed September 8, 2011).

Tucker, Elizabeth. 2009. "Guardians of the Living: Characterization of Missing Women on the Internet." In *Folklore and the Internet: Vernacular Expression in a Digital World.* Edited by Trevor J. Blank. Logan: Utah State University Press, 67–79.

CHAPTER 4

CONSPIRACY THEORIES

In the last decades "a popular paranoia" has emerged: a paranoia that questions—half-seriously, half-cynically—the versions of events told by science or government authorities.

—Campion-Vincent (2005b, 104)

In her book review of *Conspiracy Theories in American History: An Encyclopedia*, Veronique Campion-Vincent refers to the summary penned by the historian David Brion Davis in the preface to the book, stating that he highlights how the situation has developed since the 1960s when "excesses of the paranoid style appeared to be aberrations in the past" that affected only extremists. In the twenty-first century, however, those excesses are reaching nearly everyone, and the broadening abyss of suspicion combined with increased pessimism and cynicism prepares North Americans and many others to believe the worst about their world (Campion-Vincent 2007, 190). Davis is not the only one to state these views. "Going through a period of fashionable conspiracism" was how David Aaronovitch brands contemporary Western society (Aaronovitch 2010, 3). His premise encompasses the multiple books on conspiracy theory that "appear on the current affairs and history shelves as though they were as scholarly or reliable as works by major historians or noted academics" (Aaronovitch 2010, 3). Programs on conspiracy theory are also plentiful on television as well as presented as documentaries on the larger screen. "And such works are given the same treatment as major exercises in historical analysis or substantial pieces of investigative journalism. In fact, they are often given a better billing. Uncountered, their arguments enter popular culture" (Aaronovitch 2010, 4).

Contemporary Conspiracies

Conspiracy theory, defined by Aaronovitch, is "the attribution of deliberate agency to something that is more likely to be accidental or unintended" (Aaronovitch 2010, 6). He claims that this belief in conspiracy theories is harmful, distorting people's view of history, the present and the possible future (Aaronovitch 2010, 16). The phenomenon of conspiracism, however, cannot be explained entirely by unequal power relations, the abundance or scarcity of information, or disenfranchisement (Aaronovitch 2010, 349). The ongoing attractiveness of conspiracy theory appears to be the human compulsion to create story, particularly story that "either represents the way we think things should happen, or is the best explanation we can get of why they didn't" (Aaronovitch 2010, 354).

Paradoxically, conspiracy theories are reassuring, suggesting "that there is an explanation, that human agencies are powerful, and that there is order rather than chaos" (Aaronovitch 2010, 355).

Aaronovitch elucidates the common characteristics of pervasive conspiracy theories found in his research. Most conspiracy theories include a historical precedent; similar cases, regardless of their antiquity, are brought forth to bolster the believability factor of the latest argument or theory being presented to the population. These theories, usually politically populist, maintain that the current actions, like the ones in the past, are undertaken by a small power elite in opposition to the mass population. "Most conspiracy theories try to unmask a powerful, dangerous, all-appropriating elite who seek nothing less than unilateral rule and a presumed nefarious regimentation of the populace that includes slavery of mind and spirit" (Goldzwig 2002, 498). Most of the persuasive theories employ expert witnesses, often celebrities or specialists whose status is exaggerated, to validate the theories and, particularly since 2001, ask questions. "The theorist is just asking certain disturbing questions because of a desire to seek out truth, and the reader is supposedly left to make up his or her mind" (Aaronovitch 2010, 11). Another feature of these theories is "death by footnote." Aaronovitch explains this as academic credibility that is formulated through a dense mass of detailed and often undifferentiated information and laid out as an academic text (Aaronovitch 2010, 13). Flexible arguments within the conspiracy theories, referred to as "convenient inconvenient truths," facilitate the inclusion or exclusion of new and inconvenient data, bolstering the original truth of the theory. Aaronovitch discovers that conspiracy theorists, even those in safe environments, believe that they were under surveillance and endangered at all times (Aaronovitch 2010, 10–14).

In his book on conspiracy theories in the United States, Mark Fenster defines conspiracy theory as "the conviction that a secret, omnipotent individual or group covertly controls the political and social order or some part thereof" (Fenster 2008, 1). Fenster claims that two propositions dominate discussions of conspiracy theory: that it circulates solely on the margins of society and predominates American political culture (Fenster 2008, 1). In the first proposition, conspiracy theorists are considered political extremists, unsavoury characters and unstable. Fenster asserts that both propositions are correct with a relatively small number of Americans believing that a grand conspiracy is the causal engine of politics and history, and a much larger number engaging in conspiracy theory at some level, either for pleasure or as a potential explanation for personal or global events. "Both claims, however, agree that conspiracy theory, in its dangerous conception of power, nationhood, and history, represents a dire threat" (Fenster 2008, 2).

> Totalizing conspiracy theories frequently lack substantive proof, rely on dizzying leaps of logic, and oversimplify the political, economic, and social structures of power. Structural, institutionally-based inequities in the distribution of power, capital, and resources, and the manipulation and abuse of state power to establish, maintain, and extend political control, do not constitute conspiracy in the sense that conspiracy theorists would describe (as some anomalous, apocalyptic moment within a heretofore perfect democratic republic). Rather, they constitute the political economic consequences of capitalism and an inevitably imperfect system of politics and governance. More dangerously, conspiracy

theories can express—and in American history frequently have helped organize—virulent hostility to racial, ethnic, religious, sexual, or political Others. (Fenster 2008, 11)

Theo Meder states that some contemporary legends, rumors and tall tales might contain a grain of truth and that, in many cases, there is a connection between these tales and the general conception of reality, validating people's beliefs in the tales (Meder 2009, 258). Similar to these types of tales, contemporary conspiracy theories resonate as possible and plausible, but are never proven (Campion-Vincent 2005b, 104). Conspiracy theories rely on a nexus of belief, combining plausible elements into a "totalizing discourse." Once the beliefs are acknowledged by the public, they make disorder orderly by relating the situation to general assumptions regarding human motivation. "Conspiracy theories can explain large swaths of an otherwise ambiguous world; they are transcendent explanations, unlocking a closed world with a cleverly forged key. The power of a conspiracy theory is that it connects rumors with documented, official facts" (Fine and Ellis 2010, 53).

Conspiracy theories follow an established structure when providing satisfactory rationalizations for non-routine and non-explained public events. A specific agent or agents is always identified as is the clear motivation for the agents' behaviour. The named agent is always evil, the outcome destructive and the agent controls important resources clandestinely acting with powerful allies and therefore the action was unstoppable (Campion-Vincent 2005b, 104–5). As Campion-Vincent points out, extremist views have always been with us but what is less ancient are the echoes that are produced in the general public by these conspiracy theories.

> In food contamination stories, the villains are often the greedy corporations, which behave as enemies of the people in their unchecked quest for profit. They have replaced the foreigners, lepers, and Jews who used to be accused of poisoning water in the great epidemics of yesterday. (Campion-Vincent 2005b, 113)

In the aftermath of any disaster, political legends typically follow a pattern of crisis management, blame and conspiracy after the immediate events and their results were processed by the pubic (Fine and Ellis 2010, 51).

The first stage in this process includes that of improvised news, questioning others about what they had heard, comparing notes and preparing to take some type of action. Once a measure of stability resumes, the legends and rumors change their focus. Fine and Ellis suggest that relevant inspiring tales about tragedies and triumphs are sought after by people to provide the event with emotional resonance and moral significance. "At this point, they also pin blame on those who are obviously responsible, painting these villains in dark shades" (Fine and Ellis 2010, 52).

The next stage, when the legends and rumors become more elaborated and nuanced, is that of the conspiracy theory (Fine and Ellis 2010, 52). "A conspiracy may be real or imagined, but the process is the same; a chain of apparently unrelated events or actions is linked to reveal concerted actions and intentions to cause all sorts of social, economic, political, religious, and moral problems" (Goldzwig 2002, 492). Fine and Ellis assert, along with other scholars, that conspiracy theories begin with one simple core premise: history has always been shaped by evil elites, the actual identity of which has continuously altered over time and place (Fine and Ellis 2010, 55).

An important element regarding conspiracy theories is that they are rarely responsible for people disliking a group for whom people had no animosity. They, instead, reinforce specific prejudice and disdain, always located within the context of belief (Fine and Ellis 2010, 55). Recently, because this context of belief incorporates major distrust of official spokespeople, the government and the media, conspiracy theories flourish as they never have before.

> Mulder and Scully's confrontation with the intrigue and the horror of extraterrestrials and their attempts to uncover the government conspiracy to cover up their existence [in *X-Files*] is made more plausible, if not credible, by a specific and very real background and context: the lack of full disclosure in governmental circles, whether it be citizen suspicion in the wake of Vietnam and Watergate (where the government was caught lying) or in the nether worlds of places like Ruby Ridge and Waco where continuing revelations of seeming half-truths siphon off the small credibility reserve government has left. (Goldzwig 2002, 495)

A recent call for papers for the conference Conspiracy Theories in the Middle East and the United States: A Comparative Approach, held at the Freiburg Institute for Advanced Studies, Germany (January 13–15, 2011) stated that these theories flourish in highly diverse environments answering to vastly different human needs, desires and imaginations.

> The rise of the United States to the leading imperial power has gone hand in hand with a proliferation of conspiracy theories that located the conspiring forces within the federal government or big companies. The theories that have thrived in the Middle East, by contrast, imagine foreign conspirators, because the region has been on the receiving end of the international power system in the nineteenth and twentieth centuries. (January 25, 2010)

A brief examination of a wide variety of conspiracy theories in various countries demonstrates that the "evil" antagonists of these theories basically fall into these two distinct categories depending on the country in which the conspiracy theory originated.

Debunking or debating conspiracy theories is not one of the concerns in writing this chapter. Instead, brief commentaries are offered on some of the most prevalent examples of conspiracy theories in today's Western society, from governmental activities in diverse countries to universal health issues and to the end-of-the-world prophesies.

World Trade Center, September 11, 2001

Numerous contemporary legends and conspiracy theories rose in the aftermath of the September 11, 2001, attacks on the World Trade Center. Most of them focus on the demolition of the towers; but others incorporate stock trading, ethnic profiling and vanishing aircraft. Speculation abounded that the Wall Street trading on stocks directly affected by the attacks proves that some people knew about the attacks in advance. According to others, United Airlines Flight 93 did not crash in a Pennsylvania field but simply vanished, perhaps after being shot down by a fighter jet. Another segment of the population claims that it was an American missile and not American Airlines Flight 77 that crashed into the Pentagon.

Three main threats are offered as explanation for the attacks: all Arabs, not just a few terrorists, were responsible for this attack and were planning others as part of a jihadist war; powerful Jews in general and the Israeli Mossad were behind the attacks; and the attacks were known about or caused by the American government itself. "While the first explanation gained the widest public support in the United States, the others gathered communities of believers as well, and the final explanation proved to be very hardy indeed" (Fine and Ellis 2010, 57). While numerous theories are attributing blame, others concentrate on the destruction of the towers themselves. Theorists propose that the twin towers could not have collapsed from the impact of the airplane alone and that the collapse of Tower 7, which was not hit by an aircraft, was the result of professional demolition.

In his investigation on conspiracy theories, Aaronovitch explores the power of the Internet in the offering of "a mass of undifferentiated information, some of it authoritative, some speculative, some absurd" (Aaronovitch 2010, 232). One example is the construction and circulation of material devoted to 9/11 revisionism.

> Cheap movies, often made using materials not cleared for copyright, made and narrated by nonprofessional filmmakers, have been posted on Google video, YouTube, and other sites specializing in moving pictures. Invariably, such items make the same claims to accuracy and balance as do mainstream TV programs, but have been concocted with the smallest fraction of research and resource, though no little ingenuity. (Aaronovitch 2010, 232)

The continuing amount of information, misinformation, data, speculation and articles written about all aspects of the 9/11 disaster prompted this brief exploration of some of the conspiracy theory and theorists associated with this latter speculation, the professional annihilation of Tower 7. In Robert Blaskiewicz's interview with Richard Gage, founder of the group Architects and Engineers for 9/11 Truth about the alleged controlled demolition of Tower 7, he writes:

> "Suddenly on the afternoon of September 11," Richard tells me, "this building drops symmetrically, smoothly straight down into its own footprint, in the exact manner of a classic controlled demolition. . . . We are told that this is destruction by normal office fires, and if you look at the fires in that building in they were . . . small and scattered. I mean if the building is going to collapse due to fire, which has never happened to a skyscraper at all in the history of skyscrapers, it's going to fall slowly, gradually, and over into the path of least resistance." (Blaskiewicz 2011)

Gage also cites, as evidence for his theory, molten iron, chemical evidence of thermite/thermate in the dust and nanothermite composite explosives, or pyrotechnics, found in the entire World Trade Center dust sample (Blaskiewicz 2011).

There is not a consensus among the conspiracy theorists on the topic of the World Trade Center disaster. The web-only film series, *Loose Change*, which argues that the findings of the 9/11 Commission are erroneous, had already been viewed 10 million times by the time a *Vanity Fair* article (August 2006) mentions that it may be the first Internet blockbuster. According to the five different versions of this film which allegedly base their claims on records of the devastation, the attacks on the World Trade Center were planned and conducted by elements within the American government. *Loose Change 2nd Edition Recut* (2006) begins with a look at historical precedence of suspicious and questionable behaviour by the American government followed by examinations of several elements of the World Trade Center conspiracy controversy. The film endorses the belief in the controlled demolition theory, citing eyewitness reports from several people near the buildings during that fateful moment, and claiming that the towers are the first steel buildings alleged to collapse due to fire and that an audio recording captured the sound of two distinct explosions at the time of the collapse. Accompanying the legion of viewers is a variety of different sources offering criticism and debunking of the films, including the U.S. Department of State which published an article "Loose Change Debunked" (March 2007), various journalists, researchers, scientists, engineers and members of the 9/11 Truth Movement. This latter group, established in 2004, one of several organizations and individuals who question the acknowledged reports of the September 11, 2011, attacks, suspect that the American government and mainstream media were engaged in either, or both, covering up the truth of the attacks or involved in them from the very beginning. According to the membership, which asked for an impartial investigation into the attacks, motivation for the complicity includes the initiation of war in Afghanistan and Iraq and the opportunity to curtail civil liberties within their own borders.

Another organization focused on the destruction of the Twin Towers and Tower 7, Architects & Engineers for 9/11 Truth, founded by Richard Gage in 2006, is composed mainly of architectural and engineering professionals who support the controlled demolition theory. This organization also demands an independent investigation into the attacks, including an inquiry into the possible use of explosives. Scholars for 9/11 Truth, founded in 2005, is a group of individuals of varying backgrounds and expertise who reject the mainstream media and government account of the attacks. Dissent within the group soon led to the creation of another organization, Scholars for 9/11 Truth and Justice, formed in 2007. The group also supports the conspiracy theory that the three towers in the World Trade Center were destroyed through explosive demolition. Several members of this organization publish papers in reputable science and engineering journals offering scientific evidence of the validity of their claims. *The Journal of 9/11 Studies*, a peer-reviewed, open-access, electronic-only journal, covers engineering, physics, chemistry, mathematics and psychology research related to the events of September 11, 2001. Their initial mission, as stated on the website, is to provide an outlet for evidence-based research that may not have otherwise been published "due to the resistance that many established journals and other institutions have displayed toward this topic" (http://www.journalof911studies.com/). As they now believe that the case for falsity of the official explanation has been well established, they encourage all potential contributors to send their papers to the more established journals, which might be more readily available to other scientists. The most recent of the available 61 articles on the website, as of this writing, was published on February 2011.

As Fine and Ellis point out, research on rumor begins with the study of rumors in crisis, in war or after a natural disaster; and the September 11 rumors and tales fit the same pattern, amalgamating hope, fear and anger. "Not since World War II have we had such a profusion of rumors that generated such conflicted emotions" (Fine and Ellis 2010, 203).

Other rumors circulating immediately after the September 11 attack, and still having an impact a decade later, are racially specific: groups of Arab Americans allegedly publicly celebrated the attacks; an Islamist terrorist warned his non-Arab girlfriend to stay away from the Twin Towers on September 11; Arabic taxi drivers disappeared from the streets of lower Manhattan; and predictions of specific dates when another attack would occur such as dates revered by the American public: July 4, Halloween and the Friday after Thanksgiving. "After anthrax letters were sent, rumors warned of poisonings, including Coca-Cola, toxic samples of perfume or lotion, deadly sponges, or diapers" (Fine and Ellis 2010, 23). Other contemporary legends connected to the attacks such as the theft of U-Haul trucks, UPS driver uniforms or Costco candy for reprehensible goals are addressed in various discussions within this book.

Chupacabra

Perhaps one day an actual unknown mystery beast will be captured dead or alive, but until then there's more than enough speculation, folklore, and myth to keep the belief alive.

—Radford (2011, 97)

The first reported attacks of this goatsucker beast, draining all of the blood from eight slaughtered sheep through two holes in its neck, occurred in Puerto Rico in March 1995. Madelyne Tolentino, an eyewitness in Canovanas, Puerto Rico, reported seeing the creature in August of the same year. The chupacabra's red eyes, apparently having the ability to hypnotize and paralyze their prey, allow the creature to leisurely suck the blood. "Unlike conventional predators, the chupacabra sucks all the animal's blood (and sometimes organs) through a single hole or two holes" (Monstropedia). The resulting mass hysteria, fuelled by the mass media, locally and globally, helped spread the stories and, consequently, there were additional sightings worldwide in March of the following year. "The TV talk show *Christina* [*sic*], the Spanish-language Univision network's popular counterpart to Oprah Winfrey, featured the chupacabra, and it was the media attention from this exposure that seemingly caused the migration of Chupamania into Mexico and the United States" (Coleman and Clark 1999, 62). The broadcast almost immediately spurred a sharp increase in reports from Mexico, Latin America and Spanish-speaking areas of the United States (Radford 2011, 166). The Chupacabra legend transformed from a local legend into an international phenomenon (Jordan 2008, 2). An important newslore factor regarding the chupacabra is that the majority of the initial reports circulating in Puerto Rico were written by Ruben Dario Rodriguez, a reporter for *El Vocero* (Radford 2011, 40). When the legend first spread to Mexico, the Mexican media turned the creature into a political figure, utilizing it to express feelings about the nation and the leaders. Eventually, the frequency of sightings and attacks in Mexico followed the pattern established previously in Puerto Rico; as social conditions improve and the strain upon society lessens, the number of sightings lessens (Jordan 2008, 71). However, the sensationalized and alarmist news reports continued to spawn more sightings, until the chupacabra was known and recognized worldwide, in newslore and in popular-culture appearances.

Three different physical forms have been applied to Chupacabra in the various sightings. The best known, identified by Madelyne Tolentino, is approximately five feet tall, a bipedal creature with long claws and a row of spikes down its back. It is also described as a mammal from the Canidae family, a four-legged creature closely resembling a dog or coyote. The third, a catchall category, basically includes any unusual animal, alive or dead, that anyone reported seeing or thought might be the Chupacabra (Radford 2011, 4). Investigations into most of the sightings found that the animals thought to be chupacabras are dogs, foxes or coyotes with mange, a skin disease caused by parasitic mites (Kruczy 2010). The sightings and stories about the chupacabra flourish until almost any story, regardless of its credibility, would be believed somewhere. "This social climate of few facts and sensationalist tabloid headlines combined with wild rumor and gossip to create a perfect breeding ground for a mild form of mass hysterical in which ordinary events (such as attacks by dogs on pets or livestock) were interpreted in extraordinary ways" (Radford 2011, 9). Radford states that most of the reports of sightings fall into four distinct categories: they are either fictional; they are so sensationalized that no factual knowledge remains about the actual sightings themselves; the sightings are of other creatures that have nothing to do with the chupacabra; or they are sightings of dead livestock that have no overt connection with the vampiric nature of the beast or the beast itself (Radford 2011, 13).

George Eberhart, librarian for the Center for UFO Studies and editor of *American Libraries*, offers nine possible explanations for the chupacabra that ranges from emerging folklore to paranormal origins and beyond. He does not, however, mention conspiracy theories, a rationale proposed by other authors and discussed below. Eberhart asserts that, as folklore in the making, the stories of the chupacabra, made up, misinterpreted, repeated and embellished, are spread by contagion (Eberhart 2002, 108). On the other hand, they could be ritual killings by practitioners of Santeria or gang members or have paranormal origins such as aliens, genetic experiments gone awry, freshwater Merbeings or black magic (Eberhart 2002, 108).

Numerous animals that have been misidentified also figure prominently in rationalizations for the chupacabra sightings: the long-tailed weasel, feral domestic dogs, escaped Rhesus monkeys, the false vampire bat and the band-winged nightjar (Eberhart 2002, 108). Eberhart points out some inconsistencies to these animal theories. The long-tailed weasel, for example, feeds on small mammals but is not native to Puerto Rico. Some Rhesus monkeys, brought to the area for research purposes, did escape from a La Paraguera facility in the 1970s but they are known to eat insects, shots, fruit, seeds and, occasionally, a small animal but nothing as large as a goat. The false vampire bat limits its prey to birds, other bats and small rodents. The night-flying, insect-eating Band-winged Nightjar is said to have contributed to the sightings because of its name in Spanish: *chotacabras* (Eberhart 2002, 108).

Benjamin Radford believes that the sightings will continue, and they have done so as the quantity of references to this topic in recent e-mails attests. These new sightings continue the pattern described by Radford: "Each new sighting will make national, maybe even international, headlines (often accompanied by photos), crowing 'Chupacabra Found!'; the new dead beast and its owner will become a minor celebrity, hounded by press, gawkers, and a curious public" (Radford 2011, 97). Any scientific investigation and analysis reveals the animal as a diseased canid, and the matter rests until the next incident. In actual fact, the word "chupacabra" became the catch-all phrase for a Hispanic bogeyman and any strange animal seen or found, with or without a vampiric association (Radford 2011, 177). In a review of Radford's book, Bjorn Carey cites the author's belief that the chupacabra sightings and beliefs are "the result of a perfect storm of urban legend-brewing conditions" and, as one of the first mythical beasts discovered in the Internet age, advanced exponentially (Carey 2011).

Chupacabra and Other Contemporary Legends

Major themes that emerge from the ever-expanding literature on the Chupacabra include conspiracy theory, links to organ thefts and shoddy research practices. Shoddy research practices are not a focus of this discussion but exploring conspiracy theories, organ thefts and cryptozoological connections in the research are important.

Chupacabra and Conspiracy Theories

> As U.S. popular culture was often one of the nation's chief international exports, it is no surprise that symbols aboard used to demonize and denounce the United States might be formed from its own culture reshaped and recombined into a new form.
>
> —Jordan (2008, 23)

In his thesis on the chupacabra as an icon of resistance to American Imperialism, Robert Michael Jordan explains that many of the descriptions given by the first witnesses, the locations of the supposed attacks and the local theories regarding the origins point to an association with the sustained American presence in Puerto Rico (Jordan 2008, 24). There is, in the descriptions, distinct associations with the industrial pollution of the contaminated ground water and soil resulting from leakage from the industrial plants or waste storage facilitates. The terror of intense environmental danger is reflected in the depictions of the creature which are particularly precise regarding their stench. "Rather than possessing the traditionally demonic odor of sulphur or brimstone, the Chupacabra was repeatedly described as smelling of 'battery acid,' 'Malathion (a widely used pesticide),' and 'paint thinner' " (Jordan 2008, 24). The locations of the reported attacks tend to be near irrigation canals, lakes and rivers, in traditionally rural areas encroached by new urban or industrial growth, or around the numerous American military facilities in the area (Jordan 2008, 25). Many of the local population in areas where the chupacabra was sighted believe that it is the unholy creation of secret American government experiments gone awry (Radford 2011, 4). Regardless of the country of the sightings, the United States is overwhelmingly perceived as the ultimate source of the creature society (Jordan 2008, 63). Theorists claim that the chupacabra is the result of genetic or medical experiments by the American military which, like the Rhesus monkey in the 1970s, escaped from its confines to wreak havoc (Jordan 2008, 25). The conspiracy theorists and most of the general population in Puerto Rico feel that the chupacabra is most likely an escaped beast, while those in Chile claim that their government conspired with NASA and the American military to create this dangerous creature regardless of explanations put forth by professionals and investigators (Radford 2011, 175).

> Little wonder, then, that the occasional attempts by governmental officials to quell fears and calm citizens are often met with dismissals and jeers. One of the hallmarks of conspiracy theories is that

they cannot be effectively disproven: any evidence that negates or undermines the theory is itself part of the conspiracy. For those who are certain that the chupacabra exists, no amount of evidence or arguments will prove to them otherwise. There will always be explanations they refuse to accept, preferring fanciful fables over simple scientific truths. (Radford 2011, 175)

The chupacabra also shares numerous physical characteristics with aliens, or at least the aliens that are depicted in the popular American science-fiction films and television shows aired in the 1990s. A program showing crude film footage of an "alien autopsy" that supposedly took place inside the Roswell Air Force Base in 1947 was shown on both the Fox and Telemundo television networks in the summer of 1995, just at the time of the first mass sightings in Puerto Rico. The people's distrust of the American presence on the island meshed well with the suggestion that the military installations could secretly house otherworldly creatures (Jordan 2008, 23). And, as Radford points out, whether the Chupacabra was the result of a top-secret American government genetics experiment or an extraterrestrial, most explanations share the common theme of conspiracy, making the chupacabra unique in this regard. He reassures his readers that neither Bigfoot nor the Loch Ness monster have been cited as conspiracies created by the American government (Radford 2011, 175).

While many experts feel that the universality of the Chupacabra sightings lay in the existence of similar environmental, social, economic or political conditions in the countries in which the creature hunted, and that these conditions are brought about by the fears of globalization and the American juggernaut, what rationale explains the recent sightings in the United States itself? Recent Chupacabra sightings have been reported in Texas, Minnesota, Maryland and Kentucky, and in various locations in Russia. Truly the Chupacabra, rooted in conspiracy theory and anti-American sentiment, continues to be "a contradictory and bizarre amalgamation of vampiric monster, folk myth, and chameleon" (Radford 2011, 3). There are also nods to other conspiracy theories such as cattle mutilations and Armageddon. The chupacabra phenomenon was initially linked to the wave of cattle mutilation legends emerging out of the American Midwest in the 1970s and 1980s because of the mysterious deaths of the goats (Koven 2008, 73). James Lloyd, founder of the Christian Media Network ministry, explains in his booklet *Chupacabras: The Devil's Genetics* how the arrival of the chupacabra was predicted in Bible prophecy signaling the start of Armageddon. He links the arrival of the Chupacabra with the monsters mentioned in Revelations 9: "The locusts looked like horses prepared for battle" (Radford 2011, 53). According to Radford, Lloyd believes that Chupacabras are created through genetic engineering as a weapon to attack humanity alongside demons collectively named Legion (from the Gospel of Mark 5:9) (Radford 2011, 54). It is easy to agree with Radford when he asserts that "from its roots as a vampire to its role as an agent of Armageddon and symbol of American imperialism, the chupacabra has a rich history" (Radford 2011, 55).

"The Fat Stealer"

The Peruvian creature, *likichiri*, the "fat stealer," that attacked people as they slept in the highlands of the Andes Mountains, is associated with the possible origins of the Chupacabra. This creature painlessly removes the fat from its victims through long, thin slits in its victims' sides which promptly heal. Since the victims are not aware of the extraction and the subsequent healing of their own skins, they usually die because they do not seek immediate treatment to survive. Radford points to the fact that natural body fat, in the Andean highlands, is essential for survival in that extremely cold environment (Radford 2011, 29).

Spanish historian Crisobal de Molina reported, in 1571, that rumors circulated among the Indians of the central Andes that the Spanish explorers did not arrive in Peru seeking gold, but human fat to be exported to Europe to cure specific diseases. According to Radford, the contemporary likichiri sells the collected fat to international corporations, mostly American, to be used for plastic surgery and the development of anesthetics (Radford 2011, 30). The comparison to the likichiri lies in the reality that when the Chupacabra took the life of valuable livestock, it dried not only the blood, but by extension, the livelihood of poor farmers and ranchers (Radford 2011, 31).

Cryptozoology Connections

> *Switch on your cable TV and skim through the channels for history and science and you see dozens of programs about unexplained creatures. El Chupacabra, Nessie, the Yeti, the Mothman, Bloody Mary, La Llorona, the Hobbits, Champ . . . they all get airtime in specials that promise to unlock the secrets of these unknown beings. Sadly, none of these shows ever do what they promise. Instead they collect the facts, they interview the witnesses, they have scientific analysis done on what few pieces of physical evidence can be collected, and then they wrap up with a cryptic statement like, "we don't know whether these creatures are out there . . . but the belief remains."*
>
> —Mayberry and Kramer (2009, xvii)

Paranormal investigator Joe Nickell reports on a discussion with journalist Gabriel Alcalde of Santa Rosa that the rumored animal deaths due to mutilation were found to be attributed to natural causes by the National Service for Food and Agriculture (SENASA) and the Veterinary College of the Center of the Province of Buenos Aires. The report of the investigation concluded that "under direct and close observation, it could be ascertained that the injuries to the tissues and organs were caused by predators. Histological studies done on the carcasses showed conclusively that no special tools had been used to produce the cuts" (Nickell 2006). Gabriel Alcalde points out that many Argentines deny the scientific evidence, believing instead the stories concocted by the media. "He told me that he felt the real mutilation was that which had been done to critical thinking" (Nickell 2006).

The Chupacabra is included in numerous reference sources on cryptozoology including Michael Newton's *Encyclopedia of Cryptozoology*. Newton offers popular descriptions of the Chupacabra as well as a catalogue of sightings in Puerto Rico, Guatemala, Mexico, Florida, Spain, Arizona, Texas, California, Costa Rica, Portugal, Brazil, Argentina, Chile and Nicaragua. He concisely summarizes the various theories concerning the identity of the creature. The Chupacabra can be considered a supernatural entity, an extraterrestrial, a normal predator, a human practitioner of occult blood rituals or an outstanding example of mass hysteria (Newton 2005, 105). Radford asserts that in the short time span since it was first sighted, it has become a global phenomenon and the world's third best-known monster after Bigfoot and the Loch Ness Monster (Radford 2011, 4).

Grease "Yakas" or Devils in Sri Lanka

He sneaks in through windows in the dead of night, his body shining with grease, garbed in black. His motive is always dire—from stealing valuables to rape. He is a slippery customer; impossible to catch because of the grease he is covered in.

—Wickrematunge (2011)

Traditionally, grease devils are merely slippery thieves but the reputation of the current rendition is much more sinister. Reports of the Grease Devils, or "Kreese Pootham," in Tamil and "Thel Yaka" in Sinhala, flooded e-mail boxes as this chapter was being written and, although their story has not been completed at this time, it is necessary to mention it here. Fears of the people in Sri Lanka are heightened by the stories and then exploited by several people who, through ostensive behavior, pose as the Grease Yaka in order to commit robberies according to police reports. "The so-called 'grease yaka' suspects who have been apprehended are ordinary people who were behaving suspiciously, or in the case of the 16-year-old Badulla youth, breaking the law using the persona of a mythical devil to frighten people" (Wickrematunge 2011). Numerous people have died and others been hurt in the incidents of violence and vigilantism that spawned as a result of this contemporary legend. People have been arrested for spreading the rumors as well as acting them out.

As the fear spread, the details of the stories became wilder and more horrifying. Conspiracy theories abound as villagers blame the security forces for launching or fostering the Grease Devil assaults. The charges are denied but the violence continues (Haviland 2011). There is ambiguity about the nature of these alleged intruders. Some stories claim that some criminals were seeking female blood for ritual purposes; other tales attribute "bionic" or superhuman powers to the intruders (Haviland 2011). Others believe that the phenomenon is a type of mass hysteria resulting in the outbreak of social panics rather than the result of real, physical attackers. There seems also to be an ethnic dimension in the stories as well, as those reporting the attacks are Muslim or Tamil rather than from the majority Sinhalese community (Haviland 2011). Meetings with area politicians, army officers and the president was called on September 6, 2011, to end this "unhealthy trend" as the Grease Devil fear continued to grip the people of Jaffna (Coleman 2011). In most cases, however, the reactions by vigilante groups, armed forces and the media to the fears, anxieties and attacks of the general population caused even more violence and tension (Aruna 2011).

While there are general features in the reports of this panic such as the targeting of women, the cuts and scratches to hands or breasts, and the elusive nature of the perpetrators, the Grease Devil seems to take on localized qualities in each of the communities where it manifested (Aruna 2011).

Where there are concerns about militarization the Bogeyman is thought to be an army operative or deserter, for those who mistrust institutions charged with maintaining law and order it seems the police are freeing captured suspects, and worries about the

implications of deepening Sino-Lanka ties lead others to speculate
that the "Grease Yaka/Mystery Man" is Chinese or using superior
imported technology to elude capture. For those troubled by the
entrenchment of the current regime the figure is an attempt to
remain in power, either by means of blood sacrifice or by the more
mundane (but no less feared) continuation of the state of
emergency ... Those supportive of the current regime perceive
an unseen hand of opposition parties, foreign governments or an
Eelamist diaspora behind the incidents or stories. (Aruna 2011)

While the phenomenon was just emerging as this book was written, there are
no examples of it in popular culture, as of yet, but there was a furor over
Facebook pages for the Grease Yaka and Grease Devil. Apparently the Sri Lankan
government requested the administrators of Facebook to launch an investigation
about the users who created the page as well as those individuals who "liked" it
on Facebook. At that time the page had over 3,500 followers and a video of a man
being assaulted on the assumption that he was a Grease Devil ("Sri Lankan
Grease Devil"). When checking Facebook on September 21, 2011, neither page
was still available. There are several other pages referring to the Grease Devil, but
none of those pages had more than 20 people following them.

Organ-Theft Narratives: The Stolen Kidney

*While in today's world human organs are subject to removal
and redistribution, the* idea *of organ transplantation preceded
its technological possibility.*

—Campion-Vincent (2002, 33)

Organ-theft narratives, defined as legends in which eyes, kidneys and other
organs are stolen from living people, resulting or not resulting in death following
the theft, began circulating vigorously with the development of organ transplants
and the availability of immunosuppressant drugs aiding in successful organ transplants (Campion-Vincent 2001, 185). Three categories of these legends are identified: the "Baby Parts" story, *sacaojos* (eye robbers) stories, and the stolen kidney.
All three types of organ-theft narratives are linked to a growing awareness of the
existence of a global traffic in human beings.

The "Baby Parts" legend, the theft of Third World children's organs, is also
linked to the traffic in children that accompanied the development of international
adoption. The legend, circulating in the 1980s, asserts that children presumably
adopted by foreign parents are actually taken by unscrupulous traffickers, ending
up in clandestine hospitals where they are harvested for their organs to be used in
transplant operations benefiting the rich (Campion-Vincent 2002, 34). The theft of
street children's eyes, *sacaojos* stories, connect with the maltreatment of the homeless poor and street children, in which these victims are left to die after, their hearts,
kidneys and livers, along with their eyes, are also stolen. Both of these subgenres of
the legend appear in Latin America, reflecting the poverty and violence of the countries and the dominance of the United States over the area (Campion-Vincent 2001,
185). The resurfacing of these legends prompted new investigations, but the subsequent findings establishing that such practices do not occur are less publicized.
These legends often explain missing children, the presence of white foreigners or

the general ill-health of children (Donovan 2004, 61). In more affluent countries, the "Stolen Kidney" legends involve careless and misfortunate travelers but now these variants are diffused all over the world. "Stolen Kidney" legends are strongly linked to two social problems: social unease towards organ transplants and the reality of legal organ trading in several countries (Campion-Vincent 2001, 194). This legend also reflects the fears of the rich towards the poor in distant lands, mirroring the anxieties of the poor in those countries to the rich (Campion-Vincent 2002, 42). Gillian Bennett considers organ-theft legends, legends of the cannibalization of the body, the most prominent legend in the last decades of the twentieth century, "specifically, the illicit taking and trading of bodies and their organs for cash, research, or transplant surgery" (Bennett 2005, 189).

The Stolen Kidney

> *"The Kidney Heist" offers a good example of how the oral tradition of an urban legend dries up as popular culture absorbs it ... in about nine years "The Kidney Heist" went from complete narrative legend to a mere quip, and from oral tradition to the Internet and popular culture.*
>
> —Brunvand (2004, 6)

When the "Stolen Kidney," frequently referred to as the "Kidney Heist," is discussed in *Tales, Rumors, and Gossip* (de Vos 1996) in some detail under the broader heading, "Threats to Our Children," the legend usually refers to the disappearance and murder of children from poor homes or orphanages. During the ensuing years, the alleged organ thefts have been conducted on a much more diverse population and in even more varied settings. However, the mistrust of the general population towards official denials of the thefts has not changed in the least. The tacit assumption that a large network of underground facilities with corrupt personnel exists to process and deliver stolen organs provides a foundation for widespread belief in this legend (Donovan 2004, 61). Debunkers of the legend are proactive, accusing those circulating the legend of causing social harm (Donovan 2004, 61). As Donovan points out, these proactive debunkers "claimed the moral high ground and could be considered themselves moral entrepreneurs, promoting both faith in medical practitioners and voluntary organ donation (Donovan 2004, 62). For example, in the position statement released in 1997 from the United Network for Organ Sharing, the organization maintains that this "persistent and totally false urban myth" gained new life and notoriety thanks to the Internet, and the setting is often a popular tourist destination such as New Orleans or Las Vegas. "Many people who hear the myth probably dismiss it, but it is possible that some believe it and decide against organ donation out of needless fear" ("Position Statement" 1997). Campion-Vincent asserts that the two different modes of reference to this legend, allusion or full description, correspond to the measure of acceptance. A full description, she states, "expresses indignation and seeks to convince others, trying to prove that the alleged horrors really do exist," while an allusion, presupposing that the legend is well known and factual, "can be used as an example or argument to reinforce the main theme of one's discourse. One is then using a datum on which everybody agrees (Campion-Vincent 2005a, 95).

Chip and Dan Heath, in *Made to Stick*, claim that the "Stolen Kidney" is one of the most successful contemporary legends in the past 15 years (Heath and

Heath 2007, 4). A retelling of the legend and a discussion of its popularity and memorably formulates the onset of their entire discussion. They maintain that three basic elements of this story "made it stick" in the minds and imaginations of people: unexpected outcome, concrete details and an emotional response from the audience. The highly *unexpected* outcome of a man stopping for a drink and ending up with one kidney, told with a lot of *concrete* details such as the ice-filled bathtub and the weird tube protruding from the lower back, creates a great deal of *emotion*: "fear, disgust, suspicion" (Heath and Heath 2007, 15). The e-mailed warning, "Travellers Beware," went viral in the latter part of January 1997. The warnings of a well-financed, highly organized gang operating in various major American cities drugging business travelers to harvest their kidneys to sell them on the organ transplant black market were received with horror, fear, dismay and disbelief. In quick order, the earlier variants became localized to Las Vegas, for much the same reasons alluded to in the discussion, later in this chapter, on the "Wendy's Chili" Hoax, before moving on to New Orleans and beyond (Mikkelson 2008). Other adaptations to the legend include directives regarding calling 911 and the "chain letter-like" instructions to immediately forward the warning to as many people as possible. "As many urban legends do, this one plays upon our fears. Fear of travelling to distant cities and thus being out of our element. Fear of being ill and desperate. And most of all, fear of being a victim of random crime" (Mikkelson 2008).

Variants of this legend are told for other reasons as well. By telling this story, mothers, uncomfortable about talking to their sons about sex, focus overtly on the drinking issue while still warning their sons about sexual concerns, as these tales mostly comment on the danger from the woman (Whatley and Henken 2000, 162). "If the 'Welcome to the wonderful world of AIDS' legends have lost their impact in warning men against sex with strangers, these theft for transplant stories infuse fear of new dangers into one-night stands" (Whatley and Henken 2000, 160). Gary Alan Fine and Bill Ellis agree, asserting that "the organ-theft rumors critique gender roles, revealing male anxiety that they may be the victims in sexual encounters" (Fine and Ellis 2010, 179). Fine and Ellis liken this aspect of the stolen kidney legends to rumors spread about tourism and the lack of sleep, "for it is during sleep that the villainous can vanish or can anaesthetize the victim. For the middle class, this lack of control is equivalent to the powerlessness of the poor (Fine and Ellis 2010, 198).

Campion-Vincent's analysis of organ theft narratives has revealed that—even as social conditions connect to the narratives have remained constant—the scary tales disappear, become less topical and are restricted to limited circles. The same process has been observed in the case of satanic abuse, where the accusations now operate in small subcultures and no longer raise concern in society at large (Campion-Vincent 2005b, 117).

The Stolen Kidney and Conspiracy Theories

> *Nowadays the mad doctor is more often represented as belonging to a conspiracy-prone oligarchy for whom humans are simply material for experimentation.*
>
> —Campion-Vincent (2002, 36)

This legend has encountered a great deal of mass-media debunking in recent history, but the insistence of a moral prohibition against spreading the story does not seem to hinder its cyclical appearances on the Internet. This is mainly because of the expressions of distrust of medical establishments that both work miracles but change the limits of life and death through that very progress (Campion-Vincent 2002, 35). "Both in legends and in popular culture more generally, doctors emerge as potential criminals who give life and wholeness to some individuals by stealing it from others" (Campion-Vincent 2002, 34). Campion-Vincent, who has researched and written extensively about organ-theft narratives, emphasizes that horror legends, defined as exaggerations and elaborations springing up around disturbing facts, situations of social conflict and mistrust between social groups, play an important part as a tool for alerting public opinion when a new social problem appears (Campion-Vincent 2005a, 170). "Often encouraged by propagandists, who find in these worrying and sensational stories a means of mobilizing the masses in support of their own objectives, horror legends appear, one after the other, adapting themselves to the diverse historical circumstances of the time"(Campion-Vincent 2005a, 170). The horror legends of organ thefts are created and maintained even now by the exploitation of these propagandists and the media industry who utilize the stories for commercial advantage in selling stories (Campion-Vincent 2005a, 192). The legends are also created and disseminated as a symbol of social unrest, danger and distrust of the governments, organizations and medical establishments actively denouncing them as contemporary legends. The events articulated in these legends are still considered plausible by many of the lay public throughout the world (Campion-Vincent 2005a, 193). Perhaps, also, the fact that these legends make frequent appearances in fictional narratives aids in promoting the belief of organized organ-theft rings. In the fictional world, the technical impracticalities of forced organ removal are overcome through current medical corruption or future technological development in futuristic settings (Donovan 2004, 78).

> The conviction that organized organ theft occurs remains strong in the realms of folk and popular culture. First, transplants profoundly threaten our definitions of identity and the boundaries between life and death. Second, they invest god-like technological powers and authority in the medical establishment without resolving important ethical questions. Finally, they dramatize the unequal access to medical care that continues to exist in the Third World and in industrialized countries such as the United States. As long as these concerns and conditions persist, the legends will continue to circulate—if not for factual credibility, then as symbolic expressions of important and unresolved moral issues. (Campion-Vincent 2002, 45)

"Wendy's Chili" Hoax

> *A patron dining at a Wendy's fast food outlet found a human finger in her bowl of chili.*
>
> —"Getting the Finger" (2006)

While technically not a conspiracy theory, the discussion of this hoax is included here because of the numerous connections made by reporters and others with the "Stolen Kidney" contemporary legend and the connections to the sin-filled environment of Las Vegas as well as an example of the media as spin doctors.

The entry regarding this hoax labels the quote from the article, "Getting the Finger," as false, whereas it is actually true—but it should have included the information that the patron had placed the finger in the chili herself. As the entry explains, claims of human body parts in food products are the most horrifying of contaminated-food legends because of the strong societal taboo against cannibalism and the idea of death or dismemberment by an industrial accident ("Getting the Finger" 2006). The news of the actual discovery of the fingertip in the food rocked the news airways, showing up on numerous news broadcasts and in even more newspaper articles. By reviewing the news reports detailing Anna Ayala's arrest for grand larceny, it is readily apparent that many news stations used footage from a single station. "As a result of the similarities in the narrative presentation, viewers from cities across the country would have seen similar, if not the very same, narrative presentations of food contamination" (Plummer 2009, 52). Plummer reports that at the beginning of 24 of the 99 news transcripts, reporters identify the suspect as "a Las Vegas woman." According to Plummer, the wording, vastly different from "a woman from Las Vegas," creates the sense that she is one of the anonymous residents negatively influenced by life in large American cities, symbolic of Las Vegas and representing a sinful female type (Plummer 2009, 52).

> [Contemporary] legends involving Las Vegas in particular focus on the role of prostitution and sexuality in this town and its effects on unwary out-of-towners, many of whom are male. While the parallels between these narratives and the story of Wendy's chili and Anna Ayala do not seem obvious, the contemporary legends and news reports both illustrate the framing of food contamination in terms of gender. (Plummer 2009, 53)

Plummer continues her discussion about contemporary legends set in Las Vegas by commenting on the "Kidney Heist" discussed earlier in this chapter. Plummer's conjecture is that the implications in the "Kidney Heist narratives" set in Las Vegas not only reflect a variety of concerns with large cities, female sexuality and lust, but also present the image of a "Las Vegas woman" as a sort of sociopath, surreptitiously stealing human body parts for personal, monetary gain (Plummer 2009, 53). "This construction of a "Las Vegas woman" then is commonly understood in terms of urban legend and media image. Therefore naming Ayala a "Las Vegas woman" is also a way of connoting her questionable integrity, dangerous morals, and possible criminal status" (Plummer 2009, 54). Plummer considers the story of Wendy's contaminated chili as an allegory for the effects of gambling on traditional American business and corporate structure (Plummer 2009, 55).

The criminal act committed by Ayala is based on ostensive action, building on existing contemporary legends about food contamination. "She enacts a theme prevalent in contemporary legend and thus negotiates the space between consumer and food industry" (Plummer 2009, 63). The disgusting and sensational content of her actions meant that it was ready-made for broadcast. By implying the possible taboos committed by Ayala in the process of contaminating food, news broadcasts cast her as a cannibal, grave robber or murderer. "This diminished her onscreen presence as an individual with agency and instead presented the image of a depraved individual" (Plummer 2009, 66). Police determined that the finger belonged to an associate of her husband's who, after losing his fingertip in a work-related accident, apparently gave it to a co-worker to settle a debt. Ayala and her husband, Jaime Placencia, pled guilty to conspiring to file a false claim and attempted grand theft in September 2005. In January 2006, Placencia was sentenced to 12 years in prison, while Ayala was sentenced to 9 years ("Getting the Finger" 2006). She served four years of her term and, according to an article in the *Mercury News*, was banned for life from the Wendy's food chain (Newman 2010).

Plummer's research on food contamination narratives in the news media demonstrates that they do not necessarily alter opinions about food, but because these narratives often involved placing blame on individuals or groups, they change the way people view ethnic groups, children, immigrants, vegetarians or people outside their respective communities, and the way the individuals approach their own social roles (Plummer 2009, 9).

H1N1 Pandemic

> *Instead of weakening the B.S. movement, the information and misinformation explosion gave it more strength. If you advanced a conspiracy theory in the 1980s, it might catch a ride on the word-of-mouth express, or it might just die. If you put forward a conspiracy theory in the 21st century, it'll live on the Internet forever.*
>
> —Roeper (2008, ix)

During the 2009 influenza scare, there were numerous conspiracy theories circulating about both the disease and the vaccination to protect people from the disease. Concerns, theories, warnings and contemporary legends circulated by e-mail and on reputable health websites. Headlines such as "H1N1's True Toll Not Shown by Death Tally, Picture May Take Months to Come Clear" pointed to the ongoing confusion of many people to the hype and conflicting information disseminated by government and health officials. The headline above was followed by the common question: "Wondering why public health officials are making a fuss about a virus that has so far killed so few people?" (Branswell 2009). The debunking website, Hoax-Slayer, reported the alarmist and inaccurate warnings about the flu, stating that some of the e-mails citing confirmation by the Centers for Disease Control and Prevention and Johns Hopkins Hospital claimed that the virus was already wiping out villages in Asia and was set to kill 6 out of 10 people when a mutated version reached North America (Hoax-Slayer). Within their debunking argument, they assert that spreading blatant misinformation about H1N1 is counterproductive and irresponsible, spreading fear and alarm that could lead to panic (Hoax-Slayer).

A widespread e-mail falsely attributed to Dr. Vinay Goyal among others regarding "Swine Flu Prevention Tips" swamped e-mail boxes as well during this time. Several websites discussed each of these tips for validity and harm. David Emery concluded that of the six tips included in the messages, only two were recommended by the Centers for Disease Control and Prevention and the World Health Organization. Neither of these tips is specific to H1N1 and, in fact, both are based on common sense: frequent washing of hands and avoidance of touching one's own eyes, nose or mouth (Emery "Dr. Vinay Goyal"). A malicious e-mail circulating at the same time referred to the creation of a personal H1N1 vaccination profile on the cdc.gov website. This was a phishing lure which redirected users to a downloadable executable and harmful computer virus ("CDC Vaccination Profile" 2009).

The reason, however, that this topic is included as an example of a conspiracy theory is another series of e-mail warnings regarding the ingredients of the vaccine itself. According to the e-mail this author received from a concerned and well-meaning friend, the Australian government used $100 million to purchase swine flu vaccine that many experts believed was several times more dangerous than the swine flu itself, citing the possible side effect of Guillain-Barre syndrome and the fact that the vaccine was fast-tracked by pharmaceutical companies without proper assessment as examples of this danger. An article in the *New Scientist* addresses these claims as false and misleading. Contacting the Guillain-Barre syndrome was indeed a faint possibility as there were actual occurrences of this happening in 1976 with other influenza vaccines, but, the article reassured its readers, the chances of contacting the disease was much lower than the risk of contacting the deadly flu virus. The conspiracy theorists also claimed that the dangers inherent to the flu were not made known to the public in order to avoid panic and that martial law would be put into effect in order to handle the panic when it came. Snopes.com assured their readers that these types of statements are commonly found, almost verbatim, in all manner of unsubstantiated alarmist e-mails that cover scenarios from Y2K-related chaos to the United States surrendering its sovereignty to the United Nations ("Flu the Coop" 2009).

The fact that this pandemic did not reach the dangerous proportions as was projected may mean that future pandemic warnings will be ignored. However, we can be reassured that the anxiety-ridden, paranoid and harmfully malicious responses to the medical and governmental warnings will be immediate. For more information on this issue please consult Andrea Kitt's book, *Vaccinations and Public Concern in History: Legend, Rumor and Risk Perception* (Routledge, 2011), which was still in publication as this entry was composed.

Doomsday Prophecies

Western civilization barely finished celebrating the fact that the Y2K (the millennium bug) did not fulfil its anticipated promise when the doomsayers were facing another major catastrophe, the end of the world as prophesied by the Mayan calendar or, even before December 2012, by Comet Elenin.

2012 Mayan Prophecy

> *Over the past year or so, many people have suggested that the year 2012 will bring some sort of significant change, either catastrophic disaster . . . or perhaps a new age of enlightenment.*
>
> —Radford (2010)

December 21, 2012, is considered an ominous date for many people who follow the theory of cataclysmic or transformative events occurring as various astronomical alignments and numerological formulae proposed. Theorists suggest that this date marks the end of the world with the arrival of the next solar maximum, a collision with a black hole or passing asteroids. Others interpret the prophecy as the transition for this planet and its inhabitants in a positive physical or spiritual transformation, marking the beginning of a new era. Numerous scholars, however, dismiss the entire concept of cataclysmic events occurring at that time, and Mayanist scholars, in particular, assert that there are no predictions of impending doom found in any of the classic Mayan beliefs or calendars. Scientists and astronomers deny the validity of the apocalyptic forecasts as well.

However, numerous people refuse to accept the claims of these experts, citing that the prophecy is accurate and inevitable. Countless Internet sites, YouTube videos and blog entries continue to endorse the conspiracy of misdirection and silencing that had been occurring on this particular issue. Two examples of websites employing the idea for commercial purposes are 2012 Mayan Prophecy Store, a small business owned by Pakalian Group of Mexico, Mayan experts promoting their indigenous culture values (http://www.printfection.com/2012mayan), and the 2012 Supplies Company (http://www.2012supplies.com/d/) that sells essential supplies for survival such as dried foods, radiation tablets and water purifier kits and has a comprehensive listing of books and full-length videos on the topic. According to this website, the family-owned business is the world's first 2012 survival supply website distributing survival and sustainable-living supplies and information in preparation for the uncertainty of today, 2012 and beyond. It also maintains the Official 2012 Countdown to the end of the Mayan Long Count Calendar.

Along with a prominent online presence, the 2012 Prophecy has been the subject of numerous television programs, films and books. The History Channel aired several special series such as *Decoding the Past* (2005–7), *2012, End of Days* (2006), *Last Days on Earth* (2006), *Seven Signs of the Apocalypse* (2007) and *Nostradamus 2012* (2008). *2012 Apocalypse*, aired by the Discovery Channel in 2009, explores the possibility that massive solar storms, earthquakes, extraordinary volcanic action and other drastic natural events might occur in 2012. The disaster film *2012* (2009) had an advance promotion campaign that went viral. Television spots and websites from the fictional "Institute for Human Continuity" contend that preparation for the end of the world is essential. Apparently, since these promotions did not mention the film itself, many viewers believed the advertisements to be real and contacted authorities in panic. Ironically, as scientific paranormal investigator Ben Radford reported, the film, basically a retelling of the biblical flood story, has nothing to do with the date 2012: "The 2012 angle made a perfect hook for the film: Why not tie it in with the supposed end of the world, allegedly tied to the end of the Mayan calendar in 2012?" (Radford 2010). Due to the plethora of literary titles investing in this topic, only one extremely popular title, Dan Brown's *The Lost Symbol* (2009), is mentioned.

The film and companion book, *2012: Science or Superstition*, are available on the accompanying website, which had been created with anticipated, but unrealized, fanfare. The documentary film, available for purchase as a download or DVD, began in 2007 to answer questions about the Mayan prophecy. The filmmakers claim to avoid "the type from the likes of the History Channel and the Hollywood studios," interviewing leading researchers, writers and scientists in the field regarding the upcoming date, December 21, 2012 (http://www.2012sos.net/).

During their research, the filmmakers realized that despite the seemingly endless supply of resources related to the 2012 phenomenon, no book captures the broad spectrum of opinion, research and myth regarding the prophecy. In order to fill this void, they asked author Alexandra Bruce to build on the film and create an insightful, detailed analysis of the phenomenon. They quote her book, stating that "the 2012 meme has evolved beyond any debates about the relevance of the Maya Long Count calendar to the lives of contemporary human beings. 2012 is about us on planet Earth at this time" (http://www.2012sos.net/). The website includes information on the book and the film and an extensive listings of resources on the topic.

My daughter reports that when she went to rent this movie when it was first released, the store clerk was a bit spooked, informing her that when the DVD first arrived at that location, there were three on file, none had been checked out and none could be found (de Vos, personal communication).

Perhaps one of the most inventive outcomes from this prophecy is the invitation from Mexican tourism to Americans to visit the Mayan ruins. The tourism campaign includes a countdown to the calendar's conclusion and recommendations to visit the archaeological sites in the states of Campeche, Chiapas, Yucatan, Quintana Roo and Tabasco. "Our interpretation of the Mayan calendar is reverse to what many people speculate," Rodolfo Lopez-Negrete, the chief operating officer for the Mexico Tourism Board, on a swing through Los Angeles with other top Mexican officials this summer, said. "Our focus will be on growth and prosperity instead of the end of the world" (Schmidt 2011).

Comet Elenin

> On Internet conspiracy sites, this comet is being blamed for the March 10 Japan earthquake and tsunami, and it is supposed to either hit the Earth or knock us off our axis in September.
>
> —Morrison (2011)

A friend of ours gave my husband and me a bundle of articles printed off the Internet about the dangerous predictions regarding this comet. He was very concerned that our way of living was going to be horrifically altered as a result of this comet. Unfortunately for his authority, the articles were all from conspiracy sites, with very little credibility for this researcher. He explained that NASA was not allowing the truth to be told about the dangers, and I thoughtfully thanked him for anther subheading for this chapter on conspiracy theory.

Leonid Elenin, an amateur Russian astronomer, discovered Comet C/2010 X1, known now as Comet Elenin, on December 10, 2010. The non-periodic comment was estimated to reach its perihelion (closest point in its orbit to the sun) on September 10, 2011. Attracting the attention of doomsayers, 2012ers and end-of-the-world scaremongers, alarming e-mails and frightening headlines warned people about an inevitable collision with the comet with disastrous results. Coming at a time close to the 2012 prophecy caused many people to anticipate and fear the comet and, when questioning authorities on it, to decide that NASA was conspiring to hide the information from the public. Others suggested that Elenin was not a comet but perhaps a planet, a brown dwarf or a massive black hole masquerading as a comet (Morrison 2011). Morrison assured his readers that if Elenin was massive like a planet, brown dwarf or black hole, its gravity would hold onto the gas and it would not develop tail as does a comet, which sheds an extensive thin atmosphere of gas as it approaches the sun (Morrison). But as the September date passed uneventfully, astronomers also discovered that the comet was disintegrating and fading away after being hit by a solar flare on August 20.

However, these further observations have not shut down the doomsayers who predict earthquakes, three days of darkness or a collision with Earth. Checking on articles published just before and just after the heralded date, an even larger plethora of hits on this topic was discovered online. Actively debunking the misinformation and apprehension being disseminated about Comet Elenin, Australian astronomer and blogger Ian Musgrave addressed several concerns regarding conspiracies. His response to the question regarding NASA or the government hushing up the possibility of a collision between the comet and Earth was "Which government?" "Amateur astronomers worldwide are following this comet and continually talking to each other. They have the programs to work out where the comet is going. If the comet was coming anywhere near us, the amateur community would be first to know, and there is no keeping them quiet" (Atkinson 2011). NASA Senior Scientist and Director of the Carl Sagan Center for Study of the Origin of Life, David Morrison, also tried to deflect anxiety in his online article. In answering questions, Morrison maintains that instead of refusing to comment or hiding information on the comet, there was no reason for NASA or the media to be commenting on this small, faint comet as the only people observing and tracking the comet were amateur astronomers. "There is a lot of craziness circulating on the Internet, from people who either don't know much about astronomy or are intentionally making up stories to frighten gullible people" (Morrison 2011). One question, regarding NASA's fear that the comet might knock the International Space Station out of orbit, received from "an inside source," which was why the space flights ended, concluded with "I want to know if I am falling for the conspiracies trap. Where are these people getting their 'updated calculations,' and who is this 'inside source'? I truly dislike when people post these things in order to frighten others" (Morrison 2011). Morrison's response:

> There is no "inside source" from NASA. That is a standard technique of conspiracy websites: make up some story and then attribute it to a secret unnamed source so no one can check up on the claim. I don't know details, but you are partly correct that the NASA Buzzroom website was taken down because of the video claiming that the comet orbit had changed. Also, other people had posted several offensive videos that had nothing to do with NASA or space. Because of these inappropriate postings, the entire Buzzroom website was taken down. I too get lots of offensive messages, but I don't post them. It is important that you be able to trust what you read on a government website. (Morrison 2011)

As with other very current events, there had not been enough time for the story of Elenin and the conspiracies surrounding it to surface in popular culture, except for the countless websites, Vimeo and YouTube videos and the ubiquitous Facebook pages.

Debunking Conspiracy Theories

> *The availability of debunking information, however, does not automatically stop its spread, as there may be reasons besides credibility that might motivate one to pass along a rumor.*
> —Fine and Ellis (2010, 10)

As mentioned previously, it is not my focus to debunk conspiracy theories but, frequently, the targets of these conspiracies feel the need to speak out. Recently, the authors of an article in the *Economist* magazine demonstrated that if "Middle East rumors" is entered in the Google search engine, the first page shown is the page of the Coke website dedicated to debunking contemporary legends about their supposed collusion in the Israeli plot to undermine Islam and to crush Palestine. This result was certainly still the case when the search was replicated. The authors of the article, who supposed the first link would be to websites regarding conspiracy theories, quote experts Derek Rucker and David Dubois, of the Kellogg School of Management, and Zakary Tormala, of Stanford Business School, suggesting that Coke should stop responding to the contemporary legends as the responses just increase their shelf life. The Coke web page now serves as a magnet for search engines. It is rumors that remain in the memory of people, not the denials (Sternberg 2011). "As information is passed around, important qualifiers are lost. A rumour may start as 'I'm not sure if this is true, but I heard that . . . ' Then it evolves into: 'I heard that . . . ' Finally it becomes: 'Did you know that . . . ?' Even when no one intends to spread falsehoods, they spread" (http://www .economist.com/node/18114835.) The article states that other companies such as McDonald's (hamburgers containing worm meat), Procter and Gamble (satanic links) and the various ongoing legends regarding Facebook and its founder, Mark Zuckerberg, need to follow their sage advice (http://www.economist.com/node/ 18114835).

The fabric of rumors, conspiracy theories and contemporary legends involves not only hidden beliefs but also real changes in attitudes, and it serves as a barometer of these changes (Fine and Ellis 2010, 10). Debunking conspiracy theories, specifically, seems fraught with unintentional conflict with those who strongly believe in these tales.

Conspiracy Theories in Popular Culture

> *Whole sectors of literature and media now draw their substance from the prosperous industry of conspiracy theories. Personal involvement in conspiracy theories often takes the form of play mixing humor and distance with paranoia and belief.*
>
> —Campion-Vincent (2005b, 107)

"The specter of conspiracy circulates in the fictional trappings of movies, television shows, popular novels, video games, comic books, and even in an increasingly gullible and market-driven news media" (Fenster 2008, 1). Fenster discusses Dan Brown's novel, *The Da Vinci Code* (2003), as a prime example of conspiracy theory in fiction and part of a "wave" of conspiracy theory in popular culture (Fenster 2008, 6). "The novel's conspiracy theory thus is doubly about information; the characters and readers both gather information to learn *about* a conspiracy and then they learn that the conspiracy itself is about the conspiratorial suppression and disclosure of information" (Fenster 2008, 6). Fenster claims that at least 20 books attempted to debunk or explore further the conspiracy contained within the covers of this book and, subsequently, the film (Fenster 2008, 7).

> *The Da Vinci Code*'s heady mixture of fact, fiction, and conspiracy has led both Catholic and Protestant church leaders to worry that readers are unable to separate the spiritually and historically true from the fictional fantastic and may ultimately come to question their faith based on nothing more than paranoid fantasies about hidden secrets. (Fenster 2008, 7)

Chupacabra in Popular Culture

While the resurgence of the political left in Latin America may have been benefi-
cial for its people, it was not so good for the legendary Chupacabra. What has grown
exponentially, instead, is appearances of the beast as part of popular Latino culture.
Hundreds of Internet web pages, festivals, restaurants, costumes, films, television programs and artistic renditions in music and paintings, as well as an annual bicycle race
through Ciudad Juarez. take their names from the Chupacabra (Jordan 2008, 78).
Manufactured products such as toys, T-shirts, books and other merchandise also
reflect the popular fascination with the creature. For the first decade after the first sighting in Puerto Rico, the folkloric idea of the creature was the focus of articles and non-
fictional reports. It was not until about 2005 that the first non-fiction writing on the
Chupacabra emerged, but not as the bloodthirsty goatsucker since the vast majority
of Chupacabra literary appearances are in sanitized form in children's books
(Radford 2011, 47). "There are no references to cow-raping, slime-spewing, gory carcasses, or real danger to children. Most treat the chupacabra as mere myth, a wink-
and-nod creature only a step or two removed from unicorns and dragons" (Radford
2011, 48). The earliest of these titles, published in English, is by Marie G. Lee. Her
book, *Night of the Chupacabras* (New York: Avon Camelot, 1999), is intended for
readers between the ages of 9 and 12. Another book, aimed at the same readership,
is Terry O'Neill's *Chupacabras* (Farmington Hills, MI: Kidhaven, 2007). Lloyd
Wagner's *Chupacabras: Trail of the Goatsucker* weds the idea of contemporary
legends, legend tripping and the Chupacabra in this novel for the same reading age.

Several picture book versions have also been recently published. *Juan and the
Chupacabras* by Xavier Garza (Houston, TX: Piñata Books, 2006), *The Fairy and
the Chupacabra and Those Marfa Lights* by James A. Mangum and Sidney Spires
(Houston, TX: John M. Hardy, 2008) and Eric A. Kimmel's *The Three Cabritos*,
illustrated by Stephen Gilpin (New York: Marshall Cavendish, 2007), are intended
for younger readers. The latter title is a reworking of The Three Billy Goats Gruff,
set in the southern United States with a Chupacabra replacing the troll as the adver-
sary. Eric Kimmel in his author's note states, "Chupacabra is a legendary creature
who attacks farm animals at night. Chupacabra was first reported in Puerto Rico.
Subsequent sightings followed in Florida, Texas and Mexico. There is absolutely
no scientific evidence that Chupacabra exists. So they say." Rudolfo Anaya's
young-adult novels deal with the legendary Chupacabra in a more realistic manner.
Curse of the ChupaCabra (Albuquerque: University of New Mexico, 2006)
involves a university professor whose interest in Chupacabra folklore leads her to
Mexico to investigate a man's death blamed on the goatsucker, only to discover that
the Chupacabra is used by drug runners trafficking in methamphetamines (Radford
2011, 47). The sequel, *ChupaCabra and the Roswell UFO* (Albuquerque:
University of New Mexico, 2008), has the professor travel to Roswell to stop genetics experiments involving aliens and Chupacabras. "This plot has echoes of the science fiction film *Species*" (Radford 2011, 48). One title in the "Maggie Quinn: Girl
vs. Evil" series by Rosemary Clement-Moore focuses on the Chupacabra. *Highway
to Hell* (New York: Delacorte, 2009) has Maggie Quinn revealing the identity of the
actual predator in a tiny Texan town. The demon antagonist is called a Chupacabra
throughout the novel even after it is rightly identified. "There is a great scene where
the towns people are describing the monster and they all have a different
description ... except for the red glowing eyes" (de Vos, personal communication).

Other literary reworkings and adaptations include the play "Chupacabra,"
included in the anthology *Caribbean Mythology and Modern Life: Five One-Act*

Plays for Young People by Paloma Mohamed (2003), which draws on characters from various Latin American mythologies in dealing with HIV/AIDS in the context of Caribbean culture. A special edition of *The Fantastic Four*, published by Marvel in 2007, set in Puerto Rico, reveals the Chupacabra to be a beast under the control of the Fantastic Four's nemesis, the Mole Man (Radford 2011, 48).

The cinematic and televised Chupacabra certainly predates its literary counterparts. The 1997 *X-Files* episode "El Mundo Gira" (season 4, episode 11) aired just after the full flush of chupacabra sightings and news reports were beginning to slow down, but the writers appropriated only the name, as their depiction did not conform to any of the known legendary traditions. "The chupacabra story is here fused with both alien invasion and werewolf lore: in other words, the episode violates most of the verisimilitude with the oral tradition" (Koven 2004). However, as with the literary reworkings of the goatsucker legend, most of the television and film reworkings appeared in the last decade.

In discussing the filmic depictions of Chupacabra, Radford acknowledges them as cryptids, categorizing chupacabras with Bigfoot and the Loch Ness monster (Radford 2011, 45). He also recognizes that most of the films featuring Chupacabra are grade-B splatter films, fairly recognizable by their titles: *El Chupacabra* (2003); *Chupacabra Terror* (2005); *Bloodthirst: Legend of the Chupacabra* (2003); *Bloodthirst 2: Revenge of the Chupacabra* (2006); and *Legend of the Chupacabra* (2007) (Radford 2011, 46). Written by Cameron Graham, the film *Mexican Werewolf in Texas* (2007) relates the story of four teens in a small Texas town that is plagued by mysterious killings. The adults in the town, mired by racial unrest, accuse each other of the crimes, but the four teens band together to kill the beast and save their town. In this reworking the Chupacabra is identified as a mythical Mexican werewolf. Radford remarks that the only films that treat the Chupacabra as an object of mocking and humor, a source of comedy, are those from Latin America. The films produced in North America treat the Chupacabra as a genuine threat and object of fear and horror. "It seems that, as with the chupacabra in a larger contents, it is mostly foreigners—not locals—who take the creature seriously" (Radford 2011, 47). Not exactly everyone in North America, perhaps as seen in the direct-to-video animated film *Scooby-Doo and the Monster of Mexico* (2003), set in Veracruz, Mexico, where the Scooby-Doo gang are visiting a friend. In another example, the animated *Grim and Evil*'s episode "Aren't You Chupacabra to See Me?" (season 4, episode 9, 2005), a young boy, watching the film *The Legend of the Chupacabra* on his television set, adopts as a pet the small pink chupacabra which came to him through the television. The episode has very little to do with the legendary creature, other than adopting its name. *Crimes of the Chupacabra*, released originally only in Asia in 2009, a parental guidance adaptation of the 1997 cult monster film classic, *Guns of El Chupacabra*, has the adult content removed, replacing it with footage seen in no other version of the film.

Numerous television programs known for explorations of unexplained characters and events have focused on the Chupacabra. Most of these episodes are available on DVD, in collected collections or in segments on YouTube, popping up in great numbers when "chupacabra" is entered in the YouTube search engine. The paranormal reality television series, *Destination Truth* (season 1, episode 3), which sent its crew to Chile to investigate the Chupacabra in the second half of the program "Reopen/Chupacabra," aired in 2007. They interviewed a zoologist from the Buin Zoo who thought the attacks on the farm animals were done by a Kikay (a ferret), and a woman who had 100 of her chickens killed by the blood-sucking chupacabra with glowing red eyes in one night before they could frighten him away. DNA tests on circumstantial evidence proved inconclusive, but the program concluded with the conviction that the livestock were all killed by natural predators. In 2008, *Monster Quest: Chupacabra* (season 2, episode 8) discusses slaughtered farm animals in Puerto Rico, and sightings in Texas, Chile and Mexico, describing the creatures as a humanoid figure with large red eyes and four large fangs. Attempting to capture a live Chupacabra for testing, the program had to rely on hair and DNA samples from skeletal remains, indicating that the creature tested was a dog-coyote hybrid. Even more recently, in *Fact or Faked: Paranormal Files* (season 2, episode 5), which aired in 2011, the team travels to DeWitt County, Texas, to investigate a possible chupacabra sighting recorded by a police dashcam video in 2008. DNA evidence from a similar-looking creature was determined to be a wolf-coyote hybrid. Traveling to Argentina, another team investigates a local news video depicting a humanoid creature, subsequently revealed as a computer-generated imagery hoax.

Additional appearances of the Chupacabra in popular culture include the Chupacabra tracking app for Apple's iPads which offers evidence for both believers and skeptics with a map of Chupacabra's territory and stories told about the creature. Chupacabra is featured in RPG games such as *Read Dead Redemption*, as a fly-fishing lure and in a photoshopped photograph that went viral when their joking comment to a local newspaper was reported as an actual sighting. A search of chupacabra-related items for sale on eBay offers some measurement its popularity. Possibly one of the more bizarre items promoting the existence of the Chupacabra is its inclusion in sideshow exhibits. Radford feels that this reflected the semi-mythical status of the Chupacabra in American culture (Radford 2011, 51).

The Stolen Kidney in Popular Culture

> *The organ theft legends articulate anxieties felt in our societies in connection with modern medicine, which transgresses boundaries which had seemed immutable, and transforms our traditional conceptions about life and personality. These anxieties cannot be directly expressed in our societies, where science is officially considered to be a force for good.*
>
> —Campion-Vincent (2005a, 191)

Organ-theft narratives appear extensively in popular-culture fiction: modern thrillers embrace organ-theft intrigues, medical thrillers focus upon the evil medical establishment and political thrillers center on the victims (Campion-Vincent 2001, 207).

> In the intrigues dealing specifically with organ theft, stock elements predominate, including a powerful medical establishment that organizes recurrent malpractice (thereby ensuring a huge, free supply of comatose patients whose organs can be sold on the world market) opposed by a courageous young female doctor who relies on solid help from her devoted but dull companion to expose the criminal scheme. Firmly set within the medical universe, this "medical thriller" genre is more explicit than the legend in its critique of modern medicine, freely airing fears generated by the power to cure, kill, or maim. Thus, the deliberate killing of

patients (to save money clearly needed by the hospital or to pro-cure more bodies) is a recurrent element in the genre. (Campion-Vincent 2002, 36)

Fear of organ thefts also lies at the center of many of the horror films and liter-ature: "tales about vampires, werewolves, monsters, zombies, dissection, mutila-tions, blood suckers, and human sausage factories" (Bennett and Smith 2007, 126). The following annotations are merely a sampling of the literature and cin-ematic reworkings of this contemporary legend.

Frank Robinson's *The Donor* (TOR 2004), a medical thriller, tells the story of Dennis Heller who wakes up in a small private hospital after a minor automobile accident to discover that not only was one of his organs missing, but it was the sec-ond one that had been harvested from him. "You've been harvested, Richard. Someone stole a kidney and part of your liver for transplants. I've never heard of it happening before, least of all to the same person twice" (13). *Kiss Me Judas* by Will Christopher Baer (Viking, 1998) reworks the variant of the legend where the protagonist wakes up in a hotel bathtub filled with ice after losing one of his kidneys.

The "Stolen Kidney" is told as a contemporary legend in the 2000 episode "Fury" of *Star Trek: Voyager* (season 6, episode 23), serving as a segue to a plot involving a threat from a desperately ill alien species that must harvest human organs to survive. The updated legend relates the experience of a cadet's first time on leave on a vacation planet with the same results as the twentieth-century variants: a missing kidney (Donovan 2004, 78).

Another television series alluding to the legend is that of *Las Vegas* (season 3, episode 15). In this segment, titled "Urban Legends," the main characters enter one of the hotel rooms to find a man lying in a bathtub full of ice. He is, of course, miss-ing a kidney.

This legend also makes an appearance in the film *Urban Legend* (1998) but this time the only reason for the theft is ostensive action. The kidney, left on a bench beside the bathtub awaiting the victim's awakening, is fed to a dog when the killer finishes its murdering task.

One of the lead characters in *Jay and Silent Bob Strike Back* (2001) dreams he woke up in a tub of ice after selling one of his kidneys.

Possibly one of the most effective reworkings of the legend is the film *Dirty Pretty Things* (2001) which was nominated for an Academy Award for Best Original Screenplay and a winner of the "Best Independent British Film" in 2003. The film noir plot revolves around a shady hotel manager who purchases kidneys from the illegal immigrants who work for him and then sold them on the black mar-ket. When the front desk clerk, formerly a doctor in his home country, got involved, the hotel manager is tricked into giving up his own kidney.

References

Aaronovitch, David. 2010. *Voodoo Histories: The Role of the Conspiracy Theory in Shaping Modern History.* New York: Riverhead Books.

"Alarmist and Inaccurate Swine Flu Warning." Hoax-Slayer. http://www.hoax-slayer.com/swine-flu-fear-mongering.shtml (accessed September 21, 2011).

Aruna, T. 2011. "You Can't Catch a Bogeyman." Groundviews. http://groundviews.org/2011/08/25/you-can%E2%80%99t-catch-a-bogeyman/ (accessed September 21, 2011).

Atkinson, Nancy. 2011. "Worried about Comet Elenin? FAQs from Ian Musgrave." Universe Today, July 20. http://www.universetoday.com/87619/worried-about-comet-elenin-faqs-from-ian-musgrave/ (accessed September 21, 2011).

Bennett, Gillian. 2005. *Bodies: Sex, Violence, Disease and Death in Contemporary Legend*. Jackson: University Press of Mississippi.

Bennett, Gillian, and Paul Smith. *Urban Legends: A Collection of International Tall Tales and Terrors*. Westport, CT: Greenwood Press, 2007.

Blaskiewcz, Robert. 2011. "You Can't Handle the Truthiness: A Night Out with the 9/11 Truth Community." CSI, September 1. http://www.csicop.org/specialarticles/show/you_cant_handle_the_truthiness_a_night_out_with_the_9_11_truth_community/ (accessed September 21, 2011).

Branswell, Helen. 2009. "H1N1's True Toll Not Shown by Death Tally, Picture May Take Months to Come Clear." Health Zone Canada. http://www.healthzone.ca/Health/Newsfeatures/Article/726186 (accessed September 21, 2011).

Brunvand, Jan Harold. 2004. "The Vanishing 'Urban Legend.'" *Midwestern Folklore* 30 (2): 5–20.

Campion-Vincent, Veronique. 2001. "The Diffusion of Organ-Theft Narratives." In *How Claims Spread: Cross-National Diffusion of Social Problems*. Edited by Joel Best. New York: Aldine de Gruyter, 185–214.

Campion-Vincent, Veronique. 2002. "Organ Theft Narratives as Medical and Social Critique." *Journal of Folklore Research* 39 (1): 33–50.

Campion-Vincent, Veronique. 2005a. *Organ Theft Legends*. Jackson: University Press of Mississippi.

Campion-Vincent, Veronique. 2005b. "From Evil Others to Evil Elites: A Dominant Pattern in Conspiracy Theories Today." In *Rumor Mills: The Social Impact of Rumor and Legend*. Edited by Gary Alan Fine, Veronique Campion-Vincent and Chip Heath. New Brunswick, NJ: Aldine Transaction, 103–22.

Campion-Vincent, Veronique. 2007. "Review of *Conspiracy Theories in American History: An Encyclopedia*." In *Dossier: Rumors and Urban Legends*. Edited by Veronique Campion-Vincent. *Diogenes* 213: 169–99.

Carey, Bjorn. 2011. "El Chupacabra Mystery Definitely Solved, Expert Claims." http://www.foxnews.com/scitech/2011/03/23/el-chupacabra-mystery-definitively-solved-expert-claims/ (accessed June 27, 2011)

"CDC Vaccination Profile." 2009. Snopes.com. http://www.snopes.com/fraud/phishing/cdcvaccination.asp (accessed September 21, 2011).

Coleman, Loren. 2011. "Grease Devil Riot Kills Police." http://www.cryptomundo.com/cryptozoo-news/grease-devils/ (accessed September 21, 2011).

Coleman, Loren, and Jerome Clark. 1999. *Cryptozoology A to Z: The Encyclopedia of Loch Monsters, Sasquatch, Chupacabras, and Other Authentic Mysteries of Nature*. New York: Simon and Schuster.

de Vos, Gail. 1996. *Tales, Rumors, and Gossip: Exploring Contemporary Folk Literature in Grades 7–12*. Westport, CT: Libraries Unlimited.

Donovan, Pamela. 2004. *No Way of Knowing: Crime, Urban Legends, and the Internet*. American Popular History and Culture. New York: Routledge.

Eberhart, George M. 2002. "Chupacabras." *Mysterious Creatures: A Guide to Cryptozoology*. Santa Barbara, CA: ABC-CLIO, 106–9.

Emery, Davis. "Dr. Vinay Goyal/Dr. Oz Swine Flu Prevention Tips." About.com: Urban Legends. http://urbanlegends.about.com/od/medical/a/dr_vinay_goyal_swine_flu.htm (accessed September 21, 2011).

Fenster, Mark. 2008. *Conspiracy Theories: Secrecy and Power in American Culture*. Minneapolis: University of Minneapolis Press.

Fine, Gary Alan, and Bill Ellis. 2010. *The Global Grapevine: Why Rumors of Terrorism, Immigration, and Trade Matter*. New York: Oxford University Press.

"Flu the Coop." 2009. Snopes.com. http://www.snopes.com/medical/swineflu/asia.asp (accessed September 21, 2011).

"Getting the Finger." 2006. Snopes.com. http://www.snopes.com/horrors/food/chili.asp (accessed September 19, 2011).

Goldzwig, Steven R. 2002. "Conspiracy Rhetoric at the Dawn of the New Millennium: A Response." *Western Journal of Communication* 66 (4): 492–506.

Haviland, Charles. 2011. "The Mystery of Sri Lanka's 'Grease Devils.' " BBC News. http://www.bbc.co.uk/news/world-south-asia-14673586 (accessed September 21, 2011).

Heath, Chip, and Dan Heath. 2007. *Made to Stick: Why Some Ideas Survive and Others Die.* New York: Random House.

Jordan, Robert Michael. 2008. *El Chupacabra: Icon of Resistance to U.S. Imperialism.* Thesis for Master of Arts in History, University of Texas at Dallas.

Koven, Mikel J. 2004. The Folklore *Files*, or How *The X-Files* understands and uses folkloristics. *FOAFTale News* 59 (August): 12. http://www.folklore.ee/FOAFtale/ftn59.htm (accessed June 27, 2011)

Koven, Mikel J. 2008. *Film, Folklore, and Urban Legends.* Lanham, MD: Scarecrow Press.

Kurczy, Stephen. 2010. "Chupacabra Found in Texas: Is It a Coyote?" *Christian Science Monitor*, July 14. http://www.csmonitor.com/World/Global-News/2010/0714/Chupacabra-found-in-Texas-Is-it-a-coyote (accessed September 19, 2011).

Mayberry, Jonathan, and David F. Kramer. 2009. *They Bite: Endless Cravings of Supernatural Predators.* New York: Citadel Press.

McKenzie, Debora. 2009. "Swine Flu Myth: The Vaccine Isn't Safe—It Has Been Rushed through Tests and the Last Time There Was a Swine Flu Scare the Vaccine Hurt People. Why Take the Risk to Prevent Mild Flu?" *New Scientist*, October 21. http://www.newscientist.com/article/dn18014-swine-flu-myth-the-vaccine-isnt-safe—it-has-been-rushed-through-tests-and-the-last-time-there-was-a-swine-flu-scare-the-vaccine-hurt-people-why-take-the-risk-to-prevent-mild-flu.html (accessed September 21, 2011).

Meder, Theo. 2009. "They Are Among Us and They Are Against Us: Contemporary Horror Stories and Muslims and Immigrants in the Netherlands." *Western Folklore* 68 (2/3): 257–74.

Mikkelson, Barbara. 2008. "You've Got to Be Kidneying." Snopes.com. http://www.snopes.com/horrors/robbery/kidney.asp (accessed September 21, 2011).

Monstropedia. http://www.monstropedia.org/index.php?title=Chupacabra (accessed June 10, 2011).

Morrison, David. 2011. "Will Comet Elenin Destroy the World?" *CSI*, April 21. http://www.csicop.org/specialarticles/show/will_comet_elenin_destroy_the_earth_this_year (accessed September 21, 2011).

Newman, Bruce. 2010. "Wendy's Chili 'Finger Lady' Back in San Jose, but Banned from Restaurant." *The Mercury News.* http://freerepublic.com/focus/f-chat/2469015/posts (accessed September 19, 2011).

Newton, Michael. 2005. *Encyclopedia of Cryptozoology: A Global Guide to Hidden Animals and Their Pursuers.* Jefferson, NC: McFarland.

Nickell, Joe. 2006. "Argentina Mysteries." *CSI* 30 (2). http://www.csiop.org/si/how/argentina_mysteries/ (accessed September 19, 2011).

Plummer, Stephanie C. 2009. *Food Contamination Narratives in United States News Media.* Master of Arts Thesis, Bowling Green State University, Ohio, 2009.

"Position Statement: Debunking the Kidney Heist Hoax." 1997. United Network for Organ Sharing, February 21. http://web.archive.org/web/20010420012338/http://www.unos.org/newsroom/archive_statement_022197.htm (accessed September 21, 2011).

Radford, Ben. 2010. "2012: Not a Complete Disaster." *CSI* 34 (1). http://www.google.ca/search?q=ben+radford+%222012%3A+not+a+complete+disaster%22&ie=utf-8&oe=utf-8&aq=t&rls=org.mozilla:en-GB:official&client=firefox-a (accessed September 21, 2011).

Radford, Benjamin. 2011. *Tracking the Chupacabra: The Vampire Beast in Fact, Fiction, and Folklore.* Albuquerque: University of New Mexico Press.

Roeper, Richard. 2008. *Debunked! Conspiracy Theories, Urban Legends, and Evil Plots of the 21st Century.* Chicago: Chicago Review Press.

Schmidt, Rob. 2011. "Mexico Seeks '2012' Tourism." Newspaper Rock. http://newspaper rock.bluecorncomics.com/2011/09/mexico-seeks-2012-tourism.html (accessed September 21, 2011).

"Sri Lankan Grease Devil." 2011. UrbanLegendsOnline.com. http://urbanlegendsonline.com/2011/08/sri-lankan-grease-devil/ (accessed September 21, 2011).

Sternberg, Hannah. 2011. *Is Coca-Cola Making a Mistake by Responding to Rumors It's a Zionist-Controlled Company?* Frontpagemag.com. http://frontpagemag.com/2011/02/14/is-coca-cola-making-a-mistake-by-responding-to-rumors-it%E2%80%99s-a-zionist-controlled-company/.

Whatley, Marianne H., and Elissa R. Henken. 2000. *Did You Hear About the Girl Who . . . ? Contemporary Legends, Folklore and Human Sexuality*. New York: New York University Press.

Wickrematunge, Riasa. 2011. "The Grease Yaka Sightings: Fact vs. Myth." *The Sunday Leader*, August 14. http://www.thesundayleader.lk/2011/08/14/the-grease-yaka-sightings-fact-vs-myth/ (accessed September 21, 2011).

CHAPTER **5**

GHOSTLORE AND SCARY STORIES

> *The internet not only acts as a new conduit for the dissemina-
> tion of old and new ghost legends, it has also enabled the forma-
> tion of new communities of believers who can share, swap and
> debate their experiences. The internet has further enabled a
> new generation of ghost hunters to present their investigations
> to the public, establish reputations and construct their won
> multi-media experiences of the spirit world. Cyberspace had
> become part of the geography of haunting.*
> —Davies (2009, 248)

Legend scholars frequently offer definitions of contemporary legends that pur-
posely exclude mentions of the supernatural, the paranormal or elements of cryptozoology. However, as tellers and retellers of legendary do not differentiate these
characters and events from the corpus of contemporary legends, several of the most
popular of them are included in this chapter. As in the other chapters, the justifica-
tion for inclusion here is the presence of these tales in contemporary popular culture
in the last decade.

> Contemporary ghost lore—while rooted in tradition—is also
> wedded to and embedded in mass culture. Ghost narratives and
> supernatural beliefs are the ancestors of mass-mediated forms such
> as the Scooby-Doo cartoons (1969–1972) . . . but today they are
> marketed as mass media's creation, its offspring. However snarled
> their genealogies, mass culture ghosts and folk ghosts are clearly
> family and despite generations of rationalism and the influence of
> the enlightenment . . . , consumers still buy into the supernatural.
> (Goldstein, Grider and Tomas 2007, 2)

Annette Hill, citing Harvey J. Irwin's *The Psychology of Paranormal Beliefs*
(2009), catalogues the various aspects of the paranormal. These include superstitions (good and bad luck), Psi processes (extrasensory perception), divinatory arts
(astrology), esoteric systems of magic (magical spells), New Age therapies (crystal
powers), spiritualism (spirit communication), Eastern mystic-religious beliefs
(reincarnation), Judeo-Christian beliefs (angel communication), extraterrestrial

135

aliens (alien visitations) and crypozoological creatures (legendary monsters) (Hill 2011, 38). Hill adds traditional folkloric beliefs (vampires and werewolves) to the original list (Hill 2011, 39). Balancing the immense scope of material that could be covered with the available amount of space for this discussion, it was deemed that only a few of these aspects can be examined here.

> Recurring themes include the re-imagining of historical sprit forms or folk legends for contemporary times; relationships with loved ones or relatives who have passed to the other side; the search for evidence through personal experiences; mind, body, and spirit practices that unite various paranormal beliefs as part of personal empowerment; and a resurgence of rationalism that encourages critical thinking on paranormal claims. The process of going mainstream creates a paradox. As paranormal beliefs become part of popular culture, the meaning of the paranormal changes from something extraordinary to something more ordinary. Beliefs become lifestyle practices. But, as people become familiar with representations of the paranormal they also continue to search for unique experiences ... And in the cycle of culture, new products, services and events connect with a never-ending search for unique experiences. (Hill 2011, 64)

Ghostlore

> *The extraordinary fact about the history of ghosts is that it is not a story of decline, unlike that of those related supernatural beings witches and fairies.*
>
> —Davies (2009, 241)

As established in other chapters, technology, particularly in the forms of television, films and the Internet, brings greater access for spectators to the perspectives of ghost enthusiasts and paranormal professionals (Goldstein, Grider and Thomas 2007, 220). One of the most common ways for the public to encounter ghost stories, however, is through the myriad of collections of ghost stories available in bookstores and libraries. Paradoxically, the very fact that these collections are so accessible and popular may have lessened the public perception of the significance of paranormal and supernatural research and scholarship. "Along with the prevalence of science as a means to explain away ghost stories, the packaging of the supernatural as entertainment has helped perpetuate the notion that ghost stories are trivial—that is, all they're primarily good for is generating a few goose bumps" (Thomas 2007b, 30). But, at the same time, this ongoing fascination with ghost fiction and the barrage of images and information from the mass media and advertising has reinforced and elevated general belief in the supernatural in the general public.

> The enculturation of young children into a worldview that encompasses ghosts, haunted houses, and other supernatural entities reinforces a sincere belief in the reality of these beings in later life,

or at least reduces scepticism. Adolescents and adults who grew up hearing and telling ghost stories may very well be more likely to believe in ghosts and such than those who were not enculturated into this supernatural worldview at an early age. (Grider 2007a, 138)

Ghost stories are particularly popular around Halloween, both in the media and with oral storytellers. While some stories come up in casual conversation, others are related much more formally, in cemeteries, on stages or electronically. The stories encompass chilling memorates, warnings and thrills and frights guaranteed to frighten audiences. For college students, however, the relating and listening of tales of ghostly lovers, suicides, violent deaths and other attributes of ghost tales perform a quasi-initiatory experience that assists their expansion of a more intricate sense of self (Tucker 2007, 94).

Numerous literary genres resulted from this ongoing fascination with the uncanny. The gothic novels of the eighteenth and nineteenth centuries, involving sinister monks, innocent young women, dashing young men and haunted castles and cathedrals, spawned a lucrative industry that continues to influence popular culture today. The ghost stories of the nineteenth century in Britain and North America incorporating séances, mediums and confrontations with ghosts reflected the rapid spread of spiritualism that was occurring at the time, while simultaneously, was indicative of the industrialization of mass culture. Magazines also published short narratives about haunted mansions, graveyards and other spectral sites (Tucker 2007, 8). These types of stories remain in publishers' catalogues since their first appearances and are reflected in popular contemporary genres such as paranormal romances and mysteries. Paranormal activities are also re-invented as reality formats, films and events that ask a never-ending series of questions about evidence. "In magazines and books the paranormal becomes a feature of personal empowerment and lifestyle choices. A resurgence in scepticism questions paranormal claims and encourages rational thinking" (Hill 2011, 6).

Jonathan Mayberry and David Kramer discuss different types of ghosts in their book on supernatural predators. The first category of ghost, a fairly conventional perception, is a spirit of a dead person who is either trapped in this plane of existence or has unfinished business to complete. Mayberry and Kramer assert that the majority of people believe that ghosts are aware of humans but not necessarily aware of their own status as a ghost (Mayberry and Kramer 2009, 241). Aware ghosts, intent on completing unfinished business such as redressing a wrong done to them in life or seeking justice for the crime that put them in the grave, struggle to make themselves known in order to injure the person who harmed them, to reveal the identity of the wrongdoer or to make their final resting place known to those still living (Mayberry and Kramer 2009, 241). Several other types of ghosts are also aware of their spectre status and interact with the living. Messenger ghosts, appearing only briefly, often bring messages of comfort to their loved ones. Wagner, in his discussion on ghosts and citing Lauren Forcella at Paranormal Investigations, labels messenger ghosts "crisis apparitions." Sometimes important and useful information is relayed to the receiver of the visitation, but most frequently, the encounter is a type of farewell (Wagner). Poltergeists, also conscious of their spectral nature, are pranksters blamed for unexplained noises, missing items and interfering with plumbing and lights at whim. Some are quite malevolent to the living (Wagner). "In recent decades, cinema has usually presented ghosts as realities, and reprised the character of the purposeful ghost, morally bound to rectifying injustice, or the ghost who desires to make one last gesture of love to the bereaved" (Davies 2009, 246).

> In general, the term [ghost] is used to describe the appearance of the souls or spirits of the dead, while the word *haunting* signifies the recurring manifestation of a ghost witnessed by someone in a certain location. A ghost is usually described as similar in appearance, if not identical, the dead person when they were living. However, not all hauntings involve apparitions. They may be auditory (relating to the sense of hearing) or olfactory (relating to the sense of smell)." (Haughton 2009, 8)

Ghosts also materialize as recordings or residential hauntings, contained by a structure such as a house, graveyard or event that plays as a continuous loop for eternity. Forcella asserts that the rationale behind the recording and cyclic replaying of these events is not understood by live humans. "Whatever the actual mechanism, it apparently possesses longevity as the encore performances of a haunting can continue for decades or longer. Generally, the haunting is a fragment or portion of an actual event" (Wagner). Mayberry and Kramer assure their readers that there is no personality attached to this type of ghost and that it is probably not a supernatural entity (Mayberry and Kramer 2009, 241). As Goldstein, Grider and Thomas remind the reader, "Technology, whether as a medium for ghosts to communicate, or as a medium for the living to communicate about ghosts, is and has always been central to ghost lore (Goldstein, Grider and Thomas, 2007, 220).

Commodification of Ghostlore

> *Advancements in technology frequently prompt revivals in their flurry of new ways to pass on traditions. In ghost lore those revivals, especially mediated by technology, reach out to involve film, television, literature, and the Internet and then feed back both into tradition as well as into new forms of interest in the paranormal.*
>
> —Goldstein, Grider and Thomas (2007, 220)

The commodification of ghostlore is most apparent in the proliferation of local, regional and national collections of ghost stories and supernatural memorates published in the last decade. This increase is most likely connected to the inexhaustible universal concentration on ghost hunting and ghost tourism. There is, of course, a great deal of overlap between these three aspects of ghost business.

Ghost Stories

> *One of the most common ways that the public encounters ghost stories is in the form of a movie or a trade paperback book; these modes of presentation frequently emphasize the entertainment value of the supernatural.*
>
> —Thomas (2007b, 30)

An increase in the commodification of ghost stories, both legends and personal-experience tales, in print collections reflects local, regional and thematic gatherings of tales for all ages of readers. "These popular published collections, intended for both profit and entertainment, are what I have termed the literary commodification of the oral tradition" (Grider 2007c, 7). In her article on collections of ghost stories in Texas, Sylvia Grider claims that the immense popularity of these collections may be changing the repertoire of the oral storytellers to conform to the fixed resources. "In many ways the status of the oral ghost story in Texas parallels the weakened oral tradition of the contemporary legend, which is generally attributed to their widespread transmission on the internet" (Grider 2007c, 7). In many ways, also, this trend parallels that of the oral folktale over a century ago; once these tales were captured in print, the oral telling made way for the reading of them and, at the same time, producing "correct" versions for the canon of tales. A quick search for ghost stories reveals a plethora of titles for virtually every state and province in North America and beyond. These collections of "true ghost stories," which often incorporate sensationalized content and frequently offer commentary on the paranormal, the afterlife, fear of death, fear of the supernatural and human skepticism, have helped shape a fixed perception of the supernatural for an entire new generation of consumers.

The commodification of this fascination of the supernatural also affects the cinematic presentations on television available to consumers with shows such as *Ghost Whisperer* (2005–present), *Medium* (2005–present) and *Supernatural* (2005–present) along with such reality shows *Ghost Hunters* (2004–present), *Ghost Hunters International* (2008–present) and *Paranormal State* (2007–9). "When it comes to distorting reality, it is the so-called reality programming, which focuses on paranormal investigations, complete with electromagnetic sensors and infrared vision, which moves Ghostlore from pure entertainment to scientific—or pseudo-scientific—exploration" (Compora 2006, 85). The appearance of reality television shows regarding the supernatural was primed for audiences by the widely popular 1999 film *The Blair Witch Project*. The initial marketing of this film incorporated the process of pseudo-ostension (hoaxing) in encouraging reviewers and audience members alike to consider the film a "true story" (Goldstein, Grider and Thomas 2007, 218). Besides reflecting an increased attentiveness of the supernatural, this film, along with its earlier counterpart *Urban Legends* (1998), aids in increased public awareness of contemporary legends (Brednich 2001, 9). The television show *Supernatural*, focusing on paranormal-hunting brothers, is frequently mentioned in discussions of various supernatural characters and creatures. This series remains quite different from many of the others in tone, emphasis and presentation but, like *Ghost Whisperer*, does not make any pretence of being anything but fiction. "[Both] deal with ghostly lore and afterlife themes, and viewers may choose to believe in these depictions, but neither of these programs overly portrays their tales as being true, or even being based on truth" (Compora 2006, 85). Unlike *Ghost Whisperer* and the others, however, *Supernatural* also increases awareness of contemporary legends for the general public. But while television and films allow viewers to vicariously and safely experience fears and anxieties about the supernatural, they cannot provide enough of the human interaction that people seem to need—hence, the distinctive rise in the popularity of ghost hunting and ghost tourism in recent years. "Ghost walks, all night ghost hunting, weekend breaks in haunted places, these are just some of the experiences to offer to tourists. Businesses and communities compete for the title of 'most haunted,' with lists for the most haunted pub, hotel, castle, village and city" (Hill 2011, 9).

Ghost Hunting

> *These dedicated men and women spend hours and thousands of dollars [usually their own] walking through old buildings and cemeteries, not because they want to, but because they have to.*
>
> —Brown (2006, xxv)

Paranormal investigation groups are not a new phenomenon. Two of the earliest groups, with illustrious founding members such as Mark Twain, Lewis Carroll and William Gladstone and still in existence today, are the Society for Psychical Research (1882) and the American branch of the Society for Psychical Research (1885). Their focus is exposing fraudulent mediums, and these groups set the standard for ghost research (Brown 2006, xviii). A resurgence of interest in ghost research, partially instigated by the popularity of the movies *Poltergeist* (1982), *Ghostbusters* (1984), *The Sixth Sense* (1999), *The Others* (2001) and *The Ring* (2002), resulted in a multitude of independent ghost-hunting groups globally (Brown 2006, xx). Alan Brown credits the television program *Ghosthunters* (2004–present) with increasing the popularity of ghost hunting as an exciting endeavour for people (Brown 2006, xx). "Advances in technology, such as digital cameras, digital voice recorders, electromagnetic field meters, and negative ion detectors, not only made it seem possible to gather convincing evidence ... but they also lent the groups using these instruments a luster of respectability" (Brown 2006, xx). The primary reason, however, behind the renaissance of vigorous interest and activity is the Internet. "Lest we think that this is only peculiar to televised ghost hunts, and perhaps a calling card of televised media, ghost hunting websites and discussions on online message boards regularly relate subjective experiences with the supernatural" (McNeill 2006, 105). *The Shadow Lands* (http://theshadowlands.net/ghost/) is the most frequently mentioned ghost-hunting website in my research; having an online presence of almost two decades, it provides listings of ghost investigation groups from Canada and the United States and contains over 16,500 postings of real experiences with the supernatural. *The Shadow Lands*, however, does not analyze legends or offer any documentation but provides leads for further research. "Websites contain films, photographs and reports of paranormal investigations. Included in the 'top paranormal sites' website is the online ghost hunting community 'ghostsamongus' which hosts live ghostcams" (Hill 2011, 54). Finding a paranormal community was limited by social mores and geography before online social media. "It was the wild success of the relatively new networking site MySpace that permitted paranormal enthusiasts to transcend the borders of their town or avoid potential embarrassment from judgmental PTA members. A paradigm shift occurred where groups could gather and ghost hunt, and attend paranormal conventions, and feel secure knowing they were with like-minded individuals" (Sagers 2010).

In his research on ghost-hunting groups in the southern United States, Brown discovers numerous similarities among the groups: they all use the Internet to promote themselves, they have all experienced negative comments from the community and they have an almost universal disdain for the director of the television program *Ghosthunters*. Most of them also take advantage of any media opportunity that may come their way from interviews, especially at Halloween, and on nationally broadcast television shows (Brown 2006, 346–47). The twentieth-century ghost hunter is depicted as a "media-friendly, maverick psychic investigator who came to each case with an open mind but who, like any good detective, treated every case as a mystery waiting to be solved rationally" (Davies 2009, 95).

> Relatively new groups that have not yet established a reputation for themselves usually confine their investigations to public places, such as cemeteries and battlefields. The more established groups, especially those who have had media exposure, have no trouble receiving invitations from private residences and historic sites. The prohibitive cost of staying at historic sites that required payment for security guards restricted a number of museums and forts that these groups were able to visit. Most of the groups do not choose outdoor sites for their investigations because of the possibility of interference from such environmental factors as insects, mist, and ambient noise. (Brown 2006, 347)

While cemeteries may be considered public places, they tend to be problematic for ghost hunters. In some areas it is illegal to be in a cemetery after dark or past sundown, as in the case of the cemetery we visited on our legend trip to Rehmeyer's Hollow discussed in an earlier chapter. In other areas, cemeteries may be lairs for homeless people, drug dealers and other criminal activity. "We suggest inviting a local police officer along with you for safety's sake. Also, if you do choose to legally investigate a cemetery, be respectful of the dead and their graves" (Gibson, Burns and Schrader 2009, 79).

Battlefields are considered viable ghost-hunting sites since there were multiple, violent deaths that should provide high levels of paranormal activity (Gibson, Burns and Schrader 2009, 79). Other suggested places for teens wishing to engage in ghost hunting include churches, theatres, schools, colleges and universities, hotels and abandoned hospitals or prisons. Visiting these sites as a ghost hunter is unlike legend-tripping adventures in attitude and focus. "Ghost hunting consists of going out in teams, to places reported, by tradition or by witnesses, to be haunted, and attempting to record, photograph, or otherwise detect supernatural presences (McNeill 2006, 96). Local folklore is often referred to by ghost hunters in validating supernatural claims. "Several hunters I contacted also spoke of looking to folklorists to find out what is 'just an urban legend' and what is not" (McNeill 2006, 99). Two recent publications on ghost hunts for young readers are published by the paranormal investigatory group the Atlantic Paranormal Society: *Ghost Hunt* (2010) and *Ghost Hunt 2* (2011). Both books are reviewed positively by major review journals such as *Kirkus Reviews*.

Ghost Tourism

> *Especially popular in October and November, ghost tours feature places rich in local tale. Jack the Ripper and tales of local murders and urban legends dominate sightseeing tours in London, Paris, Rome, Venice, Prague and Atlanta. Ghost hunts in Montreal and Savannah, cemetery walking tours in New Orleans, and Asian ghost stories in Singapore complete the selection.*
>
> —"Ghosts and Jack the Ripper" (2010)

The commodification of legend tripping resulted in a recent development in sightseeing: ghost tourism. This resurgence and fascination with ghost stories, paranormal investigations and the supernatural demonstrated by tourists is evidenced in the popular media with numerous investigative programs dealing with ghosts and the spirits of the dead. "Ghost tours join the ghost hunter clubs, paranormal-themed television shows, amateur and ethnographic ghost story collections, and ever-evolving procession of horror films in contemporary culture's seemingly endless enthrallment with the paranormal" (Thompson 2010, 79). Annette Hill agrees that ghost tourism is a growth area partially explained by increased interests in paranormal beliefs and history in contemporary culture and diversity in tourism practices. "Ghost tourism combines all three in its mix of ghost stories, folklore and memorable historical events, encounters with ghostly phenomena in jaunted locations, and ghost walks, talks and hunts in tourist destinations" (Hill 2011, 106).

Besides the advertisements for haunted restaurants, real estates, cars and all manner of other places and things publicized as ghostly, there are three main facets for contemporary ghost tourism: hotels that advertise their haunted nature in order to attract guests; ghost-hunting companies that encourage visitors to enact paranormal investigations using group vigils, Ouija boards, séances and technology in the presence of mediums and psychics; and ghost tours or ghost walks (Holloway 2010, 619). Diane Goldstein asserts that folklorists have rarely written about ghost tours, but with the gargantuan numbers of Web site hits on the topic, "scholarly conservatism and disapproval of the commodification of traditional culture is untenable" (Goldstein 2007, 204).

> To a significant extent tourism now defines where ghosts are seen ... Ghost tours and walks have recently become a popular leisure activity. ... These tours have proved particularly successful by placing heritage ghosts in a firmly urban setting, broadening tourism's more traditional association of ghosts with castles and stately homes. Haunted locations were advertised as tourist attractions in Victorian travel guides ... and in attempts to attract English middle-class visitors to Scotland by advertising places mentioned in the hugely popular Scottish novels of Walter Scott. But the tourist ghost is a largely twentieth-century phenomenon. (Davies 2009, 62)

Ghost walks or tours bring the ghosts into urban centers, "precisely the place where previous generations of tourists would not have expected to find it" (Inglis and Holmes 2003, 60). The tourist industry reformulated and repackaged the experience by creating a synergy between a visitor, place and ghost. "The visitor is now a customer, the place has a brand identity, and the ghost is a desirable lodger rather than an unwelcome guest" (Davies 2009, 64). Ghost tours generally involve a costumed guide leading visitors on foot during the evening or at night through sections of a city, telling stories of supernatural and macabre events believed to have occurred at sites along the way (Gentry 2007, 223). The tours focus on the paranormal and present tragedy in a light-hearted manner but, at the same time, often mix deep reflection with education and entertainment (Gentry 2007, 223). "Ghost tours certainly cash in on the wild and wonderful imagery of the paranormal. Rattling chains, skeletons that pop out at you as you are walking, and buckets of water thrown seemingly from nowhere during particularly chilling stories are not uncommon and neither is the extensive rewriting of traditional narratives to capitalize on entertainment value" (Goldstein 2007, 195). While some ghost tours claim authenticity, the entertainment component is a prime concern. Thus a key element of these tours is the interaction between the guide and the participants. "Through dialogue with the tour guide, tourists actively participate as authors and editors in the story presented on the ghost tour rather than merely passive consumers" (Gentry 2007, 232). As in traditional forms of legend tripping, the stories told on the ghost tour depend on the individual guides and the locations being highlighted with some of the narratives relating previous participants' experiences on the tour. The light-hearted aspect of these tours provides tourists with a comfortable distancing from the tour's inherent call for belief in the paranormal (Thompson 2010, 82). "The various popular guidebooks describing local haunted sites and inviting tourists and others to visit them . . . are a popular cultural phenomenon related to legend tripping behaviour because they are . . . based on the premise that, under the right circumstances, perhaps one can personally encounter a ghost or other supernatural being" (Grider 2007b, 186).

> The readiness of human beings to believe in things they cannot see in the conscious, daylight world is striking. We can observe the rapidity with which these ideas spread and the imaginative concepts by which such fears are expressed. Even nowadays, when vampires are largely considered to be the stuff of horror films, we find Scottish teenagers organizing vampire hunts in Glasgow graveyards. It seems that we often enjoy the sensation of fear and the investigation of a shadow, supernatural world from the safety of a cosy fireside or a large company of friends. (Davidson and Chaudhri 2001, x)

The Stanley Hotel in Estes Park, Colorado, exemplifies the popularity of ghosts, along with a connection with author Stephen King, as part of their tourist attractions. The hotel website promotes regular ghost and history tours conducted by professional and experienced tour guides to explore the history of the hotel, built in 1909 by F. O. and Flora Stanley; the hotel's famous room #217 where Stephen King, in 1974, was motivated to write *The Shining*; ghost stories and sightings; the most haunted rooms and places; and tours through the underground tunnel (http://www.stanleyhotel.com/tours/). The Stanley Hotel is considered more successful as a tourist destination than as a hotel as the daily ghost tours attract approximately 500 visitors each day (Stollznow). Allegedly haunted by at least 12 ghosts, including Freelan O. Stanley, the founder, whose ghost, attired in a tuxedo, appears in the billiards room. The hotel also contains a haunted piano playing phantom music, and a ghostly party in the ballroom. "In an unwitting historical revisionism, elements of *The Shining*'s Overlook Hotel are pasted onto the Stanley Hotel . . . Although the plot was conceived at the Stanley Hotel, it is not based on it. The mini-series was filmed there, but Stanley Kubrick's original movie was filmed in Oregon and England . . . The book's fictional ghosts have also become the resort's ghosts" (Stollznow 2009).

The Stanley Hotel has also adopted spectral history from neighbours. The previous owner of Elk Horn Lodge relayed the ghost stories to an author who needed a few more stories for the book on the Stanley Hotel and borrowed them with permission from the owner. "The Stanley Hotel's ghost stories appear to be a jumble of tales from the Elk Horn Lodge, local history blended with urban legend, staff anecdotes, and the creation of visiting psychics, guests, ghost hunting groups, and TV shows such as *Ghost Hunters*" (Stollznow 2009).

Paranormal reporter Karen Stollznow attended an investigation with the Rocky Mountain Paranormal Research Society (RMPRS) to see if the Stanley Hotel was "haunted by anything more than its reputation." Stollznow comments that the members of RMPRS called themselves "Paranormal Claims Investigators" in an attempt to have a neutral title that does not contain the perceived negative connotations of "skeptic" or the implication of "believers" with the term "ghost hunter." However, she points out, careful labelling did not help. "The word *paranormal* in their title is a neon sign portraying them as believers to skeptics, although it was adopted to keep from deterring believers by avoiding the label *skeptic*. Labels aside, they are investigators who adopt a skeptical, scientific approach to examining claims of the paranormal. Importantly, they do not dismiss claims a priori but rather assess and challenge them (Stollznow). The RMPRS, accompanied by Stollznow, researched the beliefs and claims, solved some mysteries, maintained the historical integrity of the hotel and performed valuable outreach. What they did not find was any anomalous phenomena (Stollznow 2009). This finding, of course, does not lessen the popularity of the ghost tours for people fascinated by the possibility of a paranormal encounter or the postings of experiences on YouTube.

In her examination of three ghost tour companies in Edinburgh, Joy Fraser discusses the similarities of one of the City of the Dead tours with that of the three scenes of legend tripping first established by Bill Ellis in 1981. The first scene, that of experienced group members telling new members about the reputation of a haunted local place, is represented by the guides telling their audiences the story on the way to the Black Mausoleum. Some aspects of this story are also related through the promotional material and the media coverage of the poltergeist and previous tours (Fraser 2005, 217). The concrete trip to the location and the invoking of the supernatural by prescribed activities is the second scene. The tour performance and the journey to the Covenanters' Prison and Black Mausoleum exemplifies this scene. The final scene of both the legend trip and the tour experience is the sharing of the experience after returning to "safety." Fraser observes that, at the conclusion of the tour, the guide invited the audience members to discuss any uncanny events they may have experienced while relaxing in the safety of a nearby pub (Fraser 2005, 218). "Like legend-trip participants, both guides and audience members . . . 'cultivate an atmosphere of fear' in the process of 'seek[ing] out contact with the supernatural and attendant dangers' " (Fraser 2005, 219). However,

> the use of the jumper-outer on the City of the Dead tour highlights a fundamental difference between the ghost tour and the legend trip. The tour is a commodified performance: audience members on the company's tour are required to pay for the chance of an encounter with the Mackenzie Poltergeist. In contrast to the legend-trip, where participants are usually closely interconnected, the ghost tour is characterized by the existence of clearly marked distinctions between guide and audience. (Fraser 2005, 239)

Three key ingredients for ghost tour success are identified by the ghost tour guides interviewed by Fraser. In order to be informative and entertaining, as well as effective in scaring the audience, a good tour mixes "history, humour and horror" into the presentation (Fraser 2005, 20). The selection of the locations is another key factor. The locations should not be easily located by tourists on their own and should have a claim to be genuinely haunted for maximum effect. This ghost potential offers the likelihood of audience members obtaining photographs of ghosts or other chilling encounters (Goldstein 2007, 189). In Fraser's examination of the three distinct tours, she discovers that the tours by Mercat emphasized the role of the oral storyteller as a central component of their claims for authenticity (Fraser 2005, 80). Witchery Tours, on the other hand, exemplifies "the model of tourism as a modernistic 'quest for authenticity,' . . . indicative of a cultural shift towards postmodern-or post-tourism, in which tourism comes to be seen as a playful 'game' rather than a serious quest" (Fraser 2005, 175). Although audience members are given several physical frights in the performance, they are discouraged by the guides to interpret any of the encounters as genuine supernatural activity (Fraser 2005, 178).

The third tour group, City of the Dead, structures the entire tour around the possibility of an actual encounter with the poltergeist inside the Black Mausoleum in the cemetery. Fraser states that "in the event that an 'attack' occurs on any given tour, these narrative and performance frames collapse into one another, with participants literally acting out the legend" (Fraser 2005, 180). Incidentally, there are numerous videos available on YouTube of City of Dead tours for those who either cannot go on the tour or would like to compare their experiences with those of others. Apparently in the first two years of this company's existence, members of the audience have fallen victim to over 70 alleged poltergeist attacks (Fraser 2005, 183). "As a result of the incidents experienced by participants on its tours, the newly-formed company found itself confronted with an urgent need to create a dramatic and believable history for the Poltergeist suitable for presentation on the tours, in its promotional material and in its dealings with the media" (Fraser 2005, 185). Thus this ghost tour evolves into a commodified form of legend tripping with the story of the Mackenzie Poltergeist. The resultant tale has a dual purpose, to satisfy the demand of an explanation of the phenomenon and to maintain the public's fascination and fear of it, while meshing with established local belief and local legends. "The earlier accounts also lend the Poltergeist story an added air of authenticity and believability. They enable the company to present the Mackenzie Poltergeist phenomenon as a continuation of a local supernatural folklore tradition" (Fraser 2005, 215).

> Having created its own legend in response to public fascination with the Mackenzie Poltergeist phenomenon, City of Dead provides the Poltergeist with a dramatic and believable history while maintaining a careful balance between "explanation" and "mystery" which enhances the draw of the supernatural encounter that the company promises its audiences. Significantly, it is a narrative that intersects with pre-existing local belief and legend traditions concerning supernatural activity in and around George Mackenzie's' tomb. It thereby provides an illustration of the ways in which local folkloric traditions may come to be used and adapted within the touristic context. The construction of the Poltergeist legend depends on a process of piecing together assorted fragments of information and interpretation, a process in which the fact that a particular piece of the puzzle "seems to fit" is more important than whether or not it can be proved to be true. Indeed, "the facts" may be manipulated and even invented in the interests of creating a coherent and engaging narrative. (Fraser 2005, 251)

Joy Fraser and Diane Goldstein both mention the Haunted Hike Tour in St. John's, Newfoundland, created and operated by folklorist and storyteller Dale Gilbert Jarvis. The promotional material on the website encourages tourists to take part in an "Ambulatory Theatrical Exploration of the Macabre ... with the distinguished Reverend Thomas Wyckham Jarvis, Esquire, eminent Lecturer on the Paranormal, well versed in Grimm Tales of the Vengeful Deceased, Murthers of Gruesome dispatch, Curious Manifestations of the Holy Ghost and Historical Miscellanea" (http://www.hauntedhike.com). Along with many other storytellers, I survived the haunted hike (there is a Facebook group of almost 500 members that attests to survival of these hikes over the years) at a recent Storytellers of Canada/ Conteurs du Canada conference. Rain or shine, the Reverend guides his audience through the downtown core of hilly St. John's. Amongst the umbrellas and frequent cloud bursts, we followed our appropriately dressed guide as he warned us that "this is not a tour for the faint of heart," informing us that he would not be responsible for "shortness of breath, palpitations for the heart, melancholia or even sudden death." In interviews with Dale Jarvis, he stresses that ghost tours are theatre, and his costume and presentation style emphasize the theatrical aspect of the tour. "For Dale, the theatre is what his clients want and expect" (Goldstein 2007, 196). But at the same time, he does not make up these stories, there are no jumpers coming out to frighten the audience and his marketing affirms the authenticity of his material. "It's not a haunted house, where the whole thing is fabricated" (Fraser 2005, 70). We were, perhaps, a difficult audience for Dale, all of us well versed in folklore and ghost stories, or, alternatively, a very receptive audience as we were willing to fully experience all that our guide and his tour had to offer us. And, as Goldstein maintains, "We should not be surprised that for tour patrons, character portrayals and over the top dramatisation exist side by side with less trivialized, more serious aspects of belief and personal narrative. Such a combination mirrors traditional supernatural culture in which serious belief genres and personal experiences are held in repertoire and told together with humours genres and more heavily fictionalized narratives" (Goldstein 2007, 199).

The search term "ghost tours" on YouTube on August 12, 2011, brought forth over 2,500 results from all over the world; "ghost tours, MacKenzie" produced 35 videos about the poltergeist tours with an abundance of other videos tagged on the sidebar; "MacKenzie Poltergeist" yielded over 50 videos; 26 videos were found by searching "Mercat tours"; while searching for "St. John's Haunted Hike" generated only 1 video, "Ghosts of Signal Hill," posted approximately one month previous to the search.

Ghost Legends Revisited

> We found that stories are still alive and well even in our modern scientific world, and that ghost and death lore, far from being a dying folk style, is still a part of contemporary society not limited by race, creed, class or rural/urban status.
>
> —McCormick and Wyatt (2009, 6)

The legends in this section were discussed in detail in my previous book on contemporary legends. When *Tales, Rumors, and Gossip* (de Vos 1996) was written, there were so many academic discussions on "La Llorona" and "The Vanishing Hitchhiker" that I dedicated two separate chapters to the two legends.

Since that time, additional research and reworkings of the two tales, and others, have materialized. The subsequent discussions, while referring to some extent to the material presented in that earlier book, focuses on the material published after 1996.

"La Llorona"

> *A ghostly female figure who haunts the canals, creeks, and rivers, wailing loudly as she searches for the spirits of her children whose deaths were the direct result of her madness or spontaneous conscious decision to get rid of them by drowning.*

Nasario Garcia introduces his discussion on La Llorona by stating that she was one of the most popular and well-known figures in Latino folklore, particularly for those of Mexican descent. Young children and adolescents "may not be intimately familiar with the details regarding this roving woman of the night, who searches for the children she allegedly drowned or repents of some other mysterious transgression, but at least they have heard of her" (Garcia 2007, 293). Anne-Marie Hall affirms this familiarity, stating that every child she interviewed in the rural school believes that at least some part of the La Llorona legends are true as they have been told the stories by reliable family members (Hall 2006, 395).

> *La Llorona* demonstrates how the oral tradition works: Certain legends are constantly rewritten but their archetypal features remain intact. . . . The notion of mothers doomed to suffer is constant in all the stories. The idea of salvation and entrance into heaven despite some sinful stains on one's soul is the core theme in almost all versions of the legend. Whether from alcohol, infidelity, or sin and damnation, the lessons are cultural warnings, modernized or adapted for each child's world (Hall 2006, 395)

Garcia considers this continual awareness of the wailing woman a notable exception in the modern age that is far removed from interest in traditional folklore, and mentions the interest of educators, librarians and storytellers in the story and figure of La Llorona as an emerging cultural awareness that occurs within and without the contemporary Latino population.

> La Llorona has been labelled everything from a ghost to an old hag, a murderer, an adulteress, and a bogeywoman. Some adults have invoked her name in much the same way as they have the *aguelo*, her counterpart, the bogeyman, to scare children into obedience with stories of this sad figure who roams the countryside, wandering among rivers and arroyos and scaring both children and adults (mostly men). (Garcia 2007, 294)

Shirley Arora researched the ways children up to age 12 are affected by, react to and relate the Llorona story. She states that:

> For many individuals of Spanish-speaking—particularly Mexican—background, initial acquaintance with the Llorona comes in early

> childhood and in the form of warnings on the part of parents and other care givers not to stay outside after dark, or not to go near the river, or the canal, or some other local body of water, "because the Llorona is there looking for her children and she might mistake you for one of them and carry you off." (Arora 2000, 29)

While the most typical elements of the legend integrate infanticide, death by drowning, divine punishment, everlasting remorse and the weeping or wailing figure, the theme of infanticide, at least in the United States, became less prevalent in recent times. "To some extent this change may represent a deliberate attempt on the part of some parents to 'soften' the legend ... and make it less disturbing for the children, while still preserving the capacity of the Llorona to serve as an effective threat figure" (Arora 2000, 38). Hall recommends that educators in the United States should encourage students from Mexico to talk, write and read about their indigenous beliefs as, she discovered, La Llorona "is not a story, it is real" (Hall 2006, 400). "In these Mexican schools, through the writing and speaking of sixth-grade students, I found the magic of local legends and the oral tradition of the *abuelas* (grandmothers) to be a significant part of the curriculum" (Hall 2006, 400).

Children do not necessarily appreciate the softening of the legend. Arora discovered that death by drowning has been supplemented in the tales told by children. La Llorona's children are now being stabbed or burned to death, their heads chopped off with an axe or even shot to death in the versions children related (Arora 2000, 39).

> In the case of the Llorona, there is evidence of an evolution from parent-invoked threat figure to peer-invoked "scary being" whose frightfulness derives in part from the degree of belief shared with the adults who play a significant part in the children's lives. There is likewise a progression from cautionary being invoked merely by name to a figure with a "story" whose details serve to capture and hold the child's imagination and, to the degree that the story reflects elements of the child's own world, to enhance the reality, and therefore the fearfulness, of the threat that the Llorona represents. (Arora 2000, 31)

Narrators of all ages portray La Llorona alternatively and simultaneously as a bogeyman, ghost, goddess, metaphor, legend, person and a symbol (Perez 2008, 2). Stephanie Serrano agrees that one of the prime functions of the folkloric La Llorona is that of a modern-day bogeywoman, "initially beautiful, but ultimately hideous and ghastly ... her tale also serves as a means for curtailing inappropriate displays of femininity in favor of appropriate ones—be a good mother, be a good wife, and comply with dominant notions of proper femininity" (Serrano 2009, 3). La Llorona legends teach young males to view women as temptresses, affirming the sexual agency of women, symbolizing their behaviour as dangerous to males as it threatens male access to, and control over, women's bodies (Perez 2008, 28). Young females learn that sexuality, when acted upon, may result in despair and eternal punishment (Perez 2008, 28). For both genders, the threat of a thieving mother taking them away from the security of their "real" mothers and their home underlines much of the comprehension of this cautionary legend.

Serrano discovered in her research that the figure of La Llorona does not fit neatly into the familiar context of vindictive and scornful woman obsessed with the man in her life but instead haunts the texts by traversing varying sexual orientations, ages, agendas and emotions. (Serrano 2009, 10). "If we continue to view the myth of La Llorona through a stagnant, conservative, and fixed lens, her story cannot be revolutionary. Recognizing the inventive possibilities of this tale garners tremendous import when considering the real world confines that enclose and stunt the contributions of Chicanas in the U.S." (Serrano 2009, 11). Others agree with this position. "Whether cultural producers represent or revise the legend, position La Llorona as a champion for her people, or turn her toward new narrative possibilities, what matters is that for approximately five centuries she has held a powerful place in the cultural and political imaginations of her people" (Perez 2008, 208).

> Thirty-five years ago, La Llorona remained largely a part of oral stories, but the figure has wandered out of this genre onto pages, canvases, celluloid, and even into cyberspace where, in a substantial change in the narrative's structure, we must instead look for her. Complicating this movement is the fact that La Llorona is used now around the world to sell or promote everything from coffee and women's underwear to films and academic conferences. (Perez 2008, 2)

In 2002 a television commercial for milk, created by Los Angeles Hispanic film students for the California Milk Processor Board, won a silver award in the Ad Age Hispanic Creative Advertising Awards. The commercial is a darkly comical spin on the La Llorona legend, emphasizing only her ghostliness and her weeping as she glides past a couple sleeping in their home, a book of stories about La Llorona resting on the man's chest. The ghost's unhappiness is abated when she finds a carton of milk in the refrigerator but soon returns when she discovers that the milk carton is empty. The television commercial may be viewed on YouTube: Got Millk: La Llorona (the spelling error of "milk" is part of the title). The goal of the overall campaign was to increase milk consumption of young-adult consumers. The recognition of the amusing substitution of milk for La Llorona's lost children depends on the audiences' familiarity with the story. "Without this information, the production loses much of its impact, as demonstrated by the reaction of Anglo viewers who thought the ad was a promotional tie-in to a film about a ghost" (Perez 2008, 60). My Canadian students did not understand the reference to this contemporary legend when they viewed this commercial until the legend was discussed in class. La Llorona has obviously not fully migrated this far north from her traditional haunting arena. Unfortunately, while the commercial was popular, attested to by numerous blog entries and Facebook hits, it did not make any significant impact on the sale of milk in the Latino youth market. Spanish speakers were not the only intended audience as the commercial also ran in English-speaking markets so, while the intended increase in milk consumption may not have been realized, the commercial did disseminate the legend to a wider and diverse audience (Perez 2008, 62).

There are countless sites regarding this legend that explain variants of La Llorona's origin story but even more that offer a forum for people to include their own experiences with La Llorona. There are over 122,000 images that can be found doing a simple Google search. Unfortunately for the scope of the possible research available, this survey is limited to English-language sites. *Legends of America:*

A Travel Site for the Nostalgic & Historic Minded (http://www.legendso famerica.com/gh-lallorona.html), for example, offers a wide variety of personal-experience narratives from people of all ages. There have been also several exhibits and conferences on the topic of La Llorona in the past decade. One recent multimedia exhibition, "La Llorona Unfabled: Stories to (Re)tell to Little Girls," at the Galeri de La Raza in San Francisco, finished April 16, 2011. Paintings, drawings, videos, a public art project and a digital mural were some of the formats showcasing the La Llorona image and story. In his review of the exhibit, Matthew Harrison Tedford states that it is "fierce and intrepid, but it is not naive. The Latina body is under assault—from culture, labor and policy. La Llorona persists" (http://www.artpractical.com/review/la_llorona_unfabled_stories_to_retell_to_little_girls/, June 6, 2011.

"The Vanishing Hitchhiker"

> One night a man met a woman in the neighbourhood, and the pair went to the cemetery for a tryst. She borrowed a jacket from him but then suddenly ran away. He followed, searching for her. Eventually he found his jacket at a crypt bearing a picture of a young woman who was entombed there. It was the same young lady!
>
> —Nickell (2006)

Joe Nickell comments that the guide who told him the above version of the "Vanishing Hitchhiker" in Argentina felt the authenticity of the story was dubious since there was a general absence of pictures of the deceased at the tombs of Recoleta. He draws definite parallels to the "Vanishing Hitchhiker" legend with the meeting of the couple, the young lady's sudden disappearance, the cemetery as the destination and the scene of revelation incorporating the jacket and photograph. "Thus, the Recoleta tale is simply another variant of the ubiquitous legend which has antecedents as far back as 1876" (Nickell 2006).

> Nowadays, the legend of the Vanishing Hitchhiker seems a more complex, diffuse and subtle story than it did fifty years ago to its first researches. There can be no certainly about its age, the search for its origins has long since been abandoned as futile, and it appears to be much more widely distributed and culturally variable than was at first suspected. The result is that it is now best regarded, not as an easily definable type, but as a more diffuse complex of related stories. Even so, its themes and motifs are both so adaptable and so ubiquitous that it is difficult to draw maintainable boundaries between it and other stories about numinous or supernatural beings interacting with living mortals on roads or similar liminal places. (Bennett 1998, 12)

Barbara Mikkelson offers an example of the legend collected on the Internet in 1998. She states that the appeal of these stories lay in the nature of the encounter—an accidental interaction with the supernatural. "Such tales underscore the belief that representatives from the spirit world can be encountered at any time and by anyone. Adding to the horror factor is the specter's passing for a living person"

(Mikkelson 2011). This adds to the appeal as well, she reflects, since it makes it easy to believe that one would not easily recognize a ghost if one encountered it. "Belief in roadside ghosts like the Vanishing Hitchhiker is not that different from many indigenous folk beliefs and perhaps not that different from a deeply held archetype of human emotion: the inability to let go of deceased loved-ones by those who remain living" (Johnson 2007, 32).

Examples of the "Vanishing Hitchhiker" have been categorized as diverse types of ghostlore in the literature: disappearing ghosts and returning ghosts. Disappearing ghosts manifest themselves in human form rather than by creating disturbances, making eerie sounds or moving objects." Some of these ghosts are seen only in particular conditions or settings, probably associated with their earthly life, while others may be encountered at various places ... the most common type of "disappearing ghost" story is that of the vanishing hitchhiker"(McCormick and Wyatt 2009, 29). However,

> perhaps the Vanishing Hitchhiker legend is best understood in the context of ghost lore as a whole, where it fits in well with the tradition of the ghost who returns briefly to the land of the living in order to settle unfinished business, to continue an activity they were known to pursue during their lifetime, or most relevantly, in terms of Vanishing Hitchhiker stories, to escape from their in-between, luminal state and find rest. Whatever its true origin, the fact that the Vanishing Hitchhiker is still discussed and reported today indicates the motif still has meaning and relevance in the folklore and urban legend of modern 21st-century society. (Haughton 2009, 98)

Gillian Bennett categorizes the hitchhikers themselves in two large overall groupings rather than the four types enumerated earlier by Beardsley and Hankey, discussed in chapter 13 of *Tales, Rumors, and Gossip*. Beardsley and Hankey's four types are:

- Type A, the most common variant of the story, involves the hitchhiker, picked up on the road, vanishing while in the vehicle and the unexpected revelation that the hitchhiker had been dead all the time.
- Type B includes stories in which the hitchhiker, often an elderly female, prophesies disaster or the end of a war. The essential differences between these two types is that the hitchhiker here is elderly and the journey takes place in the daylight hours.
- Type C, similar to Type A, differs in the location of the original meeting with the hitchhiker in that she is usually picked up at a dance or other place of entertainment and leaves an article behind in the vehicle when she vanishes.
- Type D stories are those in which the hitchhiker is later identified as a deity (de Vos 1996, 334–38).

Bennett's two major groupings, supernatural entities or numinous beings, are further subdivided according to the way the significance of the hitchhikers is discovered when they exhibit "a non-natural alternation between being there and not-there (the disappearance which has given the stories their title)" (Bennett 1998, 4).

> The storyteller ... needs to supply some secondary proof which the traveller (and the story audience) will accept as conclusive. So, in the most familiar forms (the story as told recently in regions

of the western world that have a Protestant Christian religious tradition) numinous beings tend to reveal special powers such as
prophesy, and supernatural beings (in this case invariably ghosts)
tend to leave a personal possession on their grave as a token, or
ask to be taken to a specific destination where a train of circumstances will later provide proof that they are in fact dead.
(Bennett 1998, 4)

Elements of the current hitchhiker of the contemporary legend that have
remained constant since the first folkloric examinations almost 70 years ago include
the female archetypical hiker, the way most of the ghosts meet their demise from
traffic accidents, either from being inside the vehicle or from being a pedestrian,
and the random innocent nature of the victims (Bennett 1998, 8). Bennett analyzes
the ultimate destination of the hitchhiking ghosts. "In stories where the ghosts leave
a token in the cemetery . . . it is plain they are going back to their graves" (Bennett
1998, 8). The other ghosts, however, seem to be haunting the scene of their deaths,
unable to find final rest and endlessly repeating the cycle of their journey. Bennett
determines that the destination-giving hikers can be seen as dying with unfinished
matters on their mind that force them to return to the land of the living in an attempt
to complete their tasks (Bennett 1998, 9). "They could be read as dying before they
could enjoy some simple human pleasure—a dance, fatherhood, marriage, a family
reunion, homecoming, and so on. Their haunting—rather than being the re-
enactment of the familiar joys of life (as in older ghost traditions) or the desperate
search for an exit from an existential maze . . . is the compulsive enactment of pleas-
ures denied" (Bennett 1998, 10).

Bennett and Smith, in *Urban Legends*, subdivide the vanishing hitchhiker
tales into six major subtypes according to their definitive destinations and
purpose:

- Home-going ghosts: The ghost is encountered in a desolate place. She wants to
  return home where there is always a grieving parent waiting for her, to show the
  traveler a photograph and/or give an explanation for the ghost's attempted journey
  (Bennett and Smith 2007, 289).
- Party-going ghosts: The ghost, usually a young girl dressed in party attire, is picked
  up by a young male who is going to the party. This version usually ends with a "coat
  on the grave" sequence of events where the ghost identity is discovered the following day. "Some of these stories strongly recall traditions about vampires and she-
  devils who seduce unwary men. They have similarities to the 'Devil at the Disco'
  legend about girls who go to dances and unwittingly dance with the devil (though
  with the roles reversed)" (Bennett and Smith 2007, 292).
- Coat on the grave ghosts: This less common variant begins and ends like the stories
  of the party-going ghost but has the same middle section as stories of the home-
  going ghost with the hitchhiker being picked up near a cemetery and vanishing from
  the car while it is still moving. This variant has a more traditional feel than the other
  versions as the ghost appears during the night and must return to her grave at the
  break of dawn (Bennett and Smith 2007, 295).
- Jesus on the Thru'way: Instead of giving directions or asking to be taken home, this
  hitchhiker issues a prophesy about the end of the world or the second coming, or
  announces that he is Jesus (Bennett and Smith 2007, 296).
- Hitchhiking prophets, saints and aliens: These are non-human hitchhikers who ask
  for a ride and then mysteriously vanish. Examples include the goddess Pele in
  Hawaii, the Three Nephites of Mormon tradition and others who offer warnings,
  give help or make predictions (Bennett and Smith 2007, 297).

- Double prophesy: Very popular during World War II, the mysterious hitchhiker makes two prophesies: the first one about world affairs, often predicting the end of the war, and the second one, offered as proof of the truth of the first one, about the presence of a corpse in the car at the end of the journey (Bennett and Smith 2007, 300).

"Resurrection Mary"

In addition to the Malaysian *langsuyar*, the Russian "vanishing mother," and the English ballad "The Suffolk Wonder" briefly discussed in *Tales, Rumors and Gossip*, one major traditional ghost that belongs in this category was not addressed in that discussion.

The best-known and oldest ghost story in Chicago is Resurrection Mary, a vanishing hitchhiker type of supernatural phenomenon. This young woman has been hitchhiking from the Willowbrook Ballroom to Resurrection Cemetery since the 1930s when she was killed in a hit-and-run accident on her way home from a dance. There are several different versions of Mary's story: one follows the traditional vanishing hitchhiker scenario, but a more disturbing version involves a driver attempting to miss her as she darts in front of the car but ends up hitting Mary regardless, who then runs back into the cemetery. There sightings of this ghost have been reported up until the late 1980s. In the last decade, several low-budget horror films based on this legend and employing the Resurrection Mary label have been released; Michel Lansu wrote and directed the 2005 adaptation, and Sean Michael Beyer wrote and directed his version in 2007.

"Humans Can Lick Too" or "Doggie-Lick"

Similar to "The Roommate's Death," a young woman, oblivious to a grisly killing taking place in front of her, later realizes the danger with a chilling comment left by the murderer. Be it dog or roommate which ends up on the slab, the real horror of the moment is focused on the girl who survives (Aren't You Glad You Didn't Turn on the Light?"). This contemporary legend circulated as an e-mail chain letter in 2001, and is one of the most frequently posted legends on YouTube. It also is featured in a wide variety of films and television shows such as *Campfire Tales*, *Urban Legends: Final Cut* and *Supernatural: Family Remains* (Season 4, Episode 11). Bennett and Smith include an elaborated variant in their discussion on this legend. The young girl is aware of a murderer at large, and because of this knowledge takes her dog, Rover, to bed with her, instructing him to lick her hand once if the murderer is on the street, twice if the murderer is on the lawn, three times if he is in the house and four times if he is in her room. She ignores the first three licks but, after the fourth lick, immediately gets up and switches on the light. There is no sign of the murderer, but she finds her dog hanging from the showerhead, stabbed in the chest, with the message written for her in the dog's blood: "People can lick too!" (Bennett and Smith 2007, 60).

More Ghostlore

In addition to the contemporary legends already discussed in the previous section, commentaries concerning other ghostly apparitions have surfaced in the media in recent years.

Phantom Vehicles and Haunted Roads

Generally, contemporary accounts of haunted roads involve two distinct types of phenomenon: apparitions of people, as exemplified by the "Vanishing Hitchhiker" and the vanishing victim; and apparitions of vehicles. The vanishing victim involves a vehicular accident where the driver runs into someone only to discover that the "victim" of the accident has vanished (Haughton 2009, 121). The current roadside ghosts are "folkloric signifiers of the increasing cultural importance of the car over the last fifty years, and the psychological significance of the car crash as a modern tragedy" (Davies 2009, 249). Davies wonders if the present ritual practice of memorial crosses at the locations of fatal accidents will act as focal points for the generation of new hauntings. "If so, they would be poignant successors to those commemorations of roadside tragedy in centuries past—the gibbet and crossroad ghosts" (Davies 2009, 249). The main characteristic of ghostly vehicles is their sudden inexplicable appearance or disappearance before witnesses. Sometimes these vehicles are vintage models, and these accounts are closely connected to stories of spectral coaches, popular in the eighteenth and nineteenth centuries in Great Britain (Haughton 2009, 121). The current renderings of the tales are "often connected with fatal car crashes, accidents, or more rarely, murders. However, many accounts, especially of ghost cars, are urban legends if not outright hoaxes, as is evidenced in the fashion of filming staged sightings of 'ghost cars' and showing the results on video- sharing Websites such as YouTube" (Haughton 2009, 122). According to surveys conducted in Britain, the M6 is considered the most haunted highway in the United Kingdom. The area around Bachelor's Grove in the Chicago area is considered rife with ghostly vehicles (Haughton 2009, 123). This abandoned cemetery, a prime location for legend trippers, has numerous websites and YouTube videos dedicated to its ghostly nature.

Haunted Houses

> *The quintessential "haunting experience" is entering a haunted house, either literally while legend tripping or figuratively while telling or listening to a ghost story.*
>
> —Grider (2007b, 143)

Almost every North American neighbourhood and community has a haunted house, one that sits neglected, forlorn and vigilant and is the genesis of many frightening tales and dares. Other buildings, lived in and vacant, gain the reputation for being haunted based simply on their close resemblance to the iconic haunted house of oral tradition and literature (Grider 2007b, 149). These buildings, or specific parts of buildings, and natural areas such as forests and caves, are imbued with mysterious and haunting histories. The stories continually are embellished, dramatized and localized until each of these locations has their own back story or stories. The interplay between the oral tradition and popular culture invests the haunted house with the power of an almost universally recognized cultural icon (Grider 2007b, 168). As Sylvia Grider explains, "Each new generation of American children is acculturated annually at Halloween with a whole panoply of supernatural information, including the appearance and significance of the haunted house" (Grider 2007b, 168). Each subsequent Halloween season is inundated with increased numbers of books, movies and artifacts perpetuating and strengthening this cycle of knowledge and awareness of the haunted house. And each Halloween season, as well, sees an increased number of young people testing their courage by sneaking up to, or into, the houses in question. Unfortunately, as seen in the discussion on legend tripping in Chapter 2, this has the possibility of tragedy in the making.

Haunted Bathroom Narratives and "Hanako-san"

Stories about haunted toilets, focusing on either the bathroom hosting a ghost or on a specific toilet that is haunted, are universal. Despite their widespread appearances, however, bathroom ghost stories have been a marginalized narrative in an already trivialized genre. "We tend to overlook haunted bathroom stories because we don't seem them in the iconography associated with the haunted house, which tends to focus on attics and basements" (Thomas 2007b, 36). Haunted bathroom ghost stories told by children may help to prepare them for the more frightening tales, told by young adults, about malevolent beings, such as Bloody Mary, that assault those who ritually summon them (Grider 2007a, 132).

> Instead of being a frivolous but interesting waste of time or a mechanism for dealing with external fear, the real meaning behind the toilet ghost stories may be that characters such as the "White Lady," "Bloody Mary" and all her other toilet ghost manifestations are actually creating this sense of fear in the first place. So, rather than being a mechanism for dealing with real, malicious and possibly life-threatening situations, they may be more about dealing with irrational fears triggered within children at a particular stage in their development. These stories, therefore, may actually be an outward manifestation of the developing human mind itself. (Armitage 2006, 22)

Jeannie Thomas speculates that bathroom ghosts represent an updating of the traditional supernatural motif of hauntings taking place near bodies of water, in this case, plumbing instead of a river or lake (Thomas 2007b, 37). This motif is employed by J. K. Rowling, of Harry Potter fame, with her character of Moaning Myrtle, the ghost haunting the girls' bathroom at Hogwarts School of Magic. Perhaps, other than "Bloody Mary" and "Moaning Myrtle," the most prominent institutional public toilet ghost hails from Japan: Hanako-san. Regardless of her fame, she is not the only toilet ghost in Japan and not the most frightening either as she can be easily avoided if one stays away from her toilet stall. According to some tales, she protects children from other toilet ghosts (Meyer 2010).

The legend of Hanako-san varies from school to school, but contains commonalities. The basic story relates the way the young girl died in the toilet stall. She is alternatively killed by an intruder or in a bombing raid during the war, murdered by a parent who had abused her, or committed suicide in that setting. It is generally established that she died in the third stall of the third-floor girls' bathroom, and to summon Hanako-san a person must knock on her toilet stall three times asking, "Hanako-san, are you there?" Once she has affirmed her presence, in a quiet, little girl's voice, the toilet stall door opens and when the student investigates, "the ghost of little Hanako, wearing a red skirt and with her hair done up in an old-style bun, will pull her into the toilet and down to Hell" (Meyer 2010). She appears without summoning as well, materializing when a person runs out of toilet paper. Her query, "Which do you want—red paper or blue paper?" offers a serious dilemma: if one chooses red, that person bled copiously to death; choosing blue means that the victim would be strangled. The answer "Neither" would save the potential victim. Taro, Hanako's boyfriend, inhabits the boys' bathroom and the two socialize at night when no one was around (Thomas 2007b, 36).

"Kuchi-sake-onna, the Slit-Mouthed Woman"

> Usually she wears a large mask and asks people, "Am I beautiful?" If they say "Yes," she will remove the mask, say "Even like this?" and show her mouth. If you see that and try and escape, she will come after you, and kill you with a scythe. She is exceedingly fast and can soon catch anybody, but she has the weakness of not liking the odor of pomade, so if you say "pomade," it is said that you can escape her.
>
> —Foster (2007, 701)

One of the most well-known urban legends in modern Japan since the 1970s, with new origin stories emerging to be relevant for contemporary society, is that of "Kuchi-sake-onna." "In the modern version, her disfigured face is sometimes caused by botched plastic surgery, other times by environmental pollution, which also gave her seven toes on each foot" (Freeman 2009, 159). She has different elements attributed to her in various parts of Japan: in Gifu she lives in a hut near the water supply; in Kitaku (a district of Tokyo), she has a red sports car, can run at least 72 kilometres an hour and can be stopped by an offering of a hard candy known as *bekko-ame*; in Kanagawa, there are various chants and challenges that would stop her; and in Hokkaido, she is a tall, slender, beautiful woman who wears a raincoat and can run 100 kilometres an hour (Freeman 2009, 160). Throughout Japan there are also diverse ways to escape her, but those often reported as the most effective are by offering her candy, running into a record store or chanting the word "pomade" (*pomado*) three times (Foster 2009, 185).

Michael Foster investigates this new yokai (literally demon, spirit or monster) that first appeared in Japan in 1979. In his writings on her history and influence on Japanese folklore and popular culture, Foster asserts that the academic discussions in Japan focused on the oral versions of the legend but, by considering contemporary social concerns and gender issues, "Kuchi-sake-onna" has developed into "a figure of resistance who speaks meaningfully of female subjectivity against the backdrop of the Japanese women's movement" (Foster 2007, 700). His findings contain similarities to those revolving around modern interpretations and considerations of "La Llorona" discussed earlier in this chapter.

Foster maintains that this dreadfully real and terrifying image presented in this legend breathed life into the nostalgic media character that the yokai had become. "Kuchi-sake-onna herself soon became a media star, placed by Mizuki and others into a long lineage of female monsters. Yet she was simultaneously a living being, at once modern and authentic. Her brief but influential appearance proved that yokai could still haunt the late-twentieth-century urban landscape" (Foster 2009, 164). She is configured as a modern avatar of the established Japanese folkloric demon women and, because she was considered yokai rather than criminal, she provides a "concrete" bridge between the Japanese people of today and their folkloric ancestry.

> Fueled in part by a nostalgic drive to discover a persistence of folkloric tradition in urban and suburban settings, motifs are combed

> for historical connections to earlier legends and other monstrous women. The scythe, for example, as a tool emblematic of pastoral tradition, metonymically imbues its possessor with traditional rural connections ... the ritualistic invocation of pomade links this men's hairstyling gel with the apotropaic powers of certainly plants traditionally used to ward off evil spirits and other pests. (Foster 2007, 702)

There are several key motifs present in almost all the variants of the legend. She is always a young woman, often very attractive, who arouses terror because, according to scholar Komatsu Kazuhiko, translated by Foster, "she works powerfully on their tacit understanding with regard to how much effort women must expend on their own 'beauty,' how much they are controlled by it, as well as how difficult it is for a woman not considered beautiful to live in this world" (Foster 2009, 195). While there are a variety of reasons given for her mouth being slit from ear to ear, this attribute is key not only to her description but also to much of the academic speculation surrounding the implication of the sexual connotations and the motif of the vagina with teeth, or *vagina dentate*. As Foster writes, "The relevance of this motif to Kuchi-sake-onna—with the clean white cotton gauze of the mask covering a hidden slit, and the simultaneous desire and fear associated with seeing what is normally concealed—does not take a great stretch of the imagination" (Foster 2009, 195). Foster quotes feminist film critic Barbara Creed as saying that female genitalia may be considered frightening for two reasons: they "appear castrated" and they "appear castrating."

> With her gaping red-lipped mouth (sometimes portrayed with sharp teeth), Kuchi-sake-onna articulates a visceral image of the castrating mother, the femme fatale, the insatiable sexual predator; she invokes the intimate connection between desire (*Am I pretty?*) and disgust (*Even like this?*), between the pleasure principle and the death drive. And just as the mouth threatens to dismember and devour, so too the accompanying knife or scythe conveys a similar symbolic power to mutilate (castrate). (Foster 2009, 195)

The ubiquitous face mask, covering only half her face, erases her mouth completely until the literal unveiling takes place. The mask, worn by Japanese people today, is used when the person is ill and does not wish to contaminate others or to protect the wearer from contagion when others are ill such as during the SARS outbreak in 2002. Frequently, it is worn as a sign of resistance (Foster 2009, 198). Foster concludes that consideration of these defining and overlapping key characteristics—gender (she is a woman), sexuality (the slit mouth), aesthetic consciousness ("Am I pretty?") and resistance (the mask)—meant that Kuchi-sake-onna symbolized the women's liberation movement in Japan during the late 1970s (Foster 2009, 198). However, Foster maintains, the treatment in academic and popular circles as a modern, urbanized avatar of ancestral Japanese yokai means that very little attention was focused on the rationale behind the contemporary issues surrounding her appearances in everyday Japan. "Kuchi-sake-onna" legends articulate children's fears, the dangers of rapid industrialization and unchecked pollution, and gender concerns regarding the role of women in contemporary Japanese society (Foster 2009, 183).

The relationship between the "education mama," or "helicopter parents" as they are known in North America, and Kuchi-sake-onna, however, has been suggested by some Japanese scholars. Education Mama turned monster in her confrontations with children on their way home from school or on the streets between school and cram school (supplementary evening schools for elementary through precollege-age students) may have reflected the anxieties and pressures of children towards their own mothers (Foster 2007, 706). "In many of the versions of the legend, it is enroute to cram school that children are confronted, and the Slit-Mouthed Woman herself is usually portrayed as being in her twenties or thirties, an appropriate age for the mother of a young child" (Foster 2007, 706).

> The legend of Kuchi-sake-onna circulated with great vibrancy for about six months, after which the excitement surrounding this frightening woman began to die down. But she has certainly never disappeared. In early-twenty-first-century Japan, she has become legendary. For scholars, she provides a paradigmatic contemporary legend or rumor; in popular culture she is a stock character in horror movies, listed alongside other yokai in bestiary-like compendia, and still occasionally discussed by school children. (Foster 2009, 201)

Campus Lore

> *Often, though not always, campus legends describe things that happened late at night, when darkness and fatigue alter people's perceptions. Usually these events are alleged to have happened years, months, or at least weeks before the time when the story is told.*
>
> —Tucker (2005, 1)

Many students beginning post-secondary education are confronted with a confusing set of new policies, regulations and rules and state their concern over ambiguity through contemporary legends (Major 2008, 240). Research by Elizabeth Tucker, James McCormick and Macy Wyatt, and others indicates that reports of supernatural and other scary phenomena on campuses in the United States has increased in recent years.

> Students are now sharing their stories and experiences via e-mail, text messaging, and postings on blogs. At most institutions, people now accept reports of ghostly events as part of their heritage, and don't hesitate to share stories. Some schools ... have even established Web sites for sharing these stories. (This is certainly a change from sharing ghost stories around a campfire on a dark night!) (McCormick and Wyatt 2009, 132)

The ghost stories entertain and educate students: "When students gather to tell ghost stories, they get to know one another better. Although ghost stories have more than one kind of meaning in a college setting, they primarily initiate entering students into a new community and a new stage of life" (Tucker 2007, 4). Suicide victims are some of the most prominent ghosts on college campuses, particularly on campuses with bodies of water, bridges and towers. These ghostly legends reflect the intense academic and social pressures of the students (Tucker 2005, 33). Legend trips to cemeteries, séances and other experimentations with the supernatural also give young adults a chance to encounter their fears while at the same time challenge authority (Clark 2003, 63).

Tucker found that campus tales involving witches tend to be local rather than part of wider legend cycles and that these legends express attitudes towards social deviance and power, both within and outside of the college (Tucker 2005, 36). Witches from outside the college community are usually strange, deviant women who offended society by committing murder or perpetrating other crimes (Tucker 2005, 37). Witches contained within the college parameters also symbolize social deviance and tend to preserve older ideas of witchcraft as malicious magic and practitioners as subverting the established order (Tucker 2005, 38). Frequently, female professors are considered witches by their students.

"Smiley Gang"

Author and illustrator Nina Matsumoto incorporated a segment with Kuchisake-onna in her manga *Yokaiden 2*. She explains to her mostly non-Japanese reading audience that the "slit-mouthed woman is a scary, lonely lady with a Glasgow smile and a severe need for assurance" (Matsumoto 2009, non-paginated). Matsumoto's allusion to the Glasgow smile refers to the contemporary legend known also as the "Smiley Gang" or "Chelsea Smile" that circulated in the Netherlands and throughout the rest of Europe since 9/11. Similar to the questions asked in the Japanese contemporary legends explored earlier, the following questions are asked of the potential female victims of the gang members or other villains of the Smiley Gang legends:

"Gang rape or a smiley?
"Do you prefer to go home laughing or crying?"
"Smiley, chessboard or rape?
"Do you want to be raped or to laugh for the rest of your life?" (Burger 2009, 278)

Early variants of legends about knife-wielding youth gangs threatening mutilation were reported in Scotland and the United States in the 1950s and 1960s. The Chelsea Smilers were legendary soccer ruffians who terrorized the United Kingdom in the late 1980s. Peter Burger traced the history of this legend in France, where it had been circulating since 1999 and had appeared in the novel *Le sourire de l'ange* (*Angelic Smile*) by Emilie Freche (2004) and in Belgium and Spain. In Belgium, e-mailed warnings circulated since 2002 and were a major force in spreading the legend (Burger 2009, 280) while the variant in Spain, known as the "Clown's Smile," had mutilation as a punishment for snitches or a humiliation for members of rival gangs (281). "All these legends have in common the identity of the perpetrators (a youth gang with distinctive attire, often driving a distinctive vehicle), their underage victims, the trick question, the barbaric mutilation, and the panic they spread on schools and university campuses" (Burger 2009, 281).

The legend panic about a youth gang bent on rape and mutilation traveled through the Netherlands in 2003 (Burger 2009, 276). Burger follows the hoax warnings as they were forwarded by e-mail and proliferated on message boards, Usenet and weblogs, collecting a hundred threads discussing the Smiley Gang and involving around 1,000 users (Burger 2009, 277). There was also wide media coverage, mostly regional and local newspapers, local, regional and national radio, and regional and national television (Burger 2009, 278). While the identity of the gang members demonstrated some variation when the legend began circulating, it soon narrowed down to Moroccans. "This is a striking example of Gary Alan Fine's 'Goliath Effect' at work. In the Netherlands these days, Moroccan adolescents are the folk devils du jour" (Burger 2009, 279). In other countries, as Burger points out, different minorities are cast as the bogeymen of the legend.

> In public discourse on ethnic crime, legend and news are inextricably connected. The present case-study of post 9/11 gang rape legends in the Netherlands features cases of news items that turn out to be legends, cases of gang rape that turn out to be legend-inspired hoaxes; police officers and other officials mistakenly spreading legends, and the emergence of gang rape legends keeping step with new reports of an ethnic crime wave. The legends and the various acts of ostension can be read as a public response to media discourse on gang rape as a new and ethnic crime. (Burger 2009, 290).

This contemporary legend became intertwined with stories about Dutch Moroccan girls being punished for not wearing a veil. A story posted on numerous blogs states that

> The German journalist Udo Ulfkotte told in a recent interview that in Holland, you can now see examples of young, unveiled Moroccan women with a so-called "smiley." It means that the girl gets one side of her face cut up from mouth to ear, serving as a warning to other Muslim girls who should refuse to wear the veil. In the Muslim suburb of Courneuve, France, 77 per cent of the veiled women carry veils reportedly because of fear of being harassed or molested by Islamic moral patrols. (http://islamin europe.blogspot.com/2006/12/smiley-veil-and-urban-legend.html September 2, 2011)

"The Hook"

> *A couple's late night make-out session is cut short when they hear a warning on the car radio about an escaped killer with a hook instead of a hand. Because of her fear that the killer may target them, the girl insists on being driven home immediately, much to the disgust of her companion. Upon arriving at her house the boy finds a bloody hook hanging from the passenger side car door handle.*

In his review of Matt Clark's *Hook Man Speaks*, author Daniel Handler (Lemony Snicket) points to the fact that the Hook Man is among America's most enduring contemporary legends and has been given plenty of academic credibility (Handler 2001). He mentions Jan Harold Brunvand's work regarding the legend but as Brunvand asserts:

> Perhaps because of the legend's improbably tidy plot, most tellers narrate the story nowadays more as a scary story than as a believed

legend. Folklorists are divided about whether "The Hook" represents simply a warning story about staying out late in an unknown environment, or whether its details may signify sexual meanings, including symbolic castration of the threatening and deformed phallic symbol—the hook-outside the car at the same time that the boyfriend is trying to "get his hooks into the girl" inside the car. (Brunvand 1999, 95)

Hayden Blackman, in his entry included under the heading of "Enigmatic Entries," claims that the Hook is a maniacal sociopath reported in virtually every portion of North American. "He is described as a large, overbearing fiend who delights in causing misery and death ... Like many monsters, the Hook prefers to terrorize and murder children and teenagers, especially those parked along lovers' lanes on dark and stormy nights" (Blackman 1999, 218). Blackman sardonically recommends that, in order to spot "The Hook," legend trippers should wait along secluded roads late at night, bringing along teenagers to act as bait while hiding in the bushes waiting for his approach (Blackman 1999, 218).

Bennett and Smith recognize this legend as a classic, stating that it has been a major influence on "slasher" movies (Bennett and Smith 2007, 65). There have been copious instances regarding commodification of this legend including comic strips, films and television programs and popular compilations of legends and horror stories for readers of all ages. This happens so frequently that the very image of a hook hanging from a car door handle suggests, for most people, the entire genre of contemporary legends. "Although this image destroys the suspense necessary for the legend versions, it highlights the fact that 'The Hook' is known even better nowadays as a simple scary story rather than a believed account of something that really happened. Parodies of urban legends almost inevitable allude to this story as well, making it in a sense the archetypal example of the genre" (Brunvand 2001, 200).

"The Suicide Rule"

> *A standard college regulation specified that a student whose roommate committed suicide automatically received a 4.0 grade point average for the current school term.*

Contemporary legends about suicide also circulate widely on college campuses. These legends "dramatize suicide, warning students about the dangers of self-destructive behavior" (Tucker 2005, 138). Some of the legends involve a student becoming aware of a ghost of a previous occupant of the residence who had committed suicide, while others describe ghosts that haunted bridges, towers and other liminal places on campus encouraging living students to end their lives as the ghosts had done in the past (Tucker 2005, 138). Barbara Mikkelson, in her discussion on this legend in Snopes, affirms that it is a false story (Mikkelson 2011). Variations of the legend include the type of death required for the automatic mark. While murdering one's own roommate does not qualify, almost any other type of death does. In other variants, the roommate does not have to expire, but the qualifying death is of any person, such as a parent, who is important in the student's life. This legend is the basis of two films released in 1998: *Dead Man on Campus* and *Dead Man's Curve*. Leo Reisberg, writing for the *Chronicle of Higher Education*, responding to the release of the two films, states that while the legend seemed absurd, it is based on an element of truth as most colleges do special things to help grieving students cope psychologically and academically (Reisberg 1998). He quotes William Fox, sociology professor at Skidmore College, who speculates that the legend emerged in the mid-1970s because it portrays college administrators as benevolent and caring, something that probably would not have been thought about college administrators before that time. It also appears in an episode of *The Simpsons* (November 19, 2000) when Bart is given straight A's by the principal on the belief that his sister Lisa had died. Several law enforcement television programs also employ this legend as part of their storylines: *Law and Order: Criminal Intent* ("Art," October 7, 2001) and *CSI: NY* ("Some Buried Bones," February 7, 2007).

Other "Lethal" Legends

Elizabeth Tucker states that of the legends about gruesome murders still circulating widely on college campuses, the three most popular ones are "The Hook," "The Boyfriend's Death" and "The Roommate's Death" (Tucker 2005, 40). "Since the rumor panic in 1968, rumors and legends of dormitory massacres have waxed and waned. The largest resurgence took place in 1998 after the movie *Urban Legend* was released. . . . While the details always varied, the message stayed the same: students, especially women, should worry about their safety on college campuses, far from home" (Tucker 2005, 40).

A variant of "The Roommate's Death" was circulating in Thailand's universities in 2007. Apparently, when one of two roommates went out late at night to buy some food, he got cut in half by a psychopath. Because his ghost felt guilty for not bringing back food for his roommate, it makes its way home. The ghost's former roommate answered the door and saw the upper torso of his friend floating there, holding out a bag of noodles for him (http://legendsrumors.blogspot.com /2007/08/thai-roommates-death.html, September 3, 2011). In another example, this legend has been combined with one about Mary Hawkins, the first director of Pemberton Hall at Eastern Illinois University in Charleston.

> Mary was a dorm mother decades ago who was the role model, All-American type of girl. One night, one of the girls on her floor couldn't go to sleep. She went up to the fourth floor of the building where there was a piano that she would play until she felt sleepy. A night janitor came from behind and raped her, and eventually tried to stab her to death. Leaving her for dead he disappeared. However, the girl was still alive and dragged herself to Mary's door where Mary opened it and witnessed the girl bleed to death. As her innocent was heart mauled by the sight, Mary went insane and hung herself in the state hospital. She and the murdered girl now haunt the halls of Pemberton. (Surbeck 2008)

"Over the years, Pemberton Hall has opened its doors, and the notorious fourth floor, around Halloween in an effort to take advantage of the story, or just to have some fun with it" (Kleen 2006, 4). No evidence has ever been found to substantiate the claim of a death ever taking place in Pemberton Hall.

> However, there is no evidence that any amount of facts will stop the story from continuing to be told, passed on, and adapted by

hundreds of students each year, especially when it directly addresses the deepest fears of EIU's female population. From doors that lock themselves, to strange electrical behavior, to unusual sounds coming from the fourth floor, generations of Pemberton Hall residents have attributed otherwise explainable phenomenon to the ghosts of Mary Hawkins and a murdered resident. (Kleen 2006, 4)

Kleen revisits the legend, and various articles and theses written about it, again in 2008. He confirms that the interest in the legend seems unabated and that it has become an obligatory inclusion in books (and websites) on Illinois ghost stories (Kleen 2008, 6).

A Contemporary Invention: "Slender Man"

He is the Slender Man, a mythical predator and Internet sensation whose greatest skill is the ability to strike terror in the hearts of teens who aren't frightened by much else ... Slender Man would make a great horror movie, but I like that you don't see him in movies or TV, that it's more like urban-legend folklore. That makes it scarier, because it seems like it could maybe be real.

—Tillotson (2011)

Recognized as a fictional contemporary legend, created by Victor Surge on the Something Awful forums, June 8, 2009, "Slender Man" has gained prominence beyond the confines of the online forum. He is most often portrayed as a malevolent entity abducting and psychologically traumatizing people after stalking them for a long while.

There is an enigmatic figure, most often seen as a tall, extremely thin man with long, strange arms, and a face that no two people see the same way (if they see any face at all) wearing a suit. Where he comes from is as much a mystery as what he wants. All that is known is that there is evidence of him existing for far longer than one would expect. Those who see him often wind up missing—or worse—with their mutilated bodies impaled upon a tree, and their organs removed and then replaced systematically. (http://tvtropes.org/pmwiki/pmwiki.php/Main/ TheSlenderManMythos)

Numerous additional stories and countless YouTube videos have since been created by fans of the character, falling into four major categories: "Marble Hornets," "Just Another Fool," "Everyman Hybrid" and "Tribe Twelve." The YouTube video series for "Marble Hornets" has been published on DVD. "Just Another Fool" is one example of a major blog while "Everyman Hybrid" and "Tribe Twelve" are Alternate Reality Games incorporating the character. Sightings of this dangerous creature have been made everywhere, from Japan to Norway and various locations in North America. "He appears to the unwitting mostly at night, and most always peering out of wooded areas or near rivers. He has also been reported to peek inside left open windows and to walk out in front of lone motorists on long uninhabited roads" (http://www.mythicalcreaturesguide.com/page/Slender +Man#fbid=yhgcM_ypNR-, September 3, 2011).

Literary and Visual Adaptations

The following annotated titles are only a sampling of the reworked contemporary legends explored in this chapter that are readily available to readers, viewers of movies and television programs and Internet users. Several older films based on contemporary legends have been reworked themselves, updated to remain relevant for a new generation. An example of this is the slasher film *Black Christmas*, originally released in 1974, and incorporating the "Babysitter and the Man Inside the House" legend. The newer rendition kept the same title and was released in 2006. This time a back story is created for the murder but, in keeping with developing technology, the phone calls are made on the cell phone of one of the victims. The calls are still coming from inside the house but no longer restricted to a land line.

"La Llorona"

American Family: La Llorona (The Weeping Woman) (Season 1, Episodes 4 and 5), 2002.
The episodes feature three intertwined La Llorona stories. The youngest son of the Gonzales family tells a traditional story to his nephew and supplements it with pictures from a fictional Internet site about La Llorona. The additional information provided by showing the fictional site makes the basic elements available to a viewing audience that may not be familiar with the legend. "The secondary, but equally important, function is to provide a narrative frame for the other stories in the episode about women who, through drug addiction and deportation, have 'lost' their children" (Perez 2008, 196).

Anaya, Rudolfo. *Maya's Children: The Story of La Llorona*. Illustrated by Maria Baca. New York: Hyperion Books, 1997.
In the author's note, Anaya explains that he wished to tell the story to very young readers without having La Llorona taking the life of her children as she does in the traditional versions. "Instead of using La Llorona as a character to frighten children—as she has been used by generations of parents—this story teaches youngsters about mortality" (n.p.)
Maya, born with the birthmark of the Sun God, is destined to become immortal. This angers Señor Tiempo (Time) so her parents hide her away from his wrath. Because she is lonely, Maya creates children from a mixture of earth, seeds and waters in a series of clay pots. Tiempo, upon discovering her sanctuary and her children, appears to her in disguise and convinces her to break the pots and throw the shards into the river to assure their immortality. Believing the stranger, Maya follows his advice and her children disappear. Crying and searching for her lost children, Maya becomes known as La Llorona, the woman who wails for her lost children.

Blackwell, Juliet. *Secondhand Spirits*. New York: Obsidian, 2009.
La Llorona is utilized as a plot device in this first entry in the paranormal mystery series, A Witchcraft Mystery, featuring vintage clothing store owner, Lily Ivory, who is also a witch.

Chasing Papi. Directed by Linda Mendoza and written by Laura Angelica Simon and Steve Antin, 2003.
This film, which did not receive critical success, attempts to utilize La Llorona as a source of humor. "The endeavour is hampered by the filmmaker's efforts to make La Llorona accessible to those familiar and unfamiliar with the tale at the expense of integrating the lore in a meaningful way into the narrative" (Perez 2008, 56).

The Cry. Written and directed by Bernadine Santistevan, 2007.

On the website for this film, where the fundamental lesson of the film is spelled out as females' responsibility to love and protect children, Santistevan enumerates numerous contemporary cases of mothers who committed infanticide in the last decade and beyond (http://www.lallorona.com/1modern.html; June 6, 2011). The website also includes background information on the genesis of the film from 1998, when the director discovered that what she at first considered a regional legend was much more prevalent than she thought. "In the end, Bernadine spends 5 years searching for La Llorona across the Americas—interviewing people who believe they have seen or heard her, collecting music, poems, and art work dedicated to her, and working with historians and Jungian psychologists who study La Llorona as a cultural phenomenon and universal female archetype" (http://www.lallorona.com/1legend.html). Based on her research, Santistevan wrote the script for her contemporary supernatural thriller in 2003.

Curse of La Llorona. Written and directed by Terrence Williams, 2007.

This horror film is the third entry in the La Llorona series created by Williams. Previous films include *Revenge of La Llorona* (2006) and *The River: Legend of La Llorona* (2005).

Dedman, Stephen. " 'Til Human Voices Wake Us." *Never Seen by Waking Eyes*. Infrapress, 2005, 119–26.

After hearing a cowboy singing a version of La Llorona where the ballad ends with the cowboy being found torn almost in half after an encounter with the weeping woman, and various other stories and rumors about the same horrific fate of others, the narrator returns to the site mentioned in the song. The narrator encounters the weeping woman and discovers the rationale behind the ghastly mutations accorded in the stories and songs. In his afterword, the author states that this story, nominated for a Gaylaxion Spectrum Award, "came from an urban myth. It's also the best erotic cross-dressing lesbian cowboy romance ghost story I've ever written. So far" (223).

Hayes, Joe. *La Llorona, The Weeping Woman: An Hispanic Legend Told in Spanish and English*. 3rd edition. Illustrated by Vicki Trego Hill and Mona Pennypacker. El Paso, TX: Cinco Puntos Press, 2004. Originally published in 1987.

Maria drowns her two children when she realizes that her husband no longer cares for her but still loves his children. She immediately repents but cannot save her children and dies on the river bank. Her ghost returns, weeping and wailing, dressed in white. Stories are told of children through the years who have been chased by the crying ghost—"and of some who have even been caught!" (n.p.)

In the author's note, Hays offers a concise history of the legend before explaining that this version is based on things he heard as a child in Arizona. "I avoid telling the tale to children younger than nine or ten years: however, if younger children are familiar with the story from their own families, they sometimes insist on hearing it" (n.p.) In the book on the Llorona figure, Domino Perez said of Hayes's rendition of the tale:

> Hayes first learned about La Llorona as a boy after his family moved from Pennsylvania to southern Arizona. He learned Spanish from his Chicano friends, who also introduced him to a rich storytelling tradition that included La Llorona. Although uncertain if he "believed" the story about the ghost woman who wandered in the arroyos crying for her lost children, he did recognize that the story "had a lot of truth in it." When he began his storytelling career, Hayes included the story of La Llorona "because he knew almost everyone loved the story of the weeping ghost as much as he and his friends did." Hayes' own Llorona story is a conventional one about a woman named Maria. Although he gives her a specific identity, it does not alter her fate within the framework of the tale. (Perez 2008, 149)

Perez feels that Hayes's book, significant for the number of copies sold (more than 70,000), its accessibility and its appeal to various audiences, is especially noteworthy because Hayes situates La Llorona in a specific cultural context and identifies her as part of a Mexican or Hispanic storytelling tradition (Perez 2008, 149). Arora affirms that this book has affected the versions of the Llorona narrated by children who have either read the book or had the book read to them (Arora 2000, 36).

Hernandez, Gilbert. "La Llorona: Where Are My children?" *Fear of Comics*. Seattle, WA: Fantagraphics, 2000, 69–72.

After the death of her husband, a young poor woman with three children turns her back on her children and eventually murders them in order to attract the attention of a wealthy patron. After a long life of pleasure, she ascends to the gates of heaven but is not allowed inside without her children. She is told that she must wander the earth until she finds them. Subsequently, she appears at the edge of waterways, taking any child to replace her own. Poverty is emphasized as a key factor contributing to the tragedy since her lack of economic resources was heightened when faced with her new financial responsibilities when she was widowed (Perez 2008, 29). This rendition is created with an adult reading audience in mind and contains language and images that may be considered objectionable for younger readers.

Lemus, Felicia Luna. *The Trace Elements of Random Tea Parties*. New York: Farrar, Straus & Giroux, 2003.

This novel provides a first-person tale of punk rock Los Angeles queer society and of family, inherited and compiled throughout life experiences. As the story of La Llorona is told to the main character by her grandmother, the character symbolizes a bad-girl spirit who goads the narrator, Leticia, to rebel, including getting a tattoo of La Llorona on her arm. In the novel La Llorona is identified as an Aztec revenant who flew in on the wind and snatched children from the safety of their beds. Perez states, however, that instead of representing a radical revision of the folklore, this portrayal of La Llorona is quite conformist: "She flies, wanders, threatens, cajoles, weeps, and eventually abandons the protagonist" (Perez 2008, 28).

Odom, Mel. *Bruja*. New York: Pocket Books, 2001.

Based on the television series *Angel*, the antagonist in the novel is a witch or *bruja* and also an embodiment of "La Llorona."

The Others. Directed and written by Alejandro Amenabar, 2001.

Winner of eight Goya awards, including Best Film and Best Director, *The Others* is the first English-spoken film ever to receive the Best Film Award in Spain's national film award ceremonies. It is not almost until the end of the film that the audience and the main character, Grace, discover the identities of the ghosts in this psychological thriller. Film viewers familiar with the La Llorona story should easily recognize this imperative part of the cinematic experience.

> Once the oppressive forces at work on [Grace] (Catholicism, war, isolation, motherhood, and disease, to name a few) are identified, points of comparison can be made between these characters and La Llorona or even Llorona figures; these comparisons allow readers to locate intersections between US/ Mexican transnational concerns and those of other national economic, social, political, and even cultural communities. (Perez 2008, 201)

"La Llorona (Woman in White)," *Supernatural*, 2005. Pilot episode.

Two versions of the Woman in White story are mixed together to create the tale of Constance Welch, drawing on the theme of unfaithfulness (or sexual activity) which, in teen horror films, usually dooms the character to die an untimely death. In this pilot episode of the series, seeing Constance Welch is a definite sign that death was imminent.

> Like the White Rock Lake ghost, she was a vanishing hitchhiker. She'd ask for a ride home, and if you gave her one, you found yourself at an old aban- doned house out in the middle of nowhere, and you weren't going to have to worry about getting home. Also, in this case, the spirit—Constance Welch— was a suicide. She'd drowned her kids and then jumped off Sylvania Bridge. Sometimes suicides turn into angry spirits who aren't focused on the people

who did them wrong in real life. They're just lost and hurting, and over time
that turns dark, and they start going after anyone who vaguely resembles the
people who might have driven them to suicide. (Irvine 2007, 12)

Turgeon, Carolyn. "La Llorona." In *Haunted Legends*. Edited by Ellen Datlow and Nick
Mamatas. New York: Tor, 2010, 139–54.

Karen, a mother grieving for her dead son, sees a young woman in white walking along
the ocean several times from her hotel window while in Mexico. The young woman fasci-
nates her so Karen tries to find out who the woman is and why she feels a connection with
her. Despite denials and warnings about the woman from people at the hotel, Karen continues
her quest until one night when she comes upon the woman crying. Discovering that the crying
woman is La Llorona does not dissuade Karen. Eventually, she follows La Llorona to the
shore, and then, into the sea. "She looked back to La Llorona, confused, and now she saw,
stretching out behind her, countless other women, all of them crying, reaching out toward
the water, toward their children" (153). In the afterword, the author briefly mentions the many
variants of this popular legend in Central and South America. In some, the author states, "she
can only be seen by people who are about to die" (154).

"The Vanishing Hitchhiker"

Berman, Steve. *Vintage: A Ghost Story*. Binghamton, NY: Haworth, 2007.

> The seventeen-year-old narrator of this first-person novel meets a ghost on a
> deserted highway: a young man, killed in 1957, who is featured as the local
> legend of the area. "I know your ghost." She laughed. "Well not know him,
> but know of him. As soon as you mentioned 47. It's an old urban legend
> around here ... every kid in town knows that his ghost keeps trying to get
> home. We all want a glimpse. Last time I was out there looking for him
> was back in junior high with some friends and we all hid in the woods. I fell
> asleep." (13)

Along with the emotional upheaval of friendship, love, identity and suspense, the
reader experiences the thrill of legend tripping and the dread of loneliness and homophobia
on the journey with the nameless main character in this powerful and vivid story. A portion
of the royalties is dedicated to two charities that work to prevent gay teen suicides. The novel
was nominated for the Andre Norton Best Young Adult Science Fiction and Fantasy Novel
award in 2007.

Cadigan, Pat. "Between Heaven and Hull." In *Haunted Legends*. Edited by Ellen Datlow and
Nick Mamatas. New York: Tor (2010): 289–301.

A hitchhiker, picked up by two women who giggled incessantly, bemoans his fate in
this first-person narrative. Their driving skills are chaotic and dangerous, and eventually the
two women stop halfway on a bridge and push him out of the car into the fog. He falls, finds
himself on the side of a road that he recognizes and immediately begins hitchhiking once
again. The hitchhiker is unknowingly repeating a cycle from which he cannot be released.
The author, in the afterword, describes a car trip taken with Ellen Datlow, one of the editors
of this anthology. Like the two women in the story, Ellen and Pat got lost traveling from
London to Scarborough, but unlike the characters, they did not pick up a hitchhiker. The
author states that in a perfect world, the adventure they shared would have been this one.
"A Phantom Hitchhiker, after all, would have no trouble hitching all around the world. If
the Web can spread computer viruses, why can't GPS spread phantoms?" (300).

Dedman, Stephen. "Probable Cause." *Never Seen by Waking Eyes*. Infrapress, 2005, 17–22.

The narrator tells and then discusses the legend of the Vanishing Hitchhiker with the
hitchhiker he has picked up. "The way I see it," he continued, "there's *always* going to be a girl
hitchhiking along the highway, right? That's not just probable, it's almost inevitable" (17). His
discussion about probabilities, hitchhikers and death offers a chilling ride to the reader.

Warren, Kaaron. "That Girl." In *Haunted Legends*. Edited by Ellen Datlow and Nick Mamatas. New York: Tor, 2010, 33–43.

In an interview with patients at St. Martin's, the narrator hears a chance comment from one old woman sitting quietly by herself. Repeatedly, she states, "I am that girl." After listening to her and investigating her story, the narrator decides that it was just that, a story. "Taxi drivers love to tell stories of the things they've seen, the people they've picked up. I dismissed it as an urban myth, but I heard it again, and again. Always a brother, or a best friend, and they always told it with a shiver, as if it hurt to talk" (38). Eventually, after a long absence, the narrator returns to St. Martin's and, while in a taxi, finds herself accompanied by "that girl" who vanishes when the taxi passes the cemetery.

In the afterword to her story, the author explains that in actuality there is a cemetery across the road from the psychiatric hospital and that her own house overlooked the cemetery. "When I first moved in, I used to tell taxi drivers, 'The house near the cemetery.' I realized this frightened them; they checked their mirrors all the time, making the road even more dangerous than it usually is" (43).

"Resurrection Mary"

Braunbeck, Gary A. "Return to Mariabronn." In *Haunted Legends*. Edited by Ellen Datlow and Nick Mamatas. New York: Tor, 2010 185–97.

In a series of interrelated scenarios, Braunbeck relates the story of an old man filled with remorse from accidently hitting and killing a young girl near Resurrection Cemetery, and the legend tripper years later who recorded a ghost's conversation in the same location. It is a chilling tale made even colder by the winter setting. The author's afterword emphasizes his fascination with ghost stories from a very young age. "The idea of being alone on the road at night, in your car while *something* supernatural and not at all nice followed you or, worse, was in the car *with* you, tantalized by young imagination" (196).

"The Hook"

Clark, Matt. *Hook Man Speaks*. New York: Berkley Books, 2001.

> In raising questions about Hook Man's obsolescence, *Hook Man Speaks* functions not only as commentary on the nature of the circulation of contemporary legend but proffers the literary repositioning of Hook Man as a necessary replenishment of the legend itself. (Berthold 2008, 349)

In his first-person narration, the Hook Man of contemporary legend explains his legendary status as well as his exploration for his sense of self. Much of the novel is constructed as a discussion between the narrator and the folklore professor Dr. Brautigan, an allusion to novelist Richard Brautigan, beginning with a clarification from the Hook Man of a Brautigan article published in *Harper's*.

> It was with some concern, however, that I studied your observations on what sundry neuroses the Hook Man may possess that drive "him" to attack helpless lovebirds. You see—and I hope you will believe me when I tell you that this is not a joke—I am the Hook Man and am in no way whatsoever like the psychological profile you fabricated. For one thing, my sexual history is hardly bizarre. I have never been "involved" with any of the deviant types you list." [Leonard Gage, The Hook Man] (39).

Several additional contemporary legends play a significant role in the novel, particularly "The Kentucky Fried Rat" Lady, the narrator's love interest. Her story, apparently perverted somewhat in the retelling, revolves around the fact that she suffers from diabetes, causing her to lose feelings in her extremities (31). There is also an enraged comparison and competition, encouraged by Dr. Brautigan, between the narrator and "The Axe Man," "a killer who dresses up like a little old lady to wait in mall shoppers' darkened parked cars" (65). "The Axe Man" is also referred to as "The Hatchet Man" and "The Hairy-Handed Hitchhiker." "Students who have seen *Urban Legend* (1998) and other movies that parody campus killings understand the ludic nature of 'hatchet man' legends, which dramatize people's fears. Back in the late 1960s, however, this legend ["Hatchet Man"] was likely to shock and scare those who heard it" (Tucker 2005, 91).

Other contemporary legends that receive a mention from the author include: the selling of the Porsche for $500, the dead man's car, ghostly hands at the railway crossing, the choking Doberman, the Mexican Pet and the Vanishing Hitchhiker, in this case the Hitchhiker triplets.

> These stories, they're like a harmless but unstoppable virus. Everybody is susceptible, even the sceptical. Sometimes I'll hear some cockamamie gang initiation baloney between hands, and the next week it gets printed in the newspaper as truth. Except the gang's name is changed. Maybe it's a different body part they have to chop off. Casinos are the breeding ground for more than greed. (80)

Berthold asserts that the paradigmatic space in the novel was not that of the lovers' lanes of the legend, but that of Dr. Brautigan's folklore class (Berthold 2008, 352). He maintains that the novel's importance derives from the author's recognition of the availability of contemporary legend to metafiction reworkings and that "despite their generic differences, contemporary legend and metafiction function as comparable forms of gaming" (Berthold 2008, 359). Unfortunately, the author of this enthralling novel published only this one novel before he died of cancer in 1998, at the age of 31.

Campfire Legends—The Hookman. GameHouse Studios Eindhoven, 2009.
    A Hidden Object adventure game based on the legend of the Hook begins with the story, featuring Christine, told by a group of young girls telling stories around a campfire. The player, taking the role of Christine, has to find a series of items in the cabin in the woods to survive the escaped killer known as Hookman.

Miller, Geoff, and Rory Veal. *Lovers Lane* (1999).
    Two lovers were murdered at the local lover's lane on Valentine's Day 13 years previously. The killer, wielding a hook, was incarcerated in a nearby institution for the criminally insane, but this year he escapes. His targets are the children of the victims who had been married at the time of their murder, but not to each other.

Stranger, James. *The Chromium Hook* (2000).
    This short film, winner of the "Best Minnesota Short Film 2000" and the Best Comedy Short at the Magnolia Film Festival (Mississippi) and deemed hilarious and detailed by the Rochester Film Festival, examines the stories behind the truth of this contemporary legend in a small American town. It is based on a short story by Ron Carlson by the same name from *The Hotel Eden Stories* (Norton, 1997).

"Hook Man," *Supernatural* (Season 1: Episode 7), 2005.
    This episode blends two very popular "parking" contemporary legends—"The Hook" and "The Boyfriend's Death"—with a third well-known legend, "Aren't You Glad You Didn't Turn on the Lights." The Winchester brothers aid a girl whose date had been a victim of the "Hook Man" earlier on. The girl is being terrorized by the Hook Man, who also attacks and murders her roommate, leaving the ominous message for the girl written in blood on the wall.

"Hanako, the Toilet Ghost"

This legendary figure from Japan appears in a number of anime series. In *Dirty Pair Flash* she is a hologram of a dead girl with a baby emanating from one of the stalls. She so frightens Kei that she starts shooting at everything. By the end of the episode, the hologram is stuck in the on position, and when one girl says that they can't be rid of her, Hanako smiles a wicked smile. While in *Haunted Junction*, she is one of many ghosts that haunt the school along with the characters "Red Mantle and Blue Mantel," distinct elements of the Hanako folklore itself.

Esuno, Sakae. *Hanako and the Terror of Allegory.* 4 volumes. Los Angeles: Tokyo Pop, 2010–11. English translation of *Hanako To Guuwa No Teller*, first published in Japan, 2004.
    In the context of this shonen series aimed at older teens, an allegory is a living manifestation of a contemporary legend. Hanako, the toilet ghost, is one of three main characters in this series. She is a techno-savvy female capable of traveling from toilet to toilet in able to aid in the fight against malicious or vengeful allegories such as the axe-wielding bogeyman under the bed, the slit-mouthed woman and others not discussed in this book. The third volume includes the contemporary legend of "red paper, blue paper" referred to in the earlier discussion on Hanako. Hanako's back story and ultimate deliverance is the centre of the fourth and final volume of this series which, along with the various Japanese contemporary legends, explores the roles of the author and reader in creating viable and living characters. These latter "allegories" include "Kokkuri San," the Japanese version of the Ouija board, a form of spirit divination worked with a coin and a piece of paper with individual letters of the hiragana alphabet arranged in a circle. "The game of "Kokkuri San" is the subject of the films *Shinsei no Toilet no Hanako-san* (1998) and *Kokkuri* (1997).
    "Teke Teke," another popular Japanese contemporary legend, is the ghost of a young female who, after falling under a train, was cut in half, leaving her with only her upper torso. She pulls herself along with her claw-like hands, creating the "teke teke" sound, and hunts young people with a sickle, creating the next Teke Teke. In this series, she is thought to cause a chain of murders by having each victim of a train accident return to push another victim into the path of a train. It is established that all of the victims are actually members of a suicide club with the leader of the club meeting an ironic death.
    A comic version of "the pact with the devil" or "a demon in the mirror" is also explored in the series. When Kanae, the only "ordinary" main character in the series, wishes that she was a mega pop star, she creatively escapes the clutches of the wish-granting demon by continually elaborating on her wish.
    "Gap Girl," a contemporary legend about a woman hiding in gaps in walls and furniture, is based on traditional folklore from the Edo era. "The image of peering out from a gap also shares a common motif with the 'Man under the bed' ... originally imported from abroad and the original story of a robber underneath a parked car shifted to the inside of a house" (Esuno 2011).

"Kuchi-sake-onna"

Besides being mentioned in the film *Ringu*, there are a plethora of allusions to the character in anime and manga produced in Japan. There are mentions in *Occult Academy*, *Narato*, and *Hell Teacher Nube* and in the video game *Revelations: Persona*. The motifs of the legend already discussed continue to be transmitted to children and young adults particularly through the manga and anime produced by Mizuki Shigeru. Mizuki, a specialist in the stories of yokai and renowned for his Japanese horror manga, appreciates the links between the character and classical yokai. "At the root of yokai is the big mouth opened wide as if to say, 'I'll bite you!' She appears at the time one meets demons; that is, you meet her in the evening after school. She has a tool that can give you a shock, such as a scythe, and words such as "pomade" are the protective spell ... She has everything [necessary to be a yokai]" (Foster 2009, 190).

Asby, Romy. *The Cutmouth Lady.* Simiotext, 1995.
    This collection of short, intertwined and somewhat autobiographical short stories regarding Asby's childhood in Japan includes a woman with a surgical mask who scared children.

Carved. Directed and written by Shiraishi Koji, 2007.
    The film depicts the character as an abusive mother who receives her injuries from her son and becomes a supernatural child killer. "Like most female ghosts, the Slit-Mouthed

Woman as immaterial ghost does not have the power to attack the living; instead, she possesses other mothers in order to carry out her bloody deeds" (Balmain 2008, 133). In the film, as in the legend, the Slit-Mouthed Woman constantly asks whether she is pretty, but only her son hears her. The film begins with a short montage of scenes of children discussing the rumor of this creature, interspersed with three short vignettes of ordinary family life, continuing with the theme of this contemporary legend. "These scenes introduce us to a common trope in contemporary Japanese horror: the displacement of the traditional extended family by the fragmented nuclear family in which gender roles have become confused" (Balmain 2008, 135).

Kuchisake-onna (1996).
    In this film the character's slit mouth is the result of plastic surgery gone awry.

Kuchisake Onna (2007).
    In this film the slit-mouthed woman seeks her victims with a pair of scissors.

Matsumoto, Nina. *Yokaiden 2*. New York: Del Rey, 2009.
    Young Hamachi's pursuit for Yokai, Japanese spirits, almost results in a tragedy when, in an attempt to acquire a specific mirror, he comes face-to-face with a young woman wearing a mask over the lower half of her mouth. When she asks him if she is pretty, the astute reader would easily recognize the slit-mouth woman. In order to escape the quandary caused by the correct answer to her question, Hamachi discovers that the correct answer is "so-so."
    In a word from the author, Matsumoto explains that Kuchi-sake-onna cannot be pacified and that the correct answer in the 1970s when the legend first circulated was "You're average." That answer was transformed to "so-so" when the legend revived in 2000. "It supposedly leaves her confused as to how to respond, and you can use that time to escape" (non-paginated). "Matsumoto incorporates her seamlessly into centuries-old folklore, and in the process acknowledged Koji Shiraishi's 2007 film about the character, *Carved*, as a touchstone that Japanophiles as well as fans of the macabre, dark fantasy, and pop culture itself would do well to know" (http://www.graphicnovelreporter.com/content/yokaiden-2 -review)

Recommended Resources

Retellings of scary stories and contemporary legends aimed at a young-adult reading audience continued to flourish in the past decade. The following stories, although based on contemporary legends, are not part of the public domain and therefore cannot be told or adapted without permission from the copyright holder. The stories can be shared through reading, however. People wishing to retell these tales can create their own adaptations after reading a number of different reworkings to get the general feel of the story structure and the freedom of creativity that is expressed by the various authors.

"Aren't You Glad You Didn't Turn on the Lights"
Christensen, Jo-Anne. "The Message." *Campfire Ghost Stories*. Edmonton, Alberta: Ghost House Books, 2002, 45–48.

"The Boyfriend's Death"
Christensen, Jo-Anne. "The Scratching." *Campfire Ghost Stories*. Edmonton, Alberta: Ghost House Books, 2002, 61–66.

"The Dare"
Christensen, Jo-Anne. "A Grave Mistake." *Campfire Ghost Stories*. Edmonton, Alberta: Ghost House Books, 2002, 70–76.
Schlosser, S. E. "The Pitchfork." *Spooky Canada: Tales of Hauntings, Strange Happenings, and Other Local Lore*. Guilford, CT: Insiders' Guide, 2007, 72–78.

"The Devil at the Dance Hall"
Loya, Olga. "The Vain Girl and the Handsome Visitor: Based on a Mexican Urban Legend."
In *The August House Book of Scary Stories: Spooky Tales for Telling Out Loud*. Edited by
Liz Parkhurst. Atlanta, GA: August House, 2009, 16–21.

"The Hook"
Christensen, Jo-Anne. "The Hook." *Campfire Ghost Stories*. Edmonton, Alberta: Ghost
House Books, 2002, 22–25.
Tingle, Tim, and Doc Moore. "The Lady with the Hook." *Texas Ghost Stories: Fifty
Favorites for the Telling*. Lubbock: Texas Tech University Press, 2004, 218–19.

"Killer in the Back Seat"
Christensen, Jo-Anne. "The Warning." *Campfire Ghost Stories*. Edmonton, Alberta: Ghost
House Books, 2002, 32–37.

"La Llorona"
Christensen, Jo-Anne. "The Weeping Woman." *Campfire Ghost Stories*. Edmonton, Alberta:
Ghost House Books, 2002, 67–69.
Morel, Mary Kay. "The Night of the Weeping Woman." In *13 Scary Ghost Stories*. Edited
by Marianne Carus. New York: Scholastic, 2000, 107–16. Previously published as *That's
Ghosts for You: 13 Scary Stories*.
Tingle, Tim, and Doc Moore. "La Llorona." *Texas Ghost Stories: Fifty Favorites for the
Telling*. Lubbock: Texas Tech University Press, 2004, 25–28.
Tingle, Tim, and Doc Moore. "La Llorona at Mission Concepcion." *Texas Ghost Stories:
Fifty Favorites for the Telling*. Lubbock: Texas Tech University Press, 2004, 181–85.

"The Mall Rat"
Christensen, Jo-Anne. "The Helpful Stranger." *Campfire Ghost Stories*. Edmonton, Alberta:
Ghost House Books, 2002, 76–80.

"Room for One More"
de Vos, Gail. "Room for One More." In *Ghostwise: A Book of Midnight Stories*. Collected
by Dan Yashinsky. Charlottetown, Prince Edward Island: Ragweed, 1997, 87–90.

"The Roommate's Death"
Young, Richard, and Judy Dockery Young. "Outside the Door." In *The August House Book
of Scary Stories: Spooky Tales for Telling Out Loud*. Edited by Liz Parkhurst. Atlanta, GA:
August House, 2009, 96–98.

"The Stolen Liver"
Rucker, James "Sparky." "Johnny and the Dead Man's Liver." In *The August House Book of
Scary Stories: Spooky Tales for Telling Out Loud*. Edited by Liz Parkhurst. Atlanta, GA:
August House, 2009, 104–9.
Schlosser, S. E. "Where's My Liver?" *Spooky Canada: Tales of Hauntings, Strange
Happenings, and Other Local Lore*. Guilford, CT: Insiders' Guide, 2007, 44–48.

"The Vanishing Hitchhiker"
Christensen, Jo-Anne." The Hitchhiker." *Campfire Ghost Stories*. Edmonton, Alberta: Ghost
House Books, 2002, 14–21.
Jarvis, Dale. "The Girl on the Train." *The Golden Leg and Other Ghostly Campfire Tales*. St.
John's, Newfoundland: Flanker, 2007, 92–96.
Jarvis, Dale. "The Vanishing Hitchhiker." *Wonderful Strange: Ghosts, Fairies, and
Fabulous Beasties*. St. John's, Newfoundland: Flanker 2005, 137–38.

Kelly, Amy, ed. "Hitchhiker." *Spooky Campfire Stories: Spooky Outdoor Tales for All Ages.* Helena, MT: Falcon, 2000, 73–83.

Schlosser, S. E. "The Wallflower." *Spooky Canada: Tales of Hauntings, Strange Happenings, and Other Local Lore.* Guilford, CT: Insiders' Guide, 2007, 89–94.

Stone, Ted. "The Bus to Winnipeg." In *Ghostwise: A Book of Midnight Stories.* Collected by Dan Yashinsky. Charlottetown, Prince Edward Island: Ragweed, 1997, 91–96.

Teitelbaum, Michael. "The Hitchhiker." *The Scary States of America.* New York: Delacorte, 2007, 10–18.

Tingle, Tim, and Doc Moore. "The Lady in Black." *Texas Ghost Stories: Fifty Favorites for the Telling.* Lubbock: Texas Tech University Press, 2004, 185–88. This variant offers a tragic back story for the woman trying desperately to return home to her child and husband and to prove her innocence.

Tingle, Tim, and Doc Moore. "The Lady of White Rock Lake." *Texas Ghost Stories: Fifty Favorites for the Telling.* Lubbock: Texas Tech University Press, 2004, 175–81. This version relates several different futile attempts for Julie to reach her home in the intervening years before this specific narrator relates the tale.

Tingle, Tim, and Doc Moore. "Prom Queen." *Texas Ghost Stories: Fifty Favorites for the Telling.* Lubbock: Texas Tech University Press (2004): 189–93.

References

"Aren't You Glad You Didn't Turn on the Light?" 2006. Snopes.com, http://www.snopes.com/horrors/madmen/lighton.asp (accessed September 5, 2011).

Arora, Shirley L. 2000. "Hear and Tell: Children and the Llorona." *Contemporary Legend* n.s. 3:27–44.

Armitage, Marc. 2006. " 'All about Mary': Children's Use of the Toilet Ghost Story as a Mechanism for Dealing with Fear. But Fear of What?" *Contemporary Legend* n.s. 9:1–27.

Balmain, Colette. 2008. *Introduction to Japanese Horror Film.* Edinburgh: Edinburgh University Press.

Bennett, Gillian. 1998. "The Vanishing Hitchhiker at Fifty-Five." *Western Folklore* 57 (1): 1–17.

Bennett, Gillian, and Paul Smith. 2007. *Urban Legends: A Collection of International Tall Tales and Terrors.* Westport, CT: Greenwood Press.

Berthold, Michael. 2008. "Fictionalizing the Folkloric: Matt Clark's *Hook Man Speaks.*" *The Journal of American Culture* 31 (4): 349–60.

Blackman, W. Haden. 1999. *The Field Guide to North American Monsters: Everything You Need to Know about Encountering Over 100 Terrifying Creatures in the Wild.* New York: Three Rivers Press.

Brednich, Rolf W. 2001. "Where They Originated . . . Some Contemporary Legends and Their Literary Origins." Paper presented at ISFNR Congress, Melbourne, Australia. http://www.folklore.ee/folklore/vol20/legends.pdf (accessed October 19, 2010).

Brown, Alan. 2006. *Ghost Hunters of the South.* Jackson: University Press of Mississippi.

Brunvand, Jan Harold. 1999. *Too Good to Be True: The Colossal Book of Urban Legends.* New York: Norton.

Brunvand, Jan Harold. 2001. *Encyclopedia of Urban Legends.* New York: Norton.

Burger, Peter. 2009. "The Smiley Gang Panic: Ethnic Legends about Gang Rape in the Netherlands in the Wake of 9/11." *Western Folklore* 68 (2/3): 276–95.

Clark, Lynn Schofield. 2003. *From Angels to Aliens: Teenagers, the Media, and the Supernatural.* Oxford: Oxford University Press.

Compora, Daniel P. 2006. "Ghostly Attractions: The Ghostlore of Television, College Campuses and Tourism." *Contemporary Legend* n.s. 9:83–95.

Davidson, Hilda Ellis, and Anna Chaudhri. 2001. *Supernatural Enemies.* Durham, NC: Carolina Academic Press.

Davies, Owen. 2009. *The Haunted: A Social History of Ghosts.* New York: Palgrave Macmillan.

de Vos, Gail. 1996. *Tales, Rumors, and Gossip: Exploring Contemporary Folk Literature in Grades 7–12*. Westport, CT: Libraries Unlimited.

Esuno, Sakae. 2011. "Folklore commentary." *Hanako and the Terror of Allegory*, vol. 3. Los Angeles: Tokyo Pop.

Foster, Michael Dylan. 2007. "The Question of the Slit-Mouth Woman: Contemporary Legend, the Beauty Industry, and Women's Weekly Magazines in Japan." *Signs: Journal of Women in Culture and Society* 32 (3): 699–726.

Foster, Michael Dylan. 2009. *Pandemonium and Parade: Japanese Monsters and the Culture of Yokai*. Berkeley: University of California Press.

Fraser, Joy. 2005. *Never Give Up the Ghost: An Analysis of Three Edinburgh Ghost Tour Companies*. Master of Arts Thesis, Department of Folklore, Memorial University of Newfoundland.

Freeman, Richard. 2009. "In Search of Yokai!" *Dark Lore*, vol. 4. Brisbane, Australia: Daily Grail, 129–61.

Garcia, Nasario. 2007. *Brujerias: Stories of Witchcraft and the Supernatural in the American Southwest and Beyond*. Lubbock: Texas Tech University Press.

Gentry, Glenn W. 2007. "Walking with the Dead." *Southeastern Geographer* 47 (2): 222–38.

Gibson, Marley, Patrick Burns and Dave Schrader. 2009. *The Other Side: A Teen's Guide to Ghost Hunting and the Paranormal*. Boston: Houghton Mifflin Harcourt.

"Ghosts and Jack the Ripper in City Discovery's Top 10 Halloween Destinations." 2010. http://www.prurgent.com/2010-10-26/pressrelease127356.htm (accessed October 28, 2010).

Goldstein, Diane E. 2007. "The Commodification of Belief." In *Haunting Experiences: Ghosts in Contemporary Folklore*. Edited by Diane E. Goldstein, Sylvia Grider and Jeannie Banks Thomas. Logan: Utah State University Press, 171–205.

Goldstein, Diane E., Sylvia Grider and Jeannie Banks Thomas. 2007. *Haunting Experiences: Ghosts in Contemporary Folklore*. Logan: Utah State University Press.

Grider, Sylvia Ann. 2007a. "Children's Ghost Stories." In *Haunting Experiences: Ghosts in Contemporary Folklore*. Edited by Diane E. Goldstein, Sylvia Grider and Jeannie Banks Thomas. Logan: Utah State University Press, 111–40.

Grider, Sylvia Ann. 2007b. "Haunted Houses." In *Haunting Experiences: Ghosts in Contemporary Folklore*. Edited by Diane E. Goldstein, Sylvia Grider and Jeannie Banks Thomas. Logan: Utah State University Press, 143–70.

Grider, Sylvia. 2007c. "The Literary Commodification of Texas Ghost Stories." *FoafTale News* 67 (May): 7.

Hall, Anne-Marie. 2006. "Keeping *La Llorona* Alive in the Shadow of Cortes: What an Examination of Literacy in Two Mexican Schools Can Teach U.S. Educators." *Bilingual Research Journal* 30 (2): 385–406.

Handler, Daniel. 2001. "Was That a Scraping Noise?" *New York Times*, October 14. http://www.nytimes.com/2001/10/14/books/was-that-a-scraping-noise.html (accessed September 2, 2011).

Haughton, Brian. 2009. *Lore of the Ghost: The Origins of the Most Famous Ghost Stories throughout the World*. Franklin Lakes, NJ: New Page.

Hill, Annette. 2011. *Paranormal Media: Audiences, Spirits and Magic in Popular Culture*. London: Routledge.

Holloway, Julian. 2010. "Legend-Tripping in Spooky Spaces: Ghost Tourism and infrastructures of Enchantment." *Environment and Planning D: Society and Space* 28:618–37.

Inglis, David and Mary Holmes. 2003. "Highland and Other Haunts: Ghosts in Scottish Tourism." *Annals of Tourism Research* 30: 50–63.

Irvine, Alex. 2007. *The Supernatural Book of Monsters, Spirits, Demons, and Ghouls*. New York: Harper Entertainment.

Johnson, John William. 2007. "The Vanishing Hitchhiker in Africa." *Research in African Literatures* 38 (3), 24–33.

Kleen, Michael. 2006. "Pemberton Hall." *Legends and Lore of Coles County, Illinois* 1 (8): 1–4.

Kleen, Michael. 2008. *The Legend of Pemberton Hall*. Charleston, IL: Black Oak Press, 1–6. Available online at http://makleen.files.wordpress.com/2009/05/the-legend-of-pemberton-hall-by-michael-kleen.pdf.

Major, Claire Howell, and Nathaniel Bray.2008. "Exam Scams and Classroom Flimflams: Urban Legends as an Alternative Lens for Viewing the College Classroom Experience." *Innovative Higher Education* 32: 237–50.

Matsumoto, Nina. 2009. *Yokaiden 2*. New York: Del Rey.

Mayberry, Jonathan, and David F. Kramer. 2009. *They Bite: Endless Cravings of Supernatural Predators*. New York: Citadel Press.

McCormick, James, and Macy Wyatt. 2009. *Ghosts of the Bluegrass*. Lexington: University Press of Kentucky.

McNeill, Lynne S. 2006. "Contemporary Ghost Hunting and the Relationship between Proof and Experience. *Contemporary Legend* n.s. 9:96–110.

Meyer, Matthew. 2010. "A-Yokai-A-Day: Hanako-san (or 'Hanako of the Toilet')" http://www.matthewmeyer.net/blog/2010/10/27/a-yokai-a-day-hanako-san-or-hanako-of-the-toilet (accessed July 29, 2011).

Mikkelson, Barbara. 2011. "Grade Expectations." http://www.snopes.com/college/admin/suicide.asp (accessed September 3, 2011).

Mikkelson, Barbara. 2011. "The Vanishing Hitchhiker." http://www.snopes.com/horrors/ghosts/vanish.asp (accessed June 14, 2011).

Nickell, Joe. 2006. "Argentina Mysteries." *CSI: Committee for Skeptical Inquiry* 30 (2). http://www.csicop.org/si/show/argentina_mysteries/ (accessed September 5, 2011).

Perez, Domino Renee. 2008. *There Was a Woman: La Llorona from Folklore to Popular Culture*. Austin: University of Texas.

Reisburg, Leo. 1998. "Hollywood Discovers an Apocryphal Legend." *The Chronicle of Higher Education*, September 11. http://www.snopes.com/college/info/asuicide.htm (accessed September 3, 2011).

Sagers, Arron. 2010. "Paranormal Pop Culture." August 31. http://www.ghostvillage.com/resources/2010/features_08312010.shtml (accessed September 5, 2011).

Serrano, Stephanie. 2009. *No More Tears: La Llorona at the Crossroads of Feminism, Postmodernism and Futurity in Chicana Theory and Criticism*. Doctor of Philosophy Dissertation, Arizona State University.

Stollznow, Karen. 2009. "The Stanley Hotel: An Investigation." *CSI: Committee for Skeptical Inquiry*, December 21. http://www.csicop.org/specialarticles/show/stanley_hotel_an_investigation/ (accessed September 5, 2011).

Surbeck, Liz. 2008. "Column: Pemberton's Legend, Mary." *The Daily Eastern News*, October 31. http://media.www.dennews.com/media/storage/paper309/news/2008/10/31/Opinions/Column.Pembertons.Legend.Mary-3517405.shtml (accessed September 3, 2011).

Thomas, Jeannie Banks. 2007a. "Gender and Ghosts." In *Haunting Experiences: Ghosts in Contemporary Folklore*. Edited by Diane E. Goldstein, Sylvia Grider and Jeannie Banks Thomas. Loga: Utah State University Press, 81–110.

Thomas, Jeannie Banks. 2007b. "The Usefulness of Ghost Stories." In *Haunting Experiences: Ghosts in Contemporary Folklore*. Edited by Diane E. Goldstein, Sylvia Grider and Jeannie Banks Thomas. Logan: Utah State University Press, 25–59.

Thompson, Robert C. 2010. " 'Am I Going to See a Ghost Tonight?': Gettysburg Ghost Tours and the Performance of Belief. *The Journal of American Culture* 33 (2): 79–91.

Tillotson, Kristin. 2011. "Tall, Skinny, Scary—and All Up in Your Head." *StarTribune*, April 26. http://www.startribune.com/lifestyle/120717934.html (accessed September 3, 2011).

Tucker, Elizabeth. 2005. *Campus Legends: A Handbook*. Westport, CT: Greenwood Press.

Tucker, Elizabeth. 2007. *Haunted Halls: Ghostlore of American College Campuses*. Jackson: University Press of Mississippi.

Wagner, Stephen. "Ghosts: What Are They?" About.com: Paranormal Phenomena. http://paranormal.about.com/od/ghostsandhauntings/a/Ghosts-What-Are-They.htm (accessed September 3, 2011).

CHAPTER **6**

A MEETING WITH THE DEVIL AT THE CROSSROADS: A CONTEMPORARY LEGEND?

"Every crossroads has a story," proclaims the large bold lettering in an advertisement on the back cover of the November/ December 1996 issue of Living Blues magazine promoting the state of Mississippi as a tourist destination. ... the ad relates the experience of going to Mississippi to get in touch with the spirit of Robert Johnson. "Supposedly he went down to a crossroads and sold his soul to the Devil to play like that," the narrator explains. It should not be surprising that the state of Mississippi uses the story of Robert Johnson at the crossroads as a way of promoting tourism. The story has proven its extraordinary appeal and exceptional commercial value over and over again.

—Lipsitz (1997, 39)

When researching ballads for the book *Stories from Songs*, Robert Johnson was frequently mentioned, so much so that I decided to spend a little more time with him and his story. Robert Johnson was a Mississippi Delta bluesman who, with his recording 29 songs in the 1930s, influenced the growth of the blues and the development of rock and roll. He died young and fuelled various myths and legends, most notably that he sold his soul to the devil in exchange for his musical skills (Schroeder 2004, 1). At the same time, in other readings, in television programs and on the Internet, references and reworkings about others selling their souls with the devil at meetings at various crossroads became increasingly abundant.

Because of this resurgence of stories, not all of them referring to Robert Johnson or the Delta crossroads, but almost always featuring a musician and a stringed instrument of some sort, I began to wonder if this tale has entered the realm of contemporary legend. In this investigation, the development of the legend as discussed by historians and folklorists is explored and the elements of this legend are compared to the features of contemporary legends outlined in Bennett and Smith's *Urban Legends* (2007). Similar legends connected to the crossroads motif and to the legendary Robert Johnson himself are also examined. The plethora of reworkings of this motif in popular culture and the commodification of it outside of print and filmic media are also a primary focus of this research.

> There's no doubt that the devil myth contributed to Johnson's continued popularity, keeping him relevant in the world of Marilyn Manson, Stephen King, and "Hellboy" (Beifuss 2008)

The Development of the Crossroads Meeting Legend

> *A short life, a death under murky circumstances, and a body of recorded work consisting of but 29 songs only added to that legend. So did the preternatural quality of his guitar playing, the bone-deep sadness of some of his music and lyrics, the haunting quaver of his smooth, high voice, and the dark symbolism of his songs. In some respects, you could say that Johnson is the James Dean of the blues, an artist whose tragically foreshortened life and small if brilliant body of work make him a figure of great romantic allure.*
>
> —DiGiacomo (2008)

In the late 1920s, years before the legend was attached to Robert Johnson, William Bunch, known professionally as Peetie Wheatstraw, a name taken from a folklore character also utilized by author Ralph Ellison in *Invisible Man*, emphatically professed that he had been to the crossroads and had sold his soul to the Prince of Darkness in exchange for success as a musician. But according to music historians, the specific story of selling one's soul to the devil for musical proficiency was, at first, most commonly associated with Tommy Johnson (no relation to Robert) who lived in Hazlehurst, Mississippi, where Robert Johnson also lived for a time. Tommy Johnson's brother LeDell, quoted in David Evans's biography published in 1971, relates the particulars of this meeting:

> If you want to learn how to play anything you want to play and learn how to make songs yourself, you take your guitar and you go to where a road crosses that way, where a crossroads is. Get there, be sure to get there just a little 'fore twelve so you'll know you'll be there. You have your guitar and be playing a piece sitting by yourself. You have to go by yourself and be sitting there playing a piece. A big black man will walk up to there and take your guitar, and he'll tune it. And then he'll play a piece and hand it back to you. That's the way I learned how to play anything I want. (Evans 1971, 22–23).

While most biographers and researchers agree that Tommy Johnson's posthumous claim, via his brother's memory, precedes that of Robert's meeting with the devil, musician Steven LaVere argues that the crossroads legend regarding Tommy Johnson did not jump from one bluesman to the other, but that Robert Johnson's crossroads allusions derived from Robert's own life. As evidence, LaVere cites an interview with Willie Coffee and Johnson's mentor Ike Zinermon (Zinnerman or Zimmerman), who said he (Zimmerman) "learned to play guitar while sitting on tombstones at midnight in graveyards" (Graves 2008, xv). Some claim that he was the devil, and many area bluesmen had no problem accepting this rationalization (Patterson 2004, 5). Cat Yronwode, on the other hand, attributes the transference of the legend from the original "deal maker" Tommy Johnson to the Robert Johnson legacy to Robert Palmer in his book, *Deep Blues*, "probably because Robert Johnson was so much better known and Palmer thought it made a better story" (Yronwode).

One of the most fascinating aspects of this study is the dedication of researchers to either proving or debunking Robert Johnson's alleged meeting with the devil at the crossroads. There is never, however, any suggestion that the tale may be a contemporary legend that attached itself to Robert Johnson's name through localization and familiarity. Perhaps this is because much of the speculation and debunking of this legend preceded the current familiarity with contemporary legends. Although mention of both the devil and the crossroads frequently shows up in Johnson's musical repertoire, his claim to meet with the devil has always been attributed to a FOAF, friend of a friend, and the actual particulars of this alleged meeting have been amplified and adapted as the discussions progressed through time and the media. Blues historian Gayle Dean Wardlow states that "the continuing saga of Robert Johnson selling his soul to become the masterful blues legend that he was, has not itself been factually investigated" (Wardlow 1998, 196). Wardlow concludes, after carefully reviewing the lyrics and the literature leading up to the 1988 movie *Crossroads*, that it was the movie that enhanced the myth for a worldwide audience. In fact, "the present-day myth that Robert Johnson sold his soul to the devil at a cross roads in exchange for phenomenal guitar skills has no single source. This tall tale was developed in full view by blues writers, not in private, by unnamed folk" (Wardlow 1998, 203).

Historical Development of the Robert Johnson Variant

Research on the origins of this legend inevitably leads to a single essay, "Hell Hound on His Trail: Robert Johnson," by jazz critic Pete Welding, published in 1966 in *Down Beat* magazine and later reprinted in the journal *Blues Unlimited*. The essay was the start of all the Faustian mythology with a partial quote attributed to Johnson's early mentor Son House as the first explicit suggestion of a deal between Johnson and Satan. Conversely, in Julius Lester's lengthy interview with Son House, published some months before Welding's essay, "House spoke at length about Johnson's rapid development as a guitar player but never said anything about the devil's getting involved" (Pearson and McCulloch 2003, 89). As House apparently told the story, young Johnson was a mediocre guitar player who used to sneak out of his family's house and show up at parties around Robinsonville whenever House and his sidekick Willie Brown were providing the music. Eventually, House said, Johnson ran away from home to escape the drudgery of farm work and the tyranny of his stepfather. When he returned, just six months later, House recalled he could play faster and better than either of his two former mentors—and proved it by showing them up at one of their own gigs. In an attempt to understand how Robert Johnson could have quickly acquired such speed and talent, House later suggested that he might have "bartered his soul to the devil." When this story circulated through popular culture in the 1960s, the myth of Robert Johnson selling his soul at a Delta crossroads was born (Pearson and McCulloch 2003, 31).

As quoted in the Welding essay: "House suggested in all seriousness that Johnson, in his months away from home, had 'sold his soul to the devil in exchange for playing like that.' " This attributed quote troubles subsequent researchers since

Welding never confirmed his source for the devil quote or any of the other extensive quotes attributed to House; he never published a full interview with House; and no tape or transcript of an interview with House has surfaced since Welding's death. Actually, most informants remember that Johnson was away from Robinsonville for several years, not six months, and that by the time House saw him again he was already an old hand at playing jook joints (small country stores turned into dance halls on the weekend), house parties and street corners. Far from having gotten a quick fix of hoodoo magic, he had put his talent and considerable drive during this period into learning his craft, and had studied under the guitarist Ike Zimmerman. House's starry-eyed wannabe had in fact made himself into a seasoned professional with time and considerable effort.

On the basis of House's questionable quote to Welding, cultural historian Greil Marcus, in the first edition of *Mystery Train* (1975), hypothesizes that Johnson did sell his soul and then elaborated on the symbolic consequences. "Well, they tell a lot of stories about Robert Johnson. You could call that one superstition, or you could call it sour grapes. Thinking of voodoo and gypsy women in the back country, or of the black man who used to walk the streets of Harlem with a briefcase full of contracts and a wallet full of cash, buying up souls at $100 a throw, you could even take it literally" (Marcus, 1997, 28). The chapter on Johnson in *Mystery Train* offers the first extended argument that the artist believed his soul belonged to Satan. Most of the literature and popular culture documents linking Johnson to a devil deal were produced after its publication (Pearson and McCulloch 2003, 92). Robert Palmer's *Deep Blues* (1981) (there is a documentary film by this title as well, with Robert Palmer as narrator, I believe) romanticises Robert Johnson's experience at the crossroads. His book contains a single quote, subsequently frequently re-quoted, from an unidentified source, an unsupported assumption, a bit of hearsay about one of Johnson's guitar mentors and a chilling account of what Johnson might have imagined had he gone to the crossroads in the middle of the night and heard strange noises in the distance. Pearson and McCulloch state that William Barlow, in *Looking Up at Down: The Emergence of Blues Culture* (1990), maintains, without any apparent foundation for the statement, that Johnson was known to have encouraged the legend. Barlow comments: "It is important to note that the Devil is the ultimate trickster in Johnson's blues, a reincarnation of Legba at a Delta crossroads" (Pearson and McCulloch 2003, 49). Johnson used the icon of the devil, insists Barlow, as cultural resistance reaffirming African custom and tradition. This theory changes the interpretation, for him, of the meaning of the devil image from one of a cautionary tale for all sinners to that of a heroic tale of a cultural warrior fighting the power structure with his music (Pearson and McCulloch 2003, 49). But as Pearson and McCulloch remind their readers, this ultimate trickster figure, as identified by Barlow, made a manifestation in only one of Johnson's recorded songs, "Me and the Devil Blues" (49). The mischievous character of the devil, in various guises, pervades numerous oral narratives recorded in Alan Lomax's *The Land Where the Blue Began* and Zora Neale Hurston's *Mules and Men*. Although the idea of the devil as trickster is well established in folklore, there is not a great deal of agreement among historians regarding Barlow's idea of Robert Johnson as a heroic cultural warrior.

> Yet all the qualities that seem to qualify the legendary artist Robert Johnson as a romantic hero do not actually apply to the historical Robert Johnson, whose identity changes had nothing to do with

walking away from the security of bourgeois society, whose pur-
suit of pleasure and emotional intensity compensated for his sys-
tematic disenfranchisement as a worker, citizen, and racial
subject, whose art had less to do with his own originality than with
his mastery of shared social codes and forms of expression, and
whose life and art were shaped at every stage by economic and
commercial considerations. (Lipsitz 1997, 48)

Folklorist Blaine Waide points out that while the iconic images of the devil
permutated African American folklore, Johnson's white fans consider him to be
the sole proprietor of the imagery (Waide 2009, 68).

Robert Johnson's contemporaries were interviewed on numerous occasions
about the alleged meeting. Johnson's former sweetheart, Willie Mae Powell, maintained that she heard about the crossroads deal not from Johnson but from
Honeyboy Edwards, who did not remember (or at least he did not mention) the
crossroads legend until it became part of the popular culture iconography surrounding Johnson. Willie Coffee, in a filmed interview with Stephen LaVere, said that he
would have laughed off any soul-selling claims by Johnson because Johnson was
such a jokester. LaVere believed that Coffee was an effective debunker. However,
in a conversation with Mack McCormick, who studied the life of Robert Johnson
for half a century, researcher Gioia reports him saying:

When I went to New Orleans in the late 1940s to visit some record
collectors, they told me that same story. You need to remember that
almost nothing had been published on Robert Johnson at that time.
A little bit had been written around the time of the "Spirituals to
Swing concert," and a couple of record reviews had appeared, but
they were full of mistakes. Yet these record collectors had heard
about Robert Johnson selling his soul to the devil. I subsequently
heard the same story within the black community. The fact that
the same story circulated among these two groups—groups that
had very little contact with each other—impressed me. It suggests
that the story had deep roots, probably linking back to Johnson
himself. (Gioia 2008, 163)

Several of Johnson's relatives also told McCormick that Robert had sold his
soul to the devil and claimed they knew the exact backcountry crossroads where
the deal was made. "The Devil came there," said one, "and gave Robert his talent
and told him he had eight more years to live on earth" (Palmer 1981, 113).
Christine Levecq, in her examination of Walter Mosley's novel *RL's Dream*, asserts
that "it is probable that Johnson encouraged the story of a Faustian pact, and his
various references to the devil in his lyrics would only feed it more" (Levecq
2004, 241). In the Hollywood feature film *Crossroads*, the legend reaches its
present accepted form blending the Robert Johnson premise, the devil pact lore
and the Mississippi crossroads. Today tourists come to Mississippi to find the cross-
road(s), obviously believing the legend enacted on film to be factual (Wardlow
1998, 204). There are now tourist attractions claiming to be "The Crossroads" in
Clarksdale and Memphis. The legend was further cemented in mass consciousness
with the film *O Brother Where Art Thou* directed by the Coen Brothers, which
incorporated the crossroads legend and a young African American blues guitarist

named "Tommy Johnson" who had sold his soul to the devil, with no other biographical similarity to the real Tommy Johnson or to Robert Johnson. As an example of how far the belief in this legend has gone, the *New York Times* review of the movie describes this character as "a reference . . . to the real-life bluesman Robert Johnson" (Wald 2004, 272). However, as music historian Ted Gioia reminds us, "we can study the traditional stories of individuals making 'deals with the devil' at great length, without it bringing us one whit closer to understanding why this account was attached to this specific individual, Robert Johnson" (Gioia 2008, 163). The image of Robert Johnson as a darkly tormented man who wanted his contemporaries to believe that he had made a deal with his soul had eclipsed the person and his music (Pearson and McCulloch 2003, 52).

In an article published in February 2011, Philip Mlynar interviews three generations of blues musicians regarding their viewpoints on Robert Johnson and the meeting with the devil tale. Cedric Burnside, grandson of R. L. Burnside, heard the story from his grandfather when he was seven years old. He found it scary, but also found it difficult to believe because no one had seen the devil. "I just know what's on television, just horns and stuff—so it's kinda hard to believe a guy can sell his soul to the devil. But he do got great music out of it" (Mlynar 2011). Todd Park Mohr, from the current generation of blues players, does not believe it happened, asserting that the story points to something significant: the conflict and the connectedness between the religious traditions and blues traditions (Mlynar 2011). Lightnin' Malcolm, on the other hand, did believe the legend when he first heard it.

> When you talk about the crossroads, I always tell people you're at the crossroads every day of your life. You can do right or do evil. Even in my life growing up—I grew up in the culture of the church in the 90s, and they still believe the blues to be the devil's music. So a guy like Robert Johnson, he loved the blues but he wanted to do what the church expects you to do, so I think he took on that persona—"I'm working for the devil, then." That was hype at the time: Somebody say they saw him playing the blues and really pulling the spirit out of himself, and they couldn't understand that power if they didn't see it in church. If they saw that power in a juke joint where people are drinking, they thought he had to sell himself to the devil to tap into that imagery. (Mlynar 2011)

Antecedents to the Robert Johnson Variant

> *Up until the early twentieth century the ghosts of suicides were also commonly thought to haunt crossroads due to the practice of burying their bodies in the highway and driving a stake through their chests. This profane form of burial was probably quite widespread in early modern England, though evidence is scarce as there was no requirement to record burials outside the churchyard or in unconsecrated ground. However, numerous cases were reported in eighteenth-century newspapers and periodicals, suggesting the continuation of a long-standing tradition.*
>
> —Davies (2009, 51)

In Western European belief systems, the use of the crossroads as a symbol of Satan's presence came from the concepts of being the final resting place for suicides and those unworthy of being buried in hallowed ground. As the bodies were buried, stones and other objects were tossed upon the corpses to show Christian contempt for their selfish deaths. There were no grave markers, just the footsteps of "unsuspecting travelers who, unknowingly would help obliterate the memory of the unfortunate remains sequestered within their narrow cells underneath the crossroads (Patterson 2004, 5). A recent study by Robert Halliday explores the practice of suicides buried at the crossroads in England. He states that although the law stipulated that a suicide be buried in *the king's highway*, the crossroad by a parish boundary was most often selected as the preferred site and the best remembered location. "It is suggested that this derived from a belief that the four roads would puzzle the suicide's ghost, preventing it from returning to haunt its home" (Halliday 2010, 82). An act of Parliament (July 8, 1823) replaced the roadside burial with interment without ceremony in churchyards between nine in the evening and midnight (Halliday 2010, 89). Halliday contemplates that after the roadside burial ceased to be a legal process, the folklore associated wayside graves with shepherds and Gypsies: "Like the suicide buried by the road, they exist on the margins of society" (Halliday 2010, 89).

Handbooks of magic from the Middle Ages mention the crossroads as a place to conjure the devil and perform other supernatural rites. The motif of "Magic Power at crossroads" is denoted with a motif number, D1786, by Stith Thompson (Garry 2005, 338). This belief in the power at the crossroads may have been directly related to the ancient crossroad deities Hecate and Hermes from Greek mythology. But since there is no direct connection to the meeting at the crossroads in these chronicles, we will go elsewhere to look for antecedents.

Amongst blues experts who have taken a serious interest in this matter, the most common response is to explain the crossroads tale as a carryover of African belief systems. The tradition of making a pact at the crossroads in order to attain supernatural prowess was neither a creation of the African Americans nor an invention of blues lore, but originated in Africa and was a ritual of Voodoo worship (Finn 1986, 215). The most frequent connection is made to Legba, but other trickster-gods have also been referred to in various discussions on the devil at the crossroads. According to Dahomean myth, Legba became the chief of all the gods (*vodun*) because of his skill as a musician. The creator Mawu-Lisa presented his/her children with a gong, a bell, a drum and a flute, and decreed that whoever could play all of the instruments and dance to them at the same time would be the leader. His siblings all failed, but Legba was the first to master the art of music. All human musicians have since been considered his children (Marvin 1996, 588). Legba presides over crossroads, bridges and doorways, and shrines dedicated to him can be found at these liminal sites from Nigeria to Brazil, Cuba, Haiti and the United States—wherever West African religious traditions survived. In voodoo, the crossroads symbolize the portal to the spiritual world. This portal, or gate, must be approached with caution and appropriate prayers for supernatural aid, commencing with a salutation to the god who guards the crossroads (Taylor 2008, 11). It remains the most important setting for the specific hoodoo ritual to learn a skill such as playing a musical instrument, or becoming proficient in dancing, public speaking, throwing dice or whatever anyone chooses.

> As this ritual is usually described, you bring the item you wish to
> master—your banjo, guitar, fiddle, deck of cards, or dice—and
> wait at the crossroads on three or nine specified nights or

mornings. On your successive visits you may witness the mysterious appearances of a series of animals. On your last visit, a "big black man" will arrive. If you are not afraid and do not run away, he will ask to borrow the item you wish to learn. He will show you the proper way to use the item by using it himself. When he returns it to you, you will suddenly have the gift of greatness. (Yronwode)

Yronwode asserts that the idea of selling one's soul to acquire the sought-after gift is not an element in this ritual. In the non-"soul-selling" variants, the crossroads spirit is paid either with a silver coin for the bequest or with no cost at all after one had faithfully and without fear attended the crossroads for the acceptable number of nights and days. She also establishes that because the man who met people at the crossroads shared qualities with and derived from a number of African crossroad spirits, there is a tendency to equate the crossroads' "big black man" (meaning the actual color, not a brown-skinned person) with Legba. However, this association is unheard of in the oral folk tradition (Yronwode).

Harry Middleton Hyatt conducted extensive fieldwork among African American communities in the South during the late 1930s. His research, eventually published in a weighty five-volume 4,766-page collection, includes 73 accounts of musicians (and other individuals) going to the crossroads to secure supernatural skills. These stories fall into two categories: "how-to instructions," and legends about people who attempted the fateful negotiation, most of them losing their nerve and running away, underscoring a traditional function of such stories as cautionary lessons in what not to do. Folklorist Newbell Niles "Barry" Puckett also collected stories of selling one's soul in exchange for musical talent, luck in gambling and the like, "including one attributed to a New Orleans conjurer who suggested the following sequence for aspiring guitar players:

If you want to make a contract with the devil . . . Take a black cat bone and a guitar and go to a lonely fork in the roads at midnight. Sit down there and play your best piece, thinking of and wishing for the devil all the while. By and by you will hear music, dim at first but growing louder and louder as the music approaches nearer . . . After a time you feel something tugging at your instrument . . . Let the devil take it and keep thumping along with your fingers as if you still had a guitar in your hands. Then the devil will hand you his instrument to play and will accompany you on yours. After doing this for a time he will seize your fingers and trim the nails until they bleed, finally taking his guitar back and returning your own. Keep on playing; do not look around. His music will become fainter and fainter as he moves away . . . You will be able to play any piece you desire on the guitar and you can do anything you want to in the world, but you have sold your eternal soul to the devil and are his in the world to come. (Puckett 1926, 556)

Folklorist Cecilia Conway publishes a more current example told by the North Carolina guitarist Willie Trice in the seventies. Trice said his uncle had gone to the crossroads to learn banjo from the devil but was frightened by an apparition with bright red eyes and balls of fire coming out of his mouth. In language typical of the legend, Trice declared "he couldn't stand it and ran on home" (Conway 1995, 77).

Early literary evidence of the early popularity of the legend can be found in two short stories. The protagonist in "The Devil and Tom Walker" (Washington Irving, 1824) makes a pact with "a man of color" sitting on a stump in a swamp. Critics have remarked that the work is based upon actual folktales prevalent during the early 1700s in New Hampshire and Massachusetts, areas having little or no black cultural influence.

Stephen Vincent Benet's "The Devil and Daniel Webster" (1936), with a similar plot, was ironically published the same year as Johnson's first session in San Antonio at which he recorded his "Cross Road Blues." Because Johnson's own songs inspired so much speculation about a supernatural connection, legend sleuths have been on the outlook for hard historical evidence of a link between the artist and old folk beliefs about voodoo, hoodoo and "the devil's music."

Should It Be Considered a Contemporary Legend?

> *Every culture has its legends—one could argue that this is what makes for a culture. The legend of Robert Johnson selling his soul at the crossroads is one of ours. The "us" being present day, urban, literate, mostly white music fans. It is a legend carried on by the Rolling Stones, by heavy-metal bands, by blues guitarslingers, by journalists, by filmmakers. It is a potent and intriguing legend, and says a great deal about our yearnings and dreams. Just as the legend of the brilliant young musician who traveled to big cities, made records, wore fancy clothes, and never had to pick cotton ever again says a great deal about the yearnings and dreams of black people in the Mississippi Delta of the 1930s. We are all romantics in our fashion.*
>
> —Wald (2004, 276)

Ian Inglis, in his analysis of contemporary legends associated with popular music and musicians, claims the major difference between the more traditional contemporary legends and that of the world of popular music is the element of attribution. "The myths of popular music come laden with details—dates, settings, addresses, names, ages, descriptions. And the details remain constant with each telling" (Inglis 2007, 593). Over time, these precise and detailed accounts become convincing facsimiles of the historical truth, or "factoids" (Inglis 2007, 594). "The simple reality is that the Johnson legend—the whole selling-his-soul-at-the-crossroads business—cannot be eradicated at this late date; it belongs to the people now, and the fact that people embrace it as part of American music history is as important as the question of whether it is true" (Marcus 1997, 188).

Inglis postulates a fourfold typology of storytellers for the contemporary legends involving musicians and popular music, dependent on the motivations, which varied in intensity, vested in the storytellers. These are the believer, the cynic, the entertainer and the expert. The believer genuinely believes, or at the very least, hopes that the legend is true. "In exactly the same way that attempts to question accounts of alien abduction and imminent UFO invasion, or the many reported sightings of Bigfoot and the Loch Ness Monster, only add to the vigor with which those claims are defended, so too within popular music suggestions that believers may be mistaken or misguided typically result in a consolidation of the beliefs in question" (Inglis 2007, 595). The cynical storyteller, conversely, believes the legend to be false and, when telling the legend, illustrates its absurdity, ridiculing the logical inconsistencies and emphasizing the gullibility of those who accepted it as true (Inglis 2007, 596). The person for whom the legend is nothing more than a delightful and unusual narrative to tell to others in much the same way that a joke is told is labelled the entertainer (Inglis 2007, 596). The expert is the person invested in his or her stock of "cultural capital" and who increases it with each retelling, often claiming a personal association with the source or the subject of the legend (Inglis 2007, 597).

Another major difference is that, unlike the more traditional contemporary legends, these contemporary legends contain very little in the way of cautionary warnings or guidance for behavior. Rather, they stand by themselves as independent narratives told to amuse, shock and impress the audiences (Inglis 2007, 602). "Their real significance lies therefore not in their particular details, but in their general role as sources of images, ideas and information which run counter to, undermine, and challenge 'official" discourses' " (Inglis 2007, 602).

The legend surrounding Robert Johnson and his famed meeting at the crossroads can be easily accepted as a contemporary legend according to Inglis's findings. All four types of accounts have been encountered in the research about Johnson but, however popular the correlation of this legend has been to the personality of Robert Johnson in the past, a myriad of "meeting with the devil at the crossroads" stories with musicians who are not Robert Johnson has also been found. To see if this popular legend can be categorically considered a contemporary legend, aspects of the meeting at the crossroads legend are compared with features of contemporary legends as discussed by Gillian Bennett and Paul Smith in *Urban Legends: A Collection of International Tall Tales and Terrors.*

A smattering of examples of other musicians making the trek, metaphorically if not in actuality, include John Lennon, Led Zeppelin, Bob Dylan and Katy Perry. Joseph Niezgoda theorizes that John Lennon made a deal with the devil, not at the crossroads per se, but a deal nonetheless. "Short of that physical evidence [written contract], we can only rely on religious doctrine and occult knowledge, and on John's own words to Tony Sheridan at the height of The Beatles' popularity: 'I've sold my soul to the devil' " (Niezgoda 2008, 185). Previously, in his reading of the rock band Led Zeppelin, Stephen Davis reports rumors circulating in the 1970s that members of this band "sold their souls to the Devil in exchange for their instant success, their addictive charisma, their unbelievable wealth" much as Robert Johnson had done (Davis 1997, 4). Bob Dylan talks about going to the crossroads to get his musical ability in the documentary film *No Direction Home—Bob Dylan* (2005). The excerpt is posted on YouTube at http://www.youtube.com/watch?v=rJ5joCwAoo8 (August 21, 2011). In an article on Katy Perry's reinvention of herself, Steve Leftridge reports that apparently she "met the devil at the crossroads and sold her soul to him in exchange for the devotion of electro-pop's most platinum-lined producers" (Leftridge 2010). While the various elements from this legend and the elements offered substantial correlation, does the speculation that the musicians themselves fostered the personalization (localization) of the legend shift the findings? As Everett and Narvaez comment: "many blues artists assumed a Devil relationship or identity in the lyrics of their songs, and several of these may have used such associations as mechanisms of self-promotion" (Everett and Narvaez 2001, 39). They also point out that the musicians may have used these supernatural connections for purposes of security in physically threatening

Table 6.1 Meeting with the Devil at the Crossroads as a Contemporary Legend

Features of Contemporary Legends	Meeting with the Devil at the Crossroads
Outrageous content in everyday setting	While much of the research on the Robert Johnson story attempted to confirm the fateful meeting, the actual premise is, in my opinion at least, fairly outrageous.
Anonymous	Although much of the research points to Son House and Pete Welding as the originators of the story, there is no actual evidence to confirm the conversation, and much evidence to demonstrate that the story, in one form or another, had been "floating" around for centuries in both the Old and the New World.
Multiplicity	The tale has been continually told, adapted and modified even before the recent resurgence of literary and filmic reworkings.
Time frame	Set in the here and now and always claiming to be new. In the case of Robert Johnson, the time frame was definitely limited to historical evidence, but the new versions of the story are, for the most part, contemporary.
Truth	Bennett and Smith stated, "It is almost impossible to be absolutely certain whether the events described in an urban legend ever took place, and most attempts to track the origin of a legend have failed" (xvii). Yet the truth of this particular legend had been the heart of many of the discussions about Robert Johnson. Pearson and McCulloch, when talking about their writing of a book about Johnson, particularly the story that he acquired his talent in a trade with the devil, reported: "Nobody loves a debunker, especially when the debunking involves one of the most captivating legends in American music history" (Pearson and McCulloch 2003, ix).
Belief	There are still legions of people who believe in the truth of the meeting and, in an exemplar of legend tripping, search for the crossroads themselves. The crossroads of U.S. 61 and U.S. 49 in Clarksdale is where most blues tourists pay their respects. Of course—as with ancient Roman tourists setting off to find "sites" from Greek myths—the location of Johnson's crossroads is not exactly something that can be proven. Even Memphis uses the "crossroads" theme. Its promoters claim that Beale Street in Memphis is the actual location.
Usually told as narratives with a story structure	The "original" story of Robert Johnson and his meeting at the crossroads has been told and embellished by storytellers of all kinds, and in all types of forms: poetry (song), short stories, novels, picture books, comic books, films, television programs and, more recently, on the Internet where you can purchase not only products commemorating meetings with the devil at the crossroads but an actual meeting with Old Scratch himself!

environments (Everett and Narvaez 2001, 40). The association with the powerful entity perhaps enables these musicians, and others, to weave themselves protective coverings from their own selves as well as from their fans.

Related Legends

While copious folklore regarding both the devil and Robert Johnson exists, only a few related legends that are more or less specific to the meeting the devil at the crossroads story line are highlighted here.

"Pact with the Devil"

Messages, articles and blog entries containing the phrase "pact with the devil" flood the Internet at almost any occasion in recent times, making reference to diverse topics such as environmental disasters as floods, hurricane, and tsunamis, and governmental policies and promises. The pact between the devil (Satan or other demons) and a person results in the exchange of that person's soul for diabolical favors, enacted anywhere and anytime. It is best exemplified by the legend of Faust and the figure of Mephistopheles. Examples are so plentiful that it was awarded its own category in the Aarne-Thompson typological catalogue of folklore tale types—AT 756B: "The devil's contract." Well-known folktales that include this pact with the devil idea are "The Maiden without Hands," "Bearskin" and "Rumpelstiltskin."

The legend also appears countless times in popular culture including enduring stories and poems by Nathaniel Hawthorne, e.g., "Young Goodman Brown" (1835); Edgar Allan Poe's "The Bargain Lost" or "Bon-Bon" as it was later entitled (1832); and Stephen Vincent Benet for both his short story "The Devil and Daniel Webster" (1937) and the poem "The Mountain Whippoorwill (Or, How Hill-Billy Jim Won the Great Fiddler's Prize)" (1925). "The Devil and Daniel Webster" is based on the short story "The Devil and Tom Walker" written by Washington Irving (1824), while "The Mountain Whippoorwill" is the genesis of Charlie Daniel's famous song "The Devil went Down to Georgia."

> No contemporary song better illustrates the persistence of the "Devil as fiddler" than the 1979 country-rock hit "The Devil Went Down to Georgia" by the Charlie Daniels Band. The Devil encounters a young man "who plays the fiddle hot" and challenges him to a musical duel, the outcome of which is unexpected: After centuries of bargaining, humankind has finally produced a musician whose natural skills surpass the Devil's. (Sullivan "Instrument of the Devil")

On a related note, "The Devil Went Down to Georgia" is the last song in the video game *Guitar Hero III: Legends of Rock*. A heavy-metal version of the song, the fiddle playing is performed on electric guitar by Steve Ouimette. The pact with the devil is found in other games as well: *Warcraft: Orcs & Humans*, *Grim Grimoire*, *Deception* and *The Legend of Zelda: Twilight Princess*. Popular films incorporating the pact with the devil include *Rosemary's Baby* (1968), based on the novel of the same name by Ira Levin; *The Little Mermaid* (1989); *Ghost Rider* (2007); and the two films directly incorporating the meeting at the crossroads pact, *Crossroads* (1986) and *O Brother, Where Art Thou?* (2000). A well-maintained and inclusive entry on the deal with the devil can be found at the Television Tropes & Idioms website at http://tvtropes.org/pmwiki/pmwiki.php/Main/DealWith TheDevil (August 27, 2011).

The pact with the devil has been associated with musicians from a very early time, such as Niccolo Paganini (1782–1840), a violinist of such astounding ability that people believed he could have achieved such skill only through supernatural means. He played with such ferocity and eccentric facial contortions that he seemed possessed by some unnatural force. Some observers claimed to see the devil standing next to him as he played. Paganini apparently rejected his demonic reputation, but his connection with the legend, like Johnson's, took hold. Paganini's life almost became a blueprint for other musicians similarly afflicted with extraordinary talent. Early blues-inspired rock artists, among them the Rolling Stones, Cream and Led Zeppelin, perpetuated this mystical aspect as well. Heavy-metal artists consciously adopted Paganini's nineteenth-century virtuoso image in their powerful stage presence, styles of hair and clothing, and musical pyrotechnics. The electric guitar provides a modern high-voltage equivalent to the violin.

Everett and Narvaez quote Charles Wolfe regarding the labelling of the fiddle as the "Devil's Box" in the southern United States. New Protestant converts apparently destroyed their instruments as part of their conversion (Everett and Narvaez 2001, 28). They also reference a 1943 article by folklorist Herbert Halpert as documenting that other instruments such as the flute, the pipes, the banjo and the guitar have been associated with the devil and that magical musical transactions have long been elements of European and North American folklore (Everett and Narvaez 2001, 29). An infamous instrument associated with the devil is the Hardanger Fiddle from Norway. The fiddle, similar in design to the violin, has eight or nine strings instead of four and is often highly decorated. Originally blamed for immorality and wantonness and wild goings-on at wedding parties, it was called the Instrument of the Devil since superstition had it that the only way you could become a great fiddle player was to trade your soul to the devil (European Roots 2004). This type of fiddle was forbidden to be played in churches until the end of the 1950s, while the playing of violins was not suppressed at all. The unmistakeable sound and emotional responses felt by both the musician and the audience are often attributed to the devil as well. The association with dark magic also resulted in the destruction of thousands of fiddles during the nineteenth century. "This is one of the primary reasons that today's fiddlers have more contemporary instruments. It is also the reason that the few existing old ones are kept in sealed cases, like biological specimens" (George). The powerful and unique sound of this fiddle is utilized in the soundtracks of *The Lord of the Rings: The Two Towers*, *The Lord of the Rings: The Return of the King*, *Fargo* and the Japanese animated film, *Tales from Earthsea*.

> The 19th century violinist Ole Bull from Bergen made an important link between rural music and the more refined classical scene in the towns. He was hugely inspired by the Hardanger fiddle and started collaborating with the fiddler Myllarguten. They gave many concerts together in the mid-19th century. One newspaper said that Myllarguten was "a revelation from the world of the mountains," while others claimed, of course, he'd learnt to play from the Devil, in exchange for one of his fingers. The two musicians gave concerts in Oslo, Copenhagen and Stockholm. Myllarguten left behind several fiddles and a beautiful fiddle case

from 1856, big enough for three of his instruments. Today, Ole
Bull's home at Lysøen near Bergen is a major tourist attraction.
(European Roots 2004)

"Robert Johnson Curse"

*In their position as cultural texts, the materials of popular music
(songs, performances, recordings) continually offer themselves
for interpretation. "Meaning," however defined, is contingent,
malleable, transitory, and reached only through subtle negotiation. The idea that any text, musical or otherwise, possesses a
single, absolute "meaning" is difficult to sustain, since it rests
on an assumption that it contains a deliberate message, which
is decoded by the reader in the way it was encoded by the producer, and which is accepted uncritically.*

—Inglis (2007, 601).

Countless references to "Cross Road Blues" are used as corroboration to
Johnson's meeting with the devil at the crossroads, but a closer look at the lyrics
themselves seem to negate this popular conclusion. The most literal reading of the
lyrics describes an actual experience. "Johnson finds himself alone at a country
crossroads, attempting to flag a ride as the sun sets. He has ample reason to be afraid.
He's in a part of the country where he isn't known. If a white law officer or a passing
redneck discovers him there, he could be jailed or worse" (Palmer 1981, 126).
Trying to hitch a ride at a crossroads was a commonplace practice for many people
since vehicles had to slow down at a crossroads, offering a likely possibility that
they may also stop to pick up at hitchhiker at the same time. Since no one stopped
for the hitchhiker in this song, the singer seeks spiritual assistance but not from the
devil: "Asked the Lord above " 'Have mercy, now save poor Bob, if you please.' "
    The Robert Johnson curse, or more specifically a curse relating to perfor-
mances of the lyrics of "Cross Road Blues," apparently led to individual calamity
for musicians, primarily Eric Clapton, the Allman Brothers, Lynyrd Skynyrd, Led
Zeppelin and Kurt Cobain, who sang the song over the years. Curse theorists point
to the various tragedies that these, and possibly other musicians who did live coverings of Johnson's song, experienced. Within a few years of recording "Crossroad
Blues," for example, Eric Clapton and the band Cream disbanded, and years later
Clapton had tragedy strike with the death of his two-year-old son. Duane Allman
was killed in a motorcycle accident at a crossroads near Macon, Georgia, in 1971,
while a few years later, band member Berry Oakley died in another motorcycle accident less than a mile from where Duane had been killed. Two of the members of
Lynyrd Skynyrd died in an airplane crash in 1977. Also in 1977, Robert Plant
(Led Zeppelin) lost his son to septic shock. Kurt Cobain was apparently considering
reworking his own version of "Crossroads Blues" for his band, Nirvana, when his
life came to an end, possibly by suicide or murder. "It seems that the curse didn't
stop at Cobain's death. Two people, one former Cobain employee and a Seattle
cop widely reviled for having botched the death site investigation, have both followed Cobain to the grave" (http://www.abovetopsecret.com/forum/thread329611/
pg1; August 19, 2011).
    The idea of a curse related to a specific piece of music is not unique to "Cross
Road Blues" either. The music for the song "Gloomy Sunday" was composed by
Hungarian pianist and composer Rezso Seress in 1933. The lyrics, written by

Laszlo Javor, recounted the singer's mourning of the death of a lover and contemplation of suicide. There have been contemporary legends regarding the suicide of people who had connections to the song. While the composer Seress did commit suicide in 1968, and Billy Mackenzie, lead vocalist of The Associates, committed suicide in 1997, there has not been a flood of others doing the same thing. Artists who have recorded this song include Billie Holliday, Lou Rawls, Elvis Costello, Sinead O'Connor, Bjork, Kronos Quartet and hip hop artist Chance Calaway but, to further stoke the fires, Ricky Nelson's rendition was released posthumously. Bill Ellis, in an e-mail to the ISCLR, states that "Gloomy Sunday" had an ominous reputation for inspiring hundreds of suicides in Budapest and the United States where it was allegedly banned from radio because of concerns regarding its sinister nature (Ellis 2010). Ellis's comments are in response to a contemporary legend circulating in the Philippines during February 2010 regarding Frank Sinatra's classic "My Way."

> The authorities do not know exactly how many people have been killed warbling "My Way" in karaoke bars over the years in the Philippines, or how many fatal fights it has fueled. But the news media have recorded at least half a dozen victims in the past decade and includes them in a subcategory of crime dubbed the "My Way Killings." The killings have produced urban legends about the song and left Filipinos groping for answers. Are the killings the natural byproduct of the country's culture of violence, drinking and machismo? Or is there something inherently sinister in the song? (Onishi 2010)

Onishi's article explains that most of the "My Way" killings reportedly occurred after the song was performed out of tune, but that other equally popular songs, sung badly, have not provoked killings. While the contemporary legend is just that, many people now refuse to perform the song, just in case it was true.

"Club 27" or "The Forever 27 Club"

Apparently Robert Johnson is a founding member of this specialized club of musicians who died at the age of 27. "Johnson's premature death at the age of twenty-seven seems to have developed a bizarre pattern that would later claim many of rock's legendary performers, and like Johnson, some of those death's hint at 'murder most foul' " (Patterson 2004, 219). Illustrious members include five major rock musicians who died between July 3, 1969, and July 3, 1971: Janis Joplin, Jim Morrison (Doors), Brian Jones (Rolling Stones), Jimi Hendrix and Al "Blind Owl" Wilson (Canned Heat). Additional "members" include Ron "Pigpen" McKernan (Grateful Dead), Pete Ham (Badfinger), Kurt Cobain (Nirvana) and, at the time of writing this entry, Amy Winehouse. Information about their deaths can be found at sites such as "Forever 27," http://www.forever27.co.uk/forever/, and Wikipedia, http://en.wikipedia.org/wiki/27_Club (August 20, 2011). Eric Segalstad and Josh Hunter's book *The 27s: The Greatest Myth of Rock & Roll*, published in 2008, explores this contemporary legend in detail.

When Amy Winehouse died in the summer of 2011, there were numerous articles, postings, discussions and debunkings regarding the "Club 27" legend. Dr. David Sack, MD, addiction specialist and CEO of Promises Treatment Centers, states that "the 27th year of one's life tends to be a passage between unbridled youth and the sobering reality of adulthood. People with a substance abuse problem tend to have a harder time breaking through to the other side, relatively intact" (Sack 2011). He maintains that the deaths are more likely the result of early drug or alcohol problems than the actual number of years. However, neither types of substance were found in the autopsy performed on Winehouse. Alan Cross, in *The Ottawa Citizen*, states in his article on the death of Winehouse,

> The legend of "The 27s" starts, it appears, with the death of the legendary bluesman Robert Johnson on August 16, 1938. After allegedly selling his soul to the devil at the crossroads, Beelzebub came to collect in the form of a jealous husband who gave Johnson a bottle of whiskey spiked with strychnine. His death wasn't exactly voluntary (Cross 2011)

Charles Soule and Renzo Podesta focus on this contemporary legend in their comic book series and graphic novel compilation, *Twenty-seven: First Set* (Image Comics, 2011). The premise behind the series is a reworking of the motif of famous musicians dying at the age of 27, the infamous "Club 27." Included in this first story arc are several references, textually and visually, to the main character meeting the devil at the crossroads as well as a complete story dedicated to Robert Johnson's meeting with the devil. The protagonist, Will Garland, is a guitar legend who has lost not only his way but the use of his left hand at the age of 27. Garland finds salvation with a shaman but quickly discovers that the price is, in due course, membership into the famed 27 club.

"Two Guitars"

This contemporary legend, categorized by "Guitar Man" on Snopes.com ("Guitar Man" 2010), declares that after a musician finally masters an extraordinarily difficult guitar part that he heard on a recording, he discovers that the recording had been made using two guitars. The reverse variant of this legend involved Rolling Stones guitarist Keith Richards who assumed, upon listening to a recording of Robert Johnson, that he was listening to Johnson and an accompanist. "Listening to Johnson you often swear two guitarists are playing, not one. His long fingers reached for notes other guitarists could only dream of, while his penchant for slide guitar and 'walking' bass riffs gave his style a remarkably rich language of notes, tones, and sounds. No wonder people thought he made a deal with the devil" (Santelli 2004, 29). Dave Rubin, leader of the team that transcribed Johnson's songs for the guitar instructional *Robert Johnson: The New Transcriptions*, states that "when you get to 'Crossroads' and 'Preachin' Blues'—oh my God, forget it. It sounds like three guys playing" (DiGiacomo 2008).

Commodification of the Meeting at the Crossroads

> *The story makes for great drama: a Faustian bargain . . . no wonder it has been written up in countless books and articles and has even supplied the plot for a Hollywood movie. And the story won't be forgotten anytime soon, if only because it makes for good business, too. A writer for Esquire captured the mood perfectly when he entitled his article on the reissue of Johnson's*

music, "Satan, Now on CD." Packaged in this manner, Robert
Johnson becomes the Marilyn Manson or Ozzy Osbourne of
his day. Who can deny that a tabloid angle like this sells loads
of CDs to folks otherwise little concerned with the niceties of
prewar acoustic blues? And it sells more than just music.

—Gioia (2008, 160)

Daniel Lieberfeld, in 1995, considered the commercialization of blues culture
that had taken place since the 1980 release of the *Blues Brothers* film and the widespread recognition of the blues music scene as a source for major tourist revenues.
He states that "defining and distorting other people's culture is the dubious preroga-
tive of the culturally dominant . . . and dominant cultures remain the frame of reference, even when presenting or appreciating other cultures" (Lieberfeld 1995, 219).
He refers to an enthusiastic review of the Robert Johnson recordings as an indica-
tion of the fantasy of bridging black and white cultures through the blues world.
This tendency to believe in this "fantasy" has been inflated by the popularity of
another blockbuster film with a much stronger connection to Robert Johnson.
"The memory of Robert Johnson has been central to the commodity-infused folk
revival of the postmodern period, which has become synonymous with the film *O*
Brother, Where Art Thou?" (Waide 2009, 15). In Benjamin Filene's article exposing the consequential commodification of Johnson and blues culture as a result of
the popularity of this latter film, the cultural historian declares that the danger of
appropriating a folk culture at a distance was that it "becomes just one in a series
of fashion products that savvy consumers of global culture try on and discard—like
hip-hop jeans, rain-forest body lotion, and Indonesian sarongs. . . . Roots becomes
another brand, 'authenticity' another accessory" (Filene 2004, 61). Others have
articulated related viewpoints regarding the appropriation of the crossroads story
with this romantic image of Robert Johnson acquiring his prowess as a musician
in a deal with the devil at the crossroads obscuring the realistic segregated South
in Johnson's time. "This romanticism plays an important role in the possessive
investment in whiteness, because it maintains the illusion that individual whites
can appropriate aspects of African American experience for their own benefit without having to acknowledge their structural relationships with actual African
Americans" (Lipsitz 1997, 40). Nick Tosches comments that it was not Johnson's
music that contributed to him being the most mythic of all bluesmen but the
"legends involving a horrid end through evil spell or demonic possession, attributed
to blacks but loved by whites" (Tosches 2001, 207).

In the ensuing years since his life and death, Robert Johnson evolved into
someone totally unrecognizable and unfathomable. In this section, the visible
commodities available to virtual and actual consumers at this point in time, directly
following the 100th anniversary of Robert Johnson's birth are examined. Several
items, such as the program for the 1998 conference, remain online as reminders of
past events in the celebration of his influence, but not necessarily, as we have seen,
of the man himself.

Legend Tripping and Pride of Place

Clapton and his band mates actually first heard the reference to
Rosedale in the "supernaturally benign" "Travelin' Riverside
Blues." Hearing Johnson sing, "Lord, I'm goin' o'Rosedale,

> *gon' take my rider by my side," they excerpted this line and*
> *reinserted in into their version of "Crossroads Blues," further*
> *constituting Robert Johnson as an assembly of his various per-*
> *sonas and appearances, a patch work quilt stitched together*
> *out of many disparate shards of memory.*
>
> —Waide (2009, 78)

At least three identified settings around northern Mississippi have been associ-ated with the crossroads where Robert Johnson apparently met the devil so many years ago. All of these are distinctly marked and marketed to tourists from all over the globe. The crossing of highways 61 and 49 near Clarksdale is indicated with a triangular traffic island adorned with a tall pole and three identical oversized repli-cas of a blue electric guitar, an instrument Robert Johnson did not play (R. Lewis 2011).

Steve Cheseborough, in his tribute to legendary sites relevant to the Delta blues, includes numerous references to Robert Johnson's birth, life, death and, of course, the meeting at the crossroads. Towns mentioned, with directions given for those who wish to travel to the sites, include Robinsonville, the tiny town "where young Robert Johnson bombed out when he took the stage at a jook joint where Son House and Willie Brown were playing" (Cheseborough 2009, 58), and Friar's Point, mentioned in Robert Johnson's "Traveling Riverside Blues." Cheseborough reports that it was in Friar's Point that Muddy Waters saw Johnson play and was intimidated by his fierceness and musicality (Cheseborough 2009, 66). One of the points of interest for Friar's Point is Hirsberg's Drug Store where Waters apparently heard Johnson playing on a bench in front of the store. Consumers can purchase T-shirts commemorating that event inside the store which has remained in the Hirsberg family since 1935. The city and area around Clarksdale warrants a sizeable entry in this guidebook with the main point of interest being the crossroads that many believe is the authentic site for the Johnson legend.

> Type in "Robert Johnson Crossroads" and you're offered a
> YouTube clip of Johnson singing Cross Road Blues (it's been
> watched more than 6 million times), a long Wikipedia entry on
> Johnson's tragic life and a detailed account of the myth from a
> fan (crossroads.stormloader.com). Add "Clarksdale" to a "Robert
> Johnson Crossroads" search and the first entry is "How to Locate
> the Devil's Crossroads of Robert Johnson in Mississippi"
> (ehow.com/how_4899581_locate-crossroads-robert-johnson
> -mississippi.html) with specific instructions and excellent advice to
> stop at the Delta Blues Museum in Clarksdale and "get completely
> immersed in the history of this music genre." Mind you, the myth
> always suggested Johnson met the Devil on the delta flatlands out-
> side town. Today you'll find the "crossroads" are in Clarksdale
> itself, opposite a gas station and indicated by two huge guitars sit-
> ting on a pole in the middle of the road. (Elder, 2011, http://
> www.brisbanetimes.com.au/travel/hound-dog-and-other-hits
> -20110817-1ixox.html#ixzz1Vaf35LN1)

In actuality, the frequently suggested location of the intersections of Highways 49 and 61 in Mississippi is anachronistic since the crossroads did not exist during

Johnson's lifetime; but the small town of Rosedale is another popular possibility according to many blues fans. Unfortunately, for those devotees determined to discover the fateful crossroads, this location originated in Cream's cover of the song, not Johnson's original. However, that fact does not hinder the publicity machine. "A group of locals [in Rosedale] has recently formed the Crossroads Blues Society, with an annual one-day Crossroads Blues Festival. They also hope to erect a monument to Robert Johnson (already the most-monumented bluesman, with markers in Hazlehurst, Morgan City, and Quito) in the Rosedale courthouse square" (Cheseborough 2009, 120). Ironically, the most revered crossroads for legend trippers is the one in Beulah, near Rosedale, made famous because it was the location for the filming of the crossroads segment in the 1986 movie *Crossroads*. Cheseborough maintains that since it was the movie *Crossroads* that popularized the meeting at the devil concept, the crossroads at Beulah that figured in the film could be considered the real one (Cheseborough 2009, 122). Throughout rural Mississippi the intersections of the most important roads in each area were locally referred to as "the crossroads." "Since Robert Johnson was a rambling guy, it is impossible to tell which crossroads he is talking about, if any in particular, in his song" (Cheseborough 2009, 83).

The Greenwood area, associated with the tragic early death of Robert Johnson, also receives attention in Cheseborough's guidebook. It is also the site of the court case that decreed Claud L. Johnson as Johnson's official progeny. This legality was not undertaken until after the 1990 release of the CD compilation as it "began putting money into the Johnson estate" (Cheseborough 2009, 133). This is the site as well of Steve LaVere's Greenwood Blues Heritage Museum. LaVere collected royalties from artists who recorded versions of Johnson's songs and was the main force behind the 1990 compilation. He continues to own the rights to the two only known photographs of Johnson. Most legend trippers also make their way north of Greenwood to Robert Johnson's grave where a marker was placed as late as 2002. This is the third graveyard acknowledged as the final resting place for Johnson because the exact location of his burial was never recorded on the death certificate. Seeing as there was an eyewitness who confirmed the burial at this site and since she was not in the least interested in making any money from her account, Cheseborough concludes that this grave site is the correct one. Quito, identified as the site of Johnson's grave in an article published in *Living Blues* magazine in 1990, was, at that time, just an unmarked patch of land identified by one of Johnson's ex-girlfriends who insisted that since he was in Hell, he wouldn't appreciate flowers, much less a tombstone (Cheseborough 2009, 145). Apparently not everyone agreed with her and a marker now exists there as well. Morgan City had also been considered the location of Johnson's grave as there is a Zion Church in the area, the only specific place name mentioned on Johnson's death certificate.

> Johnson has two or three more grave markers than any other blues artist, and many more words inscribed on the stones. He also gets more gifts left at his graves . . . Johnson's draws jewelery, notes scrawled on food-stamp tickets or other kinds of paper, CDs by obscure artists (perhaps left by the artists themselves, hoping that some of Johnson's spirit will penetrate their music), pencils, cigarettes, flowers, beer cans, pretty stones, and of course guitar picks. (Cheseborough 2009, 147)

When the marker was placed in the Mount Zion Baptist Church in Morgan City in 1991, Pastor James Ratliff was quoted as stating, "Isn't it wonderful that somebody that sold his soul to the devil can do so much good for the church?" (Marcus 1997, 188). The text on this monument was taken verbatim and utilized in Hazlehurst's Robert Johnson monument erected in that town square. "Memorial bricks in front of the monument include one for H. C. Speir, the Jackson record store owner and talent scout who recommend Johnson to Vocalion Records" (Cheseborough 2009, 206).

Recently, various communities proudly employed their connections to Robert Johnson to raise awareness of poverty and hardship in their areas; or perhaps it is the various news reporters who utilized the association as part of their newslore. The following two pertinent and diverse examples reflect this thematic approach. The headline for the article covering the American Recovery and Reinvestment Act grant for Lake Perry Martin near Rosedale states: "Town immortalized by blues legend get stimulus funds for popular lake." Phil Kloer, author of the article, though reporting on the 2010 project grant, writes about the widespread legend of Johnson selling his soul to the devil for supernatural mastery of the guitar as part of the story line (http://www.mnn.com/earth-matters/wilderness-resources/stories/town-immortalized-by-blues-legend-gets-stimulus-funds-for-popular-lake; August 21, 2011). He also quotes Steven Johnson, Robert Johnson's grandson and vice president of the Robert Johnson Blues Foundation, regarding Robert Johnson feeling honored that the project is taking place and that he would have been very supportive too. Walt Grayson, when writing about the Mississippi waterways, states that the river and culture it fostered is the springboard for much of the lore and legend of Mississippi itself, including "legends of bluesmen selling their souls to the devil at the crossroads at midnight. The Great River Road was one of the roads in that crossroads legend" (http://www.wlbt.com/story/14710924/look-around-mississippis-waterways; August 21, 2011)

Robert Johnson Blues Foundation Headquarters and Museum

The foundation (http://www.robertjohnsonbluesfoundation.org/) located in Crystal Springs, Mississippi, dedicated to preserving the music and memory of Robert Johnson through the provision of art education, competitions and scholarships, is sponsored by Sony Music Entertainment. Registered members of the website participate in discussion forums, one of which features the myths surrounding the musician including the devil at the crossroads legend. Along with a collector's edition of the complete original masters recordings, the foundation offers three T-shirts for sale: "Hellhound," "Crossroads" and "Crest." The "Crossroads" design features two crossed guitars with the highway signs "61" and "49" on either side of them with the text "Robert Johnson" and "The Crossroads" at the head and foot of the design. It is intriguing that the word "Crossroads" does not conform to the spelling that accompanied Robert Johnson's own recording of the song but that of subsequent blues and rock and roll artists. The website offers current news, such as a campaign for the re-issue of the 1994 U.S. commemorative postage stamp featuring Johnson, and upcoming events in this centennial year.

Not everyone, however, was pleased with the issuing of the first stamp. "Placed into a museum of national heritage, he was disremembered into an icon of national identity; as a stamp, a special commodity bearing the endorsement of American official culture, the USPS subsequently froze this nostalgic rendering of his memory in a laminated snapshot that circulates with market value" (Waide

2009, 100). Johnson, who was "wearing a button-down shirt with thin suspenders and holding a guitar, stares at the lens with eyes that look both defiant and haunted. A cigarette dangles from his lips, and although the guitar is only partially visible, his long left-hand fingers can be seen forming an indeterminate chord on the guitar's neck" (DiGiacomo 2008). There were numerous outcries regarding the removal of the cigarette from the iconic photograph when it was rendered as a 29-cent stamp.

According to Cheseborough, the museum is run by Robert Johnson's grandson, Steven Johnson, and at times, Steven's father, Robert's grandson Claud, also visits the place. The museum contains numerous guitars donated by Robert Lockwood Jr., the only person who learned guitar directly from Robert Johnson, and a piano that Johnson himself supposedly played. The museum acquired the piano from a local joint where, apparently, Johnson played piano as one of the Freetown Boys along with Tommy Johnson and James Adams (Cheseborough 2009, 205).

"Hellhound on My Trail: Robert Johnson and the Blues" Conference (September 26, 1998)

The conference was the third instalment of the Rock and Roll Hall of Fame and Museum's American Music Masters series celebrating the lives and careers of people considered early influences on rock and roll music. Robert Johnson had been inducted into the Rock and Roll Hall of Fame in 1986 in the "early influence" category. This particular conference series included museum exhibits, lectures, music, performances, film, and a conference focusing Robert Johnson. The event, along with the examination of his musical influences, considered the mythology surround Johnson's life and death. The program for this series can be accessed at http://rockhall.com/education/outside-the-classroom/american-music-masters-series/1998-robert-johnson/ (August 22, 2011).

Recordings

What remains of the man and the myth that engulfed him is his music. Tall tales of Robert's life and exploits can monopolize any conversation about him, but in the end, it is his legacy of songs that will endure.

—J. Lewis (2006, 47)

Robert Johnson recorded 29 songs in two sessions: three days in a hotel room in San Antonio, November 1936, and two days in an office building in Dallas, June 1937. The initial recordings had a very limited print run as they were considered "race" records, marketed only to African American audiences and not available in record stores outside of the general area. After they sold out, his recordings remained out of print until the 1961 release of *King of the Delta Blues Singers* (Columbia), followed by *King of the Delta Blues Singers, Vol. II* in 1970. With the release of the first volume came a renewed interest in the Delta blues artists of the 1920s and 1930s as researchers and journalists attempted to discover more about their lives and music. "Johnson 'was the toughest case to crack,' " claims blues researcher Gayle Dean Wardlow, the first person to track down an actual document pertaining to Johnson: his death certificate, found in 1968. "The record indicated that Johnson died at the age of 26 on August 16, 1938—the same month and day that would claim Elvis Presley in 1977—although it is believed today that Johnson was actually 27" (DiGiacomo 2008). Frank Driggs, the producer of *King of the Delta Blues Singers*, in an effort to tap into the romantic imaginings" of the early 1960s blues and folk revivalists, placed "Cross Road Blues" at the beginning of the album, "immediately drawing the listener's attention to tracks that alluded to the Devil and the crossroads imagery, which were not songs that were relatively popular with Johnson's contemporaries, and thus would not necessarily have incited an African American memory of the late blues singer" (Waide 2009, 59). Driggs's marketing plan was successful, and the white folk revivalists, knowing nothing about the artist, started filling the gaps in his story with the adventures narrated in his songs, stories that supported the romantic yearnings to discover a new American past (Waide 2009, 59). A recent commentary on the marketing of this first album (the original songs were all released as 78-rpm singles) states that the collection portrays Johnson as "the epitome of the stereotypical backporch bluesman, tormented by demons that drove him to an early death," while in actuality, Johnson was "a sophisticated modernist; a young ambitious and supremely gifted performer who listened to a wide variety of popular music and synthesized it into an original style" (Kot 2011). The two albums were released as a two-LP set, *King of the Delta Blues Singers*, in the United Kingdom in 1985. These albums had an immense impact on a generation of British musicians, including Eric Clapton. In his memoir, *Clapton: The Autobiography*, Clapton writes: "At first the music almost repelled me, it was so intense and this man made no attempt to sugarcoat what he was trying to say, or play" (DiGiacomo 2008).

In 1990 an omnibus two-CD set, *The Complete Recordings*, was released containing all 41 known recordings of the 29 songs. *King of the Delta Blues Singers* was remastered for compact disc, with the first volume appearing in 1998 and the second in 2004. Johnson's biggest-selling recording, "Terraplane Blues," sold about 5,000 copies in his lifetime. The first volume of *King of the Delta Blues Singers*, with 16 of his songs, sold around 20,000 copies, and since its 1990 release, *The Complete Recordings* has sold 1.5 million copies (R. Lewis 2011). Johnson has emerged as the biggest-selling pre-war blues artist of all time resulting in a second rebirth of interest in his music and his mythical history. Posters, T-shirts and other promotional paraphernalia flood the marketplace. And, as a direct result of this increased awareness, Robert Johnson was chosen for the 1994 commemorative postage stamp. On the occasion of the 2011 centennial, Columbia/Legacy released *Robert Johnson: The Complete Original Masters—Centennial Edition* which includes, among other items, a hardbound vintage book with sleeves housing the 78-rpm vinyl-disc replicas originally released by Johnson and a booklet; a newly pressed double CD of all the takes of the 29 songs recorded in 1936 and 1937; a second double-CD set compiled of rarities from the vaults of Johnson's contemporaries; and the DVD of the 1997 documentary film, *Can't You Hear the Wind Howl?*

Besides the countless recordings of Robert Johnson's songs, predominantly "Sweet Home Chicago," "Cross Road Blues," "Hellhound on My Trail" and "Love in Vain," there have been a number of tribute recordings dedicated to Robert Johnson. These include Eric Clapton's *Me and Mr. Johnson* (2004) and two albums by the Peter Green Splinter Group: *The Robert Johnson Songbook* (1998) and *Me and the Devil* (2001). In the wave of the centennial, Big Head Todd and the Monsters recorded a tribute entitled *Big Heads Blues Club: 100 Years of Robert Johnson* (Ryko/Big Records) including revered bluesmen David "Honeyboy" Edwards, B. B. King and Ruthie Foster. "Honeyboy" Edwards, the person who saw Robert Johnson as he was dying, died August 30, 2011.

Johnson's song "Cross Road Blues," because of its historical significance, was inducted into the Grammy Hall of Fame in 1998. Through its close association with Johnson's alleged meeting at the crossroads with the devil, the song came to represent the legend itself.

YouTube and Internet Presence

> *Visible in places that offer everything from encyclopaedic facts to interpretative essays, merchandise sales to promotional materials, and the services of at least one impersonator, Robert Johnson is alive and well in cyberspace.*
>
> —Schroeder (2004, 136)

A quick search at the end of August 2011 on YouTube for "Robert Johnson" and "Cross Road Blues" resulted in over 300 hits, a search for "Crossroads" over 21,000 hits, for "devil at the crossroads" over 1,500 hits and for "Robert Johnson" over 7,000 hits. A similar search on Google for the same search terms resulted in more than 10,000 hits each time. There is truly a plethora of resources, not all applicable or worthwhile, easily accessible on the Internet. There also are countless concrete and intangible products available with just a click of the mouse. Perhaps one of the oddest, but at the same time most understandable, products available is the eBay item from author and voodoo practitioner Doctor Snake who, in 2003, was auctioning his services to help musicians gain fame and fortune by emulating Robert Johnson and making a pact with the devil at the crossroads. Snake provided a "genuine Devil's contract" but, in the accompanying disclaimer, none of this was as Satanic as it may have seemed since the devil is, in reality, more a teaching spirit that gives a person access to his or her inner genius. Doctor Snake chronicled his own bargain in his book *Voodoo Spellbook* (St. Martin's Press). A revised edition of this title is being released in November 2011.

> Popular music has proved to be an especially fertile ground for the propagation of such stories; whether by word of mouth, through fanzines, or across the Internet, the (often dramatic) urban legends of popular music have been, and continue to be, generated to ever wider audiences. (Inglis 2007, 591)

Several websites that merit mention include:

- "Robert Johnson's Deal with the Devil and the Crossroads Curse," available at http://www.hauntedamericatours.com/cursed/ . The site includes a "vision" as told by Henry Goodman of the "Meeting with the Devil at the Crossroads" that fleshes out the meeting with vivid details, dialogue and background information on the legend, Robert Johnson and the "curse" associated with musicians recording "Cross Road Blues." The "vision" creatively concluded with the devil sending Johnson on his way, referring to several of Johnson's recordings, saying "Go on, Robert Johnson. You the King of the Delta Blues. Go on home to Rosedale. And when you get on up in town, you get you a plate of hot tamales because you going to be needing something on your stomach where you're headed."
- "The Crossroads by Daniel Leary," available at http://thebluehighway.com/blues/crsrds1.html. Leary examines and interprets the "mythic narrative" of the meeting at the crossroads between the devil and Robert Johnson. His background information on rural southern history, race records and hoodoo are well researched and presented.

- "Museum of Pop Archaeology: Exhibit 15: Meeting the Devil at the Crossroads." Available at http://museumpoparch.blogspot.com/2008/05/exhibit-15-meeting-devil-at-crossroads.html. Several anecdotal tongue-in-cheek discussions between the devil and musicians such as John Philip Sousa, Robert Johnson and Kevin Federline.
- How to Locate the Devil's Crossroads of Robert Johnson in Mississippi: http://www.ehow.com/how_4899581_locate-crossroads-robert-johnson-mississippi.html (accessed August 30, 2011).

Various 2011 centennial celebrations, in the form of articles, tributes, blog entries and other commentary, flooded the Internet in May of 2011 leading to the numerous celebrations planned in honor of the birth date of Robert Johnson on May 8. One of Robert Johnson's peers, Davis "Honey Boy" Edwards, participated in the tribute to Johnson and his music in Greenwood, Mississippi, the town where Johnson was confirmed to be buried. NPR produced a program, "Robert Johnson at 100, Still Dispelling Myths," available at http://www.npr.org/2011/05/07/136063911/robert-johnson-at-100-still-dispelling-myths (accessed August 30, 2011). Material on the site includes an eight-minute radio segment, the transcript for that segment and background information on the man, his music and above all the mythical tale of selling his soul at the crossroads.

> But the myth about Johnson persists, in part because it helps sell records. Steve Berkowitz is a producer at Sony Legacy, which is reissuing Johnson's music again, this time in a new centennial edition: "That was always the heart and soul of the marketing plan," Berkowitz says. "We always knew the music was great. But a guy sells his soul to the devil at midnight down at the crossroads, comes back and plays the hell out of the guitar, and then he dies. I mean, it's a spectacular story."

The radio segment incorporates sound bites from the movie *Crossroads* as well as blues researchers Barry Lee Pearson, Frank Driggs and Elijah Wald, and excerpts from interviews with Son House and Johnny Shines from the documentary *Can't You Hear the Wind Howl?* Robert Johnson is also heard from with brief excerpts from several of his songs.

Another, perhaps dubious, honor to Robert Johnson's centennial was the "Hellhound on My Ale" super-hoppy brew created by Dogfish Head Craft Brewery. Brewery founder Sam Calagione states that the limited-quantity ale honors Johnson's guitar work as it was "so complex and full that his one guitar sounded like two. His voice and lyrics were as distinct as his guitar playing, and stood out as distinct beyond the other blues musicians of the day. Beyond that you have the legend of Johnson selling his soul to the devil in return for mastery of the guitar. We wanted to make an ale that paid tribute to all that" (http://blues.about.com/b/2011/05/09/dogheads-hellhound-on-my-ale-inspired-by-robert-johnson.htm; accessed August 22, 2011).

Reworkings of the "Meeting with the Devil at the Crossroads"

> *The image of Johnson prevailing today—the Johnson legend—borders on allegory. He has been cast as the unsophisticated but ambitious young musician who, in one fateful moment, sells his soul to the devil, or at least chooses to believe he as, and who*

thereafter flashes all too briefly across the American musical landscape, a genius possessed by self-destructive impulses who leaves behind a small but utterly singular musical legacy: blues lyrics laced with Faustian imagery, recordings of a voice imbued with supernatural foreboding, and little else.

—Pearson and McCulloch (2003, 2)

Before delving into the multitude of reworkings on the Robert Johnson story, and more specifically, the legend of a musician gaining his musical fame and talent from a bargain made with a supernatural character at a crossroads, in film, television programs, novels, plays, short stories, graphic novels and picture books, here is a sampler of texts that offer allusions to the legends themselves.

Allusions and Brief Mentions

Musicologist Gerald Kubik, when speaking of the difficulties he had in finishing his book *Africa and the Blues*, remarks that "Robert Johnson appeared to me . . . and proposed a simple solution to my problem: I had better sign up with the devil and I would finish the work successfully" (Pearson and McCulloch 2003, 63). Pearson and McCulloch also point to an article published in *Tennis* magazine suggesting a possible parallel between John McEnroe and Robert Johnson, "each selling his soul to the devil in order to make violently graceful black magic with his instrument" (Pearson and McCulloch 2003, 63). Others have alluded to the idea of the meeting at the crossroads in their own compositions.

Musical Allusions

A minute sampling of these tunes, all of which are available for one's listening pleasure on the Internet, demonstrate both the diversity of artists and the allusions to the meeting the devil at the crossroads legend in the lyrics.

Tracy Chapman. *Crossroads*. "Crossroads" (1989). This song, used as the soundtrack for "Point of No Return" in *Supernatural* (Season 5: Episode 18), incorporates the symbolism of the meeting with the devil as a personal commitment, from the narrator's point of view, to be true to herself. "Demons they are on my trail / I'm standing at the crossroads of hell."

Clutch. *From Beale Street to Oblivion*. "The Devil & Me" (2007). The lyrics refer to a dispute between the protagonist and the devil: "The devil and me had a falling out / Violation of contract beyond a shadow of a doubt."

The Issacs. *Big Sky*. "Walk On" (2008). This gospel song counsels the audience, that "When the devils at the crossroads trying to make a deal, Walk On."

Marla B. *Destiny Meets Devil at the Crossroads*. "Destiny Meets Devil at the Crossroads" (2006). The song relates a personal experience of someone other than Robert Johnson meeting the devil at the crossroads.

Tom Waits. *The Black Rider*. "Crossroads" (1993). The song appears on both the soundtrack and in the play of the same name. This song was co-written by William S. Burroughs for the play based on the German opera, "Der Freischutz," which is based on a German supernatural folktale. The play premiered in Germany on March 31, 1990, with the world English-language premiere occurring in my hometown of Edmonton, Alberta, at the International Fringe Festival. The song relates the experience of George who "found himself out there at the crossroads moulding the devil's bullets."

Literary Allusions

While the majority of the remaining part of this chapter is dedicated to concrete reworkings of the meeting at the crossroads legend, the following brief excerpts demonstrate the popularity of the contemporary legend and the assurance, by most contemporary authors, that their readers will readily understand the sometimes subtle references.

Arnold, J. D., and Richard Koslowski. *BB Wolf and the Three LPs*. Atlanta, A: Top Shelf, 2010.

Although neither Robert Johnson nor the meeting with the devil at the crossroads motif is referred to in this graphic novel for mature readers, there is a strong emotional identification with the Johnson story when reading about Barnabus Benjamin Wolf's tragic adventures with the Littlepig family. BB Wolf, a Mississippi farmer, father, husband and innovative and pioneering bluesman was not the ruthless and deranged killer he was thought to be by the general public. This tale sets the record straight, relating the story of racism, murder, revenge and the blues through the lens of a classic folktale.

Coleman, Reed Farrel. *The James Deans*. New York: Plume, 2005.

This throwaway comment, made by the narrator, a white private investigator, in a private conversation in this mystery novel set in 1983, is never clarified by the author for his possibly perplexed readers either.

"He made detective. You know that, right?"
"Yeah, and Robert Johnson mastered the blues. I wonder if it was worth the price."
Larry looked perplexed, but didn't ask for an explanation. Good thing, because he wouldn't
      have gotten one. (Coleman 2005, 67)

Gilman, Greer. "Jack Daw's Pack." In *The Year's best Fantasy and Horror: Fourteenth Annual Collection*. Edited by Ellen Datlow and Terri Windling. New York: St. Martin's Griffin, 2001, 306–23. First published in *Century* (Winter 2000) and subsequently published in *The Year's Best Fantasy & Horror: Fourteenth Annual Collection*, edited by Ellen Datlow and Terri Windling (St. Martin's, 2001), and in Greer's *Clouds and Ashes: Three Winter's Tales* (Small Beer Press, 2009). It was a finalist for the 2001 Nebula Award and the 2001 Locus Poll Award for best Novelette.

Michael Swanwick asked Gilman in an interview about her character Jack Daw.

> Okay, let's move into the actual text. "He is met at a crossroads on a windy night ... a man in black ... with a three-string fiddle in his pack." When I hear that Jack Daw, characterized as "a witty angry man, a bitter melancholy man," is a fiddler one might meet at a crossroads at night, and later that he's a gambler, I can only conclude that he's the Devil. Or maybe it's better to call him the Lord of the World. He's also, I believe, the only supernatural entity that appears only as himself. What's his part in all this? (Swanwick 2000)

Gilman explains that Jack Daw only wished he was so powerful but he is only an upstart god desiring to be much more than he is in reality. Swanwick obviously is familiar with the variant that the devil himself was a musician.

Jackson, Alice. "Cuttin' Heads." In *Delta Blues*. Edited by Carolyn Haines. Madison, WI: Tryus, 2010, 50–76.

The term "cutting heads" is frequently found in discussions regarding the crossroads legend and, most frequently, when discussing the movie *Crossroads* (1986). It refers to an impromptu duel or showdown with musical instruments, "a kind of street competition in which blues musicians would stand on opposite corners and see whose music drew the largest crowd. There came a time when Robert [Johnson]'s fame led his playing partners to claim that they were Robert Johnson because they knew his name alone would attract an audience" (Lewis 2006, 46).

> Faye Mae's older brother Levon had confided to her that Granny had known Robert Johnson before he up and found himself down at the Crossroad, trading songs with the Boogey Man. Levon had told her the story last Halloween, and while she wasn't certain of its truthfulness, she suspected that it had some basis in fact. (51)

Another reference, later on in the story, refers to the character's deep connection to Johnson and his story.

> "I promise on Robert Johnson's grave and the night he made his deal with Mr. Devil," said Faye Mae, quoting one of Granny's favorite sayings. (63)

Kadrey, Richard. *Kill the Dead*. New York: Eos, 2010.

This sequel to *Sandman Slim*, for mature readers, follows Stark's adventures once he left Lucifer's realm. Stark, known as Sandman Slim, is not human but a Nephilim; the offspring of a fallen angel and a human mother. He has all the power of a Nephilim, but still is not strong enough to fight black magician Mason Faim, who dispatches him to hell for over a decade to reside with Lucifer. As Lucifer is an active character in the novel, there are many references to people trading their souls to him for a wide variety of gains. While it does touch upon deals with musicians, there was no explicit reference to Robert Johnson but, when talking about the Beatles:

> "You knew them? They didn't make a deal with you, did they?"
>   He gives me a look.
>   "Don't be ridiculous. Pete Best wanted to make a deal back in Hamburg, but he was already out of the band, so who cared?" (111)

Lister, Michael. "Death at the Crossroads." In *Delta Blues*. Edited by Carolyn Haines. Madison, WI: Tryus, 2010, 162–80.

Lister creates the settings of both the present and the past juke joints while, at the same time, making pointed commentary regarding the commodification of the legend.

> The tourist fed the hungry jukebox and Robert Johnson's "Cross Road Blues" began to play. "Real original," Jerry said in the direction of the tourist, but not directly to him. "Nice choice. You just come from the big blue guitars or are you on your way? It's not really *the* crossroads you know. Hell, it ain't even *a* crossroads." (164)

And again:

> "It was a real juke—not like this place. Not like all this shit they're trying to market to tourists—that ridiculous Crossroads sign . . . corporate owned blues clubs . . . Real jukes started as a place for black sharecroppers to escape their painful existences in a time when Jim Crow kept 'em out of the white joints," he said. "On the outskirts of town in shacks or somebody's house, they offered cheap entertainment, a chance to socialize and share each other's burdens . . . It's why the blues ain't just music, gotta be caught, not taught, and jukes not somethin' some corporation can do." (169)

Love, Jeremy. *Bayou: Volume One*. New York: Zuda, 2009. Love, Jeremy. *Bayou: Volume Two*. New York: DC Comics, 2010.

Told from the perspective of a young girl, *Bayou* addresses the serious issues of racism and history in the southern United States in the 1930s. The story line, incomplete at the time of this writing, weaves history, fantasy, folklore and setting together to follow Lee as she attempts to save her father from an unjust hanging. There are several subtle allusions to Robert Johnson in the first volume, but this is stepped up in the second volume, along with the appearance of a very evil Stagolee.

Vaughn, Carrie. *Kitty Goes to War*. New York: Tor, 2010.

In a conversation about fires in the area with the main character, Kitty, a caller on radio talk show queries: "My friend Stacy who's kind of a witch said it's because it was on a crossroads, and, something demonic must have happened there, one of those deal-with-the-devil-type things, and the energy overflowed and incinerated it. Could she be right?" (1).

Willingham, Bill, Matthew Sturges and Andrew Robinson. "Jack O'Lantern." In *Jack of Fables* Issue 16 (December 20007).

The cover of this Halloween special issue states "the devil gets a small kickback every time you purchase a copy of . . . Jack of Fables." In a similar tongue-in-cheek approach, the stand-alone story describes the many different deals made by Jack and various devils to extend his already immortal life.

Cinematic Allusions

References to meeting the devil at the crossroads appeared on various television series dealing with the paranormal. Two prominent examples are the shows *True Blood: Burning House of Love* (Season 1, Episode 107) and *Charmed: The Devil's Music* (Season 2, Episode 4). In *True Blood* the reference is made when Tara and her mother meet the medicine woman to exorcise the demon out of her mother. The reference in *Charmed* surfaces when the band manager makes a deal with a demon (Masselin) to attract popular bands to hire him to manage them.

Literary and Visual Adaptations

> *It's in literary fiction, though, more than film or critical analysis, that Johnson seems to be finding a true second home. Though sophomoric fictional riffs or short stories on Johnson have been common fare for decades (T. Coraghessan Boyle's breathless "Stones in My Passway, Hellhound on MY Trail" is an early example), the first work of lasting value was probably Stanley Booth's "Standing at the Crossroads," a nine-page "playlet" written in response to Greenberg's Love in Vain.*
>
> —Marcus (1997, 186)

The entries in this section, organized by format, work the crossroads meeting legend in an extensive diversity of ways for a variety of audiences.

Novels

Alexie, Sherman. *Reservation Blues*. New York: Atlantic Monthly Press, 1995.

In the acknowledgements for this novel, Alexie notes that he wants to especially acknowledge the influences of the film *Crossroads* and the memory of the real Robert Johnson as, without his music, none of the story contained in the novel would exist. *Reservation Blues* begins with Robert Johnson showing up at the Spokane Indian Reservation where the only person who will talk to him is Thomas Builds-the-Fire. In the novel, Johnson apparently does not die in 1938 but has been wandering around trying to get rid of his guitar, cursed in his infamous bargain with the devil at the crossroads. Johnson leaves Thomas his guitar when he follows Thomas's advice, making his way up to see Big Mom living on a nearby mountain.

> Old and tired, he had walked from crossroads to crossroads in search of the woman in his dreams. That woman might save him. A big woman, she arrived in shadows, riding a horse. She rode into his dreams as a shadow

on a shadowy horse, with songs that he loved but could not sing because the Gentleman might hear. The Gentleman held the majority of stock in Robert Johnson's soul and had chased Robert Johnson for decades. Since 1938, the year he faked his death by poisoning and made his escape, Johnson had been running from the Gentleman, who narrowly missed him at every stop. (6)

Johnson's guitar is the catalyst for the novel's characters to form a band and travel beyond the confines of the reservation while learning about the world and themselves in the process. The fact that none of the members of the band has any musical talent is a moot point as Johnson's guitar has retained its magical power regardless of who holds it. Unfortunately, it also inflicts burns on those hands. And, to make matters even more audacious, the guitar is a sarcastic communicator. Alexie's humor illuminates his candid approach to life for contemporary musicians and Native Americans as well as popular culture's reciprocal consumption of Native American cultures in the process. He also provides his own variant regarding Johnson's alleged meeting with the devil at the crossroads. When Johnson agrees to trade what he loved the most, freedom, to be the best guitar player ever:

"It's done," said the Gentleman and faded away. Johnson rubbed his eyes. He figured he'd been dreaming ... So he turned around and walked back towards Robinsville. He'd only been gone for a few hours. Nobody would even notice he'd left, and he was foolish for leaving. He'd forget about the guitar and play the harp with Son House. Johnson vowed to become the best harp player that ever lived. He'd practice all day long.
"Where you been?" Son House asked when Johnson walked into the juke joint. House sat in a chair on stage.
"What you mean?" Johnson asked. "You act like I been gone forever. I just walked out to the crossroads. Then I changed my mind and came back."
"You been gone a year! Do you hear me? You been gone a year!"
Stunned, Johnson slumped into a chair on the floor below House and laid his guitar on his lap. He heard an animal laughing in his head.
"Don't you know where you been?" House asked.
"Been at the crossroads," Johnson said. He looked down at his guitar. He looked at House (265).

Ojibway author and storyteller Richard Wagamese editorializes that Native people related to blues music because the blues, like them, were born of a displaced people made to feel unwelcome in their imposed new surroundings. The blues were born of loneliness and desperation. "It's music, and in the clack of the skeletal bones of Robert Johnson that serve as its meter, you can mask the political with passion" (Wagamese 2008). The soundtrack, *Reservation Blues*, written and recorded by Sherman Alexie and Jim Boyd in 1995, is still available through iTunes and CDBABY.

Ashford, Barbara. *Spellcast*. New York: Daw, 2011.
Maggie Graham ends up at the crossroads, both literally and figuratively, when she fled Brooklyn and stumbled on the Crossroads Theatre in Vermont, reigniting her love of acting. But the Crossroads Theatre offers much more than just summer musicals: mystery, magic, search for identity and for romance itself. While there is no devilish influence here, there is definitely something uncanny at work.
Barbara Campbell, writing as Ashford, received positive reviews for this paranormal romance that became much darker than she had originally anticipated writing. When she typed the four words, "Welcome to the Crossroads," the tone and ending were transformed (Ashford 2011). A sequel was forthcoming at time of this entry.

Atkins, Ace. *Crossroad Blues*. New York: St. Martin's Press, 1995. (Reprinted by Busted Flush Press, 2009).
Part-time detective and instructor of blues history at Tulane, Nick Travis searches for a Tulane colleague who disappears on a quest for an unknown Johnson recording in the town of

Greenwood in the Mississippi Delta. Johnson's life, music and death are an integral part of this first entry to the Nick Travis mystery series but his alleged deal with the devil is not a focus of either Travis or his author. The anniversary 2009 edition includes a short story, "Last Fair Deal Gone Done," nominated for the 2010 Edgar Mystery Award and the Anthony Award. This story, using the title of one of Robert Johnson's songs, is available on-line at http://bustedflushpress.blogspot.com/2009/12/original-ace-atkins-short-story-excerpt.html (accessed August 3, 2011). There is no crossroads reference in the short story that acts as a prequel to the novel, *Crossroad Blues.*

> "No," Fats said. "What I got, pod'na, is a fair deal. Just like Robert Johnson said, 'Last Fair Deal Goin' Down.' You know about Johnson?"
> "Sure."
> "He sure played a weird guitar. I've always tried to make my sax do that. But it just ain't the same.

Boyett, Steven R. *Mortality Bridge*. Burton, MI: Subterranean Press, 2011.

According to the intriguing cover blurb for this novel, it remixes the stories of Orpheus, Dante, Faust and the Crossroads legend, in a brutal, unpredictably funny quest "across a Hieronymus Bosch landscape of myth, music, and mayhem; and across an inner terrain of addiction, damnation, and redemption." Not for the faint of heart, this horrifying and horrific journey is intended for mature readers. The novel begins with a letter the narrator, Niko, receives on a parchment, delivered by an Achaian during a recurring cycle of events where Niko slowly began to regain his memory.

> Here's the short version. Your name is Niko. You're a real true Rock Star. The reason you are is because you signed a deal with us a long time ago. We'll skip the fact that you've got the chops to have made it to the top without us. Your problem, not ours." (16)

When Niko's lover, Jem, is struck with a terminal illness, he decides to travel to the underground to re-negotiate the deal he had once made. "He went down to the Crossroads with his contract by his side" (29). The journey, horrific and grotesque, connects him with the worse and best of humankind but, always, giving him a bit more understanding of himself, his dreams and the world itself. Numerous allusions and concise retellings of classical mythology dot the narrative landscape as do bloody images and the frequent use of strong language. The intertwining of all of these underground stories creates a fascinating journey for the reader as well. "He doesn't even try to beat the rap the way they do in all those deal with the devil stories, because the Greeks didn't have a heaven and hell. Just an underworld where everyone ends up. Nowadays who knows what old Orpheus would do?" (109). As Boyett explains on his website,

> The original idea was to tell a muscular, action-packed novel that was essentially an extended chase scene from start to finish. But "the tale," as Tolkien once wrote, "grew in the telling"—from a straightforward action-adventure to a deeply felt and lyrically written examination of the power of myth, free will, duty, and redemption, and even of the ways in which language itself shapes our perceptions, thoughts, and abilities. ("Mortality Bridge")

In the acknowledgements, the author states that he hoped the readers familiar with Dante's *Inferno*, the myth of Orpheus "and familiar descent-motif stories–along with the legend of Faust, the blues legend Robert Johnson and the Crossroads, and many related deal-with-the-devil myths, folk tales, songs, and movies" would indulge his mash up of elements that he perceives as mutual and archetypal (419). He also states that wherever possible, he tried to acknowledge the sources in the text itself. According to both the acknowledgements and the website, maps of the Niko's above-ground journey will be available for interested readers. At the time of this writing, the map section is still under development.

Bunce, Elizabeth C. *A Curse Dark as Gold*. New York: Arthur A. Levine, 2008.

Essentially a reworking of the Rumpelstiltskin folktale, this winner of the William C. Morris Debut Award given by the American Library Association, and a host of other literary awards, also intertwines elements of the meeting with the devil at the crossroads into her novel. When a deal made by her ancestors to keep the family mill running is discovered in a stack of old correspondence, Charlotte has to counter the generations-old curse and bargain in order for the mill, her sister and herself to survive. "Powerful magic at work in a crossways. Folk've been known to make dark bargains there—and worse" (318). Set in the early days of the Industrial Revolution in England, Bunce weaves elements of fantasy and historical fiction in this strong young-adult novel.

Elizabeth Bunce states that she thinks that she, like a lot of people, is instinctively drawn to the image of the crossroads.

> First of all, it makes such a wonderfully dramatic setting—always those four lonely roads, out in the middle of nowhere, a broken-down fence, a phantom breeze trailing by . . . so evocative. But beyond that, I think crossroads take their power from being what anthropologists call "liminal spaces"—those that cross or connect two spaces, without being completely in one or the other. Like a threshold—neither inside nor out, but both (and neither) at once, at a crossroads, the roads are going neither north nor south nor east nor west, but all—and none—of those, at the same time. This liminality naturally extends to connecting our world with the spirit world, or the world of the fey, or the underworld . . . which makes it a natural place to meet the denizens thereof.
>
> I have to admit that the crossroads in *Curse* takes it origin less from the "bargain at the crossroads" tradition than from the English tradition of other questionable goings-on at crossroads, particularly as a burying place for witches (who would presumably be confused by the multiple roads and not be able to find their way back to their victims). But of course "Rumpelstiltskin" certainly falls in to the devilish bargains tradition, especially the trick of knowing the devil's name to gain power over him. More than that, though, the crossroads echoes through *Curse* in several ways: the world is at a technological and ideological crossroads with the Industrial Revolution clashing with the folklore and superstition of the villagers. And Charlotte, like every YA protagonist, is at a crossroads of her own, neither completely adult nor child, yet something of both at the same time.
>
> And with all of that tradition and potential resonating, it's kind of an irresistible symbol. (Bunce, personal e-mail communication)

de Lint, Charles. *Spirits in the Wires*. New York: Tor, 2003.

In this urban fantasy, Charles de Lint offers the proposition that the gods and other beings are seeking haven in the unexplored world of the Internet. Wordwood, the nexus for information which appeared in earlier de Lint novels and the focus of this novel, becomes corrupted by a malicious virus, and several residents of Newford vanish into cyberspace. Folklore expert Christy Riddell, with the aid of his brother Geordie, a few friends and the bluesman Robert Lonnie, plunge into this virtual world to release their friends and, perhaps, the future.

Robert Lonnie is an extraordinarily talented guitar player who, for those familiar with Robert Johnson, has recognizable characteristics such as "those long fingers of his left hand travelling the fingerboard like the legs of a spider" (166) and his hellhounds. "Hellhounds," Robert said. "And they're not necessarily dogs. They come in all shapes and sizes. The only thing they have in common is their interest in me" (169). When Geordie comments that he would deal with the devil if that was what it took to get Christy's friend out of the virtual world, Robert speaks obliquely: "Not sure I'd recommend that," Robert says stepping out of the aisle where he'd been standing. "Dealing with the devil," he clarifies. "I'm behind you on every other count" (209). Robert later identifies his hellhounds as *les baka mal*, "hellhound spirits who like to lay proprietary claim to *les carrefours*—or at least they will at whatever crossroads they think Legba isn't watching" (287).

Grabenstein, Chris. *The Crossroads*. New York: Random House, 2008.

This middle-school-age novel incorporates elements from the "devil at the crossroads," "the Vanishing Hitchhiker" and "the Woman in White." Eleven-year-old Zack Jennings's new home is near a tree that stood at the crossroads of County Route 13 and State Highway 31. A roadside memorial has been established at the tree, the site of a dreadful bus accident 50 years before. Zack soon discovers that he had been chosen to help release the souls of the participants in that accident, tied to their earthly haunts by that very memorial. Grabenstein pays homage to other contemporary legends and legend tripping as well as additional folklore motifs and traditions such as the finding of a skeleton inside of a hollow tree in this engaging novel. As part of the action, Grabenstein explains the term "descanso" for his characters and readers.

> Spanish word for roadside memorial. In the early days of the American Southwest, funeral possessions would carry the coffin out to the graveyard for burial. From time to time, the pallbearers might set the casket down by the side of the road and rest. When the procession resumed, the priest would bless the spot where the deceased's soul had tarried on its final journey. The woman would then scatter juniper flowers and stake a cross into the ground to further commemorate the site. (66)

Winner of the Anthony Award for best children's/young adult novel, *The Crossroads* is also available as an audio book read by the author's wife, J. J. Meyers, who won an Earphones Award from AudioFile for her performance.

Jacobs, John Hornor. *Southern Gods*. San Francisco: Night Shade Books, 2011.

Jacobs's horror novel follows war veteran and private investigator Bull Ingram as he tracks down Ramblin' John Hastur, a bluesman rumored to have made a deal with the devil and whose music incites listeners to perform rites of primal lust and violence. It also follows the journey of Sarah Williams, a single mother who returns to her Arkansas roots and discovers secrets hidden away in her uncle's library. When the two paths finally intersect, this gothic story, intended for mature readers and often referred to as Lovecraftian in tone, delivers a satisfying exploration of the not-so-distant southern United States.

> Robert Johnson had a definite influence on Ramblin' John Hastur. How could he not have? However, I tried to keep away from drawing direct parallels between the two because I knew from the start that this novel wasn't going to rely upon the Christian dialecticism of God vs. Devil. I was always too worried it would come across as Ralph Macchio's movie, "Crossroads." I needed to keep Robert Johnson at arm's length. He could color and inform the story, but not be a direct example. At a certain point in *Southern Gods*, the focus on music falls away and we're left with the antagonism of malevolent forces, regardless of delivery mechanism. (Kenyon "The Monday Interview")

Milford, Kate. *The Boneshaker*. New York: Clarion Books, 2010.

The main location in this steampunk novel, intended for middle-school-age readers, is set very close to a crossroads and the remains of a ghost town. Thirteen-year-old Natalie lives in Arcane, Missouri, in the early nineteenth century with her father who tinkers with machines and has passed on his love for them to his daughter. As she learns to ride her bicycle, or the boneshaker as it was once called, she also is drawn into danger with the perpetual-motion machines built and brought to Arcane by Dr. Limberleg in his Nostrum Fair and Technological Medicine Show. To save her town and her ailing mother, Natalie has to solve the mysteries of the fair, the ghost town at the crossroads and the Civil War veteran who beat the devil with his guitar at that very crossroads. Filled with mystery, horror, humor and suspense, *The Boneshaker* takes its reader on an extremely satisfying and exhilarating ride.

Two things popped into Natalie's head. The first was a crystal-clear image of Old Tom Guyot, sitting beside a fire at the crossroads outside of town, hammering something round and gold-colored into the folded piece of metal that now held up the strings of his guitar. The second thing was what she had been trying to remember while Tom and his guitar sang with their peculiar voices. Two words: *the Devil*. (33)

Milford pays homage to Ray Bradbury's writing as well as the story of Robert Johnson's meeting with the devil at the crossroads. In an interview by Colleen Mondor, mentioning that the crossroads played a large part in the novel and that "Robert Johnson's story (which might actually be about musician Tommy Johnson) is famous among music lovers (and Americana fans)," she asks Milford what she thought about the crossroads mythos and what she learned about it while researching and writing. Milford replies that the crossroads are:

a place where you leave things behind. You come to know the road that you selected at the cost of the other three. Someday you might go back to one of those untaken ways, but there's no way to know if the road you come back to is the same as it would've been if you'd chosen it first—or if it will lead to the same place ... what I learned while researching: a musical duel is called a head cutting, and the violinist Niccolo Paganini was also believed to have dealt with the Devil to gain his amazing skills (Mondor 2010).

Kate Milford assured me, in a private message, that

I'm drawn to the crossroads for a couple reasons. As a writer of kids' fiction, I find it to be a wonderfully concrete metaphor for so many things that kids experience every day and that they inherently know may be perilous: moments of choice and of taking chances, moments of transition, even the simple, literal act of crossing the street. They may not have been asked to verbalize the idea that these everyday moments are potentially hazardous, but they often experience them as moments of anxiety. Putting words to that anxiety, using the mental picture of the crossroads to visualize what we are doing when we face tough decisions and why we sometimes feel troubled by them, can be a really comforting thing for a kid.

The other thing I love is the incredible breadth of crossroads folklore from around the world. In particular I love its dual nature. I like that for basically every example of the crossroads as a place of danger, there is a story in which it is a place of safety and that for every dreadful thing that can be done at a crossroads, there's a restorative or protective ritual that can be done there, too. It can be a place to bury the most dishonored dead, but in other traditions only the most venerated are buried there. I find that fascinating as someone who loves folklore, but I also think the idea that both the potential for good and the potential for evil can be present in something at the same time is a really important idea to present to young readers. In the end, it's what you do at a crossroads that determines the outcome. These are things that may seem obvious to adult readers, but for a kid who's eight or nine or ten, they're very powerful and empowering ideas. (Milford, personal communication)

Mosley, Walter. *RL's Dream*. New York: Norton, 1995.

The "RL" of the title refers to Robert Leroy Johnson, and it is this mythic presence that haunts both the narrator, Atwater (Soupspoon) Wise, and the reader. The novel revolves around the elderly Soupspoon's reminiscences regarding his relationship with RL to Kike Waters, a white woman in her 30s who befriends Soupspoon during his last days. "Blues is the devil's music an' we were his chirren. RL was Satan's favorite son. He made us all abandoned, and you know that was the only way we could bear the weight of those days" (140).

In their discussion, there is the mandatory query regarding the meeting with the devil at the crossroads: " 'Made a trade fo'it, Soup.' That's what he said! Give up his right eye to the blues. Made a blood sacrifice with a witch woman down Clarksdale. Soiled his hands in the blood of an animal, then goes out to the crossroads" (141). This atmospheric retelling of the life of bluesmen in the 1930s is recommended for mature readers.

Critics condemned this novel for falling into the trap of romanticizing Robert Johnson by detaching him from his socio-economic circumstances and transforming him into an individual artist who produced music almost magically and without commercial considerations (Levecq 2004, 240). The novel relies heavily on the alleged meeting with the devil at the crossroads with "references to the devil or hell punctuat[ing] practically every one of RL's appearances" (Levecq 2004, 241). "Once again, the blues are deployed as an anecdote to the shallowness of contemporary commercial culture, as an art form that is precious because it is unapproachable and unknowable, locked in the past but superior to anything we can imagine in the present" (Lipsitz 1997, 41).

Murray, Charles Shaar. *The Hellhound Sample*. Headpress, 2011.

Robert Johnson's guitar, a battered old Stella, transfers its curse and power after Johnson's death to 16-year-old James Moon, who becomes one of the great bluesmen of the next generation. The novel begins with Moon, now an old man, attempting to clear up loose ends with this family and friends as he prepares to die from cancer. Moon's father was definitely not a fan of the blues. As he told his son in 1932 in Clarksdale, Mississippi:

> "The *devil* live in the git-tar," growled Solomon Moon. "And the worst music you can play on the git-tar is the *blues*. That's what that man was playin'. The *blues*. The devil's own music. Every blues singer work for the devil. An' out of all the blues singers around here, that man is the evillest of 'em all . . . I find you on the street listening to the man who *sold* his *soul* to the *devil*, just standin' there not even sayin' a prayer to save yourself while he try to take *your* soul too!" (3)

Of course, the musician is none other than Robert Johnson, and when James "Blue" Moon left home to make his own way as a blues musician, the early experience of hearing Johnson never leaves him. Nor did the unwitting deal he makes to gain the guitar. The reader never knows if Blue made a deal with the devil in order to obtain his legendary talent, but the copious references to Johnson, the devil and the crossroads aid in the atmospheric journey taken by Murray's characters and, by extension, the reader.

In his "Hellhound Liner Notes," Murray explains the genesis and journey of the novel itself. He also maintains that

> Furthermore, I don't believe, in any rational or literal sense, that there was anything supernatural about the life or death of Robert Johnson. The myth of the crossroads is just that: a myth . . . but it still provides a metaphor which won't go. I don't believe—not *really*—that Robert Johnson sold his soul to the devil at the crossroads in order to gain his uncanny musical powers, except in the sense that we all, in our various ways, make deals, knowingly or unknowingly, with our own personal devils at our own personal crossroads to facilitate the journey towards our own personal goals . . . or maybe to ensure that we never actually achieve them. I did, however, fancy speculating as to how that spectral event *might* have gone down . . . if it *had* happened. (286–87)

Filled with commentary of real musicians and others from fiction, including JP Kinkaid from the JP Kinkaid Chronicles penned by Deborah Grabien who writes her own homage to the old bluesmen in *Graceland* (Plus One Press, 2011), Murray evokes the world of blues music and musicians. Murray, an eminent music journalist and author of books on Jimi Hendrix and John Lee Hooker, is also an accomplished musician and writes convincingly of a world he knows well.

Short Stories

Bear, Elizabeth. "And the Deep Blue Sea." In *Sympathy for the Devil: Stories of the Devil.* Edited by Tim Pratt. San Francisco: Night Shade Books, 2010, 162–77. Originally published in *Sci Fiction*, 2005. Also published in Elizabeth Bear's *Breaking the Chains* (2006). Available online at http://www.elizabethbear.com/deepblue.html (accessed August 11, 2011).

    Harrie is approached by the devil to renew her bargain with him in trade for the fetal stem cell culture she is couriering across the country on her motorcycle in this post-apocalyptic short story. She refuses to bargain a second time with him but, as she realizes, she is in trouble as "every little town in Nevada grew up at the same place: a crossroads" (169). Harrie manages to ride over the obstacles and mayhem put in her way by Nick in his effort to get her to change her mind, and, even at the end, she is willing to continue to take her chances rather than to allow him access to her valuable delivery.

Bennett, Jenn. "Demon at the Crossroads." 2011. Available online at http://www.tyngas reviews.com/2011/08/ff-demon-at-crossroad-by-jenn-bennett.html (accessed August 30, 2011).

    As Bennett explained in her introduction to her story, the forfeiture of one's soul seems a fair price if one craves something with all one's heart. She mentions Robert Johnson and his legendary deal for his skill as a guitar player as an example of this act of desperation. Her series character, a ceremonial magician, owns a blues nightclub, the Crossroads, in Memphis in the 1940s, and in desperation over her failing business calls out that she will give anything to make it a success. Not surprisingly, her call is immediately answered by an attractive devil himself, Lon Butler. And, as it just so happens, "the Crossroads Nightclub isn't an arbitrary name. It's located at a crossroad, and it is midnight." As they negotiate the terms of the upcoming deal, both feel that they are holding the upper hand.

    Bennett maintains:

> The crossroads motif—the myth of an otherworldly midnight bargain—isn't necessarily a heretical act of desperation, nor is it a cautionary tale. It's about taking a risk and conquering something dark. A standoff. The devil doesn't always win, after all—Charlie Daniels is the better fiddle player. Maybe it helps that both parties meet at a liminal place between worlds, which grants the bargainer a certain amount of equal footing. Besides, the other party isn't always evil. He might even have a sense of humor, like Papa Legba, the Vodou trickster loa spirit; he's probably winking at you right now, looking forward to the challenge. (Bennett, personal communication)

de Lint, Charles. "Ten for the Devil." *Tapping the Dreaming Tree.* New York: Tor, 2002, 19–55. Originally published in *Battle Magic*, edited by Martin H. Greenberg and Larry Segriff. New York: DAW, 1998. Also available in *Ravens in the Library: Magic in the Bard's Name*, edited by SatyrPhil Brucato and Sandra Buskirk. Seattle, WA: Quiet Thunder, 2009, 43–70; and in *Sympathy for the Devil*, edited by Tim Pratt. San Francisco: Night Shade Books, 2010, 28–50.

    The much republished short story "Ten for the Devil" draws upon the crossroads myth but takes a very different road as it follows musician Staley Cross's search for her only hope of soul survival: a mysterious bluesman known as Robert. Staley's grandmother has always warned her to be careful playing her blue fiddle, but she does not take the warnings seriously until she finds herself pulled into the world of faerie and has a contest with the devil at the crossroads, with unexpected results.

Dellamonica, A. M. "Cooking Creole." In *Mojo: Conjure Stories*. Edited by Nalo Hopkinson. New York: Warner Brothers, 2003, 212–23.

    When editor Nalo Hopkinson put out her call for stories for this anthology she asked for stories that would sing. A. M. Dellamonica produces a contemporary adaptation of the meeting with the devil at the crossroads, with a culinary flare and in a Canadian locale. When Steep Dover goes to the crossroads to ask to become a famous chef, it is not his first meeting with the tall Black Man. "Cooking's a gift, the last gift. As for the rest, you're keeping what you've tried to through off. Understand?" (222). This time the deal was not going to go down without repercussions!

Dikeman, Kris. "Nine Sundays in a Row." In *Sympathy for the Devil: Stories of the Devil*. Edited by Tim Pratt. San Francisco: Night Shade Books, 2010, 280–89. Originally published in Strange Horizons, 2008. Available online at http://www.strangehorizons.com/2008/20081027/sundays-f.shtml (accessed August 11, 2011).

Narrated by the devil's dog, the story relates a young girl's endeavour to learn how to be the best card player from the devil by sitting at the crossroads, nine Sundays in a row. "If you wanta learn you somethin' go down to a place where two roads cross. Get there Saturday 'round midnight, and wait there 'til Sunday morning—do that for nine Sundays, all in a row. The dark man, he'll send his dog to watch on you while you wait" (280). The dog and his nemesis, Red Rooster, watch over the young girl, for opposite reasons. The narration focuses on smells and sounds and the dog's thoughts about his master, the Rooster and the young girl's soul, and follows one of the processes prescribed as a voodoo crossroads ritual.

Duncan, Andy. "Beluthahatchie." In *Sympathy for the Devil: Stories of the Devil*. Edited by Tim Pratt. San Francisco: Night Shade Books, 2010, 8–18. Originally published in *Asminov's*, 1997.

The story follows Robert Johnson's arrival in Hell, or rather Beluthahatchie, as Hell itself is almost full, after his death by poisoning. He has his guitar with him as well as an attitude the devil cannot quite fathom, but it does give hope to the other residents of the area as does his singing the blues. Mature language.

Gilman, Laura Anne. "Crossroads." *Fantasy Magazine*, August 2011. Available online at http://www.fantasy-magazine.com/new/new-fiction/crossroads/ (accessed August 31, 2011).

> Crossroads were bad places. Magicians and devils were bad news. Dusk and dawn and noon overhead were bad times. Every child knew that.

When John meets the man being hanged from the tree at the crossroads by the man in black, he is not sure where his responsibilities lie. Does he really want to get involved with a dispute between two magicians? But when he finally decides on his action, he plays his hand "square and fair."

Grabien, Deborah. "Down to Rosedale." To be published in *Tales from the House Band, Volume 2* (Plus One Press, 2012).

Grabien's reworking of legend of the meeting at the crossroads stands the story on end, for this time around the devil is able to tell his version of another bargain. The narrator, a minor devil, is sent by the bossman to capture the soul of Milo Staines Junior, a 22-year-old guitar player. Milo's mother, a singer, was already known to this devil, and unlike his mother, this boy has ambition. "And ambition is the key to making the deal it's my job to make." In relating his experience with Milo, the devil offers his back story and his own bargain 70 years before. "The crossroads ain't a place, junior, it's a where and why." But Milo does understand the crossroads and more than that as well. A chilling story about bargains both made and lost. "I believe I'll go down to Rosedale. They say you can still buy a house there, by the riverside."

I wish to thank Deborah Grabien for making a copy of her story available for inclusion in this chapter. When asked her about her interest in the legend, she commented:

> I'm a guitar player as well as a writer, and I've been playing the blues since I was about twelve. The concept of the devil-hocussed guitar is one I can't imagine not being fascinated by—deals with the devil are all about playing with fire, and the blues, more me, are all about processing that same fire. "Down to Rosedale" is just looking at the legend from the other side: what about the devil's point of view? What's that about . . . ? (Grabien, personal Facebook communication)

Harris, Charlaine. "Crossroad's Bargain." In *Delta Blues*. Edited by Carolyn Haines. Madison WI: Tryus, 2010, 211–26.

Ernest Washington, known as Partner in the joints where he plays guitar, is saved from being attacked and murdered by an unknown man while walking at night outside of Clarksdale. The unknown man has Partner's guitar and refuses to give it back until they reach the crossroads. "Everyone knew what happened at crossroads—especially one like this, with graves around it. Partner didn't know anyone who remembered who was buried here, or why the graveyard was located out in the middle of nothing, but there were twelve headstones marking the earth" (216). When Partner and the unknown man are joined at the crossroads graveyard by a large white woman and her pet wolf, he discovers their primary function and grabs at the chance to change his fate, save his life and become a successful musician. His eventual payment for his bargain is even more unorthodox than selling his soul.

Martine, Daniel. "Kidd Diamond." In *Delta Blues*. Edited by Carolyn Haines. Madison WI: Tryus, 2010, 258–86.

"I was finally back home in Clarksdale, Mississippi, staying at the infamous Riverside Hotel less than a mile from where Robert Johnson had allegedly made his pact with the devil at the crossroads of Highways 61 and 49" (259). Guitarist Kidd Diamond, sitting and waiting for his Hellhound to track him down, hears the knocking of the door as the devil comes to claim his due. Kidd realizes that he really does not want to belong to Satan for all eternity, no matter what promises he made when he was a poor young black man from the Delta owning only a stolen guitar. Kidd attempts to reconfigure his deal, asking questions of the devil that the devil does not want to answer. Although Kidd originally met the devil in his hotel room rather than at the crossroads, he feels the Robert Johnson story may help him revoke the deal he himself made.

> I know this, Nick. I talked to several guys over the years who knew Johnson. Guys like his cousin Tommy Johnson and Johnny Shines, both of whom owed their careers to him. And Pinetop Perkins and Honeyboy Edwards, who are still alive and perhaps the last living bluesmen who actually knew and played with Robert Johnson. None of them ever believed the legend. It was good PR for bluesmen everywhere, and for you too, Nick. It served your purposes when you dealt with lesser lights, didn't it? Guys who bought into the lie ... into the legend. I mean, when you really get down to it, I'm a derivative of the original, the real McCoy. Oh, I'm a damn spectacular derivative, but I'm not the gen-u-wine article like those guys were. Especially, Robert Johnson." (275)

Olson, Arielle North, and Howard Schwartz, retellers. "Fiddling with Fire: A Tale from the United States." In *Ask Bones: Scary Stories from Around the World*. New York: Viking, 1999, 46–50.

Lucas is following the advice of an old granny woman when he makes his way to the graveyard alone at midnight to practice his fiddle all night. She also warns him not be greedy, but it is very difficult to limit one's self when dealing with the devil who has already taught him to fiddle during that long night. Eventually, Lucas decides he needs to outwit the devil, and does, for a time.

The source notes indicate that the authors found this story in *A Treasury of American Folklore: Stories, Ballads and Traditions of the People*, edited by B. A. Botkin (1944) and that Botkin included a variant in a subsequent collection of his, *A Treasury of Southern Folklore: Stories, Ballads, Traditions and Folkways of the People of the South* (1949) (142).

Robinson, Peter. "The Magic of Your Touch." *The Price of Love and Other Stories*. Toronto: McClelland & Stewart, 2009, 25–32. Originally published in 2004.

The narrator, a jazz pianist, relates his story regarding his meeting with the old man playing an old honky-tonk piano at a junkyard at the crossroads and the narrator's acquisition of his famous tune, "The Magic of Your Touch." "Now that there was no one to stop me, no one to claim plagiarism, I had to get back to the hotel and write down the music before I lost it. As luck would have it, at the other side of the junkyard, past another set of crossroads, was a wide boulevard lined with a few rundown shops and low-life bars" (27). After many years, however, this song becomes the only one that he could play, circulating constantly in his head so that he could no longer play music, sleep or communicate with others. He finds himself back in the part of the city where it all began, and at the same junkyard, just beyond the crossroads, he sees the same old man he had murdered so many years before. "Then I saw what I should have seen in the first place: the flames weren't reflections of the brazier's glow; they were *inside* his head, the way the music was inside me" (31). The narrator had made the bargain for his soul when he stole the song and this story, his suicide note.

Robinson, in the author's notes, states:

> Obviously the variation on the Faustian "deal with the devil" (Robert Johnson at the crossroads) was on my mind, as was the nature of obsession and the corrosive nature of guilt, as in Poe's "The Tell-Tale Heart." But I didn't know any of that at the time I started writing. All I knew was that a man was wandering lost in an urban landscape that resembled something out of David Lynch's *Eraserhead*. What he would do, what would become of him, I had no idea until several hours later when the story was finished. Another thing I like about this story is that it contains elements of horror and the supernatural that do not usually appear in my work. I have always thought that if I didn't write crime I would write horror, so I was pleased to be able to include at least a touch of it here. (306–7)

Yeahpau, Thomas M. "The Storyteller." *X-Indian Chronicles: The Book of Mausape*. Cambridge, MA: Candlewick, 2006, 70–82.

This adaptation of the traditional motif of the meeting at the crossroads is told about Sayday, the Kiowas's tribal hero who features consistently in the stories told to the narrator by his grandfather. This story, however, is the creation of the narrator, to test his storytelling ability. Although the story begins in the traditional manner, Sayday soon goes to the crossroads called the Apache Y where there are three roads leading to three different villages of the Kiowas. While deciding which direction he should go, Sayday rests at the crossroads and encounters an owl sent by the Evil Spirit. Convinced that he could outwit the Evil Spirit, Sayday drinks from the four bottles he finds there. He therefore, unwittingly, introduces alcohol and alcoholism to his people, and when he dies as an old insignificant wino, "they buried him dead in the center of their land, out at the Apache Y, where the four bottles had first appeared" (78).

Poetry and Song Lyrics

McClellan, Elizabeth. "The Walking Man Goes Looking for the Sons of John: Six Cantos." *Apex Magazine* 24 (May 2011). Available online at http://apex-magazine.com/2011/05/17/the-walking-man-goes-looking-for-the-sons-of-john-six-cantos/ (accessed August 30, 2011).

According to the author, the poem is "about the Southern folkloric incarnation of the Devil, the big Black man who hangs around the crossroads and will teach you the mastery of any instrument for a price" (Philips). McClelland's eponymous Sons of John are Robert and Tommy Johnson whose careers had strong ties to Memphis. "Every location in that poem is real, from The Rock, Georgia with its one crossroads and the Black cemetery in terrible disrepair a few miles down the road, to the building with the charred roof beams where Blues Alley used to be, before it burned for the last time four days after Elvis died, to both the Shelby Street Bridges" (Philips).

Vickers, Joe. "Across the Crossroads." Available on the recording *Eastward & Onward*, by Audio Rocketry. Lyrics and digital track available at http://audiorocketry.bandcamp.com/track/across-the-crossroads (accessed October 3, 2011).

Joe Vickers was a student in my University of Alberta storytelling course a few years ago. As a musician, he was one of the few students who knew the legend of Robert Johnson and his meeting with the devil at the crossroads. Joe decided to develop his own variant of the legend for his final oral storytelling assignment. He told the tale, partially by singing and accompanied by his guitar, and soon after reworked his creation and recorded the version now available at this website and on a YouTube video.

In the written portion of his assignment, he stated that he was first introduced to the legend through the documentary of Bob Dylan in which Dylan joked that about receiving his musical talent after selling his soul at the crossroads when he was a young folksinger. A few years later, he became acquainted with the music of Robert Johnson, discovering the history of the legend traced back to his life story. Of his adaptation for his assignment, Vickers wrote:

> Essentially the story is set in present day Canada where I represent the qualities of a struggling musician, while the devil is characterized by the Dean, the manager of Scratch Records. I stumble upon the Crossroads where Dean entices me to sign to his label in return for a life of stardom and fame. An ethical dilemma ensues. I choose this story because I am a musician and understand that it requires a lot of hard work and dedication in order to develop skills and talent at any instrument. With all the time I've invested in practicing the guitar, it's entertaining to think that you could make a bargain with the devil to attain a professional level of musicianship. (Vickers, personal communication)

Graphic Novels, Picture Books and Illustrated Books

de Lint, Charles. *Seven Wild Sisters*. Illustrated by Charles Vess. Burton, MI: Subterranean Press, 2002.

> Belatedly, she was also aware that the spot where the two deer trails met might well be considered a crossroads, and there were any number of stories about the sorts of people you met at a crossroads. Like Old Bubba, ready to trade you the gift of music for your soul like he did with Robert Johnson. The fiddler didn't look like Old Bubba himself, but she wouldn't be surprised if a body came walking up and told her he was some kind of little devil man. (76)

Seven sisters get involved in a war between two different groups of fairies because of an act of kindness. During their brief but action-filled adventure, they meet with an old woman who might be a witch, an enchanted forest, a stolen princess and the fiddling devil at the crossroads. "They both grew dizzy, but before they could fall, the little man pulled them away, out of the world they knew and into his own. A moment later, all that remained at the crossroads were two open instrument cases, filled with stones" (79). This novella received a 2003 YALSA Award for Best Book for Young Adults and was a finalist for the World Fantasy Award.

Hiramoto, Akira. *Me and the Devil Blues: The Unreal Life of Robert Johnson*. 2 volumes. New York: Del Rey, 2008 (English translation).

Originally published in four volumes in Japan, beginning in 2005, this manga series was named as one of the best adult books for high school students by the *School Library Journal* and won the 2009 Glyph Comics Award for Best Reprint Publication. Unfortunately, the third volume which would complete the story has not yet appeared. Readers familiar with Robert Johnson's story will recognize both the factual and fantastical elements of this author's take on the story. RJ and factual aspects of his life and associates, authentically rendered in the darkly mysterious drawings, effectively correspond to this story of the blues, redemption and self-discovery. Hiramoto focuses on the meeting with the devil at the crossroads legend to weave his story of RJ's and Clyde Barrow's adventures in the American South in the 1930s along with existing connotations of affiliations with the devil concerning other sins: "gambling, alcohol, fornication, avarice, sloth . . . and this new plague they call the blues" (1: 36). In the essay by musician Mitsuyoshi Azuma in volume 2 of the series, Azuma writes:

Hiramoto's work can be seen as making use of the theory that Johnson sold his soul to the devil. However, as I read the story I found myself excited by the realization that Johnson's disappearance could also be seen as a kind of science fiction-esque time slip. Furthermore, pairing RJ with the gangster character Clyde gives the story almost a "road movie" like feeling." (2: 561)

The first half of volume 1 of the series reflects the musicality of Robert Johnson more so than the following story arcs. It focuses more on the life of the actual Robert Johnson than the RJ character that travels through the rest of the book. The art work must be commended; the black-and-white illustrations vibrate with music, realistic portraits and honest emotional reactions of the faces of the characters that are created with a range of styles, techniques and media.

Lewis, J. Patrick. *Black Cat Bone*. Illustrated by Gary Kelley. Mankato, MN: Creative Editions, 2006.

In his illustrated and well-researched book of poetry, award-winning poet and recently appointed Children's Poet Laureate (2011), Patrick Lewis explores the legendary life of Robert Johnson. Lewis explains that:

The early researchers mythologized Robert Johnson out of the realm of possibility. I don't mean to be overly earnest or melodramatic, but I had an aim in this book. It was to transport myself backward in time and place and try to evoke this phantom memory of Johnson's genius—and possibly to build my own very small monument to his uniqueness. Here was a fellow wrapped in the mystery of dark and violent Mississippi, and I wanted to see if I could peel away some of the shroud without in any way contributing to this grotesque mythology. (Margolis 2006, 34)

The poems explore the life of Robert Johnson while the haunting chalk illustrations offer a glimpse into the legends behind the man and his musical ability. One poem is directly related to the legend of the crossroads: "At the Crossroad, Highways 61 and 49." The lyrics to Robert Johnson's "Cross Road Blues (take 2)" follow the poem. Lewis comments on the poem in his endnotes:

Here is where the myth was born, grew wings, and took flight. Many people who know little about the blues can recite the legend of Robert Johnson's alleged pact with the devil. A young man living on a plantation in rural Mississippi, he took his burning desire to play the guitar out to this Crossroad one midnight, and there he met the devil himself in the form of a large black man. Satan tuned Robert's guitar, handed it back to him, and within a year's time, Robert became the king of the Delta blues. The cost: Robert's everlasting soul. (45)

The black cat bone of the title refers to a charm used in hoodoo. It was "one of many superstitions dealing with the use of supernatural power to aid the bearer in his quest for fame, love, and fortune" (Patterson 2004, 7). *School Library Journal*, which gave the picture book a starred review, rates it for readers, grades 6 and older. The book was awarded a special mention in the 2008 Special Bolognaragazzi award for children poetry at the Bologna Children's Book Fair, a renowned international book fair held annually in Bologna.

Soule, Charles, and Renzo Podesta. "27: Crossroads Blues." In *Twenty-seven: First Set*. Berkeley, CA: Image Comics, 2011.

Included in this graphic novel, collecting serial issues 1–4 of the title, is a bonus tale regarding a fateful meeting at the crossroads in Mississippi in 1935. Young Robert knows what he needs to trade to be the best guitar player ever but does not figure in that the deal would be made with subcontractors who offer him 36 songs, "songs to make every dame from here to Tallahassee dizzy. People will be playing them forever. But you write that last tune, you belong to the dark man. That's the deal" (n.p.). After recording 29 tunes, Robert refuses to record any more although he does have another 6 already written. He is not planning on writing any more, until, of course, he meets a young woman who offers him so much more.

Urasawa, Naoki. *20th Century Boys*. 22 volumes. Viz Media, 1999–2006.

One of the subplots of this science fiction manga story arc involves the guitar playing of the main protagonist, Kenji Endo. Early in the series, the main protagonist despaired of his guitar-playing ability.

> Well . . . I heard this way back—I forgot who said it. But it went, "Rock musicians die at the age of 27." . . . "So I always kinda felt like I'd die at the age of 27 myself. And then along came my 28th birthday . . . that really got me down . . . I was like, oh man, so I wasn't a real rocker after all. (4: 189–90).

In volume 17, Damian Yoshida, guitarist of the Thriller band the Eroim Esseims, is met at a crossroads. It was Damien who taught Kenji Endo how to play the protest song "Bob Lennon." "It appears that he may have been suffering from amnesia at this time, as he identified himself as the devil (in a reference to the real life rock legend of Bob Johnson, said to have given birth to rock music)." Several times throughout this as yet unfinished series, Robert Johnson, his music and his alleged meeting with the devil at the crossroads are referenced through allusions and illustrations, creating a mysterious element in the story line reminiscent of the one that surrounds the man himself.

Cinematic Reworkings: Movies and Television

Can't You Hear the Wind Howl? The Life & Music of Robert Johnson. Directed by Peter Meyer. Winstar Home Entertainment, 1997.

The documentary, combining interviews with re-enactments filmed in black-and-white, featuring Keb Mo' as Robert Johnson, is narrated by Danny Glover. Remembrances by Johnson's contemporary bluesmen Honeyboy Edwards, Johnny Shines, Robert Junior Lockwood and Henry Townshend along with an ex-girlfriend and other people connected to Johnson round out the picture of Johnson as both an aspiring and accomplished musician. The meeting with the devil at the crossroads narrative is discussed, but no presumption of its truth or falsity is offered. Keith Richards and Eric Clapton explain the influence the *King of the Delta Blues* album had on them and their own musical accomplishments.

Crossroads. Written by John Fusco and directed by Walter Hill. Columbia Pictures, 1986.

> It wouldn't be too far-fetched to say that a majority of today's students, by the time they reach high school, are familiar with at least some part of the Johnson myth, even if they do not immediately connect with the name or readily identify his music. (Graves 2008, 85)

The film was directly inspired by the legend of the meeting of the crossroads between the devil and Robert Johnson. The opening sequence of the film, shown in black-and-white, shows "Robert Johnson" standing on a deserted, desolate road in the middle of nowhere. The camera follows him, and the guitar he is carrying, to the crossroads where he stops and looks around nervously. The wind howls and the film fades to black. The sequence resembled the scene described by LeDell Johnson about his brother Tommy's experience (Graves 2008, 83). The next scene, in the recording studio, features the recording of "Cross Roads Blues." "The inference, if anyone catches it, is that Robert's amazing mastery of the guitar came about as the result of something sinister and supernatural that happened back at the crossroads" (Graves 2008, 84).

The story line follows young music student Eugene Martone (Ralph Macchio) and aged bluesman Willie Brown (Joe Seneca) as they attempt to locate a missing Robert Johnson song, release Willie Brown from his own deal with the devil and ultimately compare classical guitar with that of the blues. Not only does Johnson's meeting with the devil at the crossroads figure prominently in the film, the film actualizes a legend trip (in the form of a "road movie") from Memphis to rural Mississippi. The movie culminates with the famed guitar duel with the devil, by his ringer guitarist Jack Butler (Steve Vai), who has also bargained his soul for his prowess as a metal-blues guitarist, and Eugene. Eugene, through the guitar playing of Ry Cooder, wins the battle by playing a piece of classical music that Butler cannot match. "In a move that many blues fans who watched the movie found irritating, if not offensive, Lightening Boy [Eugene] abandons the blues playing at the crucial moment and whips out some of his Julliard-trained classical licks, which the competitor cannot duplicate" (Graves 2008, 84). Others comment that "heavy metal represents the contaminated culture of the music industry, while the blues appears as a precommercial form with magical powers owing to its pure and uncontaminated history" (Lipsitz 1997, 41). Ironically, the "winning" piece of music is based on the Fifth Caprice by Niccolo Paganini, one of the "original" claimants for the identity of the musician in this contemporary legend of selling one's soul for success.

The film, released as a DVD in 2004, has been credited as being more responsible for introducing the world to Robert Johnson and his music than the cover versions of his songs by Eric Clapton and the Rolling Stones (Graves 2008, 83). It is also credited for effectively perpetuating the legend of Johnson meeting with the devil at the crossroads as factual (Wardlow 1998, 200). A few supplementary notes about the film: the real Willie Brown, named in Johnson's lyrics, was a guitarist, not a harmonica player; the idea of the missing song was introduced in Samuel Charters' book *The Country Blues* (1959) (Wardlow 1998, 200); and the mysterious black man at the crossroads is referred to as Legba in the film (Patterson 2004,7).

Hellhounds on My Trail: The Afterlife of Robert Johnson. Directed by Robert Mugge, 1999. DVD released 2000.

This film chronicles the American Music Master's 1998 series and conference on Robert Johnson and includes a mixture of academic workshops and performances of Johnson's songs by various artists. "The film beautiful alternates snippets from lectures, discussions, and interviews with complete concert pieces, most of which take place in Cleveland's grand, I. M. Pei-designed building" (Levecq 2004, 239).

Metalocalypse: Blues Devil (Season 1, Episode 14), 2006.

In this episode of the American animated television series parodying and celebrating heavy-metal culture, Dethklok, the heavy-metal band, travels to Mississippi to learn about the blues. A stranger comes to teach them how to play the blues, telling them about some of the most famous bluesmen including one who made a deal with the devil. When the stranger brings the band to the crossroads to make the deal themselves their legal negotiation skills defeat the devil, causing him to walk away from the deal and the band. The band becomes inspired again, continuing on to test their blues skills on an audience. The song summons a killing tornado.

O Brother, Where Art Thou? Directed by Joel and Ethan Coen, Touchtone Pictures, 2000.

The Coen brothers' homage to Homer's *Odyssey* includes a direct reference to the crossroad legend. During their travels across Mississippi, the three protagonists pick up a hitchhiker, Tommy Johnson, at a remote crossroads. Tommy explains to the men that he went to the crossroads to trade his soul in order to acquire musical fame. "Any Johnson fan watching this movie probably thought highly of the Coens' knowledge of blues history, because many critics argue that Tommy Johnson, not Robert Johnson, encouraged the notion that he sold his soul to the Devil" (Palmer 1981: 59). According to the soundtrack's liner notes, however, Robert Johnson was the source of the character in the film (Waide 2009, 92). Following their recording of a hit song, the main protagonist, Ulysses McGill, exclaims, "Boy, I believe you did sell your soul to the Devil," verifying this explanation for the aspiring African American bluesman's talent (Waide 2009, 92).

The Search for Robert Johnson, directed and produced by Chris Hunt, 1991. Released on DVD in 2000.

This documentary produced for British commercial television and narrated by blues musician John Hammond contains testimony from Robert "Mack" McCormick, an important but unpublished Robert Johnson researcher. Hammond, son of famed record producer and talent scout John Henry Hammond who is considered by many to be largely responsible for the revival of interest in Robert Johnson, travels to places associated with Johnson and interviews several ex-girlfriends as well as blues contemporaries Johnny Shines and David Honeyboy Edwards.

> Offering what was easily the most startling piece of new information in the film, McCormick interpreted that the satanic legends about Johnson, far from being tall tales concocted by other people, were stories with which the artist consciously chose to associate himself because, as McCormick phrased it, he was "drawn to that texture of 'I am with the devil—me and the devil walking side by side.'" (Pearson and McCulloch 2003, 56)

Pearson and McCulloch quickly point out that no other researcher or subsequent material has been found collaborating McCormick's interpretation. Patricia R. Schroeder discusses the film, stating that the film was "a well-researched attempt to recover what is knowable about the historical Robert Johnson" (Schroeder 2004, 62). She also found that the objectivity of the film is partially undercut by Hammond's prominence in the film playing long passages of Johnson's songs.

Supernatural, Ongoing Television Series

Created by Eric Kripke in 2005, this supernatural drama television series follows two brothers, Sam and Dean Winchester, as they hunt demons and other paranormals in their road trips across the United States. Kripke decided that the brothers were from Lawrence, Kansas, because of its closeness to Stull Cemetery, a location famous for its urban legends, discussed elsewhere in this book. There is an enormous outpouring of writing on this series by fans, academics and news staff; some of which discusses the connection of contemporary legends and this television series. "Most intriguingly, it draws its spooky stories almost entirely from urban legends and folklore from the United States and around the world. Sam and Dean Winchester have encountered Bloody Mary, the ghost of H.H. Holmes (America's first serial killer) . . . and the story of blues legend Robert Johnson, who supposedly made a deal with the devil" (Cochran 2007).

The meeting with the devil at the crossroads legend permeates the television series.

"Crossroad Blues" (Season 2, Episode 8): The episode opens with Robert Johnson sitting on a small stage in a salon in Greenwood, Mississippi, in 1938, playing his guitar with his head down and a cigarette dangling from his mouth. There are few people in the audience, but as he plays he hears the growling of a dog outside, an eerie sound that no one else seems to hear. Seeing a dark shadow moving past the window, he is terrified. Standing with his guitar in hand, he bolts out of the room. Several people follow him and find him behind a locked door in convulsions and repeating the phrase "black dogs." Time moves forward to the present day where Sam and Dean investigate the site of two people who claimed to be haunted by hellhounds. They discover that the bar is situated on a site where a deal-making demon had been hard at work, exchanging souls for their most covert desires. When Dean summoned the demon, he discovers the truth behind his own father's death. With Johnson's "Cross Road Blues" playing in the background, the setting moves to Rosedale, Mississippi, in 1930 and Robert Johnson. Johnson puts his photograph in a box with other hoodoo items before burying it in the center of the crossroads. When he turns around, the demon is there to grant him his desire to be the best bluesman that ever lived. In a plot turn reminiscent of the Disney studios, the demon does not tune his guitar to accomplish this but instead, she gives him a kiss before vanishing. Dean makes his own way to the crossroads and buries a picture of himself in a box. He turns around to greet the demon who discusses the deal his father had made. This specific demon, an attractive female created by Kripke, is summoned by digging a hole in the dead center of a crossroads and burying a box with the seeker's photograph, graveyard dirt, a black cat bone and possibly yarrow. The script for this episode can be found at http://www.supernaturalwiki.com/index.php?title=2.08_Crossroad _Blues_%28transcript%29.

The crossroad demon continues to make her presence known in the subsequent seasons, although the Robert Johnson connection has been severed.

"All Hell Breaks Loose, Part 2" (Episode 22). This final episode in Season 2 had Dean selling his soul to the crossroad demon in order to save his brother Sam who is killed in the previous episode. This deal is to be consummated in a year's time, leaving Sam and the viewing audience in a cliff-hanging ending. The crossroad demon was killed by San in "Bedtime Stories" (Season 3, Episode 5). In "Time Is on My Side" (Season 3, Episode 15), the demon was not explicitly identified as a crossroad demon, but the demon's red eyes, the 10-year contract and the arrival of hellhounds on the night the contract comes due were indicative of her role. The fourth season had only one crossroad demon sighting in "I know What You Did Last Summer" (Episode 9). Sam summons a different crossroad demon in an attempt to trade himself for Dean. When Dean's plea is ignored by the male demon, Dean stabs him. Season 5 had three episodes that continue this particular story line: "Abandon All Hope" (Episode 10), "The Devil You Know" (Episode 20) and "Two Minutes to Midnight" (Episode 21), while Season 6 had an equal number. In "The Third Man" (Episode 3), the crossroad story is told with a twist as it is an angel, rather than a devil, that is making deals with people for their souls. "Weekend at Bobby's" (Episode 4) has Bobby turning to Sam and Dean for help when the demon Crowley refuses to return his soul as agreed. Bobby learns the true name of the devil at the crossroads which releases him from his deal with the devil. "Family Matters" (Episode 7) has only a brief mention of the powers held by crossroad demons.

Tenacious D and the Pick of Destiny. Directed by Liam Lynch, 2006.

Two friends, looking for the legendary magic guitar pick, discover that the pick was manufactured by a blacksmith from the devil's tooth after a battle between the devil and a magician. The magician cursed Satan to remain in Hell until he was complete again. Using the pick, containing the essence of the devil, allows musicians to gain the fame and love they requested. The pick disappeared for centuries but surfaces again in the southern United States with Robert Johnson. The infamous pick was rumored to be in the Rock and Roll History Museum.

The Wind Journeys. Written and directed by Ciro Guerra, 2009. English subtitles. Available on DVD.

Ignaciao Carrillo, a musician from Majagual, Sucre, decides after the death of his wife to stop playing the accordion and to return the devilish instrument, supposedly cured, to his master. He is joined in his journey by a young teenage boy who wished to emulate him. One review states that "if you admire the legend of Robert Johnson meeting the Devil at the crossroads, you may get some similar chills watching this analogous story set in South American backcountry" (http://stlbeacon.org/arts-life/180-St_Louis_Film_Festival/106374-sliff-day-8-sly-stone-and-wind-journeys; August 29, 2011).

Screenplays

Greenberg, Alan. *Love in Vain: A Vision of Robert Johnson.* 1983. Reprinted by Capo Press (1994).

The second edition has additional introductions by Martin Scorsese and Stanley Crouch and a selected discography. Greenberg also provides annotated notes for his research as the play is thoroughly grounded in historical fact as well as the crossroad legend. Greenberg places the deal with the devil in a new context and offers several alternative interpretations for his audience: Did Johnson really meet the devil in the movie theatre and follow him to the crossroads? Was the devil actually a con man, tricking Johnson into the midnight meeting? Was the entire meeting part of a dream? The screenplay, first published in 1983, is to be filmed in 2012.

Harris, Bill. *Robert Johnson: Trick the Devil.* In *The National Black Drama Anthology: Eleven Plays from America's Leading African-American Theaters.* Edited by Woodie King Jr. New York: Applause Books, 1995, 1–46. Originally written in 1992.

Harris's play utilizes the legend but rationalizes it by making the devil at the crossroads an ordinary white man in a suit and tie, perhaps a recording company executive, who is trying to exploit Johnson. Because Johnson is protective about his guitar, he refuses to let the white man tune it and instead played it furiously, expressing the misery that he knew: "the bondage, being bid for on the block, the lash, Jim Crow, the rope, the chain gang and the Klan . . . And *that's* what got the Devil, because he couldn't call none of it a lie!" (40–41). The head-cutting contest that follows offers Johnson ample instructions on becoming a master musician, beating the devil at his own game.

Selected Reworkings of "The Pact with the Devil"

Because of their relevancy and appeal to young-adult readers, two recent novels should be included here, although technically they are not referencing the crossroad aspect of the legend. Ironically, the two novels were published the same year as the contemporary legend involving the devil and the Hello Kitty brand were circulating on the Internet.

> The story is how Hello Kitty came to be . . . that a mother or father, depending on the version of the story had a child that had cancer. The parent made a pact with the devil that if the child was cured they would create a character in the devil's honor that would be adored worldwide. There are different variations but they all boil down to the point that Hello Kitty is evil and that God fearing people should stay away from any HK products as they are affiliated with the devil and devil worship. (Mikkelson 2010)

Napoli, Donna Jo. *The Wager.* New York: Holt, 2010.

In her reworking of the Italian variant of the Bearskin folktale, "Don Giovanni de la Fortuna," the former wealthy aristocrat Don Giovanni accepts a magical purse from a well-dressed stranger, knowing full well that there will be a steep price attached. He must go three years, three months and three days without washing, shaving or changing his clothes in order to win the wager. Set in 1169, the story effectively brings to life this rather unlikeable character and setting in a novel exploring personal destiny and identity.

Zafon, Carlos Ruiz. *The Prince of Mist.* New York: Little, Brown, 2010.

This English translation of Zafon's first novel, published in Spain in 1993 for young readers, follows the adventures of 13-year-old Max Carver, the son of an eccentric watchmaker who moves his family to a seafront property in 1943. The house and the people Max and his two sisters meet in the area are definitely strange as is the malevolent Prince of Mist who seems to be coming to collect on his bargain, made many years before.

Online Lesson Plans and Education Resources

> *Beyond the seminal importance of his music, the role of the devil, and of the nature of evil, in Johnson's lyrics give his work a profound cultural significance. Robert Johnson's musical tour of hell tells us much about African American culture but also the trajectory of satanic imagery throughout the twentieth century. His talent may not have come from a meeting with the devil at a deserted crossroads in Mississippi twilight. But his lyrics did come from an encounter with personal and collective darkness, an encounter that all of American culture would soon face.*
>
> —Poole (2009, 126).

Several resources offered online further explore the suggestion of the cross-roads and Robert Johnson's association with them through the legend. An episode on KEXP's (Seattle) documentary "Blues for Hard Times" is dedicated to "Crossroad Blues by Robert Johnson" and can be accessed at http://blog.kexp.org/blog/2010/03/31/kexp-documentaries-blues-for-hard-times-crossroad-blues-by-robert-johnson/ (accessed August 22, 2011). Two substantial lesson plans from PBS are highly recommended as is the lesson contributed by Susan LoGuidice to the Rock and Roll Hall of Fame Museum.

- Blues as Culture: Crossroads Blues http://www.pbs.org/theblues/classroom/intcrossroads.html (August 22, 2011). The overview on the website, for the lesson plan addressing the American National Curriculum Standards for English Language Arts, states that:

  The crossroads—and the decisions made and entities met there—are a common theme in literature, pushing readers to examine the choices and encounters that shape life experience. The theme has also been explored in blues music, most famously by Robert Johnson, who, according to bluesman Son House, must have "sold his soul to play like that." This lesson uses Johnson and his music as an entry point into the study of cross-roads literature.

- Blues in Society: A Snapshot of Delta Blues: Skip James and Robert Johnson—http://www.pbs.org/theblues/classroom/intdelta.html (accessed August 22, 2011). The overview for this lesson plan, addressing American National Curriculum Standards for Music Education, considers the question of what ultimately influences a musician's creations.

  Is it the time in which he/she lives, his/her personal experiences, the music of the time and previous times, or the image the artist hopes to convey? This lesson explores these questions by looking at the life and times of two early bluesmen: Skip James and Robert Johnson. Students consider what influenced both men, their unique musical contributions, their public personae, and their legacies.

- STI Lesson 27: I Went to the Crossroads: The Faust Theme in Music, Film and Literature—http://rockhall.com/education/resources/lesson-plans/sti-lesson-27/ (accessed August 22, 2011).

  The Faust theme, that of risking eternal damnation by selling one's soul to the devil in exchange for magical powers, can be found in virtually every genre of music as well as in literature and the visual arts. Examples utilizing this theme can be found as early as biblical times as a means of understanding humanity's place in the universe and the struggle between good and evil. This interdisciplinary lesson focuses on the life and music of bluesman Robert Johnson as a twentieth-century interpretation of this famous myth and demonstrates thematic connections between various art forms.

References

Ashford, Barbara. 2011. "Barbara Ashford Talks about the Original Ending of this Month's Spellcast." RT Book Reviews. http://www.rtbookreviews.com/rt-daily-blog/barbara-ashford-talks-about-original-ending-months-spellcast (accessed October 3, 2011).

Beifuss, John. 2008. "Memphis Author Tracks Legend of Bluesman Robert Johnson." *Memphis Commercial Appeal*, October 14. http://www.tom-graves.com/id31.html (accessed August 21, 2011).

Bennett, Gillian, and Paul Smith. 2007. *Urban Legends: A Collection of International Tall Tales and Terrors.* Westport, CT: Greenwood Press.

Charters, Samuel. 1973. *Robert Johnson.* New York: Oak Publications.

Cheseborough, Steve. 2009. *Blues Traveling: the Holy Sites of Delta Blues.* 3rd edition. Jackson: University Press of Mississippi.

Cochran, C. O. 2007. "Supernatural: Lonely Highways and Urban Legends." http://firefox.org/news/articles/442/1/Supernatural-Lonely-Highways-and-Urban-Legends/Page1.html (accessed August 31, 2011).

Conway, Cecilia. 1995. *African Banjo Echoes in Appalachia: A Study of Folk Traditions.* American Folklore Society. Knoxville: University of Tennessee Press.

Cross, Alan. 2011. "The Mystery of the 27s Deepens." *Ottawa Citizen*, July 26. http://www.ottawacitizen.com/news/mystery+deepens/5158022/story.html#ixzz1VaSxTybB (accessed August 20, 2011).

Davies, Owen. 2009. *The Haunted: A Social History of Ghosts.* New York: Palgrave Macmillan.

Davis, Stephen. 1997. *Hammer of the Gods.* New York: Berkley Boulevard Books,.

DiGiacomo, Frank. 2008. "Searching for Robert Johnson." *Vanity Fair*, November. http://www.vanityfair.com/culture/features/2008/11/johnson200811 (accessed August 21, 2011).

Elder, Bruce. 2011. "Hound Dog and Other Hits." *Brisbane Times*, August 20. http://www.brisbanetimes.com.au/travel/hound-dog-and-other-hits-20110817-1ixox.html#ixzz1Vae840ea (accessed August 20, 2011).

Ellis, Bill. wce2@psu.edu. 2010. "Song of Death: 'I Did It My Way.' " February 8. Distribution list (accessed February 8, 2010).

European Roots. 2004. "Strings of the Devil: Norway's Hardanger Fiddle." Radio Transcript. http://www.ebu.ch/CMSimages/en/NRK_Script_tcm6-17205.pdf (accessed August 26, 2011).

Evans, David. 1971. *Tommy Johnson.* Studio Vista.

Everett, Holly, and Peter Narvaez. 2001. " 'Me and the Devil': Legends of Niccolo Paganini and Robert Johnson." *Contemporary Legend* n.s. 4:20–47.

Filene, Benjamin. 2004. "O Brother, What Next? Making Sense of the Folk Fad." *Southern Cultures* (Summer): 50–69.

Finn, Julio. 1986. *The Bluesman: The Musical Heritage of Black Men and Women in the Americas.* London: Quartet Books.

Garry, Jane. 2005. "Choice of Roads: Motif N122.0.1, and Crossroads, Various Motifs." In *Archetypes and Motifs in Folklore and Literature: A Handbook.* Edited by Jane Garry and Hasan El-Shamy. Armonk, NY: M.E. Sharpe, 333–41.

George, Patrice. "Review of *Rosa i Botnen*." http://www.rootsworld.com/reviews/botnen06.shtml (accessed August 26, 2011).

Gioia, Ted. 2008. *Delta Blues: The Life and Times of the Mississippi Masters Who Revolutionized American Music.* New York: Norton.

Graves, Tom. 2008. *Crossroads: The Life and Afterlife of Blues Legend Robert Johnson.* Foreword by Steve LaVere. Spokane, WA: Demers Books.

"Guitar Man." 2010. http://www.snopes.com/music/media/guitar.asp (accessed August 20, 2011).

Halliday, Robert, 2010. "The Roadside Burial of Suicides: An East Anglian Study." *Folklore* 121 (April): 81–93.

Inglis, Ian. 2007. " 'Sex and Drugs and Rock'n'Roll': Urban Legends and Popular Music." *Popular Music and Society* 30 (5): 591–603.

Kenyon, John. "The Monday Interview: John Hornor Jacobs." http://tirbd.com/2011/08/john-hornor-jacobs-the-monday-interview/ (accessed October 3, 2011).

Kot, Greg. 2011. "Turn It Up: Bob Dylan, Robert Johnson: The Music Not the Myth." *Chicago Tribune*, May 3.

Leftridge, Steve. 2010. "Katy Perry: Teenage Dream." *PopMatters*, October. http://www.popmatters.com/pm/review/130887-katy-perry-teenage-dream/ (accessed August 21, 2011).

Levecq, Christine. 2004. "Blues Poetics and Blues Politics in Walter Mosley's *RL's Dream*." *African American Review* 38 (2): 239–56.

Lewis, J. Patrick. 2006. *Black Cat Bone*. Illustrated by Gary Kelley. Mankato, MN: Creative Editions.

Lewis, Randy. 2011. "At the Crossroads as Robert Johnson Centennial Nears." May 4. http://www.ecollegetimes.com/music/at-the-crossroads-as-robert-johnson-centennial-nears-1.2559082 (accessed August 22, 2011).

Lieberfeld, Daniel. 1995. "Million-Dollar Juke Joint: Commodifying Blues Culture." *African American Review* 95 (2): 217–21.

Lipsitz, George. 1997. "Remembering Robert Johnson: Romance and Reality." *Popular Music and Society* 21 (4): 39–50.

Marcus, Greil. 1997. *Mystery Train: Images of America in Rock 'N' Roll Music*. 4th edition. New York: Plume.

Margolis, Rick. 2006. "Blues Brother." *School Library Journal* (December):34. Excerpts offered online at http://www.schoollibraryjournal.com/article/CA6395109.html (accessed August 31, 2011).

Marvin, Thomas F. 1996. "Children of Legba: Musicians at the Crossroads in Ralph Ellison's *Invisible Man*." *American Literature* 68 (3): 587–608.

Mikkelson, Barbara. 2010. "Hello Kitty, Good-Bye Soul. http://www.snopes.com/business/alliance/hellokitty.asp (accessed September 1, 2011).

Mondor, Colleen. 2010. "Interview with Kate Milford." http://www.chasingray.com/archives/2010/05/you_come_to_know_the_road_that.html (accessed August 9, 2011).

"Mortality Bridge." http://mortalitybridge.com/about.html (accessed October 3, 2011).

Mlynar, Phillip. 2011. "The Robert Johnson Variations." *Chicago Reader*, February 10. http://www.chicagoreader.com/chicago/robert-johnson-big-head-todd-and-the-monsters-bb-king-honeyboy-edwards-charlie-musslewhite-blues/Content?oid=3217272 (accessed October 3, 2011).

Niezgoda, Joseph. 2008. *The Lennon Prophecy: A New Examination of the Death Clues of the Beatles*. New Chapter Press.

Onishi, Norimitsu. 2010. "Sinatra Song Often Strikes Deadly Chord." *The New York Times*, February 7. http://www.nytimes.com/2010/02/07/world/asia/07karaoke.html (accessed August 20, 2011).

Palmer, Robert. 1981. *Deep Blues: A Musical and Cultural History of the Mississippi Delta*. New York: Viking.

Patterson, R. Gary. 2004. *Take a Walk on the Dark Side: Rock and Roll Myths, Legends and Curses*. New York: Fireside.

Pearson, Barry Lee, and Bill McCulloch. 2003. *Robert Johnson: Lost and Found*. Urbana: University of Illinois Press.

Poole, W. Scott. 2009. *Satan in America: The Devil We Know*. Lanham, MD: Rowman & Littlefield.

Puckett, Newbell Niles. 1926. *Folk Beliefs of the Southern Negro*. Chapel Hill: University of North Carolina Press.

Santelli, Robert. 2004. "A Century of the Blues." In *Martin Scorsese Presents the Blues: A Musical Journey*. Edited by Peter Guralnick, Robert Santelli, Holly George-Warren and Christopher John Farley. New York: Harper Books, 12–59.

Sack, David. 2011. "Debunking the Myth of the Forever 27 Club." http://www.prnewswire.com/news-releases/david-sack-md-debunking-the-myth-of-forever-27-club-126789233.html (accessed August 20, 2011).

Schroeder, Patricia R. 2004. *Robert Johnson, Mythmaking, and Contemporary American Culture*. Urbana: University of Illinois Press.

Sullivan, Todd E. "Instrument of the Devil." http://industry.rachelbartonpine.com/rec_liner.php?id=06 (accessed June 3, 2010)

Swanwick, Michael. 2000. *SF Site*. "Inside Jack Daw's Pack: An Interview with Greer Gilman." http://www.sfsite.com/02b/msgg170.htm (accessed August 5, 2011).

Taylor, Greg. 2008. "Occult Rock: From Blues to Prog Rock, the Devil Is in the Details." *Dark Lore* 2:9–22.

Tosches, Nick. 2001. *Where Dead Voices Gather*. New York: Little, Brown.

Wagamese, Richard. 2008. "Moan That Particular Blues." *Canadian Dimension*, July–August. Available online at http://www.utne.com/2008-07-01/Arts-Culture/Moan -That-Particular-Blues.aspx?page=2 (accessed October 3, 2011).

Waide, Blaine Quincy. 2009. *The Green Fields of the Mind: Robert Johnson, Folk Revivalism, and Disremembering the American Past*. Master's Thesis, Folklore Program, Department of American Studies. Chapel Hill: University of North Carolina.

Wald, Elijah. 2004. *Escaping the Delta: Robert Johnson and the Invention of the Blues*. New York: HarperCollins.

Wardlow, Gayle Dean. 1998. *Chasin' That Devil Music: Searching for the Blues*. San Francisco: Miller Freeman.

Yronwode, Catherine. "The Crossroads in Hoodoo Magic and the Ritual of Selling Yourself to the Devil." http://www.luckymojo.com/crossroads.html (accessed August 21, 2011).

Epilogue

As mentioned in the Introduction, this book is an attempt to explore the effect of technology and electronic transmission on contemporary legends while, at the same time, observing the legends still grounded in the oral tradition. Particular attention has been paid to the conventional and fictive transmissions of any new tales as well as the tales included in *Tales, Rumors, and Gossip*. This is done through the examination of widely diverse topics and contemporary legends in the individual chapters of *What Happens Next*. Contemporary legends and the horror genre, legend tripping, commodification and ostensive action accorded to contemporary legends, netlore and newslore, conspiracy theories, ghostlore, devils at the crossroads and assorted cryptids all intertwine and interlock in the ubiquitous spider web that is labelled popular culture. After this exploration, I have concluded that contemporary legends are now an even more prolific force, almost invisible because of their very presence, surrounding, enveloping, offering commentary and allusions, and blending into our daily lives without any perceptible notice. It is, therefore, even more essential that people recognize these legends, understand and appreciate their history, and realize their current significance. Contemporary legends are definitely not disappearing, even if their content has remained essentially static for some time.

This was certainly brought home very strongly with the intersection of three diverse instances of contemporary legends in popular culture appearing within hours of each other a few days ago. Being a huge, longtime fan of the singer Lucinda Williams means that her 1998 recording of *Car Wheels on a Gravel Road* gets a great deal of airplay in our home but, for some reason, her lyrics for the song "Kool 2 Be 4-Gotten" did not permeate my consciousness in any significant manner. Sitting with my mouth open, I finally heard as Lucinda sang about Mr. Johnson selling his soul to the devil to play his guitar.

Turning back to the book in my lap, *Summerland* by Michael Chabon (Miramax, 2002) which I was rereading to track Taffy the Sasquatch for another project, I suddenly read that she was following the weeping and wailing of La Llorona. Knowing that Taffy has been on an emotional journey and bereavement for her own children, I worried along with Jennifer, one of the (perhaps) human children in the story, as she looks for Taffy. Jennifer states, "I'm afraid she's going to drown herself. Like La Llorona. She's been acting so *weird*" (384).

Feeling a bit weird myself now, I decide to check Facebook only to find a posting pointing to a new rendition of "Pepper Spraying Cop" art available on the Internet. This very recent example of photoshop newslore went viral almost immediately after the incident at University of California–Davis campus was first broadcast on television, November 16, 2011. It is possibly the most-recorded single event in history with still images and videos posted almost immediately afterwards on the Internet.

The photograph taken by Davis psychology student Louise Macabitas, however, became not only the most recognized image of all the ones captured that day but also the one that "birthed the Pepperspray Cop meme" (Wild 2011). Photographer Alex Wild, in his column for *Scientific American*, cites several reasons for the popularity of this particular image including the perspective of the shot, the visibility of Lt. John Pike's face, the casualness of the mid-stride motion of Pike, the visibility of the spray and the explicit roles of the people in the photograph as Police, Aghast Onlooker and Protestor. It is, as Wild points out, "a story that tells itself" (Wild 2011). Jardin agrees that it is the surreal juxtaposition of the violence in the image with Pike's "oddly casual body language and facial expression" that captures the immediate attention of the viewer (Jardin 2011). "One of the way the internet deals with that kind of upsetting dissonance is to mock it" (Jardin 2011). Jardin explains that the image and its reworkings are now memes, "a kind of folk art or shared visual joke that is open to sharing and reinterpretation by anyone" (Jardin 2011). It is, in fact, another very vibrant example of the netlore discussed in chapter 3. Because of the new ease and fluency that many people have with the Internet, this image went viral in its many forms much quicker than the "Tourist Guy" discussed earlier.

Cataloguing of the various images, still appearing at a steady rate, can be found at Boing Boing's "Occupy Lulz" (http://boingboing.net/2011/11/20/occupy-lulz.html), "Pepper Spraying Cop" (http://peppersprayingcop.tumblr.com/) and "Know Your Meme" (http://knowyourmeme.com/memes/casually-pepper-spray-everything-cop/photos?fb_ref=recommendations_memes). The treatment of these photoshopped images is diverse: pepper-spraying actions, with or without Lt. Pike, are photoshopped on classic music record covers such as Pink [Pike] Floyd's *Dark Side of the Moon* and the Beatles' *Sergeant Pepper's Lonely Heart Club Band*; classic paintings such as Picasso's *Guernica*, Leonardo da Vinci's *The Last Supper* and *The Scream* by Edvard Munch; and with television and movie icons such as *Star Wars*, *Sound of Music*, *The Lord of the Rings*, *The Simpsons* and *Sesame Street*. Pike and his pepper spray time-warps into history as well when he appears in the American Civil War, or spraying the American Constitution or at the raising of the flag at Iwo Jima.

Another interesting development at this time is the usurping or extension of the term "meme," a word that usually means an idea, behavior or usage that spreads from one person to another within the same local culture or social group. Stories, phrases, beliefs and fashions are examples of memes or "unit[s] of cultural transmission" (Dennett 1995, 345). Internet memes are concepts or phrases that spread rapidly from person to person through the global community via Internet-based forums such as e-mail, blogs, social networking sites, instant messaging and YouTube videos. And, as is immediately evident in the case of the pepper-spraying cop, photoshopping.

> Lt. Pike's infamy doesn't end with the memes. Twitter users can follow @PepperSprayCop for random, pepper spray-centric thoughts (example: "Febreeze goes against everything I believe in."). For those seeking unconventional life advice, Pepper Spraying Cop has also taken on an advice columnist persona

online. The columnist's solution for all problems? Pepper-spraying the offending individual until their eyes bleed. Harsh. (Tersigni 2011)

Readily available as well are examples of the commodification of the meme in T-shirts, posters and other bric-a-brac for purchase on, of course, the Internet.

Ultimately, my most major discovery is that it is impossible to complete any research on contemporary legends. As I was writing this book I kept extending the deadline of when I would stop collecting examples, articles, photographs, videos, suggestions and reworkings of the legends already under consideration and any newly developing ones. Charting the contemporary legend in popular culture can be a lifetime commitment. Keep in touch to see *What Happens Next!*

References

Dennett, Daniel. 1995. *Darwin's Dangerous Idea*. New York: Simon and Schuster.

Jardin, Xeni. 2011. "The Pepper-Spraying Cop Gets Photoshop Justice," November 23. http://www.guardian.co.uk/commentisfree/2011/nov/23/pepper-spraying-cop-photoshop-justice?CMP=twt_gu (accessed December 20, 2011).

Tersigni, Jaclyn. 2011. "Pepper-Spray Cop Send-Ups: Good Fun or Bad Taste?" November 23. http://www.theglobeandmail.com/life/the-hot-button/pepper-spray-cop-send-ups-good-fun-or-bad-taste/article2246845/ (accessed December 20, 2011).

Wild, Alex. 2011. "Why One Pepper-Spraying Cop Image Dominates," November 22. http://blogs.scientificamerican.com/compound-eye/2011/11/22/why-one-pepper-spraying-cop-image-dominates/ (accessed December 20, 2011).

Index

Literary Index

Legend Index

About the Author

GAIL DE VOS has been an adjunct professor at the School of Library and Information Studies, University of Alberta, Edmonton, Alberta, Canada, and a professional storyteller for over 20 years. She has an MLIS and a B.Ed. from the University of Alberta and is the author of several Libraries Unlimited titles, including *Tales, Rumors, and Gossip: Exploring Contemporary Folk Literature in Grades 7–12*; *Stories from Songs: Ballads as Literary Fictions for Young Adults*; and *Storytelling for Young Adults: A Guide to Tales for Teens*, 2nd edition.

Made in the USA
San Bernardino, CA
25 April 2013